W9-AMT-072

A Year Inland

The Journal of a
Hudson's Bay Company Winterer

A Year Inland

The Journal of a
Hudson's Bay Company Winterer

Edition and Commentary by
Barbara Belyea

Wilfrid Laurier University Press

This book has been published with the help of a grant from the Humanities and Social Sciences Federation of Canada, using funds provided by the Social Sciences and Humanities Research Council of Canada. We acknowledge the support of the Canada Council for the Arts for our publishing program. We acknowledge the financial support of the Government of Canada through the Book Publishing Industry Development Program for our publishing activities. We acknowledge the financial support of the Hudson's Bay History Foundation for this project.

Canadian Cataloguing in Publication Data

Henday, Anthony, fl. 1748-1755
    A year inland : the journal of a Hudson's Bay Company winterer

Includes bibliographical references and index.
ISBN 0-88920-343-1 (bound)

1. Henday, Anthony, fl. 1748-1755 — Diaries. 2. Hudson's Bay Company. 3. Northwest Canadian — Description and travel. 4. Fur trade — Prairie Provinces — History — 18th century. I. Belyea, Barbara. II. title

FC3211.1.H45A3 2000   971.2'01   C99-932174-9
F1060.7.H45A3 2000

© 2000 Wilfrid Laurier University Press
    Waterloo, Ontario   N2L 3C5

Cover design by Leslie Macredie. Cover photograph of the Plan of York Fort, presumably by James Isham, undated. HBCA G.2/5 (N8187). Hudson's Bay Company Archives, Provincial Archives of Manitoba.

Printed in Canada

Contents

Preface

I am grateful to Shirlee Anne Smith, former Keeper of the Hudson's Bay Company Archives, Provincial Archives of Manitoba, for initial permission to edit Henday's journal. Judith Hudson Beattie, present Keeper of the HBCA, confirmed this permission, answered many requests, and never lost faith that the edition would appear one day.

Glyndwr Williams kindly introduced Don Kennett, Henday's descendant, who allowed me to draw on his research into the Hendy family records. Ed Dahl, formerly the early cartography specialist at the National Archives of Canada, gave me valuable information on maps and watermarks. Charles V. Fiddler, principal of the Plains Indians Cultural Survival School in Calgary, advised me on the Cree words transcribed in Henday's journal.

Dale Russell shared my interest in this project from the beginning and helped immeasurably. Cole Harris, Frances W. Kaye and Olive Patricia Dickason generously agreed to read a draft version and give me their comments. Although I persisted in my own line of reasoning, I benefitted from their views and advice.

Sandra Woolfrey, former director of Wilfrid Laurier University Press, guided the edition through the stages of funding and press approval. During this long process her insight and patient kindness were exceptional. I am also grateful to Carroll Klein, managing editor, for her smooth and energetic supervision of the book in press.

I would like to thank my family and friends, who kept me going, sometimes in difficult circumstances.

Introduction

In 1754 Anthony Henday, employed by the Hudson's Bay Company as a netmaker and general labourer at York Fort, set out with a group of Natives from the plains to winter with them and promote trade at the Bayside forts. Henday's year inland, praised by York's chief factor as fulfilling all its aims, set the main pattern of HBC inland trade for the next twenty years, and persisted as one of several policies for the rest of the century. Until 1793 "winterers," who included the explorers Matthew Cocking, Samuel Hearne, David Thompson and Peter Fidler, worked to fend off rival traders and to bring more Native groups into direct relationship with the company. Geographical discoveries and the expansion of trade depended on the ability of these young men to fit in with aboriginal ways of life, to negotiate persuasively, and to keep a daily account of the places and people they met with. Their journals are the earliest empirical record of the geography, indigenous societies and trading arrangements to be found west of the Great Lakes.[1] HBC decisions affecting contact with Native groups were based in large part on the winterers' reports. Systematic coverage of Henday's route, descriptions of waterways and prairie landscape, and repeated mention of meeting Native "strangers" and French rivals promise a detailed account of the continental interior. Yet Henday's journal, the first of this series, is oddly *uninformative*, even though it adheres to the style and categories of observation recommended by the Royal Society.

Nor is much known about Anthony Henday: documentation of his life is limited to records of his baptism and his service to the Hudson's Bay Company. Henday's birth on the Isle of Wight is confirmed in the Shorwell parish register: he was christened on 24 December

---

Notes to this section are on pp. 5-6.

1725, the third of eight children born to Anthony and Mary Hendy (née Welcombe), who were married in 1721. A Church of England "Visitation" in 1725 described Shorwell as a ten-mile circuit of farmland with just over three hundred inhabitants, no papists, no dissenters, no gentlemen, no hospital, no school. Henday would have had a country upbringing in modest circumstances. His father leased property passed down in his wife's family; this land was leased in turn to the eldest boy; as a younger son, Anthony was left to make his own way. Smuggling was a frequent occupation for islanders and promised adventure; according to Andrew Graham, under whom he served at two Bayside posts, Henday was "outlawed for smuggling" in 1748. The young man drifted to London, and joined the Hudson's Bay Company in 1750.

Henday travelled to York Fort on the company's annual supply ship together with James Isham, its returning chief factor, who pronounced him "a Very Serviceable man." After three unremarkable years as a labourer, paid at the rate of £10 a year, Henday volunteered to winter on the plains with a group of "trading Indians" and to meet with "strangers" who did not have direct contact with the Bay forts. When he reappeared at York a year later, journal and map in hand, Henday was offered a new contract at £15 a year for three years. The explorer insisted on double his former salary; accordingly he was awarded a £20 gratuity and £20 a year until 1757. He tried to return to the Saskatchewan region only a few days after his arrival at York in June 1755; this attempt failed because of his companion's poor health. Henday spent a second year inland in 1759-60. No journal for this second trip is extant or even mentioned in the York Fort reports, but Henday's name appears on a Native map copied by Moses Norton, chief factor at Churchill, in 1760. During the next two years Henday served at York Fort and at Severn House, where Andrew Graham was Master. Once more he insisted on a raise in salary, to £30 a year; this time the company's directors refused. Henday sailed for England in September 1762. Having lived frugally at the Bay, to the point of irritating the supply-ship captains by his refusal to buy "Slops & Brandy" from them, Henday was able to claim most of the back pay due to him—a sum just under £113. Nothing is known of his life following his service to the HBC. The last records are of his family on the Isle of Wight: Henday's father received poor relief for several years until his death in 1771; the parish also paid his mother for minding children, and later awarded her a widow's pension.[2]

Henday's importance as a historical figure is due solely to the winter he spent west of a French outpost called Basquia, now The Pas, in 1754-55. The Hudson's Bay Company "wintering policy," beginning with Henday's year inland in 1754-55, marks a transitional period of European exploration. Increased efforts to accommodate empirical methods of gathering and analyzing evidence distinguish both the maritime and overland explorations of the eighteenth century. The day-by-day reporting and observational categories of Henday's journal place it with records of later eighteenth-century explorers such as Fidler and Thompson. His journal has been examined for the route he is said to have followed, the Native tribes he is said to have met, and the trade negotiations he is said to have attempted. The journal's empirical claims are seldom questioned despite its remarkable opacity on all these issues. Its empirical claims are deceptive. Its information—where Henday travelled, the inland Native groups he met, what trade negotiations he was able to conduct—is not easily extracted from the four texts which represent the document. Instead, textual variants and contradictions draw attention to its formal characteristics and all but defeat any attempt to resolve them into a coherent, consistent understanding of Henday's activities. It would be a mistake to attribute this lack of "transparency" to an early, mid-century crudeness which the later journals overcame: the empirical form of Henday's journal is just as sophisticated as that of the great maritime and overland explorers. Henday's journal is doubtful evidence because it has survived as four copies immune to recension. It is valuable and interesting for precisely the same reason.

A Year Inland publishes for the first time all four known texts of Henday's journal. Now historians, anthropologists and geographers who refer to the explorer and his observations can trace the variants as they occur in the four texts, and can decide on the basis of this complete record what is and is not to be accepted as "factual" and reliable information. Henday's journal and other fur-trade documents deserve more careful consideration as sources, starting points, specific sites that of themselves establish certain relationships and suggest certain possibilities.[3] If a document is used as a source, it must be a reliable text, and all the textual aspects and problems associated with it need to be fully examined and exposed. Hence the need for careful edition which not only makes texts accessible but also presents the problems attendant on using them as sources.

These cautions concerning scholarly use of sources seem self-evident because of documentary "bias"—or at the very least, because of the difference between the contemporary function of given documents and their subsequent importance as sources. We all agree, at least in theory, that the map is not the territory. But in practice we take maps at face value by equating their signs with features of the landscape. As with maps, so with verbal documents. Narratives and

journals are valued for their reference to the events and situations
"beyond words" that history, anthropology and geography analyze,
imagine and reconstruct.[4] Textual features impeding such a process
of analysis and reconstruction are seen as a "puzzle," as problems to
be "disentangled" and resolved, more often than not by tautological
reference to the situation that the source is supposed to illumine.[5]
Henday's journal tests this process because its referentiality can be
posited only at the cost of ignoring its textual characteristics.

A Year Inland invites scholars to focus for a moment on the map,
not the territory. Henday's journal is as close to pure textuality and
non-referentiality as a document with empirical claims can get; the
multiple texts frustrate attempts to glimpse Henday's "world" even
as they claim to report it. Scholars have been tempted to ignore the
textual features of Henday's journal, or to dismiss the entire document as vague and confusing. But the referential strategy of analysis
that they have employed to date is not the only one available. Rather
than measuring the explorer's "bias" by a debatable standard, or fill-
ing in textual gaps by an appeal to various kinds of ethnographic and
archaeological evidence, I examine the four extant texts in relation to
contemporary HBC documents: the other winterers' journals and the
Bay factors' correspondence. This documentary context at times con-
firms, at times questions the statements of Henday's journal by an
appeal to evidence of the same kind, which means that the degree of
methodological adjustment and consequent uncertainty is far less.
Textual features are seen not as obstacles to non-textual, informational understanding, but as clues that the journal played a role in the
Bay factors' very textual attempts to influence company policy.

The edition begins with detailed descriptions of the Henday
manuscripts, discussion of the textual problems they present, a brief
review of Canadian and American editorial practice, and an explanation of the editorial criteria used for the four Henday manuscripts.
Presentation of the four texts is supported by detailed textual notes.
Supplementary notes provide material for study of the journal and its
place in the history and anthropology of mid-eighteenth-century
North America. These supplementary notes draw on three sets of documents: first, the winterers' journals for the period 1754-74; second,
company correspondence and memoirs relating to this twenty-year
period; and third, published historical and anthropological studies
that give more than passing mention to Henday.

The final section consists of three essays reviewing the most frequently commented aspects of Henday's year inland. These essays are
tentative; they make no claim to be the last word on their subjects.
"Tracing Henday's Route" examines historians' various estimates of

the extent of Henday's explorations, and then compares Henday's with other winterers' accounts. "Indians, Asinipoets and Archithinues" reviews studies of the Native groups with whom the Hudson's Bay Company traded, either directly or through middlemen. Anthropological classifications are then compared with reference to Native groups in the journals of Henday and the other winterers. The third essay, "Uses of Henday's Journal," considers the journal's empirical claims, and then examines the four extant manuscripts in the context of contemporary HBC documents. The deliberate, open-ended inconclusiveness of this commentary invites other scholars to review their assessments of Henday's role in the fur trade, using all four copies of the journal and building on the textual awareness they require.

Notes

1 Burpee, "York Factory to the Blackfeet Country," 307-8, hints rather vaguely at the difference between non-empirical and empirical records in his contrast of Henry Kelsey's narrative and Anthony Henday's journal. Kelsey's text offers no "satisfactory proof that he reached the Saskatchewan [River] . . . The whole narrative . . . is too unsubstantial to afford any safe ground for historical conclusions. The case of Anthony Hendry [*sic*] is entirely different. It is possible to follow him almost step by step." Burpee adds in conclusion, "Hendry was the actual discoverer of the South Saskatchewan. Certainly his is the first unquestionably authentic description of the river."

2 For information on Henday's family and his early life I am greatly indebted to Don Kennett, Henday's descendant, who searched the Shorwell parish records. Stephen, 30-49, carefully traces Henday's twelve years of service to the HBC. Company records include HBCA A.1/38, London Minute Book, 24 April 1750; HBCA A.1/40, London Minute Book, 12 January 1757; HBCA A.6/9, HBC London Committee to Isham, 12 May 1755, 27 May 1755 and 12 May 1756; HBCA A.6/10, HBC London Committee to Humphrey Marten, 24 May 1762; HBCA A.11/114, Isham to the HBC London Committee, 21 May 1750, 2 September 1755 and 4 August 1756; HBCA A.11/115, Humphrey Marten to the HBC London Committee, 2 August 1761; HBCA B.198/a/2-3, Severn House journal, 1760-61; HBCA B.239/a/39, York Fort post journal, 1754-55; HBCA B.239/a/41, York Fort post journal, 1755-56; HBCA E.2/11, Henday, journal, notes to entries for 27 June and 31 October 1754; HBCA G.2/8, "Moses Nortons Drt. of the Northern Parts of Hudsons Bay . . . " (1760). See also Williams, "The Puzzle of Anthony Henday's Journal," 54, and Stephen, 30: speculations that Henday's name was French or that Henday conversed with French traders in Cree have no documentary support—cf. HBCA B.239/a/40, Henday, journal, 23 May 1755, and HBCA A.11/114, Isham, instructions to Anthony Henday, 19 February 1754.

3 Cullen: "Too many of us have lost the skill of learning history from the documents we encounter as we do our research. We no longer let the documents lead us . . . It may be that documentary editorial projects are the

last bastion of traditional historical research, where the written record is paramount and the documents lead the scholar toward a thesis that unfolds in a well-written narrative" (73).

4 Brown and Vibert, title and introduction.

5 Williams, "The Puzzle of Anthony Henday's Journal"; Stephen, ii, 70-88.

The Four Manuscripts

1754
June
y.e 26.

Wednesday fine weather, wind att W.t took my Departure from York Fort, and padled up his River, to y.e "Big Stone." — here we put up for the night.

y.e 27.

Thursday fine weather wind W.t padled up Hays River, till we came to Steel River, and then up Steel River till we came to wood partridge Creek, their we put up for y.e night.

y.e 28.

Friday fine weather wind att S.o & SW.t padled up Steel River till we came to pine Reach, their put up for the night.

y.e 29.

Saturday fine weather wind att N.o took my Departure from pine Reach, and padled up Steel River, NWBW.t and SW.t 28. miles, the woods & Land is much the same, this day past 7 falls, was obliged to Carry our things over 4 of them, the water being shoal, past 3 brushy Islands.

y.e 30.

Sunday fine weather wind att N.o took my Departure from Inclosed falls, and steered SWBW.t and NW.t 25 miles, this day past four falls, the banks are high & tall woods on both sides the River, which is about 16 poles wide and a strong Current.

Plate I: HBCA B.239/a/40

Observations on Hudsons-Bay

The following is a Journal of a Journey inland from York Fort up Hays River &c by Anthony Hendey from June the 26th 1754 to June the 23d 1755 viz.

1754
June

26. Wednesd. fine weather, wind Wt. took my departure from Yf. and paddled up Hays River to the Big Stone; here we put up for the night.

27. Thursd. fine weather, wind at Wt. paddled up Hays River till we came to Steel River, and then up Steel River to wood partridge Creek. then we put up for the night.

28. Frid. fine weather, wind S. & SW. paddled up Steel River to pine reach, then put up for the night.

29. Saturd. fine weather, wind Nt. took my departure from + pine-Reach and paddled up Steel River NBW. 25 miles; this day passed 4 large falls, the banks are high, and tall woods on both sides the River, which is about 16 poles wide, and a strong current.

+ From Yf. to this pine reach was measured in the winter 1754 by Anthony Hendey, by which knowing the distance those 3 days first, He computes the miles He goes of a day hereafter.

Plate 2: HBCA B.2/6

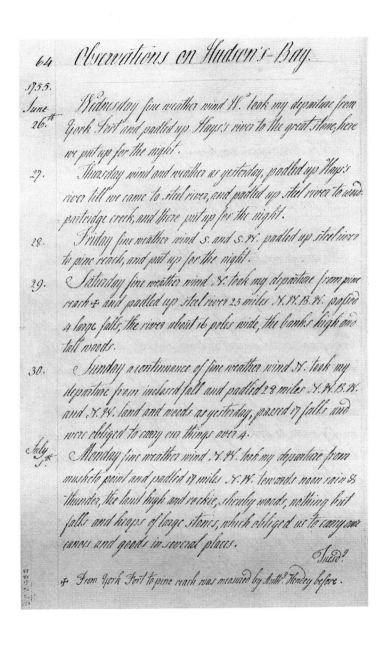

1755.

June 26th   Wednesday fine weather wind W. took my departure from York Fort and padled up Hays's river to the great stone, here we put up for the night.

27.   Thursday wind and weather as yesterday, padled up Hays's river till we came to steel river, and padled up steel river to wind partridge creek, and there put up for the night.

28.   Friday fine weather wind S. and S.W. padled up steel river to pine reach, and put up for the night.

29.   Saturday fine weather wind N. took my departure from pine reach + and padled up steel river 25 miles N.W.B.W. passed 4 large falls, the river about 16 poles wide, the banks high and tall woods.

30.   Sunday a continuance of fine weather wind N. took my departure from inclosed fall and padled 28 miles N.W.B.W. and N.W. land and woods as yesterday, passed 17 falls and were obliged to carry our things over 4.

July 1st   Monday fine weather wind N.W. took my departure from musketo point and padled 17 miles N.W. towards noon rain & thunder, the land high and rockie, shruby woods, nothing but falls and heaps of large stones, which obliged us to carry our canoes and goods in several places.

               Tuesd?

+ From York Fort to pine reach was measured by Anth⁰ Hendey before.

Plate 3: HBCA E.2/4

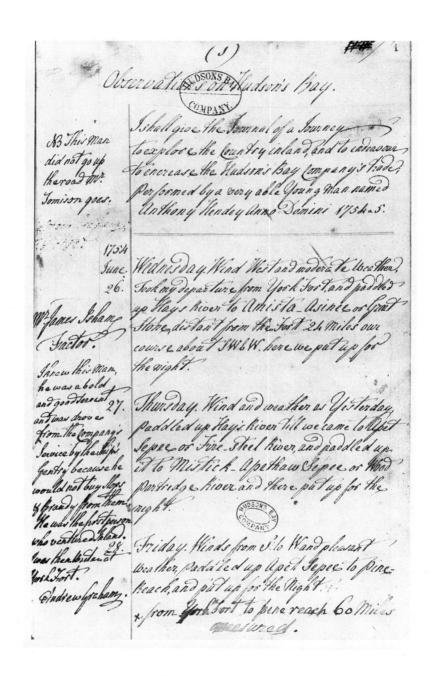

(5)

Observations on Hudson's Bay.

I shall give the Journal of a Journey
to explore the Country inland, and to endeavour
to encrease the Hudson's Bay Company's Trade,
Performed by a very able Young Man named
Anthony Hendey Anno Domini 1754 & 5.

NB This Man
did not go up
the road M.
Tomison goes.

1754
June
26.

M. James Isham
Factor.

I knew this Man,
he was a bold
and good servant
and was drove
from the Company's
Service by their Chief
Gentry because he
would not buy Slops
& Brandy from them.
He was the first person
who ventured Inland
was then Trade at
York Fort.

Andrew Graham.

Wednesday. Wind West and moderate Weather,
Took my departure from York Fort, and paddled
up Hays River to Amista-Asinee or Great
Stone, distant from the Fort 24 Miles our
course about SW&W. here we put up for
the night.

27.

Thursday. Wind and weather as Yesterday,
paddled up Hays River till we came to Apet
Sepee or Fire-Steel River, and paddled up
it to Mistick-Apethaw Sepee or Wood
partridge River and there put up for the
night.

28.

Friday. Winds from S to W and pleasant
weather, paddled up Apet Sepee to Pine-
Reach, and put up for the Night.
+ from York Fort to Pine reach 60 Miles
measured.

Plate 4: HBCA E.2/11

12

From Manuscript to Print

From Manuscript to Print

Historical claims for Henday's exploration of the western plains refer to his journal for evidence of his actions and observations. The earliest of the four extant manuscripts, all conserved in the Hudson's Bay Company Archives, is a copy sent to London a few weeks after Henday's return to York in June 1755; the latest was copied about 1782. No holograph survives; no two archival copies agree entirely on the "facts" they record. The copy dated 1782 was published in 1907, as an article in the *Transactions* of the Royal Society of Canada. Its editor, Lawrence J. Burpee, published a colleague's transcription made fifteen years before; apparently Burpee never saw the 1782 manuscript.[1] For almost a century, this *Transactions* article has been the only text of Henday's journal more or less readily available to scholars: the twentieth-century copy of a nineteenth-century copy of a late eighteenth-century copy of Henday's lost holograph journal. If this sequence of copying is hard to follow, it is doubly hard to account for the fact that Burpee's printed text has for so long been considered authoritative. Restricted access to the Hudson's Bay Company Archives may partly explain its initial acceptance. Even the number of archival copies was uncertain until Glyndwr Williams announced in 1969 that he had found four manuscripts of the journal dating from 1755 to about 1782.[2] Despite Williams's announcement, and despite his intriguing article on the four texts which appeared nine years later, there has been no rush to re-edit Henday's journal. Their awareness of the multiple texts has not prevented historians and anthropologists from making bold claims for Henday as a western explorer and a witness to Native ways of life.

Notes to this section are on pp. 31-36.

Henday is supposed to have travelled extensively in what are now the prairie provinces, to have met with Blackfoot chiefs, and to have come within sight of the Rocky Mountains. However, the four early manuscript copies contain omissions, alterations and contradictions which can easily subvert attempts to see the journal as a reliable record of the explorer's movements and observations. As empirical evidence, Henday's journal is disappointing. Its vocabulary is limited; the record of courses and distances is unreliable; its landscape descriptions are vague and repetitive; its accounts of contact with Natives are superficial and at times confusing. Instead of providing new information about inland routes and trade, it leaves the continental interior a cartographic blank, and simply repeats what was already known to the Bayside factors. Journals of the kind Henday kept are textual representations of the experiences they record: writing such journals makes the lived experiences into referential narrative statements which allow readers to learn at second hand what the writer has seen and done. In the case of Henday's journal, the relationship between text and experience is exceptionally elusive. Despite its empirical agenda and its tantalizing evocation of landscapes and cultures, references to places, people and events are so vague and contradictory that a clear sense of where Henday travelled, whom he met and what trade was carried on at the French outposts is difficult if not impossible to achieve. The temptation to force the evidence—to supply, substitute or overlook certain details—is apparent in past readings of Henday's journal. Responsible use of the journal as a reference for mid-eighteenth-century geographical exploration, Native cultures and the fur trade needs to begin with a close look at the four archival texts.

The earliest text of Henday's journal, B.239/a/40, is a folio notebook of forty-six sheets stitched into covers of heavy marbled paper measuring 32.5 cm x 20 cm. A lozenge-shaped label pasted on the front cover gives a short title, "M/ Captn Hendeys Journal/ 1754/ a/ 1755," in the bold copperplate of Andrew Graham, "Accomptant" and second-in-command at York Fort. Directed by James Isham, York's chief factor, Graham made this copy of Henday's journal for the "London Committee," the Hudson's Bay Company's governing board, to be sent with the supply ship returning to England in September of that year. The paper has a double watermark, one half with the emblem of a crowned lion encircled with the words PRO PATRIA ET USQUE LIBERTATE, the other half with a crowned circle and wreath surrounding the initials GR. Similar marbled covers with labels and the same watermark pattern characterize other York Fort records between 1750 and 1757, that is, during Isham's tenure as chief factor. The verso of the first folio carries the long title, and the daily entries begin on folio 3r; the last folio of the notebook is blank.[3] The manuscript is a neat clerical copy in which occasional errors have been carefully erased and overwritten; it is unadorned except for Graham's frequent flourished capitals. A "Draft" of Henday's route inland, drawn by Isham, originally accompanied the journal text when it was sent to London in 1755, but this map is not in the HBCA collection.

The later texts of Henday's journal are incorporated into three of ten volumes of Andrew Graham's "Observations on Hudson's Bay," a personal memoir which Graham modelled on Isham's manuscript work of the same title. Graham wrote, assembled and revised his work over a twenty-five-year period, during which he served as master of Severn House (1761-74), twice as interim chief at York (1765-66, 1771-72), and as chief factor at Prince of Wales's Fort, Churchill (1774-75), before retiring to Britain.[4] Like Isham, Graham described the landscape, flora and fauna of Hudson Bay, enumerated the Native groups who lived there and visited the forts, and commented on the customs and policies of the fur trade. Two of the Henday texts are found in the earliest states of the "Observations" (E.2/6 dated 1767-69, and E.2/4 dated 1768-69); the third is included in an undated volume (E.2/11) to which the HBCA has assigned the date 1792.

The E.2/6 text of the "Observations" is bound in vellum and contains eighty-six folio sheets measuring 37 cm x 24 cm, the last 27 folios of which are blank. The spine is stamped "O.H.B. 5." It is the second volume of a set, of which the first volume is missing. The watermark emblem is a crowned fleur-de-lis under which are the initials LVG; on the other half of the sheet is the number IV. The margins of each page are ruled in double black lines, and red ink is used for some text breaks and footnotes. The text of E.2/6 is in Graham's own hand; the cover, also in Graham's hand, is inscribed "Observations on Hudsons Bay. Book the Second. By Mr Andrew Graham. 1767-8-9." As in his nineteen-page pamphlet presented to the London Committee in October 1769,[5] much of the E.2/6 volume is taken up with Graham's discussion of trading policy; in support of his views he appends an abstract of William Tomison's journal of 1767-68 as well as a copy of Henday's journal (folios 10v-38v). The acquisition history of E.2/6 shows it to have been part of the library of Samuel Wegg, a company director as of 1772 and HBC Governor from 1782 to 1799. Since this volume outlines topics that are developed more fully in the other states, this volume appears to be the earliest extant version of the "Observations" from which the 1769 pamphlet and subsequent states were derived. While the E.2/6 copy of Henday's journal is radically different from B.239/a/40 in certain respects, in others it is closer to B.239/a/40 than the other E texts are.[6]

E.2/4 is the first volume of a two-volume set (E.2/4 and E.2/5) bound in vellum with a double line blind-stamped along the edges of the cover and a short title, partly erased: "Observations on Hudson's Bay/ by Andrew [Graham] 1768/ Iournal." The spine is stamped "O.H.B. 3."; the companion volume is stamped "O.H.B. 4." The volume is made up of ninety-three folio sheets measuring 32.5 cm x 20 cm. One half of the double watermark shows Britannia seated with a sceptre, together with a lion bearing a sword, both figures surrounded by a fence; the other half is a crown surmounting the initials GR. The recto of the first folio carries a second title followed by a table of contents on 1v and 2r. Although the text hand is not Graham's but that of an unidentified copyist, Graham's own inscription of the title page emphasizes the personal nature of the compilation and imitates Isham's note to the same effect: "Observations on Hudson's Bay by Andrew Graham many years Chief Factor; written with no other intention than for my Own Amusement, and to pass away an Idle hour in this solitary part of the world in two Books. Book 1st Anno Dom^i 1768 a 9."[7] The volume begins on folio 4r with "A Geographical description of Hudson's Straits and Bay" followed by descriptions of the Native groups who traded at the Bayside forts. Henday's journal is introduced on folio 35r as part of "A small account of the Archithinue Indians" and is copied in folios 35v-6or.

E.2/11 presents the "Observations" in a single volume bound in buckram with the spine and corners in leather; the spine is stamped "Obs. on Hudson Bay O.H.B. 11." in gold letters. There are 166 unlined pages measuring 37 cm x 23 cm, stitched into several signatures and apparently cut when bound. The watermark emblem is a crowned shield displaying a fleur-de-lis with the initials GR underneath; the other half shows the name C. TAYLOR for 144 pages (the first 72 folio numbers), then various names including EDMEADS & PINE (folios 86-89) and J. WHATMAN (folios 75, 77, 81, 83). Although differently bound, the E.2/12 volume of the "Observations" is written on the same assortment of paper stock and, as in E.2/11, the original pagination is altered. Graham's editor, Glyndwr Williams, surmises that "the two volumes were written at approximately the same time in loose-leaf form . . . a considerable reshuffling of the pages took place before they were given their final numbers and bound into two volumes."[8] E.2/11 is in Graham's hand, but relatively little of it is Graham's direct composition. Henday's journal is the first text (folios 1r-40v), followed by an abridged version of Matthew Cocking's inland journal of 1772-73, a few blank pages, Thomas Hutchins's experiments with the dipping needle and observations on cold, and thirteen more blank pages at the end.[9] A number of repeated words, omissions and corrections suggest that the E.2/11 text of Henday's journal was copied distractedly or in haste. By noting these irregularities, the reader is able to follow Graham at work on Henday's journal.

It is difficult, if not impossible, to determine the exact relationship of the four Henday texts. Unfortunately paper watermarks are poor indications for dating the manuscripts. Very generally, it can be said that until 1750 most paper used in Britain was imported from Holland, France and Italy; in the second half of the century James Whatman's paperworks, together with those of several rivals within the country, supplied many British printers. Edward Heawood's study of seventeenth- and eighteenth-century watermarks provides examples of marks like those of B.239/a/40 ranging from 1745 to 1776, of E.2/6 from 1744 and 1766, of E.2/4 from 1747 to 1766, and of E.2/11 from 1781 to 1792. Most of Heawood's watermark samples are taken from printed books, but those resembling the B.239/a/40 and E.2/4 marks are found in legal documents from southern England, while those comparable to the E.2/6 mark come from maps, a pilot and a proposal to establish longitude.[10]

In determining the relationship of the four texts, a study of the manuscript variants is not much more helpful than hunting down the watermarks. All four extant manuscripts are copies, witnesses to the lost archetype of Henday's field journal, which never became part of the company record. As we have seen, three of the texts were copied by Graham himself; the copy in another hand is found in E.2/4, possibly the earliest state of Graham's "Observations." As Williams remarks, "The more one investigates the curious business of the variant copies of Henday's journal, the more Graham emerges as a key figure in the whole affair."[11]

Williams's assessment of the manuscript relationship is that B.239/a/40, the official copy sent to London in 1755, omitted or bowdlerized key passages of the explorer's own "notes." Williams states clearly that "none of [the archival] copies can be directly attributed to him; as far as is known, not a scrap exists of the original journal or of any notes kept by Henday during his year inland." Williams speculates that Graham "acquired either Henday's original journal notes, or a copy of them. . . . A comparison of all four copies suggests that they were made from Henday's loose notes rather than from a bound journal."[12] Henday set off in June 1754 equipped with "a Compass, hand Line paper &: &"; quite possibly Henday's "Quire of Paper," sent to him in September 1754, was for his journal as well as for mapping. On the other hand, James Isham's instructions for Henday's exploration of the Nelson River in February 1754 provided a formula for entries to be noted each day in a "Wast Book." Four months later,

Isham exhorted Henday to "be Very Exact in Keeping a Journal."[13] Henday's 1754-75 journal may have been written on folio sheets stitched together, or it may have been written in another "Wast Book." Although Isham's letter and instructions leave the material condition of Henday's original record in some doubt, the manner and form of its composition seems clear. Henday wrote a journal, that is, a series of entries accounting for each day's weather, travel, hunt and social interaction. Given this calendar structure, the occasional rearrangement of entries in the E texts might be more easily explained by eyeskip during rapid or distracted copying than by the shuffling and rearranging of "loose notes." Williams further speculates that Henday tampered with his own "notes" with the aim of presenting a report of trading success to his superiors at York Fort. If Williams is right, then the text that Graham revised for inclusion in the "Observations" was a success version in the explorer's own hand, making B.239/a/40 closer to Henday's original journal than the failure version of the E texts. Williams is thus arguing that B.239/a/40 is at once "authentic" and "false."[14]

Graham's influence as copyist, compiler and commentator is clearly inseparable from all the texts of Henday's journal, yet the nature and extent of this involvement is difficult to define. From the outset, it is important to specify the generic difference between B.239/a/40, the official report sent to the company's directors, and the unofficial texts found in Graham's "Observations on Hudson's Bay." Both the report and the "Observations" can be categorized as public manuscripts: although they were not printed and published, they were circulated among influential readers. Graham presented at least one of the volumes and an executive summary to the London Committee, probably in a bid to further his career, and his notes on flora, fauna and cold were communicated to the Royal Society. But the "Observations" lacked the official character of B.239/a/40, in copying which Graham, as the clerk at York Fort and Isham's subordinate, was simply a functional link. The personal advantage Graham tried to gain by writing and compiling the "Observations" had to reflect the formulaic, professional nature of the company's official correspondence. To demonstrate his administrative role at Bay posts and his role in gathering information there, Graham copied winterers' reports into his private compilation, and referred to them as evidence of his own views on trade. How much Graham altered, redirected, even rewrote Henday's own journal to produce the three later texts found in his "Observations" cannot be decided with any precision. Even the process of preparing an annotated fair copy of the explorer's original text in 1755 must have involved certain changes, and the conditions of trade Graham faced seventeen years later probably suggested other changes. To consider the E texts as closer to Henday's lost original than the fair copy sent to London in 1755 is to ignore Graham's intervention as copyist in all four instances.

The four extant texts are rife with differences and contradictions. Even entries which record the same details—for example, the entries for 26 and 27 June; 2-4, 14, 26-28 July; 6-7, 15 August; 17-18 September—differ from each other in terms of vocabulary, proper names, turns of phrase and "accidentals" (dating, capitalization, punctuation). Williams's suggestion is that each of the "Observations" texts, like B.239/a/40, may have been directly copied from Henday's original journal. Alternatively, the "Observations" copies may be successive rewrites of the B.239/a/40 text. But indications for either pattern are slight and confusing.

Williams's argument for a common source in Henday's original journal is based on comparison of the entries for 22-23 July, 14-16 October, 27-28 December, 2 February, 15-16 and 21-25 May, and 30 May-1 June: these entries describe the French trade and the middleman system by which the Natives traded amongst themselves. It is true, as Williams maintains, that the entries in B.239/a/40 are sketchy and illogically optimistic of increased Native trade with the Bay forts, and certainly the entries in the E texts conform much more closely with the trade returns reported in the few years following Henday's trip inland.[15] There may be other signs that passages in B.239/a/40 represent alterations of the lost original journal, and that the E texts are separate transcriptions from this lost original. More than once—for example, in the entries for 24 July, 5 September, 26 October, 6 November, 4 February and 17 May—E.2/11 is closer to E.2/6 than to E.2/4. Occasionally E.2/11 includes a detail not given in any of the earlier texts: Henday's party crossed a river "in our Slender Canoes without any Accident happening" (21 August), and while hunting buffalo "the bullet we oftentimes get again" (30 December). Such details could just as easily be comments from the copyist's general knowledge as from Henday's original journal. Perhaps the most persuasive argument for a common original can be found in the pattern of combined entries in E.2/4 and E.2/11: the E.2/4 text abbreviates more incisively than E.2/11, and the dates summarized in E.2/11 represent a different selection. For example, 10-11 November, 13-14 November, 16-20 November and 28 December-4 January are combined entries in E.2/4 while each day is given a separate entry in E.2/11; again, 1-9 December, 11-15 December, 24-27 December and 6 March-22 April are combined entries in E.2/4, while E.2/11 presents a series of smaller combinations: 1, 2, 3-4, 5-7 December; 11-12, 13, 14, 15 December; 24, 25, 26-27 December; and, except for 26 March to 7 April, combined entries for only two or three days.

However, indications of successive rewriting and thus an evolving, "genetic" textual pattern are also persuasive. The E-text descriptions of Henday's mid-October meeting with the Archithinues incorporate Isham's "Notes and Remarks," which followed the B.239/a/40 journal text, directly into the journal entries. A second indication of serial rewriting is that in some entries (for example, 12, 19-21, 29 July; 9-12, 14, 17-18, 30-31 August, 23 December and 2 February), the same details are relayed in fewer words, and this tendency towards increased economy follows from B.239/a/40 to E.2/6 to E.2/4 to E.2/11. At the same time, details may be progressively altered and confused, as in the entry for 15 July. B.239/a/40 records that "this day Entered Mono ko tusky, where came to us 4 Canoes (their Leaders name Maconsko)"; E.2/6 and E.2/4 announce that Henday had arrived in "the dry or inland country" and give the leader's name as "Monkonsko," a conflation of B.239/a/40's two proper names; the E.2/11 text, which often includes the Cree names translated in the earlier "Observations" texts, states that Henday "was on the confines of the dry inland country, called by the Natives the Muscuty Tuskee," but still gives the leader's name as "Monkonsko." A third indication of successive rewriting is that the three "Observations" texts tend to minimize and/or generalize specific comments in B.239/a/40 concerning Henday's personal interaction with the Native group he accompanied (for example, 13 and 26 September, 16 May). Conversely, when the "Observations" texts amplify an entry beyond that given in B.239/a/40 (for example, 1, 14-16 October, 23 April, 15, 30 May), more often than not the added material emphasizes not Henday's individuality but his generic Englishness: he is the HBC representative opposed to French traders inland. Supplementary descriptions, such as smoking with "strangers" and hunting buffalo, are similar to passages in later fur-trade journals.

The process of editing Henday's journal is a response to two important questions: which of the four manuscripts, if any, is to be privileged as the source- or copy-text, and to what extent can editorial emendation and annotation make the journal readable and accessible? Little explicit guidance is available in the Canadian tradition of editing historical documents. From Lawrence J. Burpee's publication of Henday's and Cocking's journals in 1907-8 to editions published in the last ten years, reflection on editorial problems and choices has been cursory at best. "The historical editor has always been the poor stepchild of Clio," avers J. M. Bumsted. "To edit—even brilliantly—a lengthy manuscript or a collection of papers is regarded . . . as uncreative hackwork . . . Canada, unfortunately, has no tradition of editing whatever." As well as a shortage of funds, "historical editing in Canada suffers from . . . an absence of a clear sense of priorities . . . combined with a lack of critical criteria [*sic*]." Bumsted lists five elements of an edited text as "the minimum to be expected from an editor": "an accurate test, and some explicit statement of the transcription style to be employed; a complete text or some editorial explanation and justification of any omissions; an editorial introduction which provides an adequate context for the printed transcription, especially for the non-specialist reader; sufficient annotation to clarify obscure references in the text, including those to characters and situations given more than fleeting mention by the original author; and a full index, at least nominal and preferably including place names and subject headings."[16] Bumsted does not define "accurate test" or "complete text," while "context" is assumed to be the events, characters, setting and conditions that produced the document and that figure in the text.

The *Occasional Papers of the Champlain Society* for 1992 provides a second theoretical statement on Canadian editing, by ethno-historian and editor Jennifer S. H. Brown. This outline of editorial principles echoes American historians' views of the past three decades, notably the protest of Jesse Lemisch on behalf of previously "inarticulate" social groups.[17] Brown considers the editorial process as a series of five textual operations. First, the editor chooses a "voice" characteristic of a historically significant personality out of "an endless supply of documents." (How a "voice" issues from documents, especially the "voice" of "inarticulate" social groups, and how "historical significan[ce]" is determined are questions left unexplained.) As a second step, the editor makes a selection of texts in conformity with the restrictions of publication space and cost. Brown considers this practical consideration as arbitrary: "a portion of a man's [*sic*] writings or one phase of his career is taken to stand for his whole output or for the writer himself." Third, the editor alters the original text to accommodate a new audience—an inevitable transformation, says Brown, who even as she insists that "editors should still be as faithful as possible to texts," avoiding "substantive emendations," nevertheless approves expanded abbreviations and interpolated editorial notes of identification and clarification. Fourth, the editor further annotates the text in order to point out, for the benefit of "most readers," the "many subtle messages" of style as well as content that such readers would otherwise miss. Fifth and finally, the editor writes an introduction that is neither too detailed, nor "annoyingly minimal," but a "middle ground" that "helps readers at the outset to have an overview of the life or lives of those figures to be published and to have a sense of the origins and history of the documentary texts themselves."[18]

The recommendations of Bumsted's review and Brown's article reflect the practice of Canadian documentary editors since Burpee's day. Bumsted and Brown are agreed that the approach and emphasis of editing should be biographical, or at least "historical": the editor's job is to describe the life and explain the times of a personality or group generally considered to be an important agent or representative of events or conditions during a given period. This descriptive, explicative "context" is to surround a text made readable and accessible thanks to editorial emendations. Early editors of Canadian material gave no account at all of the manuscripts on which their edited texts were based, and their criteria for emendation were as silent as the emendations themselves. In the last twenty years, editors have become more forthcoming about the manuscripts they work on and more scrupulous about editorial interference in the printed text. Most editorial introductions include a statement of respect for original documents—a statement which prefaces a list of the changes and intrusive emendations that (respect aside) have been imposed on the edited text. In very recent editions, manuscript sources have been clearly identified and in some instances described. But although they make insistent claims that they have faithfully transcribed these sources, recent editors continue the Canadian historical tradition of fairly heavy emendation, interpolation and annotation. A century of Champlain Society editions provides an overview of Canadian documentary editing; publications of the Hudson's Bay Record Society (later volumes of which were under the general editorship of Glyndwr Williams) furnish an important parallel series. To these can be added the journals of Mackenzie, Fraser, Franchère and Vancouver edited by W. Kaye Lamb, the journals of Franklin edited by Richard C. Davis and those of his officers by C. Stuart Houston, the journals of George M. Dawson edited by Douglas Cole and Bradley Lockner, as well as my edition of Thompson's "Columbia" journals.[19]

In contrast to editorial theory and practice in this country, American documentary editing has been organized on a grander scale, and theoretical discussion has been livelier. Government funding of scholarly teams who worked for decades on the papers of eminent statesmen was parallelled by aid for "definitive" editions of important American literary figures. Institutional divisions and separate funding policies encouraged two editorial methodologies. Literary critics, championed by Fredson Bowers, insisted on scrupulous collation of all copies and claimed to honour a writer's "final intentions." Although institutionally powerful, the Bowers approach to editing was never without its critics, the most recent and persuasive of whom publish regularly in the journal *Text*.[20] Historians favoured the expanded transcriptions and extensive commentary of Julian Boyd and Lyman Butterfield, whose edition of Thomas Jefferson's *Papers* is still considered "exemplary."[21] The historians' approach, known as "documentary editing," was pursued with far less internal discussion of premises and principles. A jumpstart to historians' reconsideration of their methods and to interdisciplinary debate came in 1978 with the publication of G. Thomas Tanselle's essays entitled "Editing of Historical Documents." Tanselle condemned certain practices of documentary editing, especially heavy emendation and inadequate exposition of editorial criteria.[22] The National Historical Publications and Records Commission reacted by publishing an official study of the "crisis" in editing, and Robert J. Taylor wrote a particularly thoughtful response. At the same time, as Mary-Jo Kline attests in *A Guide to Documentary Editing*, "[i]n private, many historical editors grumbled at an 'outsider's' criticism of textual methods for materials they felt he did not understand or appreciate."[23]

In the years that followed, American practitioners of literary and historical editing tried hard to listen to each other.[24] The Society for Textual Studies, publisher of the journal *Text*, has held interdisciplinary conferences every two years since 1981. In 1983, inheritors of Boyd's project announced "a conscious decision to focus editorial work on the documents themselves" rather than on historical commentary.[25] Gary E. Moulton's edition of the *Journals of the Lewis and Clark Expedition*, published between 1983 and 1989, set a newly rigorous standard for emendation and a closer focus on texts.[26] Kline maintains that all American scholarly editors now share "the same goal . . . : how best to present cautiously emended texts that preserve as much as possible of the original's evidence, along with efficient textual and contextual apparatus that the reader might use to evaluate the editors' handiwork in both textual [literary] and historical terms."[27]

Yet the conservative, institutional pull has been stronger than any interdisciplinary queries and ventures. The Association for Documentary Editing, which issues the journal *Documentary Editing* as well as sponsoring and endorsing Kline's *Guide*, tends, in Kline's words, "to focus more narrowly on the materials of 'history.' "[28] The impulse to expand, emend and annotate is rooted in historians' traditional choice and use of documents. Lemisch protested American historians' emphasis on statesmen's papers, but did not question the assumption that editors should choose "historically significant" texts—that is, texts associated with a figure or organization whose impact and importance is *already* acknowledged. Historians work on the premise that the social subject is "greater" and more fundamental than the text, in contrast to literary scholars, whose work centres on the text. For the historian, "the most important criterion to be met by any document . . . is that it is indeed the intellectual product of the person or organization purported to be its author." Documents are "evidence for factual research"; documentary editions "add to the human store of factual knowledge"; consequently, the work of documentary editing (unlike literary editing) "imposes a special responsibility."[29] Since historians believe that "context" (in the sense of conditions or motives for writing) determines the text, editorial selection of documents is "at best a necessary evil"; the edition should be a "window to the larger collection" of all the papers associated with a given individual, organization or period.[30] Historians' confidence in these axioms appears to be unshakeable, while the "continued academic debate . . . [has] forced literary scholars to reappraise their own assumptions and techniques as editors."[31] Critics' tendency to be critical, even or especially of their own "assumptions and techniques," is in marked contrast to historians' complacency, high moral seriousness and developed sense of turf. Although Kline states that "continued academic debate has modified the tone and direction of much of the discussion . . . and has called into question the simplistic alternative of 'historical' versus 'literary' editing," this academic distinction is maintained throughout her *Guide*, even in its newly revised edition.[32] Unfortunately, history as a discipline suffers from this isolationist tendency of its practitioners, and never more than when its own "assumptions and techniques" remain unexamined.

Its disciplinary myopia notwithstanding, *A Guide to Documentary Editing* furnishes a practical overview of the tasks and stages of editing, from collection and selection of documents, to textual transcription and emendation, and finally to annotation and indexing. It provides definitions that have long been implicit and clearly sets out a range of editorial choices. As well as explaining the types of transcription and editorial signs that are most commonly used, Kline briefly explores "documentary problems with textual solutions" and here finally concedes that "literary" editing has provided models for editing complex documents. Kline summarizes these textual problems by laying down three "common sense" rules for editing manuscript materials:

1. The manuscript . . . is to be preferred over any later scribal copies or transcriptions as the source text.

2. If the original has been lost or destroyed, contemporary copies are preferred over later ones unless evidence survives to demonstrate that later copyists had access to the now-vanished original, and were more accurate than earlier scribes.

3. In general, the most nearly final version of a document is the preferred source text. Editors can take comfort in the thought that variants can and should be noted in the editorial apparatus. Significant differences between different versions of a document will not be denied the reader by choosing one of them as source text. That source text is simply the version that serves as the best working basis for the edition.[33]

Henday's journal tests these guidelines: it presents several "documentary problems" in combination and requires innovation beyond Kline's rules in order to resolve them.

Kline's first two rules for choosing source texts are based on the assumption that "[d]ocumentary editing is most clearly distinguished from traditional critical textual editing by its customary reliance on a single . . . document (the source text)." When no original exists, the editor may rely on a holograph or letterpress duplicate. "A third order of preference is given to transcriptions," which may force editors to "use more advanced methods of classical filiation to determine which [transcription] offers the soundest source text."[34] Obviously transcriptions make problematic texts, and recension is a poor alternative to reliance on an authentic text (as any classical scholar would hasten to agree).[35] Historians are understandably reluctant to conflate or emend the texts they inherit; Kline's recommendation here is perhaps surprising, given her repeated distancing from the editorial manipulations of Bowers and his school.

But as we have seen in Glyndwr Williams's essay on the four Henday texts, avoidance of one trap can lead straight to another: Williams feels impelled to choose one manuscript over the others. Williams's choice is a textbook example of Kline's second rule: he privileges B.239/a/40 as more authentic than the three E texts because it is a contemporary copy. Yet we have also seen that in copying Henday's journal into his "Observations," Graham and the unidentified assistant of E.2/4 may have had access to the lost original, and may well have transcribed important passages on trade with less alteration than was the case for B.239/a/40.

Kline's third rule, privileging "the most nearly final version of a document," does not apply because the Henday texts cannot be arranged in a clear genetic sequence. Editorial focus on one text over others, however arbitrary and however compensated by the apparatus, "denie[s] the reader" precisely this ambiguity. As Kline points out, "scholars are as lazy as other mortals":[36] when readers are faced with a format that presents one "working" text as typographically more important than others, they cannot be expected to consider other "variant" texts as parallel and worth equal consideration. If Henday's journal were to be organized as Kline recommends—that is, privileging E.2/11 and making the earlier texts into variant drafts of this "most nearly final version," the journal would not be presented accurately or adequately.

In transcribing the texts, the editor must decide whether to emend them, and if so, how much. Kline presents the traditional range of editorial options—facsimile, diplomatic transcription, expanded transcription and clear text. From one traditional option to the next, the manuscript text is more and more open to alteration, and the emendations are less and less apparent. Kline recognizes that "no . . . typeface can reproduce all the subtle distinctions" of a manuscript text; "knowing this," she advises, "the editor should choose a textual policy whose conventions do not conceal additional subtleties."[37] Her recommendation goes against the preference of many historians for expanded transcription, in which punctuation, spelling and spacing are standardized, abbreviations and contractions are written out, and superscript characters are brought down to the line. In expanded transcription, these changes are noted generally in a preface rather than at each specific occurrence, while diplomatic transcription indicates each alteration. Yet diplomatic transcription, as Kline describes it, can also produce a heavily emended text:

> Editors of diplomatic transcriptions often standardize the placement of . . . datelines, greetings, salutations, titles and the indentation of paragraphs, and they may also supply missing punctuation, expand ambiguous or archaic abbreviations and contractions, or even supply words unintentionally omitted by the author or destroyed by mutilation of the source text. But none of these corrections or emendations is made silently: each is given within a form of brackets that indicates such editorial activities.[38]

One form of editorial intrusion is replaced by another; in both expanded and diplomatic transcription, the distance between the manuscript and the transcript can be equally great. The same can be said for typographic facsimiles. Readers must fight through a wilderness of editorial signs, and if they are "lazy mortals," they will probably admit defeat and close the book.

The clear text option avoids such unpleasantness: not only are emendations made silently, but the editor is free to improve the text. In theory, such improvements result from careful study of what the manuscript author would have written under more favourable conditions, or with a sharpened awareness of audience. Bowers and his following were notorious advocates of clear text; in this format, the editor could realize the author's "final intentions" and (more to the point) produce a text that perfectly satisfied the editor's own inclinations.[39] These "literary" editors were not alone in divining authorial intentions. Kline traces the editorial logic of the *Jefferson Papers*:

> Acutely aware of the loss suffered by the transfer . . . to a twentieth-century printed page, [Boyd and Butterfield] cast about for some device that would preserve the flavor of the original materials: their solution was to print manuscript materials more or less as they would have been printed at the time of their inscription. . . . In effect, Boyd and Butterfield sought to publish volumes of documents edited as Jefferson, Rush and Adams themselves would have edited them.[40]

The editors' period "flavor" and inferred intentions could only be spurious, since Boyd and Butterfield assumed a twentieth-century relationship between manuscript and print—manuscript for a rough draft, and print for the final version. Yet most pre-twentieth-century documents were never destined for the press: not only personal letters, but business records and correspondence were drafted, copied, received and filed in manuscript. The whole archive of the Hudson's Bay Company falls into this category of official manuscript texts. Documentary editors who pride themselves on their "responsibility . . . to translate handwritten, typescript, or printed source texts into a form that their readers can trust as an accurate representation of the specific original materials they represent [e]ven when they use traditional techniques of textual scholarship"[41] need to recognize this responsibility. They need to reject the logic of clear text as well as of expanded and diplomatic transcriptions.

What options are then open to the editor of Henday's journal? Given the complex and ambiguous relationship of the four texts (and, for practical purposes, their brevity), the logical and informative editorial choice is to consider all four manuscripts as working texts. In print format, the ideal presentation is parallel columns, so that the integrity of each text is preserved, and comparison of daily entries is easily made. Less-than-ideal print solutions require an awkward choice between successive and simultaneous presentation. The manuscripts can be presented separately, so that the calendar year is repeated four times, or divided and printed as a sequence of texts for each daily entry. A hypertext format avoids these problems: readers can view the journal texts simultaneously, navigate freely from one to the other, and decide for themselves which text exhibits features relevant to their interests.[42] At the same time, hypertext redefines the concept of text by transforming traditional limits and categories into infinitely extended relationships. The hypertext access which allows free movement from one Henday text to another allows equal freedom of movement to other texts beyond those of the journal. Published, authored, dated documents as well as materially distinct manuscripts dissolve in the wider network of links to contemporary records and to histories which refer to these records as "evidence."[43] The advent of electronic texts may have made the hierarchy of text and commentary more than ever dependent on editorial choice.

In transcribing manuscript texts, an editor is well advised to follow Kline's advice and adopt "a textual policy whose conventions do not conceal additional subtleties." In this edition the texts of Henday's journal reflect a policy of literal transcription which admits very few, duly noted exceptions. Although the relationship of the four texts is exceptionally complex, individually they present few problems. Each manuscript is a clean clerical copy which shows remarkable consistency of punctuation as well as notation of dates, names and compass directions. This scribal neatness permits editorial transcription of each text with very few changes, none of which is an emendation in favour of standardization, clarification or identification. The only changes are a direct consequence of the shift from manuscript to print. Since the copyist Andrew Graham's A, M, P, S and often W are enlarged minuscules rather than distinctly shaped majuscules, size alone becomes the criterion of capitalization. Graham's C regularly falls below the line, but is so emphatic that a print capital gives a closer impression of the written letter than lower-case type. Manuscript punctuation and headings, which vary from one text to the next, are reproduced without standardization. All distinctive manuscript marks—flourishes, abnormal spacing, and words or letters obscured by discoloration of the paper—are recorded in the textual notes. Spaces in the text are indicated by blank square brackets [   ], and a very few indecipherable words by filled square brackets [xxx]. Occasional scribal lapses such as repeated or omitted words and unclosed parentheses are reproduced as they occur in the manuscripts, and the errors are recorded in the textual notes. Graham's marginal additions and interlinear revisions, most of which occur in E.2/11, are enclosed in angled brackets <   > and inserted into the neighbouring text, an operation that is fully described in the textual notes. The edited texts of Henday's journal are thus both readable and as faithful as possible to the manuscript sources. This claim is made repeatedly in documentary editions but it is very seldom justified: more than nine times out of ten, readability wins out over fidelity.[44] The price of literal transcription in this edition is the small effort required of readers to recognize abbreviations and accommodate what is to them unorthodox spelling; its reward is a near-archival experience of the textual "surface."

The textual notes furnish information on the four manuscripts and editorial procedures, while supplementary notes link the Henday texts to contemporary documents and to publications which have made more than passing reference to Henday's journal. Thus the edition presents the Henday texts together with their contemporary and scholarly contexts. Both the supplementary notes and the commentary take stock of almost a century of Henday scholarship but they remain deliberately inconclusive.

Kline maintains that good editing depends on a "trio of basic considerations . . . the nature of the documentary sources, their expected audience, and the medium in which they [the sources] will appear."[45] Edition is a kind of translation, from one form, audience and textual medium to another. But the process should not be conceived as a juggling act, each consideration pulling in a separate direction and requiring nothing but editorial compromise. Instead, fulfilment of all three considerations forms a sequence of obligations: satisfying a new audience depends on fidelity of transcription, and this fidelity depends in turn on the editor's textual awareness. The editor's job is not to anticipate narrow academic concerns or public ignorance so much as to present the document as exactly and efficiently as possible, with a minimum of editorial emendation and intrusion, and with full and detailed notice of all editorial operations. The text is thus open to readers' interpretations rather than limited by the editor's own evaluation of its "historical significance."

Notes

1 Burpee, "York Factory to the Blackfeet Country": the editorial introduction consists of Burpee's speculations on Henday's route; there is no mention of his source or of his editorial practice. Stephen, 2-13, gives an informative summary of early historical knowledge of Henday's journal. In 1894-95 Canadian historian Robert Miller Christy transcribed Henday's and Cocking's journals from HBCA E.2/11, Andrew Graham, "Observations on Hudson's Bay." Burpee published both of Christy's transcriptions as contributions to the*Transactions* of the Royal Society of Canada, 1907 and 1908.
2 Williams, ed., appendix A to Graham, *Observations on Hudson's Bay*, 335n.
3 HBCA documents are numbered on one side of the sheet, like traditional folios. Past editors have referred to simply the folio number (e.g., "1") to indicate recto, and "d" for "dorso" (e.g., "1d") to indicate verso. For the usual indication of recto (e.g., "1r") and verso (e.g., "1v") folio sides, see the *Chicago Manual of Style* 15.194: "Each folio has two sheets, or four pages. The sheets are numbered only on the front, or recto, side. The two sides of a numbered sheet must therefore be referred to as either recto (r) or verso (v)."
4 HBCA E.2/6, Graham, "Observations on Hudson's Bay": Graham's résumé of his appointments to 1767; Williams, ed., appendixes A and B to Graham, *Observations on Hudson's Bay*, 333-61.

5 Huntington Library HM 1720, Graham, "Remarks on Hudsons Bay Trade."

6 Williams, "The Puzzle of Anthony Henday's Journal," 41, 44-49, lists the four texts of Henday's journal in the order of their archival cataloguing (B.239/a/40, E.2/4, E.2/6, E.2/11), and then discusses them in this order as Journals A, B, C and D. Stephen, 60-66, does the same and infers that E.2/6 is an "amalgamation" of B.239/a/40 and E.2/4. But cf. the title-page dating of E.2/4 and E.2/6, the fact that E.2/6 is in Graham's own hand while E.2/4 is in an unknown clerical hand, the relative detail of each volume, and Williams, "Andrew Graham and Thomas Hutchins," 6.

7 Cf. HBCA E.2/1, Isham, "Observations on Hudson's Bay," dedication to the London Committee (f. 4r, no page): "I being in an Disconsolate part of the world, where thier is Little Conversation, or Divertisment to be had, I was dubious of ye too Common Malady the Vapour's, which is frequent the forerunner of other Distempers, therefore to prevent such if possable, I have in Cold Days and Long winter Nights, amus^d my self with the following Observations."

8 Williams, ed., appendix B to Graham, *Observations on Hudson's Bay*, 359. Williams chose E.2/12 as his copytext for the HBRS edition and conflated it with passages from earlier states of the "Observations." The E.2/9 state is not only comparable to E.2/12 in its choice and coverage of topics, but can also be dated more precisely: E.2/9 is copied in several hands, one of them Matthew Cocking's, and can be dated 1771-73. The E.2/10 state dates from 1773-74 and is clearly a copy of E.2/9, entirely in Cocking's hand. In the notes to this edition of Henday's journal, E.2/9 has been quoted as well as E.2/12 and earlier states dating from 1767-69 (E.2/6, E.2/4 and E.2/5).

9 Williams, "Andrew Graham and Thomas Hutchins," 8, 12-14.

10 Heawood, 26-27, 29-34 and catalogue; see also Gravell and Miller, xv-xvi.

11 Williams, "The Puzzle of Anthony Henday's Journal," 48.

12 Williams, "The Puzzle of Anthony Henday's Journal," 48, 54. MacLaren, 41-42, 56-57, perhaps expanding on Williams, insists on "field notes" as a first stage of recording a voyage of exploration; the journal, he says, was a second stage, developed from the "notes" and written up at the end of the voyage. MacLaren, 41, argues that to define the journal as first-stage writing is "imprecise"; it "exemplifies the custom of not discriminating among the stages of composition." Accordingly he assigns the term "journal" to a draft of Samuel Hearne's narrative dated 1791, overlooking the fact that an incident of Hearne's journey was included in HBCA E.2/9, ff. 133r-135r, pp. 259-63 Graham, "Observations on Hudson's Bay," almost twenty years before. The account in E.2/9 (cf. other copies in HBCA E.2/12, pp. 336-45, and HBCA E.2/13, pp. 252-57) must have been written within months of Hearne's return to Churchill in 1772. But neither the excerpt in Graham's book (all states) nor the narrative dated 1791 has the formal structure of a journal—that is, a series of daily entries written as the journey proceeds, as observations are made and as events occur. Instead, Graham's editing isolates an incident, and the 1791 narrative treats Hearne's

journey retrospectively, by emphasizing certain events and summarizing others.

13 HBCA A.11/114, Isham, instructions to Henday, 19 February 1754; Isham, instructions to Henday, 26 June 1754; Isham, letter to Henday, 4 September 1754.

14 Williams, "The Puzzle of Anthony Henday's Journal," 53, 56.

15 Williams, "The Puzzle of Anthony Henday's Journal," 52-56; cf. Stephen, 83, who considers "the evidence which Williams brought forth to support his argument [to be] limited and largely circumstantial." Stephen's own discussion, 69-87, 93, uses the same kind of evidence. Although he warns against "a natural inclination to single out the 'right' version and to blame someone [the copyist] for the 'wrong' version" (13), Stephen falls into the same trap and simply reverses Williams's conclusion. Stephen sees the E texts as "flawed" and B.239/a/40 as the "right" version: "there is no indication of [B.239/a/40] having been tampered with . . . the collective and self-contradictory account presented by [the texts found in Graham's "Observations"] have no claim over [B.239/a/40] regarding the truth about Anthony Henday's experiences in 1754-55."

16 Bumsted, 92-94. Bumsted's concern for the "non-specialist reader" is repeated in Brown, "Documentary Editing," 6-7, and Kline, 214-15; cf. Sande Cohen, 110: "the historian's infamous 'ordinary educated public.'" For an early historical discussion on editing Canadian literary texts, see Halpenny.

17 Brown, "Documentary Editing," 1-13; see also Trigger; Brown, "Ethnohistorians"; Peers, xii.

18 Brown, "Documentary Editing," 4-9. Brown insists that texts are not "transparent," and that the reader "*should* feel some distance" from the writer (original emphasis)—but cf. Brown and Brightman, introduction to George Nelson's "*Orders of the Dreamed*," 24-107: Brown's theoretical concern with genre and "distance" should be extended to all texts, including Nelson's. See Trigger, 33, on the editor's need for linguistic expertise; on "voice" and text, see Tedlock, *The Spoken Word and the Work of Interpretation*; Tedlock, "From Voice and Ear to Hand and Eye"; Cruikshank, 11-13, 18-19; cf. Derrida, *passim*, and (in a nutshell) Hartman, xx: "To see writing as silent speech is already to misunderstand it and reduce its force. . . . What complexity have we overlooked or suppressed—perhaps what threat have we warded off—by 'forgetting' writing, a forgetting that includes its reduction to the status of mere technique, to a function of voiced and prior thought?"

19 Coles, "The Decline of Documentary Publishing," and Coles, "Looking Backward, Reaching Forward"; also the editorial prefaces of the following Champlain Society publications since 1980: *Lord Minto's Canadian Papers*, ed. Stevens and Saywell, 1: xi-xii; *The St Lawrence Survey Journals of Captain Henry Wolsey Bayfield*, ed. McKenzie, ix-xii; *The Journal of Alexander Henry the Younger*, ed. Gough, xv-xviii; and *Franklin's Journals and Correspondence: The First Arctic Land Expedition*, ed. Davis, cvii-cix. Williams's editorial practice can be seen in his edition of Graham,

Observations on Hudson's Bay: several states of Graham's compilation have been conflated; spelling and punctuation have been modernized; paragraphing has been introduced. See also Lamb's editions of Fraser, Franchère, Mackenzie and Vancouver; Houston's editions of Richardson, Hood and Back; Nelson edited by Brown and Brightman; Dawson edited by Cole and Lockner; Thompson edited by Belyea.

20 See Parker; Elias; McGann, "The Textual Condition"; West; Eggert; Phelps; also Hay. Greetham, 271-417, provides an overview of "literary" editing. As a co-founder of *Text*, Greetham has furthered radically critical views of the Bowers school, although he continues to wrestle with these views. It is safe to say, however, that no "literary" editor now accepts without serious reservation Bowers's insistence on authorial intentions and clear text, and leading theorists such as McGann and Reiman have pointedly rejected Bowers's recommendations. By continuing to attribute Bowers's editorial theory to current theoretical positions and practices of "literary" editors, Kline, 20-23, 138, 192, 203, tilts at windmills and weakens her case for "historical" editing.

21 Kline, 218, points out that for decades Butterfield's *Letters of Benjamin Rush* and *Jefferson Papers* set a standard of "contextual" annotation in documentary editing; she quotes one historian's praise: "the texts and their notes took me into Benjamin Rush's world." See also Brown's case for annotation in "Documentary Editing," 6-7: since texts come down to us already "mediated" by "other forces," Brown suggests that the editor's job is to *increase* the amount of intervention—to produce an even *more* "mediated" text—with the aim of correcting "current common knowledge and comforting stereotypes."

22 Tanselle, "The Editing of Historical Documents"; see also Tanselle, "Historicism and Critical Editing," and Tanselle, "External Fact as an Editorial Problem." Taylor summarizes Tanselle's objections to 'traditional' documentary editing: "Dr. Tanselle . . . rejects any silent changes in the text, particularly any effort at modernization. He takes historians to task, for example, for regularizing punctuation or paragraphing; for silently correcting slips of the pen, such as inadvertent repetition of word or phrase; or even for dropping the dash that in the eighteenth century commonly follows a period. Silently tinkering with the text alters the spirit and mood of the original; it injects an editor's judgment or taste between reader and author. What Dr. Tanselle desires is a literal text that with suitable editorial devices includes every cross-out, interlineation, comma, capital letter, and misspelling. . . . If an editor presents private [unpublished manuscript] documents 'as anything more polished or finished than they were left by the writer, he is *falsifying* their nature.' . . . Dr. Tanselle has no patience with the readability defence" (4, original emphasis). Graff and Reagor chart historians' reactions. Schultz sees Tanselle's essay as a turning point: "in a powerful indictment of then current historical practices, G. Thomas Tanselle accused . . . historians in general of having 'no coherent textual rationale,' and of tampering inexcusably with the manuscript texts in their

transcription policies of 'modernization.' . . . [Since the early 1980s] the new generation of editors has acquitted itself well. Professionalization of editing has served the scholarly community in ways it is only slowly coming to appreciate" (339). Cf. Kline, 17-19, 137-38, 192, 194.

23 Kline, 18.

24 See Teute; Gottesman and Bennett; Dunlap and Shelley; Bowers; Voigt and Jones; McElrath; Small; Philip Cohen. For recognition of practical limits to "contextual" annotation, see Gilman.

25 Shultz, 340; Cullen, 73.

26 Moulton, 2: 8-54.

27 Kline, 23.

28 Kline, 21.

29 Kline, 94, 137, 211, 194; see also Brown, "Documentary Editing," 3; Brown and Vibert, title and x-xi.

30 Simon; Cutler; cf. Nordloh. These articles are irritatingly brief; they are statements of position rather than developed arguments.

31 Kline, 21-22. Reiman, *Romantic Texts and Contexts*, 170-71, quotes Tanselle's response to debate on editorial principles: "The basic issues that confront textual critics and scholarly editors are unchanging. . . . There will be no end to debates over these issues, because they are genuinely debatable . . . that different people hold different opinions about basic issues is not a sign of crisis; it points to a perennial situation in any challenging and lively field."

32 Greetham, 361, refers to Kline's *Guide* as discipline-specific and "promoted by the historians of the Association for Documentary Editing."

33 Kline, 96. These rules remain unchanged from the first edition, published in 1987.

34 Kline, 97-99.

35 Maas is the standard account of recension as practised in classical scholarship—see Reynolds and Wilson, 186-213, for a summary explanation. Vinaver provides clear examples of textual emendation. The work of classical scholars and medievalists is of relevance here because they address the problems particularly associated with manuscript transmission more thoroughly than documentary editors or textual critics of post-Renaissance literature.

36 Kline, 81.

37 Kline, 104 .

38 Kline, 154.

39 Cf. Reiman, *Romantic Texts and Contexts*, 167, 170, 179: "In using and analyzing scholarly editions over the years, I have become less and less confident that an eclectic critical edition is the best way to present textual information to scholars. . . . Often . . . it is more useful and efficient to provide critics and students with complete texts of two or more different stages of a literary work, each of which can be read as an integral whole, than to chop all but one version into small pieces and then mix and sprinkle these dismembered fragments at the bottoms of pages, or shuffle them at the back of the book as 'variants' or 'collations'. . . . there are

good reasons to redirect our energies away from the attempt to produce 'definitive' or 'ideal' critical editions."

40 Kline, 104.

41 Kline, 137-38.

42 For introductions to electronic texts, see Nielsen; Landow; Brown and Honeycutt; Lavagnino; Robinson; Kenny and Rieger; http://www.uic.edu/orgs/tei/ and http://ota.ahds.ac.uk (9 June 1999).

43 Kline maintains that even in hypertext, one text must be chosen "from which the links will radiate" (93): this may be true for the editor's establishment of links, but the reader can navigate freely from one to the next—otherwise hypertext would have little to offer as a medium and tool. Kline seems influenced by Tanselle's apparent conservatism; she quotes Tanselle's declaration that "[c]omputerization is simply the latest chapter in the long story of facilitating the reproduction and alteration of texts" (132). Kline insists that "the process of finding sources and maintaining control . . . follow the same principles developed in the days of manual procedures: only the methods . . . have changed" (65). Even in the 1998 revised edition of the *Guide*, she describes formerly employed "manual procedures," although it would be hard to imagine any editorial project starting up or even continuing without computers. Kline chooses to ignore the rest of Tanselle's statement: "what remains [to challenge editors] is the inseparability of recorded language from the technology that produced it *and makes it accessible*" (my emphasis).

44 Taylor: "An historical editor's real sin is saying carefully and explicitly what he is going to do and then not sticking to it" (8).

45 Kline, 70.

Texts

A Copie of Orders and Instructions to Anth^y Hendey

upon a Journey in Land, Dated att York Fort, June 26th 1754

Having intimated to the Hudson's Bay Company 1752, that in my opinion it was Requisit and wou'd be to their Interest if a proper person was sent up the Country, by wch Such a person might Enlarge and Encrease the Said Company'^s trade &c with unknown Ind^s: It is therefore the Company'^s will and pleasure answerable to their general Letter 1753 that any person that is willing and will undertake such a Journey, that I do forward the same. and as I Chuse you as a proper person for such an undertaking, and besides being willing your self, I therefore order that you be very punctuall in observing the following Instructions.

1st   Having procured a trusty home Indian, Connawapa by Name, for your Companion, you are to proceed with him, with the Captn or Leading Indian who is now at the fort, Attickosish by name, and is to sett out tomorrow the 26 Day of June, having given him Encouragm^t and promis^d him further Encouragement provisor he faithfully Discharges the trust impos^d on him; that is, to See you Safe to his Country; that is to say, the Kisckachewon, Missinneepee, Earchethinue, Esinepoet or any other Country Indians, that we have not as Yet any traffick with; and that by your presence and with your Assistance he Exhorts the Natives to Come to you, that you may Converse with them, making them presants, perswading them as much as in you Lyes to be at peace, and not to Warr, one against another, but to hunt and gett goods, and bring them to the fort, where their is a Suffitient of Sundry sorts of goods, and that your gov^r will use them Civilly, who is beloved by all Indians that as yet Knows him by his Civil treatment to them; tell them I send you to acquaint them I want to See them, I love the Indians, and that if they will all Come the following year, you will then go along with them and Lead them down the Ensuing year, with many more Such promises that occur to your memorie &c. Espetially if you Can gett a Sight of the Earchethinues, and perswade two or three to Come with you by fair means, but by no means use force, but use all you may See of Different Nations Civily, giving Each Leader a small Presant, you having such with you for that purpose, and above all be upon your Guard.

2^d You having a Compass, hand Line paper &c &c along with you, therefore be Very Exact in Keeping a Journal of your travels and observations Daily, observing the Courses, trying the Depth of water in the River or Lakes when in your Cannoe; and as you Know the Distance a Considerable way up the River, you may therefore by a Day or two at first Setting out Know how many miles you go in a Day hereafter, by which you may Compute the miles by padling or travelling by Land all the way; mind to Remark Down Every thing that occurs to your View Daily, mentioning when you Come to any River or Lake the name, when you meet with any Natives what Nation &c.

3^d Observe the Soil as you proceed, what trees, Herbs &c, mentioning in your Journal when and where; also take particular notice if their is any sort of mineral if you find any Reserve some and mention the Day and month &c and perticular Remark the place and Situation where you may find Such.

4th Observe when you pass the missineepee Country, and Down near to the Earchethinue Country, whether the great Lake is a Lake or not, or whether it is an open Sea, as I have been Inform'd by Several it is a Sea where Ships are seen to Pass by; be purtiular in Comming at the truth of this, which is a material Point.

5th When you have [xxx] and Seen all the Natives you Can, then Return taking Care to be back by the 10th of Augt at farthest, if possable Sooner, as you will have Suffitient time to travel as far as the borders of the Earchethinue Country by the 20th of July.

6th This will be Suffitient for the first time, first to Know the Situation of the Country and Indians, then please god, we may better be able to Send the following year for to winter and bring such forign Indians Down to trade, also by this Journey we shall Know partly whether their is any possability of making a Setlem^t a Considerable Distance up Nelson River, or if such a Setlement is made a Considerable Distance up Nelson River, whether or no the Indians Cou'd bring Double the Quantity of goods to the said Setlement in one Year, to what they do at presant bring to the fort in one Year.

7th It's not unlikely but the french or wood Runners, in hearing of your being amongst the Indians, may way Lay you, to prevent which, take perticular Care to make the Indians your friends, that in case They shou'd attempt Such a thing, you may be able to head the Indians against the said wood Runners, for your own preservation, but otherwise do not offer, or Let the Indians molest the Said wood runners, unless they are the first transgressors, as already observ'd.

8th I have been Severall times inform'd that the Earchethinues who are perdigious Numerious, and which is my View in Sending you to bring them to trade, has no knowledge, or at Least can not padle in Cannoes; if this be true and you have the oppurtunity of seeing some of them, Let your Guides Show and Learn them, also Exhort them to practice it, that they may be able to padle Down to the fort &c.

9th As you travel up Nelson River observe the track or branch the Indians go to out of Nelson River for to go to Churchill or to Come to York Fort, and what Distance up Nelson River as near as you can guess, what Sort of a place, whether plenty of woods or Likely for a house their &c.

10th Upon the contrary Side the french Knowing of your Com^g as mention'd in the 7th Instruction, I say they may Come to See you as a friend, make much and Invite you to their Setlement; if so, use them Kindly but upon no acc^t go with them, but Keep at a Distance for you can not be too Carefull in Regard to their fondling, artfull and Knowing Disposition.

11th As you proceed inland if you meet with any Indians who is Comming for the fort, besure to Send a note by all Such Different Indians you shall meet Coming down, as I may Know how you proceed &c.

12th I Desire you take particular notice of all these Instructions, peruse them often, that you may not fail in the performance thereof—besure to Converse with the guides as much as possable, that you may attain their Language, and by so Doing you will be the better Capable to Exhort and Encourage the Natives to trade.

13th And Lastly, besides these Instructions, take all the observations and Remarks that occur's to your View, be it Ever so trifling as you may imagine, yet all Such when I come to Examine it will be a Suffitient Satisfaction mentioning such in Your Journal, and by so doing and Encouraging and Exhorting the Natives to trade, you

may Depend upon it the Company will Suffitiently Reward you for any Service you may do the Company by such a Journey, Besides which you may Depend upon Encouragement from
　　Your Sincere friend and Well wisher,
　　　　JAMES ISHAM
Vera Copia
(HBCA A.11/114)

Journal

26 June 1754
    B.239/a/40
The Following is a Journal of a Voyage or Journey in Land, from YORK FORT up Hayes River, By Captn Anth^y Hendey from June the 26th 1754 to June the 23^d 1755.

    1754 June ye 26 Wednesday fine weather, wind att W^t took my Departure from York Fort and padled up his River to ye Big stone,* here we put up for the night.

    * this is Called Mistasinee, or the great stone.

    E.2/6
The following is a Journal of a Journey inland from York Fort up Hay's River &c by Anthony Hendey from June the 26th 1754 to June the 23^d 1755, Viz^t

    1754 June 26 Wednesd^y fine weather, wind W^t, took my departure from YF and paddled up Hay's River to the big stone, here we put up for the night.

    E.2/4
A Journal of a journey from York Fort to the Archithinue country in the years 1755 and 1756, by Anthony Hendey, being the first of the Company's Servants who went inland to endeavour to promote the fur trade <excepting the late Mr Norton, who after 3 years absence from Churchill brought the Weshepowuck Indians to trade in the beginning of this present Century>.

    1755 June 26th Wednesday fine weather wind W. took my departure from York Fort and padled up Hay's river to the great stone; here we put up for the night.

    E.2/11
I shall give the Journal of a Journey to explore the Country inland,

and to endeavour to encrease the Hudson's Bay Company's trade, Performed by a very able Young Man named Anthony Hendey Anno Domini 1754@5. <N.B. This Man did not go up the road Mr Tomison goes.>

1754 June 26. Wednesday. Wind West and moderate Weather, Took my departure from York Fort and paddled up Hays River to Amista Asinee or Great Stone, distant from the Fort 24 Miles our course about SWbW. here we put up for the night. <Mr James Isham, Factor.>

27 June 1754
    B.239/a/40
ye 27 Thursday fine weather wind W^t padled up Hays River, till we Came to Steel River and then up steel River till we came to wood partridge Creeck, their we put up for ye night.
    E.2/6
27 Thursd^y fine weather, wind at W^t, paddled up Hay's River till we came to Steel River, and then up Steel River to wood partridge Creek, then we put up for the night.
    E.2/4
27. Thursday wind and weather as yesterday, padled up Hay's river till we came to steel river, and padled up steel river to wood partridge creek, and there put up for the night.
    E.2/11
27. Thursday. Wind and weather as Yesterday, Paddled up Hay's River till we came to Apet Sepee or Fire-steel River, and paddled up it to Mistick-Apethaw Sepee or Wood Partridge River and there put up for the night. <I knew this Man, he was a bold and good Servant and was drove from the Company's Service by the Ship's Gentry because he would not buy Slops & Brandy from them. He was the first person who ventured Inland. I was then Writer at York Fort. Andrew Graham.>

28 June 1754
    B.239/a/40
ye 28 Friday fine weather wind att S^o & SW^t padled up steel River till we Came to pine Reach,* then put up for the night.
    * 20 M from the ffort, to this pine Reach was measured in the winter 1754 by Captn Hendey, by which Knowing the distance in padling there 3 days past, he Computes the M he goes of a day hereafter.
    E.2/6
28 Frid^y fine weather, wind S^o & SW^t, paddled up steel River to pine reach, then put up for the night.

E.2/4

28. Friday fine weather wind S. and S.W. padled up steel river to pine reach, and put up for the night.

E.2/11

28. Friday. winds from S. to W. and pleasant weather, Paddled up Apet Sepee to Pine Reach, and put up for the Night.*

* from York Fort to pine reach 60 Miles measured.

29 June 1754

B.239/a/40

ye 29 Saturday fine weather Wind att N^o took my Departure from pine Reach, and padled up Steell River NWbW^t and NW^t 28 miles, the woods & Land is much the same, this day past 7 falls, was obliged to Carry our things over 4 of them, the water being shoul, past 3 brushy Islands.

E.2/6

29 Saturd^y fine weather, wind N^o took my departure from pine-Reach* and paddled up Steel River NWbW^t 25 miles, this day passed 4 large falls, the banks are high, and tall woods on both sides the River, which is about 16 poles wide, and a strong current.

* From YF to this pine reach was measured in the winter 1754 by Anthony Hendey, by which knowing the distance these 3 days past He computes the miles He goes of a day hereafter.

E.2/4

29. Saturday fine weather wind N. took my departure from pine reach* and padled up steel river 25 miles N.W.B.W. passed 4 large falls, the river about 16 poles wide, the banks high and tall woods.

* From York Fort to pine reach was measured by Anth^y Hendey before.

E.2/11

1754. June 29. Saturday. Wind North and agreeable weather; Took my departure from Pine-Reach, and paddled up Apet Sepee 25 Miles NW. Passed four large falls, the River about 16 poles wide, the banks high, and tall woods.

30 June 1754

B.239/a/40

ye 30 Sunday fine weather wind att N^o took my Departure from Inclossed fall, and steered NWbW^t and NW^t 25 miles, this day past four falls, the banks are high & tall woods on both sides the River, which is about 16 poles wide and a strong Current.

E.2/6

1754 June 30 Sunday fine weather, wind N^o took my departure from enclosed fall, and paddled NWbN° and NW^t 28 miles, the woods and land are much the same as yesterday; this day passed 17 falls, and were obliged to carry our things over 4 of them, passed three brushy Islands.

E.2/4

30. Sunday a continuance of fine weather wind N. took my departure from inclosed fall and padled 28 miles N.W.B.W. and N.W. land and woods as yesterday, passed 17 falls and were obliged to carry our things over 4.

E.2/11

30. Sunday. Wind North and pleasant weather; Took my departure from inclosed fall, and paddled 28 Miles N.W.b W. & N.W. the lands and Woods as Yesterday: passed seventeen places, where the water was so shoal as to be under the necessity to carry our goods and Canoes over.

1 July 1754

B.239/a/40

1754 July ye 1st Monday fine weather Wind att NW^t took my Departure from Musketo point, and Steered NW^t 17 miles, towards noon thunder and a great deal of Rain, very high Rocky Land & shrube woods, nothing but falls and heaps of Large Stones, that we are Obliged to Lead our Canoes a mile together and Carry them & our Goods over the falls.

E.2/6

July 1 Mond^y fine weather, wind NW^t took my departure from musketo point and steered NW^t 17 miles; towards noon Thunder'd and rain'd; very high rocky land and shruby woods, nothing but falls and heaps of large stones which obliged us to lead our Canoes for a mile together, and carry them and our goods over the falls.

E.2/4

July 1st Monday fine weather, wind N.W. took my departure from musketo point and padled 17 miles N.W. towards noon rain & thunder, the land high and rockie, shruby woods, nothing but falls and heaps of large stones, which obliged us to carry our canoes and goods in several places.

E.2/11

1754 July 1st Monday. wind N.W. and moderate weather; Took my departure from Musketo-point, and paddled 17 Miles NW. A heavy rain towards noon with thunder & lightning. The lands high rocky with shrubby woods. Very shallow Water with Stones, which obliged us to carry our Canoes & Goods in several places.

2 July 1754

B.239/a/40

July ye 2^d Tuesday fine weather wind att NW^t all day, took my departure from stoney Banks and steered NW^t 23 M, the River is very Narrow & full of Large Stones, the banks are Large and Rocky, full of
Large Stones with Little or no woods, the Land Looks very barren, we
have seen neither fish nor fowl as yet, so that we are very short of provisions att present.

E.2/6

2 Tuesd^y fine weather, wind NW^t took my departure from stoney
banks, and paddled NW^t 23 miles; the River is narrow and full of large
stones, the banks are large rocks, little or no wood, the land looks
very barren; we have neither seen fish nor fowl as yet so we are scarce
of provisions.

E.2/4

1755 July 2^d Tuesday fine weather wind N.W. took my departure from
stoney banks and padled 23 miles N.W. the river narrow and full of
large stones, the banks are rockie, little or no wood, the land looks
very barren; we have neither seen fish nor fowl as yet, so we are scarce
of provisions.

E.2/11

2. Tuesday. Wind SW and very warm weather; Took my departure from
Stony-banks, and paddled 23 Miles NW. The River narrow & full of
large stones. The banks are rocky and very little woods. The land
looks very barren. We have neither seen Fish nor Fowl yet, so We are
scarce of provisions.

3 July 1754

B.239/a/40

July ye 3^d Wednesday fine weather wind att S^o took my Departure from
tickamegg Reach and steered up ye other Branch or River NW^t 12
miles, past 16 falls, where we was obliged to Carry our Canoes over
them, there being nothing but Large Rocks, we past also 30 Islands on
one of them grows small willows, pine & Birch, the banks on both
sides are Low, on which grows Small pine trees and Brush, this day
saw severall Craw fish,* and killed one Duck.

    * Captn Hendey says these Crawfish are as Large & as fine as
those in England.

E.2/6

3^d Wednesd^y fine weather, wind S^o took my departure from tickomeg
reach and paddled up a branch of Steel River NW^t 12 miles; passed 16
falls, obliged to carry our Canoes &c over them, being nothing but
large rocks, passed 30 Islands, on one of them grows small willows,

pine & Birch trees, the banks on both sides the River is low, on which grows Small pine trees, saw several Crawfish, killed one Duck.

E.2/4

3. Wednesday fine weather wind S. took my departure from tickomeg reach and paddled up a branch of steel river 12 miles N.W. passed 16 falls, obliged to carry our canoes &c past them being nothing but rocks; passed 30 Islands, on one of them grows some birch trees, the banks of the river are low on which grows small pine trees; saw several craw-fish and killed one duck.

E.2/11

3. Wednesday. Wind South and pleasant weather. Took my departure from Tickomeg Reach, and paddled up a branch of Steel River 12 Miles NW. passed much Shoal Water with rocky ground; obliged to carry our Canoes over it. Passed thirty Islands; on one of them grows a few Birch trees. The banks of the River is low on which grows Small pines. Saw several Craw-fish, and killed a Duck.

4 July 1754

B.239/a/40

ye 4 Thursday fine weather wind at SW^t, took my departure from Crawfish fall, and Steered W^t 22 M, falls much the same as the day before, the Ind^s killed 3 Beaver, here being plenty of their Houses.

E.2/6

4 Thursd^y fine weather, wind NW^t took my departure from Crawfish fall, and paddled W^t 22 miles, falls and Islands much the same as yesterday, Indians killed 3 Beaver, here are plenty of their Houses.

E.2/4

4. Thursday fine weather wind N.W. left craw-fish fall & paddled W. 22 miles, falls and Islands much the same as yesterday; Indians killed 3 beaver, here are plenty of their houses.

E.2/11

4. Thursday Wind NW. and moderate weather; Left Craw-fish Fall, and paddled 22 miles West. Falls and Islands much the same as Yesterday. Indians killed three Beaver: here are plenty of their houses.

5 July 1754

B.239/a/40

ye 5 Friday fine weather, wind W^tNW^t took my Departure from Cockel shell fall, and steered WSW^t and WbS^o 25 M. this day past 34 falls, and 22 Islands, their is not a foot of water for a mile together, killed 3 Ducks, Cannot get time to fish, for we paddle till it is dark.

E.2/6

1754 July 5 Frid^y fine weather, wind WNW^t took my departure from

cockle-shell-fall, and paddled WbS and WSW 25 miles, this day passed
34 falls, and 22 Islands, there is not a foot of water for a mile distance,
killed 3 Ducks.

E.2/4

5. Friday fine weather wind W.N.W. took my depature from cockle-shell
fall and paddled 25 miles W B S and W.S.W. passed 34 falls and 22
Islands, there is not a foot depth of water for a mile; killed 3 ducks.

E.2/11

5. Friday. Wind W.S.W. and moderate weather; Took my departure from
fortunate Fall, and paddled 25 Miles WBS & WSW. passed much Shoal
water, & twenty-four Islands: there is not a foot of water for a mile.
We are greatly fatigued with carrying and hauling the Canoes, and not
very well fed but the Natives are continually Smoaking, which I
already experience Allays hunger.

6 July 1754

B.239/a/40

1754 July ye 6 Saturday fine weather wind EbN^o took my departure
from Jack Reach, and padled 26 M WbS^o, then we Came to Atticksogohegan, or Deer Lake, att the Enterance it is a Mile wide, in the middle it is as much as you Can Decern from Side to side, in ye middle of
this Sogohegan or Lake, their are severall woody Islands and att the
sides is Low Land, and tall woods, this day Caught some Large Jack
and 3 ducks, have seen no Deer as yet.

E.2/6

6 Saturd^y fine weather, wind EbN^o took my departure from Jack
reach, and paddled 26 miles WbS, then we came to Deer Lake, at the
entrance it is a mile wide, in the middle it is as much as you can
decern Either side, low land and tall woods, and in the middle several
woody Islands; killed some large pike fish, and 3 Ducks.

E.2/4

6. Saturday fine weather wind E.B.N. took my departure from jack
reach and paddled 26 miles WbS, then we left the river and entered
deer lake. killed a good many pike and 3 ducks.

E.2/11

6. Saturday. Wind EbN and moderate weather; Took my departure
from Pike-Reach and paddled 26 Miles WbS. then We left Steel-River
and entered Attick-Sagohan or Deek Lake; killed a good many Pike, &
three Ducks, which are very acceptable.

7 July 1754

B.239/a/40

ye 7th Sunday fine weather wind att S^o took my departure from the 3

Beacon Island and Steered WSW^t 12 miles, then Came to the River on the West Side of Sogohigan, the River is 12 poles wide, and full of Islands, the banks of the River are hills & dales, and small pine trees, the depth of water very unregular, some places deep, and other places not above 6 Inches Water, padled 12 mile up the River.

E.2/6

7 Sunday fine weather, wind S^o took my departure from 3 beacon Island, and paddled 12 miles, then came to the River on the West side of the Lake, the River is 12 pole wide, full of Islands, the banks are hills and dales with small pine trees, the River very irregular, some places deep and other places not 6 Inches water; paddled 12 miles up the river. Course WSW.

E.2/4

7th Sunday wind E.B.N. and fine weather, took my departure from 3 beacon Island and paddled 12 miles W.S.W. then came at the river again and paddled 12 miles up it S.W. the banks are hills and dales on which grows small pine trees, the river 12 poles wide, the water very deep in some places, and other places not above 6 inches water and many Islands; deer lake is large, deep, and encompassed with tall woods of pine and birch.

E.2/11

7. Sunday. wind and weather as Yesterday; Took my departure from: Three-Beacon Island, and paddled 12 Miles WSW. then came to the River: The Natives are divided as to the Name of this River; however it cannot with propriety be called Apet Sepee, or Steel River. We paddled 12 Miles up it. The banks are hills and dales, on which grow small pines. The River 12 poles wide, the water very deep in some places, and in other places not six inches water, & many Islands. Deer Lake is large and deep, encompassed with tall Woods of Pines & Birch trees.

8 July 1754

B.239/a/40

ye 8th Monday fine weather wind SW^t this day padled 26 M up the River WNW^t, Islands & Rocks all ye way, this Evening Came to Monokausokohigan, att the Enterance 3 miles wide, and in the middle 20 miles wide, being as much as I Can decern from Side to Side, A high Island we put up att for the night.

E.2/6

8 Mond^y fine weather, wind SW^t paddled 26 miles up the River WNW^t Islands and rocks all the way; this Evening came to Monokaw Lake, at the entrance 3 miles wide, in the middle as much as I can decern the woods on either side; a high Island we put up at for the night.

E.2/4

8. Monday fine weather wind S.W. paddled 26 miles up the river W.N.W. Islands and rocks all the way, in the evening left the river and put up on an Island in monokaw lake.

E.2/11

1754 July 8. Monday. wind SW. and pleasant weather; paddled 26 Miles up the River WNW; Islands and Rocks all the way. In the Evening left the River, and put up on an Island in Christianaux Lake.

9 July 1754

B.239/a/40

1754 July ye 9th Tuesday fine weather wind SW^t took my departure from Egg Island and steered SW^t till ye afternoon, then we steered SWbS^o 26 M, this day past 22 Islands, the woods on them very Low, the Land on both Sides of the pound very Low, the woods thick & tall.

E.2/6

9 Tuesd^y fine weather, wind SW. took my departure from Egg Island and padled SW & SWbS 26 miles, passed 22 woody Islands; the land on both sides appears Low & woody.

E.2/4

9. Tuesday wind &c as yesterday. took my departure from egg Island and paddled S.W. and S.W.B.S. in the lake, passed 22 woody Islands and put up on one for the night.

E.2/11

9. Tuesday. Wind and Weather as Yesterday; Took my departure from Egg Island, and paddled 26 Miles SW & SWbS. in the Lake; passed twenty-two woody Islands, and put up on one for the night.

10 July 1754

B.239/a/40

ye 10th Wednesday fine weather wind NW^t took my departure from Jack Island, att the Entrance of Nelson pond, and steered WSW^t 25 Miles, when we Came to ye River on the West side which is Nelson River, goes through the middle of it; this Day past 28 Islands, the water very deep all this days paddle, the Currant but small, fine tall woods on both sides of ye River.

E.2/6

1754 July 10 Wednesd^y fine weather, wind NW. took my departure from Jack Island, and paddled WSW 25 miles, when we came to the River on the west side the Lake, passed 28 Islands, the water very deep, and little current; fine tall woods on both sides the River; killed several shad fish.

E.2/4

10. Wednesday fine weather wind N.W. took my departure from Jack Island and paddled 25 miles W.S.W. untill we came to a river on the west side the lake where we put up for the night, this is frenchmans lake or little sea and leads southward towards Severn river &c.

E.2/11

10. Wednesday. Wind NW and moderate weather; Took my departure from Pike Islands, and paddled 25 Miles WSW. until we came to a River on the West side the Lake, where we put up for the night.

11 July 1754

B.239/a/40

ye 11 Thursday fine weather wind att N^o took my departure from Shade fall* and padled 2 M up ye River, when it began to blow hard with Rain, which obliged us to put up here, 20 Canoes Came to us, gave them all a peice of tobacco, and a Letter for the Govr Mr James Isham att York Fortt, this day killed 2 ducks.

    * Shade fall takes its name from the Quantity of Shade fish, the same sort as in England.

E.2/6

11 Thursd^y fine weather, wind N^o took my departure from shad-fall, and paddled 2 miles up the River, SW: it began to blow strong with rain which obliged us to put up for the day, here 20 Canoes of Indians passed us on their way to YF with whom I sent a letter to Mr James Isham the Chief Factor, Indians caught some large pike fish, and I killed a few ducks.

E.2/4

11. Thursday fine weather wind N. took my departure from shad fall and paddled 2 miles S.W. up the river when it began to blow with rain which obliged us to put up; here 20 canoes of pegogamow and keskachewan Indians passed us on their way to York Fort, with whom I sent a letter to Mr James Isham the Chief.

E.2/11

11. Thursday. wind North and agreeable weather; Took my departure from Shad Fall and paddled two miles SW up the River, when it began to blow with Rain, which obliged us to put up. Here twenty Canoes of Natives passed us, on their <way> to York Fort, with whom I sent a letter to Mr James Isham the Chief.

12 July 1754

B.239/a/40

ye 12th Friday this day & Last night it Rain'd hard so that we padled none to day, the Ind^s drunk out 2 Cags of Brandy, when I went a hunt-

ing, and fishing Catcht five large Jack this Evening the wind shifted to
ye NW^t and Clear weather.

> E.2/6

12 Frid^y a continuance of rain, so paddled none, wind all round the
Compass, Indians drank out 2 rundlets of Brandy, and I caught plenty
of fine fish, of which I had a good belly-full, it being the first good full
meal I have had since I left the Fort.

> E.2/4

12. Friday wind S.W. and a continuance of rain, paddled none, some
drinking and others fishing, fish is our daily food.

> E.2/11

12. Friday. Wind North and, a continuance of Rain, paddled none.
Some drinking & others fishing. Fish is our daily food.

13 July 1754

> B.239/a/40

1754 July ye 13 Saturday this day padled 28 Miles SW^t and fine weather
wind att S^o, the River here is wide, and full of Small Islands, the Land
Low & poor woods.

> E.2/6

13 Saturd^y moderate weather, wind S^o paddled 28 miles SW; the River
here is wide, banks low, poor woods, and many small Islands.

> E.2/4

13. Saturday moderate weather, wind S. paddled 28 miles S.W. the river
wide with small Islands, banks low & small woods.

> E.2/11

13. Saturday. wind South paddled 28 Miles: The River wide with Small
Islands; Banks low and small woods; Our course to day SW.

14 July 1754

> B.239/a/40

ye 14th Sunday fine weather wind att SW^t this day padled 25 miles, the
water not above a foot and a half all the day, and some places was
obliged to hawl our Canoes over the stones.

> E.2/6

14 Sunday fine weather; wind SW. paddled SW 25 miles, the water not
above 1½ foot deep all this day, and some places we were obliged to
hawl our Canoes over the stones; Indians caught several pike and
shad-fish.

> E.2/4

14. Sunday fine weather wind S.W. paddled 25 miles S.W. the river in
general good water; Indians caught a good many large pike.

E.2/11

14. Sunday. Wind SW. and pleasant weather; paddled 25 Miles SW. The River in general good water; Indians caught a good many large Pike.

15 July 1754

B.239/a/40

ye 15th Monday fine weather the wind att E^t, this day padled 24 M, the water much ye same obliged to hawl our Canoes over the stones in Severall places, the River is about 20 poles wide, and full of stonny Islands, this day Entered Mono ko tuskey, where Came to us 4 Canoes (their Leaders name Maconsko,)

E.2/6

1754 July 15 Monday fine weather, wind E. paddled 24 miles SWbS. the water much the same as yesterday, obliged to hawl our Canoes over several places, the River is about 20 poles wide, and full of stoney Islands, 4 Canoes of Indians in the French interest came and smoaked with us, the Leader behaved very civilly to me; His name Monkonsko; He informed me we were entered the dry or inland Country and that I would soon see a French House.

E.2/6

15. Monday fine weather, wind E. paddled 24 miles S.W.B.S. 4 canoes of Indians in the french interest met us, their Leader's name is Monkonsko, he behaved civily and informed me that I was come to the dry inland country, and that I would soon see a french house.

E.2/11

15. Monday. Wind East and raw cold weather; paddled 24 S.Wb S. met four Canoes of Indians in the French interest; the Leaders Name Monkonsko. He behaved civilly & informed me that I was on the Confines of the dry inland country, called by the Natives the Muscuty Tuskee; and that I should soon see a French house.

16 July 1754

B.239/a/40

ye 16 Tuesday fine weather wind E^t this day padled 20 Miles SWbS then we Came to Attinum Sokahigan, it opens Large & wide, and is full of woody Islands, and the water very deep.

E.2/6

16 Tuesd^y fine weather wind E^t this day paddled SWbS 20 miles, then we came to Outtenum Lake, it opens large and wide, is full of woody Islands and the water very deep.

E.2/4

16. Tuesday fine weather wind E. paddled 20 miles S.W.B.S. then came to outtenum lake.

E.2/11

16. <Tuesday> Wind East and moderate weather; paddled 20 Miles
SWbS. then came to Othenume Lake.

17 July 1754

B.239/a/40

July ye 17th Wednesday fine weather wind SW^t this day padled 27 M
SWbS^o here is no Currant att all in this pond or Lake, it is in Length
30 Miles, and in Breadth 26 M and ye woods tall, and very Large timber.

E.2/6

17 Wednesd^y fine weather, wind SW paddled 27 miles SWbS; this Lake
is 30 miles long, and 26 miles wide, little current, and the woods
round it is tall and very large timber.

E.2/4

17. Wednesday fine weather wind S.W. paddled 27 miles S.W.B.S. on the
lake and entered a river; this lake is a good days paddle either way,
and the woods around it tall and well grown timber.

E.2/11

17. Wednesday. Wind SW. and agreeable weather; Paddled 20 Miles
SWbS. then came to a River. Othenume Lake is a good days paddle
either way; and the woods around it are tall & well grown timber.

18 July 1754

B.239/a/40

18th Thursday fine weather wind att SWbS, this day padled 26 M up
the River, the Water Showl and the River wide, the banks are high on
both Sides, no woods to be seen growing on the said banks, this day
Catcht 4 Large Jack, Course SW^t.

E.2/6

18 Thursd^y fine weather, wind SWbS^o paddled 26 miles SW up the River; the water shoal, and the River wide, the banks high, no woods to
be seen; nothing to eat but fish as yet.

E.2/4

1755 July 18th Thursday fine weather wind S.W.B.S. paddled 26 miles
S.W. up the river good water for a canoe, the river wide, banks high,
and no woods to be seen; nothing but fish to be got.

E.2/11

18. Thursday. Wind SWbS paddled 26 Miles up the River: good water
for a Canoe, the river wide, banks high, & no woods to be seen: no
provisions to be got but fish.

19 July 1754

    B.239/a/40

19th Friday wind and Weather as yesterday, this went 26 M as yesterday SWbS°, up this River is Showl water, and not above 2 poles wide, and full of weeds

    E.2/6

19 Frid^y wind and weather as yesterday paddled 26 miles SWbS. up this River, still shoal water, not above 2 poles wide and full of weeds.

    E.2/4

19. Friday wind and weather as yesterday paddled 26 miles S.W.B.S. up the river.

    E.2/11

19. Friday. Wind &c as before; paddled 26 Miles up the river.

20 July 1754

    B.239/a/40

20th Saturday fine weather wind NE^t this day padled 6 miles, when we came to a Large Ledge of willows, where we hawled our Canoes through it near a mile, and then we Came to a Large River, which ye Ind^s Called port Nelson* here the water is very deep, and the Currant Runs E^t, the River is 16 poles wide, padled 16 Mile up ye River, then we Came to a Small Branch of ye River, here we put up for the night, the banks are Low nothing but poplars, and willows to be seen.

    * a mistake of Nelson River on the 9th Instant, this being Nelson River.

    E.2/6

1754 20 July Saturd^y fine weather, wind NE. this day paddled 6 miles SWbS; when we came to a large ledge of willows, where we were obliged to hawl our Canoes thro' near a mile, and then we came to Port Nelson River as the Indians informs me, the water is very deep & the current runs Eastward, it's 16 poles wide; paddled 16 miles up, SWbS; then we came to a small branch where we put up for the night, the banks low with poplars and willows growing on them.

    E.2/4

20. Saturday fine weather wind N.E. paddled 6 miles S.W.B.S. and after hawling our canoes ¾ Mile thro' a swampy drain intermixt with willows came to port Nelson river, and paddled S.W.B.S. 16 miles untill we came to a small branch; the river 16 poles wide, water deep, and current runs E.ward, the banks are low with poplar and willows.

    E.2/11

1754 July 20. Saturday. Wind NE and pleasant weather, paddled 6 miles SWbS. and after dragging our Canoes ¾ Mile thro' a Swampy drain intermix'd with Willows, came to Nelson River <& paddled on> until we came to a small branch. The River is 16 poles wide, water deep & current runs Eastward, and low banks with Poplars & Willows.

21 July 1754

B.239/a/40

1754 July ye 21st Sunday fine weather wind W^t this day padled 2 M SWbS^o then Came to another Large River, where the french track their Canoes, here we padled 8 Miles West, and then we Came to a Large pond 10 M in Length & 8 in Breadth, then put up for this night.

E.2/6

21 Sunday fine weather, wind W^t paddled 2 miles, SW; when we came to a large River called Keskachewan where the French tracks their Canoes, here we paddled 8 miles W^t, then we came to a Lake 10 miles long & 8 miles wide, then put up for the night.

E.2/4

21. Sunday fine weather wind W. paddled 2 miles S.W. up the branch, then came to Keskechewan river on which the french has 2 houses, one of which we expect to see tomorrow; paddled up it 8 miles W. passed a large lake that helps to feed the river.

E.2/11

21. Sunday. Wind West and Fine weather; paddled two miles up the River, and then came to Keiskatchewan River; on which the French have two houses, one of which we expect to see to morrow: paddled up it 8 Miles West; passed a large lake which helps to supply the River.

22 July 1754

B.239/a/40

ye 22^d Monday fine weather wind SW^t this day padled 14 miles up ye River when we Came to the french factory.* on my arrival, two french men Came out, when followed a great deal of Bowing and Scraping between us, and then we Entered their fort (or more properly a Hogstye) for in short it is no Better, they have neither victuals nor drink, Except a Little Ruhigan, they are very Lazey, not one stick of wood anigh their house; they asked me where the Letter was, I told them I had no Letter, nor did not see any Reason for one, but that the Country belonged to us as much as them; he made ansuer it did not, and that he would detain me there, and send me home to france, I told him I knew france as well as he did, and was not afraid to go their more then himself, which Made Monsieure a Little Cooler.

  * This factory is a house or hutt about [   ] feet Long and feet Broad, 8 feet high to ye Ridge, being a Sloping Rooff, the sides Log upon Log, the top Covered with the Rhyne of trees, fastned togeather with willows, it is in 3 appartments, one for their dwelling place, one

for trading goods, and one for ffurrs, the windows Low, one to each place, all the three different housses wch Captn Hendey see are much the same for Bigness, with one Large Canoe att Each house, made Light that 2 Men Can Carry.

E.2/6

22 Mond^y fine weather, wind SW. paddled 14 miles up the River W. when we came to a French house, on my arrival two Frenchmen came out and in a very Genteel manner invited me into their house, which I readily accepted; one of them asked me if I had any letter from my Master, and where and upon what design I was going inland; I made answer I had no letter, and that I was sent to view the Country, and was designed to return in the spring; he told me the Master and Men were gone down with the furs, and that He must stop me until his return; however they were very kind, and at night I went to my tent and told the Leader that had the charge of me, who only laugh'd and said they Dar'd not: I sent them 2 feet of Brazile Tobacco.

E.2/4

22. Monday fine weather wind W. paddled 14 miles up the river W. when we came to a french house; on our arrival two frenchmen came out in a very genteel manner and invited me into their house, which I readily accepted, one of them asked me if I had any letters from my master, and where & on what design I was going inland, I answered I had no letters, and that I was sent to view the country, and designed to return in the spring; he told me the master and men were gone down with the furs and that they must stop me till they returned, however they were very kind and at night I went to my tent and told my leader that had the charge of me, who only laughed and said they dar'd not; I sent them two feet of brazile tobacco.

E.2/11

22. Monday. Wind West and fine Weather; the Musketoes are now intollerable, giving us neither peace day nor night. Paddled 14 Miles up the river West; when we came to a French house: On our Arrival two Frenchmen came to the water-side, and in a very genteel manner, invited me into their house; which I readily accepted. One of them asked me if I had any Letter from my Master, & where, and on what design I was going inland. I answered I had no letter, and that I was sent to view the Country, and intended to return in the spring. He told me the Master and men were gone down to Montreal with the Furs; and that they must detain me till their return. However they were very kind, and at night I went to my tent, and told Attickasish or Little Deer, my Leader that had the charge of me,* who smiled & said they dared not. I sent them two feet of tobacco, which was very acceptable to them.

<* Attickashish was afterwards my Acquaintance, and a valuable leading Indian. Andrew Graham.>

23 July 1754
B.239/a/40
July ye 23^d Tuesday this day Rained hard, we padled none to day, I gave the french Man & his Man some tobacco 2 feet, for some Ruhigan to Eat, when he gave me some, for att this time we had not a morsel to Eat of any kind of Victuals, att Noon fine weather wind SWbS^o.
E.2/6
1754 July 23 Tuesd^y rainy and blowing weather, wind SWbS; we paddled none to day, the Frenchman invited me to breakfast and dinner,* thank'd me for the tobacco, and made me a present of a bag of pownded dry Moose flesh.
    * The House is about 26 feet long, 12 feet wide 9 feet high to the ridge, having a sloping roof, the walls Log on Log, the top covered with Birch rhine fastned together with willows, divided into 3 apartments, one for Trading goods, one for furs, and one they Dwell in. I seed one birch rhine Canoe that would carry more than a Ship's long-boat of 500 Tuns burthen, Indians tells me that 2 Such Canoes loaded with furs are sent from this House Yearly.
E.2/4
23. Tuesday wind S.W. blowing strong with rain paddled none, invited to breakfast and dine with the french who thank'd me for the brazile tobacco and made me a present of a bag of pounded moose flesh.
E.2/11
23. Tuesday. wind SW. a strong gale, with Rain: invited to Breakfast & Dinner; thanked me for the tobacco, & presented to me Some Moose flesh.

24 July 1754
B.239/a/40
24th Wednesday fine w^r wind S^o this day padled 6 mile up ye River, then Came to a Large pond, it is 20 M in Length, & in breadth 16 M, we padled to ye further side of it & put up for ye night, y^s day past 22 Isl^ds & 2 Large falls.
E.2/6
24 Wednesd^y fine weather, wind S^o paddled 6 miles up the River W. then came to a large Lake 20 miles long and 16 miles wide, paddled WbS. to the further side of it and put up for the night; passed 22 Islands and 2 Large falls.
E.2/4
24. Wednesday fine weather wind S. paddled 6 miles W. up

Keskechewan river then left it and paddled W.B.S. across a lake then came at peatago river.

> E.2/11

1754 July 24. Wednesday. wind South and Sultry warm weather; Took my departure from the French Settlement, and paddled up Keis-katchewan River 6 Miles; the Course West: Then left it and paddled 16 Miles WbS. across a Lake; then came to Peatago River: here are the largest Birch trees I have yet seen.

25 July 1754

> B.239/a/40

1754 July ye 25th Thursday fine weather wind NW^t this day padled up a Small River 27 M SWbW^t high woods on both Sides of the River, this day killed two ducks.

> E.2/6

25 Thursd^y fine weather, wind NW; paddled up a small River Called peatago 27 miles SWbW high woods on both sides the River, Birch trees lofty and large. We all live on fish as yet.

> E.2/4

25. Thursday wind and weather as before, paddled up peatago river 27 miles S.W.B.W. large birch trees on both sides the river, we live on fish, the river is small but there are very good water as yet.

> E.2/11

25. Thursday. wind & weather as Yesterday; Paddled up Peatago river 27 Miles SWbW. Large Birch-trees on both sides the river. We still live on Fish, and are all heartily wishing for a change of food. This river is small, but good water as yet. To Morrow We shall leave our canoes & travel.

26 July 1754

> B.239/a/40

26th Friday wind and Weather as Yesterday this day padled up Peatasgo River 28 M shoul water all the way, past by 9 Islands and 4 falls, killed 2 ducks & 4 Jack, past By severall Canoes the Ind^s had Left on Acc^t of showl water.

> E.2/6

26 Frid^y wind and weather as yesterday, paddled up peatago River 28 miles SWbW shoal water, passed 9 Islands and 4 falls, also several Canoes the Indians had left on account of shoal water.

> E.2/4

26. Friday wind &c as before paddled 28 miles S.W.B.W. up peatago river, shoal water, passed 9 Islands, 4 falls, and several canoes that Indians had left on account of shoal water.

E.2/11

26. Friday. Wind and weather as before Paddled 28 Miles SWbW up Peatago river. Shoal Water: passed 9 Islands, 4 Falls, and several Canoes, the Natives had left, on account of shoal water.

27 July 1754
B.239/a/40

27th Saturday wind and weather as the 24th this day padled 2 mile further up the River Little or no Water, here we Left our Canoes and travelled in Land 4 miles SWbWt here were the Inds familys in a Starving Condition, so that we are Like to have but Little Relief.

E.2/6

27 Saturdy fine weather, wind S. paddled 2 miles further up the River SWbW; little or no water, so here we left our Canoes, and Travelled 4 miles SWbS. here were the Indians Families in a starving condition, so that we are like to have little relief as yet.

E.2/4

1755 July 27th Saturday fine weather wind S. paddled 2 miles S.W.B.W. little or no water in the river, here we left our canoes and travelled 4 miles S.W.B.S. where we found our Indians families in a starving condition, and we are not yet capable to help them.

E.2/11

27. Saturday. <Wind> W.SbW. and a continuance of very warm weather: Very shoal water. Here we left our canoes, & travelled 4 Miles SWbS. Here were our Indians Families in a starving condition, for want of food; & we are in the same condition.

28 July 1754
B.239/a/40

ye 28th Sunday fine Weather Wind SWt this day travelled 26 Miles, past two Creecks, and 2 tent places, Indians was gone from, nothing to Eat nor nothing to be gott.

E.2/6

1754 July 28 Sundy fine weather, wind SW. this day travelled 26 miles SWbS; passed 2 Creeks, and 2 Indian tent places, nothing to eat, nor nothing to be got.

E.2/4

28. Sunday fine weather wind S.W. travelled 26 miles S.W.B.S. passed 2 creeks and 2 Indian tent places, neither bird nor beast to be seen so that we have nothing to eat.

E.2/11

28. Sunday. Wind SW. and very warm weather; travelled 26 Miles

SWbW. passed two creeks, and two Indian tent-places. Neither Bird
nor Beast to be seen; so that we have nothing to eat.

29 July 1754
    B.239/a/40

1754 July ye 29th Monday fine Weather wind NW^t this day travelled 24
M nothing to kill, see a fine bed of Rasberries, which I Eat of till I was
Like to burst, and about 2 miles further we Came to where there was
the finest Berries* I ever Saw, or in short tasted , they are Like a pine
apple for finest of fruit.

    * a Sample of ye Berries I have sent home, they are ye size of a
Black Currant.

    E.2/6

29 Mond^y fine weather, wind NW; travelled 24 miles SW. seed not one
Beast, but happily met with a fine bed of raspberries, of which I did
eat till I was like to burst, and about 2 mile further we came where
were the finest berries I ever did see or taste, they are the size of a
black currant.

    E.2/4

29. Monday fine weather wind N.W. traveled 24 miles S.W. when we fortunately met with a fine bed of raspberries of which I did eat very
hearty as did the natives, two miles further we met with the finest
berries I ever eat, they are the size of our black currants.

    E.2/11

29. Monday. wind NW. and warm weather; travelled 24 Miles SW. when
we fortunately met with a fine bed of Strawberries, of which I did eat
very heartily; as did the Natives. Two miles farther, we met with
berries the size of black currants, the finest I ever eat. I, as also the
Natives, are fatigued with our two days journies, which we are obliged
to perform to come up to where provisions are to be had.

30 July 1754
    B.239/a/40

30 Tuesday fine weather wind SW^tbW^t this day travelled 22M SW^t, Levell Land, willows & fruit trees of severall sorts, this day saw two fields
of tears very thick, and full as Large, as them in England, past 2 Small
Creecks of water, killed 2 Moose.

    E.2/6

30 Tuesd^y fine weather, wind SWbS; travelled 22 miles SW levell Land,
willows and Cherry trees, and fields of tares as full and Large as ever I
see'd any in England, passed 2 small Creeks; Indians killed 2 Moose, A
Noble Feast, attended with drumming, Conjuring, Smoaking, Talking,
Dancing and Singing.

E.2/4

30. Tuesday fine weather wind S.W.B.S. traveled 22 miles S.W. level land, cherry trees and fields of tares as full & ripe as any in England; Indians killed 2 moose.

E.2/11

1754 July 30. Tuesday. wind SWbS and warm weather; travelled 11 Miles SW. level land, Cherry trees, and fields of tares are full & ripe as any in England. Indians killed 2 Moose.

31 July 1754

B.239/a/40

July ye 31 Wednesday fine weather wind NW^t this day travelled 26 M WSW^t fine Levell Land and Burnt woods, all ye way; there is nothing but stinking water for to drink, and Else for to Eat, this day Came to us ten tents of Senipoets, I went and Smoakt with them, they all promised to go with me to the fort next Spring.

E.2/6

31 Wednesd^y fine weather, wind NW; travelled 26 miles WSW; fine level land and burnt woods all the way; nothing but stinking water to drink, came to 10 tents of Asinepoet Indians; I went and smoaked with them; they promised to get furs and go with me to the Fort in the spring.

E.2/4

31. Wednesday fine weather wind N.W. traveled 26 miles W.S.W. level land and burnt woods and nothing but stinking water to drink; came to 10 tents of Aseenepoet Indians, being now entered their country I went and smoaked and talked with them to go with me to the fort in the summer, but they answered, we are more conveniently supplyed from the french houses, I said that the french gave them little for their furs, but all I said signified nothing, I found them strongly attached to the french Interest.

E.2/11

31. Wednesday. Wind NW. and fine cool weather; travelled 13 Miles WSW. Level lands & burnt woods; & there are nothing <but> Stagnated water to drink. Came to <two> tents of Asinepoet Indians. I smoaked with them, & talked with them to go down with me to York Fort in the summer. but they answered "We are conveniently supplyed from the Paqua-Mistgushewuck Whiskeheginish." that is the Frenchmens House of trade.

1 August 1754

B.239/a/40

1754 Augst ye 1st Thursday fine weather wind NW^t this day travelled 24 Miles SWbS^o fine Levell Land and tall woods, past 3 Creecks, very Little water in them, killed 2 Moose.

E.2/6

august 1 Thursd^y fine weather, wind NW, travelled 24 miles SWbS. fine level Land and tall woods, passed 3 small Creeks; Indians killed 2 Moose: The Country and weather so fine and pleasant, beyond description, I cannot think myself at present in North America.

E.2/4

August 1st Thursday a continuance of fine weather, wind N.W. traveled 24 miles S.W.B.S. fine level land and tall woods, passed 3 small creeks of sweet water; the Indians killed 2 moose; I am now in a pleasant and plentyful country.

E.2/11

Aug^st 1. Thursday Wind NW. and fine cool weather travelled 12 Miles SWbS fine level land and tall woods: passed three small creeks of sweet water. The Indians killed 2 Moose: I am now entering a pleasant and plentiful country.

2 August 1754

B.239/a/40

ye 2^d Friday fine weather wind NE^t this day travelled 20 M, the Land Hills & deals, & very Little woods, this day killed 6 Waskesw—they are as large as a Moose.

E.2/6

2 Frid^y fine weather, wind NE; travelled 20 miles SWbS; the Land Hills, dales, and little woods, the Indians killed 6 waskesew's; they are of the Moose kind, Clean made, and as tall as an English draught Horse.

E.2/4

2^d Friday fine weather wind NE. traveled 20 miles S.W.B.S. hills and dales and little woods; Indians killed 6 Waskesews, they are of the moose kind, clean made and as tall as an English draught horse.

E.2/11

1754 Aug^st 2. Friday. wind NE and agreeable weather; Travelled 10 Miles SWbS. Hills and Dales with little woods. Indians killed 6 Waskesew.

3 August 1754

B.239/a/40

ye 3^d Saturday fine weather Wind att S^o and very hott, this day travelled 21 M SWbS^o fine Levell Land and tall Cherry trees, filburds, and Nutts Large & fine, Killed 2 Moose.

E.2/6

1754 august 3 Saturd^y fine weather, wind S. and sultry hot, travelled 21 miles SWbS. fine level Land, and tall Cherry trees, filbeards and nuts large and fine; killed 2 Moose, obliged to travell hard to come up to where the Buffalou's are.

E.2/4

3. Saturday sultry hot weather wind S. traveled 21 miles S.W.B.S. level land & cherry trees on which are plenty of fruit, also plenty of nuts; Indians killed 2 Moose.

E.2/11

3. Saturday. Wind South, Sultry hot weather; travelled 10 Miles SWbS. Level land with Cherry trees, on Which are plenty of fruit, Plenty of Filberts. Indians killed 2 Moose.

4 August 1754

B.239/a/40

ye 4th Sunday fine weather wind NW^t this day travelled 20 M NW^t by reason there is no water for 3 days travell, Levell Land and tall woods all ye way, then Came to us seven tents more of Esinipoets, I went to their tents & Smoakt with them, they all in Gen^ll promised, to go to the fort in ye spring of ye year, this day killed two Moose.

E.2/6

4 Sunday fine weather, wind NW. travelled 20 miles NW. Land and woods as yesterday; Met with 7 tents Asinepoet Indians, I smoaked with them, they promised to go with me to the Fort in the spring; killed 2 Moose.

E.2/4

4. Sunday fine weather wind N.W. traveled 20 miles N.W. land and woods as yesterday, met with 7 tents of Aseenepoets, I smoaked with them, but have no hopes of getting them to the fort, as what cloth &c they have, is french; Indians killed 2 moose.

E.2/11

4. Sunday Wind NW. travelled 10 Miles NW. Land and Woods as Yesterday: Met with 7 tents of Asinepoet Indians. I smoaked with them; but have no hopes of getting them to the Fort: as what Cloth &c they had were french and, by their behaviour, I perceived they were strongly attached to the French interest. Indians killed two Moose.

5 August 1754

B.239/a/40

1754 Aug^st ye 5th Monday fine weather, wind att S^o. this day travelled 22 M W^t Levell Land & poor woods. this day killed 4 Waskesw^s.

E.2/6

5 Mond^y fine weather, wind S. travelled 22 miles W. Level Land, and poor woods; killed 4 Waskesews.

E.2/4

5. Monday fine weather wind S. traveled 22 miles S.W. level land and small hasle wood; killed 4 waskesews.

E.2/11

5. Monday. Wind South Travelled 11 Miles WSW. Level land and poor Woods: killed 4 Waskesew, or Red Deer: A Stately Animal, but the flesh coarse, and no manner equal to Moose flesh: however all is welcome to us.

6 August 1754

B.239/a/40

ye 6 Tuesday very hot wind SW^t with a great deal of thunder & Lightning, travelled none, Killed two Moose.

E.2/6

6 Tuesd^y very sultry hot weather, travelled 22 miles WSW level Land and tall woods running in ledges, crossed 3 small Creeks, which is acceptable not having seen any water these three days past.

E.2/4

1755 August 6th Tuesday calm sultry weather traveled 22 miles W.S.W. level land and tall ledges of woods, crossed several small creeks of good water which is very acceptable, not having tasted any good water these three days past.

E.2/11

1754 Aug^st 6. Tuesday. Calm, Sultry weather; Travelled 11 Miles WSW. Level lands, and tall ledges of woods: crossed several small Creeks of good water, which is acceptable; not having seen any these three days past.

7 August 1754

B.239/a/40

ye 7th Wednesday fine weather wind SWbS this day travelled 24 M SW^t Levell Land and tall woods in Ledges; Crossed 3 Small Creecks, and killed 3 Waskesw^s.

E.2/6

7 Wednesd^y wind and weather, as yesterday; travelled none, killed 3 Waskesews and 2 Moose.

E.2/4

7. Wednesday a continuance of hot sultry weather wind S. traveled none, Indians killed 3 waskesews and 2 moose.

E.2/11

7. Wednesday. Calm with very warm weather; Travelled none. Indians killed 3 Waskesew & 2 moose.

8 August 1754

> B.239/a/40

ye 8th Thursday fine weather wind att SW^t travelled none this day.

> E.2/6

8 Thursd^y a strong gale of wind with Thunder, Lightning and rain, travelled none, all hands Employed eating & smoaking, and I am not behind hand, thank God a good stomach; and as I am looked on as a Leader I have Ladies of different ranks to attend me, please to observe the Men does nothing but hunt, and we Leaders hath a Lady to hold the thogin with water to our heads when we drink.

> E.2/4

8. Thursday a strong gale of wind at N.W. with thunder, lightning and rain; traveled none, a grand feast, with smoking, dancing, drumming and conjuring.

> E.2/11

8. Thursday. Wind NW. Strong gales from NW. to NWbN. attended with thunder, lightning & rain: travelled none. All hands feasting, smoaking, drinking, dancing, & Conjuring.

9 August 1754

> B.239/a/40

ye 9th Friday fine weather wind SW^t took my departure from Wonman Sokahigan, and Steered West 6 Miles, and then we Came to Swatagan Sokahigan or Salt Lake, ye water is Salt, and Round the Edge of the Lake, their is Candid Salt, it is 12 Mile Round, and the Land is very Low & Levell, poplars & willows; then we Steered WbS^o 14 M, then put up for the night, this day killed 8 Moose their being great plenty of them.

> E.2/6

1754 august 9 Frid^y fine weather, wind SW. travelled 20 miles W. level Land with poplars & willows, passed 2 small Lakes one of which was salt, large lumps was canded round the edges of the Lake; killed 8 Moose, they are plenty.

> E.2/4

9. Friday moderate weather wind S.W. traveled 20 miles W. level land with small woods vizt poplar, alder, hasle and birch trees, passed 2 salt lakes, large lumps of salt canded laying round the edges; killed 8 moose.

> E.2/11

9. Friday. Wind SW and pleasant weather: Level land; Poplars & Willows. Passed 2 Salt Lakes large lumps of Salt candid laying round the edges Indians killed 2 Moose.

10 August 1754

B.239/a/40

1754 Aug^st ye 10th Saturday fine Weather wind att N^o took my departure from Salt plain and Steered WbN^o 4 M and put up for the day, I
went to seven feasts, they Gave me 3 tongues, and some Moose flesh,
for I have work Enough to take Care of my things, having a Large family about us att pres^t.

E.2/6

10 Saturd^y fine weather, wind N. travelled 4 miles WbN. then put up
for the day, invited to 7 Feasts, we are a large Gang at present.

E.2/4

10. Saturday fine weather wind N. traveled 4 miles W.B.N. then invited
to 7 feasts.

E.2/11

10. Saturday Wind North Fine weather; Travelled 4 Miles WbN. then
put up to feast &c.

11 August 1754

B.239/a/40

ye 11th Sunday fine weather wind att W^t. took my departure from plentyfull plain, and Steered WSW^t 22 miles, fine Levell Land and dry, for
we are obliged to go Round about by Reason their is no Water for a
great way together, but Salt water, this day Cross'd three Lakes, all of
them so Salt I Could not drink of them.

E.2/6

11 Sunday fine weather, wind W. travelled 22 miles SWbW. fine level dry Land,
and nothing but salt water Lakes, short grass and no woods of any kind.

E.2/4

11. Sunday fine weather wind W. traveled 22 miles S.W.B.W. level land,
short grass, no woods, and no water but what is salt.

E.2/11

1754 Aug^st 11. Sunday. Wind West pleasant weather; Travelled 11 Miles
SWbW Level land, short Grass, no woods, & no Water but what is salt.

12 August 1754

B.239/a/40

ye 12th Monday fine weather Wind W^t took my departure from Burnt
Hill and steered 15 M; fine Ledges of Nutt trees, Rasberries, and Cherry trees and great plenty of fruit on them, all ye Grass is very Short,
and the Land is plain, this day past 2 Large Lakes, 15 M Round, and
the water as Salt as Brime.

E.2/6

12 Mond^y fine weather wind W. travelled WSW. 15 miles; fine level land,

with nut trees, Cherry trees and raspberries, yeilding plenty of fruit; the grass very short; passed 2 Large salt Lakes.

    E.2/4

12, Monday wind and weather as yesterday traveled 15 miles W.S.W. level land with hasle and cherry trees loaded with fine ripe fruit; nothing but salt lakes.

    E.2/11

12. Monday Wind West and fine weather; Travelled 7 Miles WSW. Level land, with small black Cherry trees yielding plenty of fruit. Nothing but salt lakes.

13 August 1754

    B.239/a/40

1754 Augst ye 13th Tuesday blows hard att NW^t and Clear took my departure from Cherry Ledge, and Steered 15 M, this day past 5 Large Salt ponds, being neither Grass Nor wood Near, the water very Salt and Smells Like Brime, what wood here is dry, and Grass very Short & thick ye Indian Name for this place is Muscuty, Last night it thundered and Lightned very Much, but no Rain, this day the Ind^s killed a Waskesu—

    E.2/6

13 Tuesd^y a strong gale, wind NW. travelled WSW. 15 miles, level Land, dry woods, and short grass, passed 5 salt Lakes; we are now come to Muscuty plains; the Indians informs me I shall soon see Buffalow, and Archithinue Indians hunting them on Horseback.

    E.2/4

13. Tuesday a strong gale wind W. traveled 15 miles W.S.W. level land, short grass and several salt water lakes; we are now entered muscuty plains, shall soon see plenty of buffaloe and the archithinue Indians hunting them on horse-back.

    E.2/11

13. Tuesday. Wind West, and a strong gale; Travelled 7 Miles WSW. Level land, short Grass, Dry-woods, & several Salt water lakes. We are now entered Muscuty plains, and shall soon see plenty of Buffalo, and the Archithinue Indians hunting them on Horse-back.

14 August 1754

    B.239/a/40

ye 14 Wednesday fine weather wind att W^t travelled none to day, I went a hunting with some young men, Killed 3 Moose.

    E.2/6

14 Wednesd^y fine weather, wind W. travelled none, Young men went a hunting killed several Moose and Waskesew's, provisions good and plenty.

E.2/4

14. Wednesday moderate weather wind W. traveled none, young men a hunting killed several moose and waskesews, provisions good and plenty.

E.2/11

14. Wednesday. Wind West and agreeable weather; Travelled none. The Young men hunting, killed several Moose & Waskesew: Provisions plenty, & good food.

15 August 1754

B.239/a/40

ye 15 Thursday fine weather Wind att NE^t. took my departure from Moose Valley, & Steered West 17 M, fine Levell Land and nothing but brushe Wood of Birch, betwixt the fields of french Grass, this day saw 2 Herds of Cows, very Large, having seen none before alive.

E.2/6

15 Thursd^y fine weather, wind NE. took my departure from plentiful valley, into Muscuty plains and travelled 17 miles W. level land and Birch trees, seed two herds of Buffalow, the size of English Cows.

E.2/4

15. Thursday fine weather wind N.E. travelled 17 miles W. level land and small birch trees, seed several herds of buffaloe the size of English cows.

E.2/11

15. Thursday Wind N.E. and pleasant weather; travelled 8 Miles West; Saw several several Herds of Buffalo.

16 August 1754

B.239/a/40

1754 Augst ye 16 Friday fine weather wind att W^t took my departure from horse plain, and Steered WbN^o, this day see 2 wild horses, and two Cows, but killed none of them, and the Ind^s kill'd 6 Waskesu^s, —fine Levell Land and but one Stinking place of Water.

E.2/6

1754 august 16 Frid^y fine weather, wind W. took my departure from Buffalow plain, and traveled WbN. 15 miles, level Land with Birch, Cherry, and nut trees, passed one salt Lake, see 2 Buffalow, and 2 wild Horses, killed 6 Waskesew's.

E.2/4

16. Friday fine weather wind W. travelled 15 miles W.B.N. level land with birch, cherry and hasle trees, passed a lake of salt water, seed 2 buffaloe and 2 wild horses, Indians killed 6 waskesews.

E.2/11

1754 Aug^st 16. Friday. Wind West and moderate weather Travelled 15 Miles WbN. Level land, with Birch, Cherry and Nut-trees. Passed a lake of Salt water; Saw two Buffalo and two Horses, killed 6 Waskesew.

17 August 1754

B.239/a/40

ye 17th Saturday fine Weather wind SW^t. took my departure from Hair Hill and Steered WNW 17 M, this day Crossed a Large Hill, small shrubs on both sides, where grows Cherrys, Nutts, & poplar trees, started a Hair on the top of this Hill, as Large as any in England, killed this day 4 waskesu^s.

E.2/6

17 Saturd^y fine weather wind SW. took my departure from wild Horse plain, and travelled 17 miles WNW. crossed a large Hill full of shrubs and fine Berries like unto black currants, started a hare of size and colour as in England; killed 4 Waskesews.

E.2/4

17. Saturday fine weather wind S.W. travelled 17 miles W.N.W. crossed a large hill full of shrubs and fine berries like unto black currants, started a hare of size and colour as in England; Indians killed 4 waskesews.

E.2/11

17. Saturday. wind SW. and fine weather; Travelled 8 Miles WNW. Crossed a large hill full of Shrubs, and fine berries like unto black currants Started a Hare, of size and color like those in England. Indians killed 4 Waskesew.

18 August 1754

B.239/a/40

ye 18th Sunday fine weather wind NW^t this day the Ind^s went a hunting, and killed 3 Moose, when one of the Ind^s Came to Me said he was very Lame, I drest his foot, and he brought me a Moose Nose and some tong^s, and seemed overjoyed that they had got a docter Come to them; att this place is a fine mineral water, and as Cold as Ice Itself.

E.2/6

18 Sunday fine weather wind NW. travelled none, Young Men went a hunting, I dressed a Lame Man's foot, & he gave me a Moose nose and a few tongues; at this place a fine mineral spring as cold as Ice.

E.2/4

18. Sunday fine weather wind N.W. travelled none, young men a hunting killed several moose; I dressed a lame man's leg, he gave me a

moose nose and a few tongues, at this place a mineral spring as cold
as ice & of a bluish colour.

  E.2/11

18. Sunday. Wind NW and fine weather; Travelled none. The Young Men
hunting killed several Moose. I dressed a lame Man's leg: He gave me
a Moose Nose, which is a delicate dish, for my trouble. At this place a
mineral spring as cold as ice.

19 August 1754
  B.239/a/40

Augst ye 19th Monday fine weather Wind W^t took my departure from
Link Spaw on Musqueto plains, and Steered WNW^t 20 M fine Land and
nothing but salt water ponds all ye way, have past but 4 places of fresh
Water these 5 days past, all very Nauseous & Stink very Much. this day
killed 3 Moose.

  E.2/6

19 Monday fine weather, wind W. took my departure from mineral
spring in Muscuty plains, and travelled WNW. 20 miles; fine Land, no
woods and salt water Lakes have passed but 4 places of fresh water
these 5 days; killed 3 Moose.

  E.2/4

1755 August 19th Monday fine weather wind W. travelled 20 miles
W.S.W. fine land, no woods, several salt water lakes, have passed only 4
places of fresh water these 4 days past.

  E.2/11

19. Monday Wind West and pleasant weather; Travelled 10 Miles WSW
in Muscuty plains; fine land, no Woods: several salt water Lakes: have
passed but 4 places of fresh water, these five days past.

20 August 1754
  B.239/a/40

ye 20 Tuesday fine weather wind att W^t. took my departure from
Yeabege pond and steered N° 15 M, then we Came to a Large River,
Called Wapesu Copeto Seepie, fine Levell Meadow Land, and dry on
both Sides, Grows Hasels, poplar & willows, and high Banks on both
sides of ye River, the Ind^s killed 2 Waskesew^s.

  E.2/6

20 Tuesd^y fine weather, took my departure from salt water Lake, and
travelled 15 miles N. then we came to a Large River called Wapesew-
copeto; level Land, high banks and good woods of Birch, Poplar,
Hazel, Alder, fir, & Willow trees; killed 5 Waskesew's.

  E.2/4

20. Tuesday wind and weather as yesterday travelled 15 miles N. then

came to wapesewcopeto river, it is large and the banks are high on
which grows birch, poplar, hasle, alder and fir &c; Indians killed 5
waskesews.

E.2/11

1754 Augst 20. Tuesday. Wind West and pleasant weather; Travelled 15
Miles North; then came to Wapesewcopet River It is large, the banks
are high; on which grow Birch, Poplar, Hazle, Elder, Fir &c. killed 5
Waskesew.

21 August 1754

B.239/a/40

ye 21st Wednesday fine weather wind NW^t the Ind^s made 20 Canoes of
parchm^t Skins, and willows, for here is neither Birch nor firr, then
Crossed the River & pitcht on the other side, Caught some small fray
by Angling, the Ind^s killed two Bears, and 4 waskesw^s, the women
went a Walking brought in a parcel of fine Cherrys.

E.2/6

1754 august 21 Wednesd^y fine weather, wind NW. the Indians made 20
temporary Canoes of parchment Moose skins and willows, myself
caught a few small trout by angling, the Women went a berrie hunting, brought in a great many fine Cherries; in the Evening Cross'd the
River and lay all night.

E.2/4

21. Wednesday fine weather wind N.W. the Indian men made temporary canoes of willows and parchment moose skins, the women went a
berrie hunting, brought many fine cherrys and berrys of different
kinds, I angled a few small trout fish, and in the evening crossed the
river in our temporary canoes.

E.2/11

21. Wednesday. wind NW. and fine weather; The Indian Men made temporary Canoes of Willows, covered with parchment Moose skins. The
Women gathered plenty of excellent Berries, and Cherries: I angled a
few small Trout; & in the evening we crossed the River in our Slender
Canoes, without any Accident happening.

22 August 1754

B.239/a/40

ye 22^d Thursday fine weather wind NE^t took my departure from Wapesew Copeto; & Steered NW^t 14 M, fine Levell Land all the way, and dry
Large Ledges, all this day saw no Water till we put up, the Ind^s killed
6 Waskesew's.

E.2/6

22 Thursd^y wind NE and fine weather, took my Departure from

Wapesew-copeto River and travelled NW 14 miles; fine level land and
dry ledges of Woods, see no water till we put up at night, which thank
God is fresh and sweet; Indians killed 6 Waskesew's, they are plenty
and fine food.

    E.2/4

22. Thursday fine weather wind N.E. travelled 14 miles N.W. level land
and dry ledges of woods, seed no water till we put up at night and
that is fresh and good thank God; Indians killed 6 waskesews they are
plenty.

    E.2/11

22. Thursday. Wind NE and fine moderate Weather; Travelled 12 Miles
NW. Level land, and dry ridges of woods. saw no water till we put up at
night; and that was fresh & good, thank God. Indians killed 6 Waskesew. They are plenty and although coarse food, yet go well down with
me & my Companions.

23 August 1754

    B.239/a/40

1754 Augst ye 23^d Friday wind and Weather as Yesterday took my departure from Shenaps plain and steered W^t 25 M over a plain and then
Came to a Ledge of poplars and water, which we stood in Great need
of, having had nothing but stinking water these 2 days past, this day
attickosish went for to see for ye Earchithinue tents, we past 2 of their
places, where was ye bones and head of a Cow, wch they had killed, for
they Leave most of the bones, where they kill the beasts.

    E.2/6

23 Frid^y wind and weather as yesterday, took my Departure from sweet
water pond, and travelled W. 25 miles, level Land, no woods untill
night, then came to a ledge of poplars and sweet water, the
Archithinue Indians, had been Gone from here but a few days before,
as the Natives informed me; they know by their Horses dung and
other signs.

    E.2/4

23. Friday wind and weather as yesterday travelled 25 miles W. level
land no woods nor water till the evening; came to a ledge of poplar
and sweet water; the archithinue Indians has been here lately, we
know by their horses dung &c.

    E.2/11

1754 Augst 23. Friday. wind and weather as Yesterday; Travelled 12 Miles
West. Level land, no Woods, nor water, till the Evening: came to a
ledge of Poplars and sweet water. The Archithinue Natives has been
here lately; we know by their Horses dung and foot-steps.

24 August 1754

B.239/a/40

yᵉ 24 Saturday fine weather wind att NWbN took my departure from posten plain, and Steered WbNᵒ 12 M then we Came to yᵉ side of a Large River, Sackown by name, this River is full of sandy Islands, and Runs Wᵗ and the Currant very Strong East, and deep water Close in shore, and in breadth 2 furlongs, there is no wood but just under the banks and that small; yᵉ most part hazall and Birch.

E.2/6

24 Saturdʸ fine weather wind NWbN. took my Departure from Horse dung ledge, and travelled WbN. 12 miles, then we came to a large river Called sechonby, it is about 2 furlongs broad and full of sandy Islands, the current runs Eᵗ and very strong, and deep water, no woods but what grows on the banks, and that Birch and Hazel: this day Atticko-sish and 2 young Men went another way to look for the Archithinue Indians: here are several of their tent places.

E.2/4

1755 August 24ᵗʰ Saturday fine weather wind N.W.B.N. travelled 12 miles W.B.N. an Indian leader named Attickosish and two young men went another way to look for the Archithinues, in the evening came to sechonby river, it's about 2 furlongs wide and full of sandy Islands, the current runs E. and very strong with deep water, the banks are high and on both sides of which grows birch and hazle.

E.2/11

24. Saturday. Wind NWbN. cool weather: Travelled 12 <Miles> WbN. Attickasish my Leader, and two Young Men, went another way in quest of the Archithinue Natives. In the Evening came to Sechonby River: it is about two furlongs wide, and full of sandy Islands. the Currant runs Easterly, and very rapid: the water deep; the banks high on which grow Birch & Hazle trees.

25 August 1754

B.239/a/40

yᵉ 25 Sunday fine weather, wind Wᵗ. took my departure from Earchithinue Creeck and steered West 20 M, up yᵉ side of yᵉ River, in yᵉ Eachithinue track, fine Levell barren Land, and nothing att all to be got, but berries of which their is Great plenty of, and very fine Eating, this night Catcht some fish Like Shades/

E.2/6

[1754 august 25] Sunday fine weather, wind W. took my departure from Archithinue Creek and travelled W. 20 miles up the River in the Archithinue track; fine level land, no woods but what is growing on the river banks, but plenty of fine berries, in the Evening caught several fine shad fish.

E.2/4

25. Sunday fine weather wind W. travelled 2 miles W. up the river in the Archithinue track, level land, no woods, plenty of fine berrys, in the evening caught a few shad fish.

E.2/11

25. Sunday Wind West and pleasant weather; neither too warm nor too cold; Travelled 2 miles West up the River in the Archithinue track. Level land, no Woods but what grow on the banks: plenty of berries.

26 August 1754

B.239/a/40

Augst ye 26 Monday fine weather wind att NW^t took my departure from Low Life point, and steered WbN^o 17 M, where Came to us a poor Stike Indian with a horse Loaded with Moose flesh, which was very Acceptable to us, we not having tasted any meat for 3 days past. fine Levell Land and Barren, see 2 Cows on ye other side of the River, and they are not Returned.

E.2/6

26 Mond^y fine weather, wind NW. took my departure from shad fall, and travelled WbN. 17 miles, met an old Indian Man with a Horse loaded with Moose, which he shared amongst us:—level barren land, dry and full of fine grass, seed 2 Cows on the other side the River so deep the Young Men could not come at them.

E.2/4

26. Monday fine weather wind N.W. travelled 17 miles W.B.N. the land level, no woods but plenty of fine grass seed two buffalo feeding on the other side of the river, met an old Indian man and a horse loaded with moose flesh which he parted amongst us.

E.2/11

1754 Augst 26. Monday. wind NW and moderate weather; Travelled 14 Miles WbN. the land level; no woods; but plenty of fine grass. Saw two Buffalo feeding on the other side the River. Met an aged Man and a Horse loaded with Moose flesh, which he parted amongst us.

27 August 1754

B.239/a/40

ye 27th Tuesday fine weather wind att S^o took my departure from Shad Creeck and Steered WbN^o 16 M, then we Came to 24 tents of Esinipoets, they have plenty of Moose flesh, and some Beaver, this day past several ponds of water, and one Creeck of Running water I Catcht 17 fish, and was Invited to nine feasts of Ind^s.

E.2/6

27 Tuesd^y fine weather, wind S. took my departure from fortunate point and travelled WbN. 16 miles, then came to 24 tents of Asinepoet Indians, they have plenty of Moose and Beaver's flesh, passed several ponds & one Creek of running water; caught 17 trout.

E.2/4

27. Tuesday fine weather wind S. travelled W.B.N. 16 miles passed several ponds and one creek in which we caught 17 small trout fish in the evening came to 24 tents of Aseenepoet Indians, they have plenty of moose and beaver's flesh.

E.2/11

27. Tuesday. wind South, and warm sultry weather; travelled WbN. 16 Miles. passed several ponds, and one Creek of running water, in which we caught 17 small Trout. In the Evening came to 24 tents of Asinepoet Indians. They have plenty of moose & Beaver flesh, with which they treated us liberally.

28 August 1754

B.239/a/40

ye 28th Wednesday Blowed hard att NW, stayed for a man and his family, are not Come up yet, the Ind^s killed 2 Moose.

E.2/6

28 Wednesd^y blowing weather, wind NW. travelled none to day, Young Men a hunting, killed 2 Moose, Myself and Brother Leaders feasting and smoaking with the Asinepoet Indians by invitation.

E.2/4

28. Wednesday blowing weather wind N.W. travelled none, young men a hunting killed 2 moose, myself and brother leaders feasting &c with the Aseenepoets by invitation.

E.2/11

28. Wednesday. Wind NW a strong gale; travelled none. Young Men hunting, killed 2 Moose: Myself and Brother Leaders feasting &c with the Asinepoet Natives.

29 August 1754

B.239/a/40

ye 29 Thursday fine weather wind att West, this morning the Ind^s told me the Eachithinues had killed the man and his family, and had sculpt him, as for the truth I Cannot say; travelled none these 2 days.

E.2/6

29 Thursd^y fine weather, wind W. Old and Young Men feasting; talking, singing, dancing and drumming; one Man and a Family came to us.

E.2/4

1755 August 29th Thursday fine weather wind W. old and young men feasting with the Assenepoets.

E.2/11

29. Thursday. Wind West and weather more moderate; All hands feasting, dancing, drumming &c.

30 August 1754

B.239/a/40

1754 Augst ye 30th Friday wind and weather as yesterday, took my departure from Base Valley, and steered NW 20 M on the acc^t of being supply'd with water, for if we keep on the high land we Can neither Get victuals nor water, this day I killed a Waskesew and the Ind^s 4/

E.2/6

1754 august 30 Frid^y wind and weather as yesterday. took my Departure from Asinepoet Valley, and travelled NW. 20 miles, dry level barren land, not one stick of wood to be seen and no water to drink.

E.2/4

30. Friday wind &c as yesterday left the Aseenepoets and travelled N.W. 20 miles level barren land and not one stick of wood to be seen, and no water to drink.

E.2/11

1754 Augst 30. Friday. wind West and pleasant weather; Left the Asinepoet Indians, and travelled NW 10 Miles. Levell Barren land, not one stick of wood to be seen, and no water to drink.

31 August 1754

B.239/a/40

ye 31st Saturday this day and Last night had hard showers of Rain, & blowed hard att NWbN, took my departure from Lawrence Bosom and steered NW^t 14 M very unlevell Land all this day, up one hill and down another, one the sides of the Hills are fine Ledges of Nutts and poplar trees.

E.2/6

31 Saturd^y blowing rainy weather, wind NWbN. took my departure from thirsty Habitation, in muscuty plains and travelled NW 14 miles, then came to hills, and dales, and plenty of water, the Indians killed 4 & I one Waskesew.

E.2/4

31. Saturday blowing rainy weather wind N.W.B.N. travelled 14 miles N.W. the Indians killed 4 waskesews, and I one; we are yet in muscuty plains, plenty of good water to day.

E.2/11

31. Saturday. Wind NWbN. and blowing rainy weather; travelled 12 Miles NW. The Indians killed 4 Waskesew, and I killed one. We are yet in Muscuty plains: plenty of good water to day.

1 September 1754

B.239/a/40

Sept[r] y[e] 1st Sunday fine Clear weather Wind NNW[t] took my departure from Beaver Creeck, & steered NWbN[o] 10 M Rocky hills, and in the valleys Ledges of poplar, Birch, Cherrys, Nutts and fruit trees in abundance, this day 7 tents of the Ind[s] went another way, having yet 400 mouths to be fed daily, this day killed 3 moose, and 5 waskesew[s].

E.2/6

Sept[r] 1 Sunday cold raw weather, wind NW. took my Departure from Waskesew hill and travelled NWbN. 10 miles. rocky hills, pleasant valleys, with Birch, Cherry, Alder and poplar trees, and plenty of fine fruit; 7 tents of Indians pitcht another way, we are yet above 400 in number, two thirds of whom Lives Chiefly on fruit, Especially the Women, I have not yet forgot Great Britain so far, but I allow my Bed-fellow a share of my allowance of meat.

E.2/4

Sept[r] 1st Sunday cold raw weather wind N.W. travelled 14 miles N.W.B.N. rocky hills pleasant valleys, with birch, alder, poplar and cherry trees, with plenty of fruit; 7 tents of Indians pitched another way, we are yet above 400 in number, two thirds of whom lives chiefly on berries.

E.2/11

Sept[r] 1st Sunday. wind NW and Cold disagreeable weather Travelled NWbN. 10 Miles. Rocky hillocks, pleasant valleys, with Birch, Elder, Poplar & Cherry trees, with plenty of fruit. Seven tents of Indians pitched another way. We are yet above 400 in number, two thirds of whom live chiefly on fruit.

2 September 1754

B.239/a/40

Sept[r] y[e] 2[d] Monday fine weather the wind att NW[t] this day the Ind[s] Rested themselves for they are obliged to walk over a great deal of ground for their provisions, for the Moose are but very thin this way.

E.2/6

2 Mond[y] fine weather, wind NW. took my departure from fruit hills, and travelled NW. 14 miles, the Land the same as yesterday.

E.2/4

2. Monday fine weather wind N.W. travelled 14 miles N.W. hills and dales.

E.2/11

2. Monday. Wind NW Fine weather; travelled 12 Miles NW. Hills and Dales.

3 September 1754

B.239/a/40

ye 3^d Tuesday fine weather wind att NW^t took my departure from St Cathrines Hill, and steered NW^t 14 M, and then put up for water, it is plenty in this part, having past not one Running Creeck, these 4 days past nothing but small ponds of stinking water.

E.2/6

3 Tuesd^y blowing rainy weather, wind NW. travelled none, Young men went a hunting, killed 3 Moose and 5 Waskesew's.

E.2/4

3. Tuesday blowing rainy weather wind N.W. travelled none, young men a hunting killed 3 moose.

E.2/11

1754 Sepr 3. Tuesday. Wind NW and blowing rainy weather; Travelled none. Young Men hunting killed 3 Moose.

4 September 1754

B.239/a/40

ye 4th Wednesday fine weather wind NE^t took my departure from Swan pond, and Steered 12 M NW^t—here Attickasish Joined us again, and 2 Earchithinues, fine Levell Land and plenty of poplar and Birch and plenty of waskesews, moose and fruit in abundance.

E.2/6

1754 Septr 4 Wednesd^y fine weather, wind NE. travelled NW. 12 miles, here Attickosish Joined us again with 2 Archithinue Indians; fine level land, and fruit trees, Waskesews, & Moose plenty; Indians killed a great many, all hands Employed roasting, broiling, boiling, and feasting.

E.2/4

4. Wednesday fine weather wind N.E. travelled 12 miles N.W. here attickosish joined us again with two Archithinue men on foot; level barren land, killed a great many waskesews and moose.

E.2/11

4. Wednesday Wind NE and pleasant weather; Travelled 12 Miles NW. here Attickasish joined us again, with 2 Archithinue Natives on Horseback. Level land; killed a great many Waskesew and Moose.

5 September 1754

B.239/a/40

ye 5th Thursday fine weather Wind W^t took my departure from
Iammim Creeck and Steered W^t 14 M, fine dry Land and Levell. the
Ind^s killed a Bull, see to day a great many Weweys, Grey Geese, Swans,
& ducks in abundance, this day killed 4 Moose, we are still on Musketo plains, as the Indians tell me, which I believe is 2 hundred Miles,
since we was to have Seen the Earchithinues, the Esinepoets are very
Numerous, and the Mirtho Ind^s as they call them, but their is no odds
in ye Esinepoets and them.

E.2/6

5 Thursd^y fine weather, wind W. travelled W. 14 miles Land and woods
as yesterday; we are yet in muscuty plains as the Indians tells me, and
that the Buffalow taking the rout upwards is the reason we have not
yet seen the Archithinues; the Indians killed a Bull, seed a great many
Swans, Ducks, Cranes, white and gray Geese, the Asinepoet Indians
are plenty here.

E.2/4

1755 Septr 5th Thursday fine weather wind W. travelled W 14 miles, level
land, plenty of fruit trees, plenty of moose, waskesews, swans, cranes,
white and gray geese; here are a great many Aseenepoet Indians of
different tribes, but all talks the same language, they use bows and
arrows which are made of ash; the buffaloe has taken the rout
upwards is the reason we have not yet come up with Archithinue Indians.

E.2/11

5. Thursday. Wind West and agreeable weather; Travelled 12 Miles
West. Level land, with plenty of fruit trees. Plenty of Moose, Waskesew,
Swans, Cranes, White and Grey Geese; also a few ducks. We are yet in
Muscuty plains. Here are a great many Asinepoet Indians. The Buffalo
has taken the rout upwards, & is the reason we have not yet met with
the Archithinue Natives.

6 September 1754

B.239/a/40

ye 6th Friday wind and weather as before, took my departure from
Sandy hill, and steered WSW^t 10 M, hills, dales and Small Ledges of
wood all burnt; killed 2 Moose and 5 Waskesews, the Ind^s Gave me
some tongues and a Side of meat.

E.2/6

6 Frid^y wind and weather as yesterday, travelled WSW 10 miles, hills
and dales, and small ledges of wood all burnt, killed 2 Moose and 5
Waskesew's, met with 5 tents of mirthco (ie bloody) Indians, I gave

the Leader a foot of Brazile tobacco, and smoaked with them, they
were very kind and made me a present of a few tongues and a bladder
of fatt, I could find no difference between them and the Asinepoet
Indians, only they do not cover their private parts, they are the only
Natives that ever I seed here or other parts that does not conceal
their nakedness; Indians seemed to be afraid of them.

   E.2/4

6. Friday wind &c as yesterday travelled 10 miles W.S.W. hills, dales,
and small ledges of burnt woods, killed 2 moose and five waskesews;
met with 5 tents of mirthco (i.e.) bloody Indians, I gave their leader
half a foot of brazile tobacco, and smoked with them, they were very
kind, made me a present of tongues and fat; I could find no difference
between them and the Assenepoet Indians, only the men does not
cover their private parts, and the women altho' they wear a leather
smock that reaches almost to the knee are unacquainted with
decency, they are the only folks I ever saw that does not cover their
nakedness; my Indians seemed afraid of them.

   E.2/11

6. Friday. Wind and weather as Yesterday; Travelled WSW. 10 Miles.
Hillocks and Dales & small ledges of woods all burnt. Indians killed 5
Moose and 2 Waskesew: met with five tents of Mekesue, or Eagle Indians. I gave their leader half a foot of Brazile tobacco, and smoaked
with them: they were very kind, and made me a present of some
tongues, and a bladder full of fat. I could perceive no difference
between them and the Asinepoet Natives with regard to the language;
but one circumstance surprised me much, and that is, the Men do not
cover their nakedness; which are the only natives that does not attend
to decency. The Women are cloathed the Same as the other Asinepoet
Indians. The Natives inform me that they are a Tribe of that brave
Nation; and take their Name from Eagles being plenty in the district
they inhabit. The Leader promised to collect Furs, and go down with
me to the Fort. They never had traded with any European or Canadian. My Guides & Companions seemed afraid of them. <"Since 1755
the Eagle-eyed Indians have traded annually at York Fort, and are
highly valued. When Factor at York Fort I persuaded them to cover
their nakedness, at lest when at the factory.>

7 September 1754

   B.239/a/40

ye 7th Saturday wind att W^t took my departure from wood Creeck and
Steered W^{t}SW^t 12 M fine Levell Land & burnt woods, the Ind^s killed 7
Waskesews and see a dead Bufflow which they Call Mustuce, this day
went with the french Ind^s who took Care to Load me all ye way.

E.2/6

7 Saturd^y fine weather wind W. took my departure from Bloody Indian Ledge, in muscuty plains, were Joined with several Indians in the French Interest, Indians killed 7 Waskesew's, seed a dead Buffalow that had been wounded by the Archithinues, two of their arrows were sticking in it: Land and woods as yesterday: Course WSW^t 12 Miles.

E.2/4

7. Saturday fine weather wind W. travelled 12 miles W.S.W. land &c as yesterday, killed 7 waskesews, found a dead buffaloe with two arrows sticking in its side.

E.2/11

1754 Septr 7th Saturday. Wind West, and pleasant weather: Travelled 12 Miles WSW. land &c as Yesterday. Indians killed 7 Waskesew. found a dead Buffalo; it had been wounded by the Archithinue Natives: several of their Arrows were sticking in it.

8 September 1754

B.239/a/40

ye 8th Sunday Clowdy all day, wind att S^o took my departure from Squishe plain and Steered WSW^t 10 M fine Levell Land and Ledges of woods the Ind^s killed 3 Moose and 4 waskesew^s see to day severall pheasants & two hairs.

E.2/6

1754 Septr 8 Sunday Cloudy weather, and rain at times, wind S. travelled WSW. 10 miles, fine level land, and Ledges of woods, killed 3 Moose and 4 Waskesew's, seed several pheasants and hares.

E.2/4

8. Sunday cloudy weather with rain at times wind S. travelled W.S.W. 10 miles, level land and ledges of woods; killed 3 moose and 4 waskesews, seed several pheasants and hares.

E.2/11

8. Sunday. Wind South, with rain at times; Travelled 10 Miles WSW. Level land, and ledges of woods. Indians killed 3 Moose and 4 Waskesew. Saw several pheasants and Hares.

9 September 1754

B.239/a/40

Septr ye 9th Monday fine weather, wind att West took my departure from Connawappa Creeck, and steered WSW^t 10 M over a plain, here all Men went a hunting, killed 4 Moose, here is Small homacks of nutt and poplar trees, plenty of moose and Waskesew^s, and fine sweet Water, which has been a Great Rarity till Last night when it fell a great deal of Rain.

E.2/6

9 Mond^y fine weather wind W. took my Departure from Hare ledge and travelled WSW. 10 miles, over a barren plain, not one drop of water until night, then hommocks of poplar and hazel trees, and ponds of water; plenty of Moose and Waskesews.

E.2/4

9. Monday fine weather wind W. travelled 10 miles W.S.W. over a barren plain not one drop of water in it, then came to hommocks of poplar, ash, and hasle, and ponds of water; plenty of moose & waskesews.

E.2/11

9. Monday. Wind West, and pleasant weather; Travelled 10 Miles WSW. over a barren plain, not one drop of water in it; then came to Hommocks of Poplar & Hazle, with a few ponds of water. Plenty of Moose & Waskesew.

10 September 1754

B.239/a/40

ye 10 Tuesday wind att NW^t & fine weather, this day the Ind^s travelled none, on Acc^t of more Ind^s that is to Meet us here, and when I Came from hunting Late in the Evening, there were ten more tents of Ind^s which Left us to hunt another way, killed a Large Hee Buffuloe, such a Sight of Bones; Little flesh on him, the Ind^s killed 3 moose and 5 Waskesew^s.

E.2/6

10 Tuesd^y fine weather, wind NW. travelled none; Young men and I went a hunting, Indians killed 3 Moose and 6 Waskesews, and I killed a Bull nothing but bones, so took out his tongue and left him to the Wolves who were waiting round me in great numbers; they do not meddle with any person, we cannot afford to waste our powder and shot on them, in the Evening on our return home found we were joined by 10 tents of different Indians, but no tidings of the Archithinues.

E.2/4

10. Tuesday fine weather wind N.W. travelled none, young men and I went a hunting, they killed 3 moose and 6 waskesews, and I killed a bull that was nothing but skin and bones, so took out his tongue and left the remains to the wolves who were waiting round me in great numbers, they do not meddle with any person, but preys upon the buffaloe &c and on one another, for whenever one bleeds the others eats him up immediately, we cannot afford to waste powder and shot on them; in the evening on our return home found we were joined by 10 tents of different tribes of Indians, but no tidings of the Archithinues.

E.2/11

10. Tuesday. Wind NW and agreeable weather; Travelled none. The
Young Men & I went a hunting, killed 3 Moose & 6 Waskesew. I killed a
Bull Buffalo, nothing but skin and bone: took out his tongue, and left
his remains to the Wolves who were waiting around me in great numbers: they do not meddle with any person: We cannot afford to expend
our ammunition on them. In the Evening when we returned home,
found we were joined by ten tents of different Indians, but no tidings
of the Archithinue Natives. My feet are swelled, but otherwise, Thank
God, in Perfect health.

11 September 1754

B.239/a/40

y[e] 11 Wednesday wind and weather as yesterday took my departure
from Bufflow plain and Steered WNW[t] 15 M, fine Levell Land and plenty of ponds of water, and very Little wood, the Ind[s] killed 2 Bufflow
and 4 Waskesew[s].

E.2/6

11 Wednesd[y] wind and weather as yesterday, travelled WNW. 15 miles,
Levell land, little woods, and plenty of water good and sweet, the
greatest hardships I have yet found is the want of sweet water: killed 3
Moose, and 5 Waskesew's.

E.2/4

11. Wednesday wind &c as yesterday travelled 15 miles W.N.W. level
land, plenty of sweet water, the want of which has been the greatest
hardship I have yet suffered; killed 8 waskesews.

E.2/11

11. Wednesday. Wind NW. and cool weather Travelled 15 Miles WNW
Level land; few woods; and plenty of good water: The greatest hardships I have yet experienced is the Warmness of the weather, and the
want of Water. Indians killed 8 Waskesew.

12 September 1754

B.239/a/40

1754 Sept[r] y[e] 12th Thursday the musketo[s] are very brisk wind NE[t] took
my departure from Maiden head, and steered W[t]NW[t] 14 M, this days
travell hilly, Ridgy Land, and Small trees, this day killed 3 Bufflow, and
4 Moose, fine weather and very hott.

E.2/6

12 Thursd[y] Cold raw weather, wind NE. which is very agreeable, being
almost Eat up by the musketoes; took my departure from, maidenhead pond and travelled WNW. 14 miles, hilly rocky Land with shruby
woods, killed 3 Buffalow and 4 Moose.

E.2/4
12. Thursday cold raw weather wind N.E. which is very agreeable being
almost eat up by the musketoes, travelled 14 miles W.N.W. hilly, rocky
land and shruby woods; killed 3 moose and 4 buffaloe.

E.2/11
12. Thursday. wind NE and cold raw weather which silences the Mus-
quetoes. Travelled 11 Miles WNW hilly, rocky land, and shrubby woods.
Indians killed 3 Buffalo & 4 Moose.

13 September 1754

B.239/a/40
yᵉ 13ᵗʰ Friday fine weather wind att Wᵗ took my departure from frogg
pond and Steered NWᵗ 10 M then put up; here is Great plenty of Bufflow, I went a hunting and in one plain I saw 60 Bufflow feeding, my
companion and I singled one out; when we both fired when he Ran
directly towards us, his Breath fail'd him, before he Could Come up
with us, this day killed 7 Bufflow, and 3 Moose.

E.2/6
1754 Septʳ 13 Fridʸ fine weather, wind W. traveled 10 miles NW. fine
level Land, no woods, seed nothing but herds of Buffalow Grazing like
English Cows, killed 7, the Bulls will make at an Indian when
wounded, but He is soon out of breath being a weighty Creature, and
do affirm they are as large as an English Cow, and fine sweet eating.

E.2/4
13. Friday fine weather wind W. travelled 10 miles N.W. level land, no
woods, seed herds of buffaloe grazing like English cattle, and of the
same size, and black having a hump between their shoulders, and
short black horns; the bulls are very fierce, and will run at an Indian
when wounded; they are very fine food.

E.2/11
1754 Septʳ 13. Friday. Wind West and pleasant weather; Travelled 10
Miles NW. Level land; no woods. saw many herds of Buffalo grazing
like English Cattle: Indians killed seven. The Bulls will make towards
an Indian when wounded: The flesh is sweet but coarse.

14 September 1754

B.239/a/40
yᵉ 14ᵗʰ Saturday fine weather wind wind SWᵗ in the forenoon fell a
great Deal of Rain, we travelled none this day, Killed 4 Bufflow, this
day the Indˢ Came & Smoakt with me.

E.2/6
14 Saturdʸ fine weather, wind SW. travelled none, I went with the
Young Men a Buffalow hunting, all with our Bows & Arrows, fine sport,

we beat them about, Lodging above 20 Arrows in one Beast, so Expert
are the Natives that they will take the Arrows out of them when they
are foaming, raging, running at them and now and then tearing the
ground up with their feet and horns, until they fall down with their
wounds, killed 7 Buffalow.

E.2/4

14. Saturday fine weather wind S.W. travelled none, I went with the
young men a buffaloe hunting, all armed with bows and arrows, killed
7, fine sport, we beat them about lodging above 20 arrows in one
beast; the Aseenepoets are so expert that they will pluck the arrows
out of them when foaming, raging, and tearing the ground up with
their horns, untill they fall down with wounds.

E.2/11

14. Saturday. Wind West and fine weather; Travelled none. I went with
the Young Men a Buffalo hunting, all Armed with Bows & Arrows:
killed seven, fine sport. We beat them about, lodging twenty Arrows in
one beast. So expert are the Natives, that they will take the Arrows
out of them when they are foaming & raging with pain, and tearing
the ground up with their feet & horns, until they fall down.

15 September 1754

B.239/a/40

Septr ye 15th Sunday fine weather wind SW^t took my departure from
Barren plain, and Steered WNW^t 14 M over the plains, past one Large
Lake, killed 7 Bufflow and 3 Waskesew^s.

E.2/6

15 Sunday fine weather, wind SW. took my Departure from sporting
plain, and travelled 14 miles WNW fine level Land, no woods to be
seen, passed by a Lake, the Buffalow so plenty, oblidged to make them
sheer out of our way; also Wolves without number; lurking about after
the Buffalow, Indians killed a great many taking only what they
chused to carry, I am now stocked with tongues, we also see Moose
and Waskesews but as the Natives seldom kills them with the Bow and
Arrow, they will not shoot them with the gun while the Buffalows are
so numerous; I hope we shall soon see the Archithinue Indians, their
Horses dung and paths being pretty fresh; Seed a large Snake but
could not get it, have seen their skins stuffed and dry 7 feet long.

E.2/4

15. Sunday fine weather wind S.W. travelled 14 miles W.N.W. level land,
no wood to be seen, passed by a lake of salt water, the buffaloe so
plenty obliged to make them sheer out of our way, also wolves without
number lurking after the buffaloe; Indians killed a great many buffaloe only taking out the tongues and what else they chused to carry,

leaving the remains to be eat by the wolves; I hope we shall soon see
the Archithinues, their horse dung and paths being pretty fresh, seed
a snake.

E.2/11

15. Sunday. Wind SW and agreeable weather; Travelled 7 Miles WSW.
Level land no woods to be seen: passed by a lake: the Buffalo so
numerous obliged to make them sheer out of our way. also Wolves
without number, lurking Indians killed a great many Buffalo; only tak-
ing what they choosed to carry. I am now well stocked with tongues.
We saw a few Moose & Waskesew; but as the Natives seldom kill them
with the Bow & Arrows they will not expend Ammunition, while the
Buffalo are so Numerous. I hope We shall soon see the Archithinue
Natives; the Horse dung, and paths being pretty fresh. Saw a large
Snake but could not get at it.

16 September 1754

B.239/a/40

ye 16th Monday small Rain all day, wind att West, took my departure
from Snake pond, and Steered NW^t 12 M, then Came to ye side of a
Large Creeck called Chacutena Subee, it is full of Large stones, and
weeds; this day the Ind^s killed 5 bufflow & 2 Moose.

E.2/6

1754 Septr 16 Mond^y rainy weather, wind W. took my Departure from
Snake pond, and travelled 10 miles NW. then came to a small River
Called Chacutenow, it is full of large stones and weeds, small hazel,
birch and poplar trees growing on the sides of it. Indians killed many
Buffalow, takes the tongues and what Else they chuse, and leaves the
remainder to be eat by the Wolves.

E.2/4

1755 Septr 16th Monday rainy weather wind W. travelled 10 miles N.W.
then came to chacutanow river, it is full of large stones and weeds and
shoal, small hasle, ash, birch and poplar trees growing along the sides
of it; buffaloe and wolves without number, young men sporting among
them, only taking the tongues leaving the remains for the wolves.

E.2/11

16. Monday. wind WbN and Rimy weather; Travelled 5 Miles West, then
came to a small river called Chacutenah. It is full of large stones &
weeds; Small Hazle, Birch & poplar trees, growing on the sides of it.
Buffalo very numerous. Indians killed a great many, only taking out
their tongues, and some other choice pieces; leaving the remainder
for the Wolves &c.

17 September 1754

B.239/a/40

ye 17th Tuesday in in ye forenoon, small rain, then fine weather, wind NW^t the Ind^s went a Bare hunting, one black Bear almost killed 2 of the Men, on may Recover, its unpossible the other Can Live, for his Gutts, arm and one Eye is terribly Mangled.

E.2/6

17 Tuesd^y Wind and weather the same as yesterday, Indians a hunting, and Women busy drying meat, two young Men has got miserably tore by a grizzel Bear whom they had wounded; one may recover but the other never can, for his arm is almost tore from his Body, one Eye is tore out, and his guts are hanging out of his Body

E.2/4

17. Tuesday wind and weather as yesterday travelled none, Indian men feasting and women drying meat, two young men miserably torn by a grizle bear that they had wounded, one may recover, but the other never can, for his arm is almost tore off from his body, one eye is tore out, and his broadside laid open.

E.2/11

17. Tuesday wind & weather as Yesterday. Indians hunting Women drying Meat. Two Young Men miserably tore by a Grizzle Bear whom they had wounded. One may recover but the other never can; for his arm is almost tore from his Body, one eye is quite out, and his entrails are hanging from his body.

18 September 1754

B.239/a/40

ye 18th Wednesday the Ind^s are so bad, the rest will not travell, till they are better or dead, Killed 4 Cows; fine weather Wind att W^t this Evening Came 2 Esinepoets, told us the Earchithinues had killed 6 Ind^s and that there was a great many Ind^s very nigh us.

E.2/6

18 Wednesd^y rainy weather, wind NW. travelled none, one Indian dead and the other in a weak condition, two Asinepoets came and informed us the Archithinues had killed, and scalped 6 Indians, and that there were a great many nigh us.

E.2/4

18. Wednesday rainy weather wind N.W. travelled none, one of the wounded men dead and the other in a weak condition, two Aseenepoets came and informed us that the Archithinues had killed and scalped 6 keskachewan Indians, and that they were nigh us above 200 tents of them.

E.2/11

18. Wednesday. Wind NW and Rainy weather; Travelled none. One
Indian dead & the other in a weak condition. Two Asinepoet Natives
came to us and informed us the Archithinue Natives had killed &
scalped 6 Indians, and that there were a great many nigh us.

19 September 1754

B.239/a/40

1754 Septr ye 19th Thursday fine weather, wind NW^t took my departure
from Cunekagan Creeck and steered NW^t 14 M fine Levell Land, and
Ledges of Burnt wood, and Lakes of water.

E.2/6

19 Thursd^y fine weather wind SW. took my departure from Chacutenow River and travelled NW. 14 miles, fine Level land and ledges
of burnt woods, and several ponds of good water; left one Family to
take care of the wounded Man.

E.2/4

19. Thursday fine weather wind N.W. travelled 14 miles N.W. level land,
ledges of burnt woods and several ponds of sweet water. left one family behind to take care of the wounded man.

E.2/11

19. Thursday. Wind NW and moderate weather; Travelled 7 Miles NW.
Level land and ledges of burnt woods. Several ponds of sweet water:
Left one family to take care of the wounded man.

20 September 1754

B.239/a/40

ye 20th Friday wind and weather as yesterday, took my departure from
Esinepoet hill, and steered SW^t 12 M, this day their Came 7 tents of
Esinepoets, they brought another horse, and this day they Catcht
another, so that we have now 3 horses, Levell Land Ledges of Nutt,
and poplar trees; this day killed 5 Moose, and 4 Bufflow, the Ind^s gave
me the tongue, Nose and hart of Two Moose.

E.2/6

20 Frid^y wind & weather as yesterday, travelled SW. 12 miles, then
came to 7 tents of Asinepoet Indians, I smoaked with them, and
bought a Horse from them to carry my goods & provisions; at night
they let the Horses graze about the tents, fettering their Legs.

E.2/4

20. Friday wind &c as yesterday travelled 12 miles S.W. then came to 7
tents of Aseenepoets, I smoaked with them and have done all in my
power to get them to visit our forts but I am afraid to little purpose, they
living in this plentyfull country, and can well do without any Europian

support, but their chief objection is the long distance; I bought a horse
from them to carrie my goods and provisions, they are very tractable and
at nights they graze about the tents with their feet fettered.

E.2/11

20. Friday wind & weather as Yesterday Travelled 6 Miles SW. then
came to 7 tents of Asinepoet Natives. I smoaked with them and
bought a horse from them for a gun, to carry my Provisions &c; At
night they let the Horses graze with their feet fettered.

21 September 1754

B.239/a/40

ye 21st Saturday fine weather wind att S^o took my departure from
Horse pond, and steered SWbS^o 14 M Levell Land, Shrubby woods all
this day, killed 12 Waskesew^s and 2 Bufflow the Ind^s Gave me as much
as I could Carry home, they behave very Civill to Me all but attickasish, who is very Angry he told me because I would not give him my
Gun, that the Earchithinues would kill me.

E.2/6

1754 Septr 21 Saturd^y fine weather, wind S. travelled SWbS. 14 miles,
level Land & shruby woods, killed 12 Waskesews and three Buffalow,
the Natives behaves wery civil to me, I cannot describe the pleasant
Country I am now in; one of the Leaders who has the Charge of me
named Atickosish is a little out of humour because I will not lend him
my gun but I takes no notice, neither do I value Him.

E.2/4

21. Saturday fine weather wind S. travelled 14 miles S.W.B.S. level land,
and shruby woods; killed 12 waskesews and 3 buffaloe.

E.2/11

1754 Septr 21. Saturday. Wind South, and pleasant weather; Travelled 7
Miles SWbS. Level land and Shrubby woods; Indians killed 12 Waskesew and 3 Buffalo.

22 September 1754

B.239/a/40

Septr ye 22^d Sunday fine weather Wind att W^t travelled none to day,
the Ind^s and I went a hunting killed 6 Moose, they Gave the hart, side
and tongue of one to me.

E.2/6

22 Sunday fine weather, wind W. travelled none, Indians went a hunting killed 6 Moose, no Buffalow to be seen, seed several wild Horses.

E.2/4

22. Sunday fine weather wind W. travelled none, Indians killed 6
moose, no buffaloe to be seen, but seed several wild horses, the

natives are very kind to me as yet, only Attitckosish is a little out of
humour because I will not lend him my gun, but I take no notice, neither do I value him.

    E.2/11

22. Sunday. wind West and pleasant weather; Travelled none. Indians
hunting. Indians killed 6 Moose. No Buffalo to be seen. Saw several
Wild Horses. The Natives behave very kind to me, except my Guide
Attickashish, who is a little out of humour because I would not lend
him my gun; but I take no notice, neither do I value him.

23 September 1754
    B.239/a/40

ye 23^d Monday fine weather wind NW^t travelled none this day, went a
hunting killed 4 Moose and 3 Bufflow, we saw a Large Black Bear but
my partner was afraid to kill him.

    E.2/6

23 Mond^y fine weather wind NW. travelled none Young Men a hunting,
killed 4 Moose, 3 Buffalow and one Large back Bear, seed several Toads.

    E.2/4

23. Monday fine weather wind N.W. travelled none, young men a hunting, killed 4 moose, 3 buffaloe, and one black bear, seed several toads;
I cannot describe the fineness of the weather and the pleasant country I am now in.

    E.2/11

23. Monday. Wind NW and cold weather; Travelled none. Young Men
hunting killed 4 Moose & 3 Buffalo; also a large black Bear. Saw several Toads. I cannot describe the fineness of the Weather, & the pleasant country I am now in.

24 September 1754
    B.239/a/40

ye 24th Tuesday fine weather wind att West took my departure from
toad pond, and Steered SWbS^o 10 M Levell Land and small Ledges of
woods, I went a hunting killed a Large Hee Moose took the Hart &
Brisket for my share, and gave the Ind^s the Rest.

    E.2/6

24 Tuesd^y fine weather, wind W. took my Departure from Toad pond,
and travelled SWbS. 10 miles, level Land, with ledges of wood; I went a
hunting killed a Large Moose, took the heart and brisket and gave the
rest to the Indians; seed several magpies, pidgeons and beautiful
Woodpeckers, the size of a pidgeon.

    E.2/4

24. Tuesday fine weather wind W. travelled 10 miles S.W.B.S. I killed a

large moose, took the heart and brisket and gave the rest to the natives, level land and ledges of woods.

E.2/11

24. Tuesday. Wind West and fine weather; Travelled SWbS. 5 Miles. I killed a large moose, took the heart, & gave the remains to the Indians. Level land and ledges of woods. Saw several magpies, Pidgeons, and beautiful Wood-peckers. We are yet in Muscuty plains.

25 September 1754

B.239/a/40

ye 25 Wednesday fine weather wind WbN. took my departure from Magpie plain and Steered W^t 10 M over fine Levell Land, and Small Ledges of Brush, this day the Ind^s killed 6 Moose, and two bufflow they Gave me two tongues and a Side to my share see a magpie to day, being the first I have Seen.

E.2/6

25 Wednesd^y fine weather wind W. took my departure from Magpie ledge in Muscuty plains, and travelled W. 10 miles, over level barren Land, Indians killed 6 Moose and two Buffalow.

E.2/4

1755 Septr 25th Wednesday fine weather wind W. travelled 10 miles W. level land and small woods, killed 6 moose and 2 buffaloe, seed several mag-pies, pidgeons, and beautiful wood-peckers.

E.2/11

25 Wednesday. Wind and weather as Yesterday; Travelled 5 Miles West. Level land. Indians killed 6 Moose & 2 Buffalo.

26 September 1754

B.239/a/40

1754 Septr ye 26th Thursday fine weather wind att West, took my departure from Shrubb Ledge and Steered WbN^o 11 M this day, Hills & deals and Ledges of woods, I went a hunting and killed a fine Large Moose, and when ye Ind^s Came to me they were overjoyed, that I should kill a Moose, and no body with me, for they do not go farr without 2 togeather; one of the Ind^s brought me a Snake.

E.2/6

1754 Septr 26 Thursd^y fine weather, wind WbN. travelled WbN. 11 miles, hills, and dales and ledges of woods, I killed a Moose, and the Indians a great many, very plenty.

E.2/4

26. Thursday fine weather wind W.B.N. travelled W.B.N. 11 miles, I killed a moose and the Indians a great many.

E.2/11
26. Thursday. Wind WbN and agreeable weather; Travelled 5 Miles
WbN. Hillocks & Dales. I killed a Moose, and the Indians a good many.

27 September 1754
B.239/a/40
ye 27th Friday fine weather wind att West, took my departure from
Grass hopes plaine and steered WbN 14 M Ridgy Land & Small
homacks of woods, this day the Ind^s killed 6 Beaver 3 Moose and 3
Buffuloe, we see a Large smoack, which the Ind^s thinks is the
Earchithinues;
E.2/6
27 Frid^y fine weather, wind W. travelled WbN. 14 miles, ridgy Land, with
hommocks of woods, and small Creeks; Indians killed 6 Beaver, 3 Moose,
& 3 Buffalow; See a large smoak which we think is the Archithinues.
E.2/4
27. Friday fine weather wind W. travelled 14 miles W.B.N. ridgy land,
with hommocks of woods, and small creeks, killed 6 beaver, 3 moose
and 3 buffaloe, seed a large smoak which we think is made by the
Archithinues.
E.2/11
27. Friday. Wind West and fine weather; Travelled 7 Miles WbN. Ridgy
land with hommocks of wood & Small Creeks. Indians killed 6 Beaver
3 Moose & 3 Buffalo. Saw a large smoke which we think are the
Archithinue Natives.

28 September 1754
B.239/a/40
ye 28th Saturday fine weather wind NbW^t this day travelled none, on
Acc^t of the Ind^s Coming to Join us, to day killed 4 Buffluloe, and 2
moose, the Ind^s Brought me a Lott of good fatt Beeff.
E.2/6
28 Saturd^y fine weather, wind NbW. travelled none, several tents of
Indians joined us, made me a present of some fatt meat, and one
snake 6½ feet long.
E.2/4
28. Saturday fine weather wind N.B.W. travelled none, several tents of
Indians joined us, one of them made me a present of some fat meat,
and one snake skin dry'd and stuff'd 6½ feet long.
E.2/11
28. Saturday. Wind NW. Travelled none. several tents of Indians joined
us: they made me a present of some fat, Meat, and one dryed Snake
6½ feet long.

29 September 1754

> B.239/a/40

Septr ye 29 Sunday fine weather wind att W^t travelled none, the Ind^s not being Come up, this day some Esinepoets and one Earchithinue Came, and to morrow there are a great many more to Join us, this day the Ind^s killed 4 Buffuloe, & 6 Waskesu^s, and I killed one.

> E.2/6

29 Sunday fine weather, wind WbN. travelled none, Women dressing skins for shoes, Joined by more Asinepoets, and two Archithinues on Horse-back who informed me that the smoak is the Archithinues and that it will be 8 days walking before we come up with them, so fine and level is the Land.

> E.2/4

29. Sunday fine weather wind W.B.N. travelled none, women dressing skins for shoe leather, joined by more Aseenepoets and two Archithinues on horse-back who informs us that the smoak is 8 days journey from us, and that the grand camp of the Archithinues is there.

> E.2/11

29. Sunday. Wind WbN and indifferent weather Travelled none. Women dressing Skins for Shoes. Joined by more Asinepoet Indians, & two Archithinue Natives on Horseback; who informed us it is the Archithinue Smoke we saw: and that it will be eight days before We reach them.

30 September 1754

> B.239/a/40

ye 30th Monday fine weather wind SW^t took my departure from Countenack River and steered WSW^t 15 M this day Levell Land and Small homacks of Brush, they Came more Esinepoets and brought 4 more horsses.

> E.2/6

30 Mond^y fine weather, wind SW. travelled WSW 15 miles, level land, and small hommocks of brush-wood, joined by more Asinepoets, who hath 6 pack Horses Loaded with provisions &c.

> E.2/4

30. Monday fine weather wind S.W. travelled 15 miles W.S.W. level land and small hommocks of brush wood, joined by more Asinepoets who hath 6 pack horses loaded with provisions &c.

> E.2/11

30. Monday. Wind SW and good cool weather, and no Musketoes to trouble us; Travelled 7 Miles WSW. Level lands, & small hommocks of woods. Joined by more Asinepoet Indians, who have 6 pack-horses loaded with provisions &c.

1 October 1754

B.239/a/40

Octr ye 1st Tuesday fine weather Wind SE^t travelled none to day on Acc^t the Earchithinues Coming, and in the Evening Came 7 tents of them, and I mad their Captain a pres^t of a Knife, a Steal, a String of Beads and some tobacco, killed 4 Buffuloe & 2 Moose;

E.2/6

Octr 1 Tuesd^y fine weather, wind SE. travelled none, Came to us 7 tents of Archithinues, the Men all mounted on Horseback with Bows & Arrows, and Bone spears, and darts; gave the Leader a foot of tobacco, one fire steel, one string of beads, and one knife, and smoaked with them; by the Interpreter he said he would inform the Great Leader of my coming, and so left us.

E.2/4

1755 Octr 1st Tuesday fine weather wind S.E. travelled none, came to us 7 tents of Archithinues, the men all mounted on horse-back, and armed with bows, and arrows, and bone spears, and darts, I gave their leader a foot of brazile tobacco, one fire steel, a string of beads, and a knife, and smoaked with him; by the interpreter he said he would inform their great leader of my coming, & so left us.

E.2/11

Octr 1st Tuesday. wind SE and fine weather Travelled none. came to us 7 tents of Archithinue Indians; the Men all mounted on Horse-back, with Bows and Arrows, & bone spears & darts. I gave the Leader a foot of tobacco, one fire-Steel, A string of beads, a knife; and smoaked with them. By my Interpreter he said that he would inform their Great Leader of my coming & so left us.

2 October 1754

B.239/a/40

ye 2^d Wednesday took my departure from White Horse plain, and steered SW^t 14 M over fine pleasant Land, this day a Esinepoet (by accident) shot a Boy about 12 y^{rs} old, he died in about 2 hours, fine Weather Wind SE^t

E.2/6

1754 october 2 Wednesd^y fine weather, wind SE. took my departure from pack Horse hommock in muscuty plains, and travelled 14 miles SW. pleasant level Land, this evening An Asinepoet Indian shot a Boy about 12 years old, by accident; put up at a fine Creek of water.

E.2/4

2. Wednesday fine weather wind S.E. travelled 14 miles S.W. level land; in the evening an Aseenepoet Indian accidently shot a boy about 12 years old.

E.2/11

2. Wednesday. Wind SE and close weather, with rain at times; Travelled 7 Miles SW. Level land. In the Evening An Asinepoet Indian shot a Boy by accident. Saw several wild Goats. My feet a little swelled.

3 October 1754

B.239/a/40

Octr ye 3^d Thursday fine Weather wind NbE^t took my departure from Accident Creeck, and steered WSW^t 12 M past 2 Creecks, att the Last their is Large pines, and Birch, have not seen one pine tree Since I Left steel River, Killed 2 Moose, 6 Buffuloe, and 3 Beaver.

E.2/6

3 Thursd^y fine weather, wind NbE. took my departure from accident Creek, and travelled WSW. 12 miles; passed 2 Creeks, where was growing the Largest pine & Birch trees I have yet seen; seed several wild Goats; killed 2 Moose, 6 Buffalow, & 3 Beaver.

E.2/4

3. Thursday fine weather wind N.B.E. travelled 12 miles W.S.W. passed two creeks where were growing the largest pine and birch trees I have yet seen; killed 6 buffaloe, 2 moose and 3 beaver, seed several wild goats and asses.

E.2/11

3. Thursday. Wind NbE and close weather, Travelled 12 Miles WSW. Passed 2 Creeks where were growing the largest Pines and Birch trees I have yet seen. Indians killed 6 Buffalo 2 Moose & 3 Beaver.

4 October 1754

B.239/a/40

ye 4th Friday Blowed hard wind att NE^t took my departure from threen Valley and Steered WSW^t 10 M. this day see nothing of any Kind of wood but willows, the Land is hills & dales, here is plenty of fine ponds of water and Buffuloe in great droves Like unto Smithfield Market, I killed one and ye Ind^s killed 10.

E.2/6

4 Frid^y blowing weather, wind NE. took my departure from wild Goat valley and travelled WSW. 10 miles, hills, Dales, and willows and a great many ponds of water, Buffalow in great droves, I killed one and the Indians 10.

E.2/4

4. Friday fine weather wind N.E. travelled W.S.W. 10 miles, hills, dales, and willows, and plenty of water ponds, the buffaloe in great droves, Indians killed 10 and I one.

E.2/11

4. Friday. Wind NE and raw cold weather; Travelled WSW 5 Miles.
Hillocks Dales and Willows: plenty of water ponds: Buffalo in great
droves. Indians killed 5 & I one.

5 October 1754
   B.239/a/40

ye 5th Saturday fine weather wind att N^o took my departure from
Skunck pond, and Steered WSW^t 12 M fine Level Land, and no woods
to be seen, past 2 Creecks, one is Like to Iron Mines and Runs in
thick vains, great plenty of Buffuloe.
   E.2/6

5 Saturd^y fine weather, wind N. travelled WSW 12 miles, fine level
Land, no woods to be seen, passed 2 Creeks, and several iron mines
running in large long vains; great plenty of Buffalow.
   E.2/4

5. Saturday fine weather wind N. travelled 12 miles W.S.W. level land
and no woods, passed 2 creeks, and several iron mines running in
large long veins, great numbers of buffaloe all round us, we are still in
the muscuty country.
   E.2/11

5. Saturday. Wind North, and good travelling weather; Went 6 Miles
WSW. Level land & no woods: Passed two Creeks, & several Iron-Mines
running in large long veins. Great plenty of Buffalo. We are still in the
Muscuty Country.

6 October 1754
   B.239/a/40

Octr ye 6th Sunday fine weather wind att SW^t took my departure from
Beaver Creeck, and Steered SW^t 15 M, this day An Ind^n and I killed 6
Beaver, and the other Ind^s some Beaver & 8 Buffuloe, Came to where
we got tent poles again, we having had none for 2 days past.
   E.2/6

6 Sund^y fine weather, wind W. took my Departure from the Iron mines
in muscuty plains, and travelled SW. 15 miles, several Creeks with
plenty of Beaver, Indians killed 8 Buffalow, 20 Beaver and 3 Goats,
they are not so large as those in England.
   E.2/4

5. 6. Sunday fine weather wind W. travelled 15 miles S.W. several creeks
with plenty of beaver, Indians killed 20, & 8 buffaloe, and 3 goats, they
are not so large as those in England.
   E.2/11

6. Sunday. Wind West and agreeable weather; Travelled 7 Miles SW.

Several Creeks with plenty of Beaver: Indians killed 28 Buffalo. they are not so large as those I first met with. Two Young Men brought in 3 Goats: they are not so large as the Welch ones.

7 October 1754

B.239/a/40

ye 7th Monday fine weather wind NEbN° travelled none, nothing but smoaks all around us att a great distance, severell Single Ind^s Came to us for two days past; killed 6 Buffuloe.

E.2/6

7 Mond^y fine weather, wind NEbN travelled none, several Indians Joined us, seed the Archithinues smoak; Invited to a Beaver feast, here is a ridge of fine flint stone.

E.2/4

7. Monday fine weather wind N.E.B.N. travelled none, several Indians Joined us, seed the Archithinues smoak again, here is a ridge of fine flint stone.

E.2/11

7. Monday. Wind NEbN and fine weather; Travelled none. Several Indians joined us. I was invited to a Beaver feast: Saw the Archithinue Smoke. Here is a ridge of fine flint stone.

8 October 1754

B.239/a/40

ye 8th Tuesday fine weather wind SWbS took my departure from flint Hill, & steered SW^t 14 M fine valleys and Hills and Ledges of woods, this day the Ind^s Killed 6 Buffuloe; see severall Smoaks att a distance.

E.2/6

1754 october 8 Tuesd^y fine weather, wind SWbS. took my departure from flint hill, and travelled 14 miles SW. fine valleys, hills and ledges of woods; Indians killed a great many Buffalow, took out their tongues and what else they chused and left the rest to be eat by the Wolves; I cannot say whether them or the Buffalow are most numerous; seed several large smoaks.

E.2/4

8. Tuesday fine weather wind S.W.B.S. travelled 14 miles S.W. fine valleys, hills and ledges of woods, killed a great many buffaloe, took out the tongues and left the remains to be eat by the wolves, I cannot say whether they or the buffaloe are most numerous; seed several smoaks.

E.2/11

8. Tuesday. Wind SWbW and fine weather; Travelled 7 Miles SW. pleasant Valleys, hillocks, and ledges of woods. Indians killed a great many Buffalo, took out the tongues and left the remains to be eat by the

Wolves. I cannot say whether them or the Buffalo are most numerous.
Saw several Snakes.

9 October 1754
　　B.239/a/40

ye 9th Wednesday fine Weather wind NE^t took my departure from
Mould Hill, and Steered SWbW^t 11 M fine Level Barren Land, 16 tents
Left us for to hunt Beaver, killed 7 Buffuloe, they are Still very plenty.
　　E.2/6

9 Wednesd^y fine weather, wind NE. travelled SWbW. 11 miles, fine level
Land with plenty of Creeks, 16 tents of Indians left us to kill Beaver;
Indians killed a great many Buffalow.
　　E.2/4

9. Wednesday fine weather wind N.E. travelled 11 miles S.W.B.W. level
land with plenty of creeks, 16 tents of Indians pitched from us in different routs, killed a great many buffaloe.
　　E.2/11

9. Wednesday. Wind NE and close weather; Travelled 5 Miles SWbW.
Level land, with plenty of Creeks. 16 tents of different Natives pitched
from us different ways. Indians killed many Buffalo.

10 October 1754
　　B.239/a/40

1754 Octr ye 10 Thursday wind att S^o this day travelled none, went a
Beaver hunting Killed Severell here being Great plenty.
　　E.2/6

10 Thursd^y fine weather, wind N. travell'd none, Indians went a Beaver
killing, got a great many.
　　E.2/4

10. Thursday fine weather wind N. travelled none killed several beaver
for cloathing, 16 taken out of one house, they are very numerous
about the creeks.
　　E.2/11

1754 Octr 10. Thursday. Wind North and close weather; Travelled none.
Indians killed several Beaver for cloathing, as cold weather is aproaching. 16 Beaver were taken out of one house. They are very numerous
about the Creeks.

11 October 1754
　　B.239/a/40

ye 11th Friday wind att N^o and fine weather, took my departure from
Sea kip pond, and Steered SWbW^t 14 M and then Came to Wyskasw
River,* and Crossed it about 2 feet deep on the fall, and Runs SE^t. the

Ind^s killed severall Beaver, and 3 Moose, the River is about 20 poles wide, and Sandy Islands on both sides of the River, the soil of a [   ] Stone and Large Vein of Iron mine.

    * the Runs SE^t and NW^t and ye Currant Runs to ye SE^t

    E.2/6

11 Frid^y fine weather, wind N. took my Departure from from Beaver Creek in muscuty plains, and travelled SWbW. 14 miles, then came to a River called Wykasew,* Crossed it about 2 feet deep on a fall, the River is 20 pole wide, no woods to be seen; on both sides the River are stones of different sizes, of weight and colour like Iron, and a little distance from the River are plenty of Iron mines running in large long veins on the surface of the ground; killed several Beaver and 2 Moose.

    * Wykesew or Waskesew River is Keskachewan River, and only goes by this name in the muscuty Country.

    E.2/4

12. 11. Friday fine weather wind N. travelled 14 miles S.W.B.W. then came to waskesew river* and crossed it on a fall about 2 feet deep and 20 poles wide, on both sides the river are stones of different shape and sizes, of weight & colour of iron, and a little distance from the river are iron mines on the surface of the earth, no woods to be seen, killed several beaver and two moose.

    * This river is keskachewan river and only goes by this name in the muscuty country.

    E.2/11

11. Friday. Wind North, and cold weather; Travelled 7 Miles SWbW. then came to Waskesew River,* & crossed it on a Fall about two feet high, and much the same depth, & 20 poles wide. On both sides there are stones of different sizes and weight; quite round, & of an iron color: and a little distance from the River, are Veins of iron-ore running along the surface of the ground. No Woods to be seen. Indians killed several Beaver and 2 Moose.

    * Keskatchew and Waskesew River is all one River; and is called by the French Christianaux River, from the Lake of that name.

12 October 1754

    B.239/a/40

ye 12th Saturday fine weather wind att W^t took my departure from Waskesu River and Steered SWbW^t 16 Miles, Levell Land with Ledges of Woods, and plenty of water, killed 6 Buffuloe & 2 Moose.

    E.2/6

12 Saturd^y fine weather, wind W. took my Departure from Wykasew River, and travelled SWbW. 16 miles, level Land with ledges of woods and plenty of water, Indians killed a great many Buffalow.

E.2/4

12. Saturday fine weather wind W. travelled 16 miles S.W.B.W. level land, plenty of sweet water, and ledges of woods, killed a great many buffaloe.

E.2/11

12. Saturday. Wind West and fine weather; Travelled 8 Miles SWbW. Level land; plenty of Water; & ledges of woods. Indians killed a great many Buffalo.

13 October 1754

B.239/a/40

Octr ye 13 Sunday wind and weather as Yesterday took my departure from Earchithinue Hill and Steered SWbW^t 15 M fine Levell Land and Ledges of Brush, killed 4 Buffuloe & 2 Swans, this day Came to us 7 Earchithinues, and to morrow we are to be Joined by 16 More tents.

E.2/6

1754 october 13 Sunday fine weather, wind W. travelled SWbW. 15 miles, Level land and ledges of small woods, we were Joined by 7 Archithinues on Horseback, who informed us, that we should see the great Leader and numbers of the Archithinues to morrow; Indians killed several Buffalo, they are numerous all round us.

E.2/4

13. Sunday fine weather wind W. travelled 15 miles S.W.B.W. level land, ledges of woods, and numbers of buffaloe, killed a great many; in the evening we were joined by 7 Archithinues on horse-back who informed us we should see the great leader and numbers of the Archithinues to morrow.

E.2/11

1754 Octr 13. Sunday. Wind <variable> and agreeable weather; Travelled 7 Miles SWbW. Level land, and ledges of woods; and numbers of Buffalo. Indians killed a great many. In the Evening we were joined by 7 Archith<in>ue Natives on Horse-back, who informed us we should see the Great Leader, and numbers of Archithinue Natives to morrow.

14 October 1754

B.239/a/40

ye 14 Monday fine weather wind att NE^t took my departure from Hayes plain, and Steered SWbW^t 4 miles, when we mett the Earchithinue men on horse back 40 in number they were out on a Scout from the main body, to see if we were Enemies, when they found us friends, Attickasish, Connawappa, and 2 more of our Leaders marched att the front about 4 Mile where upon the top of a Hill I seed 200 tents, where they were pitched in 2 Rows, and an opening Right through the mid-

dle, and att ye farther End of the Street their was a Large tent pitcht
in front, where all the old Men were seated and their King in the middle,* and in the middle of the tent was full of fatt Buffuloes flesh, and
after that we had all smoakt Round Every flag had a Side of meat, and
ye rest was served all round amongst ye Ind^n men, and I had satt
before me 20 Broild tongues, then we Returned to our tent, this night
we had a high frost, and thin frost.

    * Here was the End Captn Hendeys Journey which he performed
with not a Little difficulty as May be Seen by the foregoing Remarks,
after this they only pitcht too & fro to Get furrs and provisions, till
they Came to make Canoes to Return to ye Fort in the Spring. Remarks of his hereafter/

    E.2/6

14 Mond^y fine weather, wind NE. travelled SWbW. 4 miles, then came
to us 40 Men on Horseback; they told us they were sent from the main
Body to enquire whether we were Friends or Enemies; we told them
we were friends; Atickosish, Connawappaw, Cocamanakisick, and the
rest of the Leaders walked in the front about 4 miles further, then we
came to 200 tents of Archithinue Indians pitched in 2 rows and an
opening in the middle, where we were Conducted to the Leader's
Tent, which was at one end, Large enough to Contain 50 people,
where He was seated on a clean Buffalow's skin attended by 20 Elderly
Men; He made signs to me to sit down on His right hand, which I did,
our Leader set on several grand pipes, and smoaked all round; according to their usual custom, not one word was yet spoke on no side,
smoaking being done, Buffalow flesh boiled, were handed round in
willow baskets, and I was presented with 10 Buffalow's tongues; Atickosish then informed Him that I was sent by the Great Leader who
Lives down at the great waters to invite His young Men down to see
Him, and to bring with them Beaver and Wolves, and they would get
in return powder, shot, guns, & Cloth &c; He made little or no
answer, more then it was far of, and that they could not paddle; then
they entered upon indifferent subjects, untill we were ordered to
depart to our tents, which were ready pitched about a quarter of a
mile from them.

    E.2/4

14. Monday fine weather wind N.E. travelled 4 miles S.W.B.W. then
came to us 4 men on horse-back, they said they were sent from the
main body to enquire whether we were friends or foes, we told them
we were friends, after ordering us to proceed no nearer they set out at
a full gallop, and presently returned with orders from their King for us
to proceed towards the Camp, and to pitch our tents at a proper distance, on which Attickosish, Connawappaw, Cockamanakisick, and

the rest of the leaders walked in the front about 2 miles further, then we came to 200 tents of Archithinue Indians pitched in 2 rows, and an opening in the middle, where we were conducted by a party of horse-men to the leaders tent, which was at one end and large enough to contain 50 people, where he was seated on a clean buffaloe skin and attended by 20 elderly men, he made signs for me to sit down on his right hand, which I readily obeyed; our leaders set on several grand pipes and smoked all round, according to their usual custom not one word was yet spoke on no side; smoking being over, buffaloes flesh boiled were handed round in willow baskets, and I was presented with 10 buffaloes tongues; Attickosish then informed him that I was sent by the great leader who lives down at the great water to him with the pipe of friendship and other presents, and by his permission to invite down his young men with beaver skins &c, and that they would get in return guns, powder, shot, cloth and tobacco &c; he made little answer, only said, that it was far off, and they could not paddle in canoes, then we entered on indifferent subjects untill we were ordered to depart to our tents, which in the interim our women had pitched about a quarter of a mile from them.

    E.2/11

14. Monday. Wind NE and close moderate weather; Travelled 4 Miles SWbW. Then came to us four men on Horse-back; they told us they were sent from the main body to see whether we were Friends or Ene-mies. We told them we were Friends. Attickasish, Canawappaw, Coka-manakisish, and the other of our Leaders walked in front about 4 miles farther then we; came to 200 tents of Archithinue Natives, pitched in two rows, and an opening in the middle; where we were conducted to the Leader's tent; which was at one end, large enough to contain fifty persons; where he received us seated on a clean Buf-falo skin, attended by 20 elderly men. He made signs for me to sit down on his right hand: which I did. Our Leaders set on several grand-pipes and smoked all round, according to their usual custom: not one word was yet spoke on either side. Smoking being over, Buffalo flesh boiled was served round in baskets made of a species of bent, and I was presented with 10 Buffalo tongues. Attickasish my Guide, informed him I was sent by the Great Leader who lives down at the great waters, to invite his Young men down to see him and to bring with them Beaver skins, and Wolves skins: and they would get in return Powder, Shot, Guns, Cloth Beads, &c. He made little answer: only said that it was far off, and they could not paddle. Then they entered upon indifferent subjects, until we were ordered to depart to our tents, which were pitched about a full quarter of a Mile without their lines.

15 October 1754

B.239/a/40

ye 15 Tuesday fine weather wind SE^t. Last night a white frost, this day
was Spent in feasting att all their tents, they have plenty of tobacco,
as they of their own and paint of severall Colours, they think Little of
our tobacco & paint

E.2/6

15 Tuesd^y fine weather, wind SE^t froze a little last night, Women
Employed dressing Beaver skins for Cloathing; at 10 o'clock I was
invited to the Leaders tent when by an interpreter I told Him what I
was sent for, and perswaded him to allow me to carry down some of
His young Men to the Fort where they would get guns, powder, and
shot, and be kindly used; He made answer it was far of, and that they
could not Live without Buffalow's flesh, and that they never would
leave their Horses, and mentioned many more obstacles, which I
thought was very Just, the Chief of which was that they never wanted
provisions; He made me a present of a handsome Bow & arrows, and
in return I gave Him a knife, 4 strings of beads, and several other
sorts of trading goods that I had with me; so Departed and took a
view of the Camp. their tents were pitched closs one to another in two
regular Lines which formed a broad street open at both ends, the
Horses are turned out to grass, their Legs being fettered; or when
wanted are fastened to lines cut of Buffalow's skin that stretches
along, and fastened to stakes drove in the ground; they have hair halters, Buffalow skin pads, & stirrups of the same; the Horses are fine
spirited Creatures, about 14 hands high the largest, and tractable; the
Natives are good Horsemen, and kills the Buffalow on them: these
Natives are dressed much the same as the others, but more clean and
sprightly; they think nothing of my tobacco, and I think as little of
theirs, which is dried Horse Dung; they appear to be under proper discipline, and obedient to the Leader, who orders a party of Horsemen
morning and evening to reconnoitre and other parties to bring in provisions: they have other Indians beyond them who are their Enemies,
they are also called Archithinues and by what I can learn talks the
same Language and hath the same customs &c; they are like the rest
of the Natives murthering one another slyly; seed several pretty Girls
that had been taken in war, and many dryed scalps with long black
hair displayed on long poles round the Leaders tent: they follow the
Buffalow, and that they may not be surprized by the Enemy Encamps
in open plains; their firing is turf and dried Horse-dung; their
Cloathing are finely painted with red paint like unto English red oaker, but they do not mark nor paint their faces.

E.2/4

15. Tuesday fine weather wind S.E. froze a little in the night, our women employed dressing beaver skins for cloathing, about 10 o'clock I was invited to the Archithinue leaders tent, where being seated next him, I presented him the pipe of friendship and the other presents, and by an interpreter I told him what I was sent for, and desired him to allow some of his young men to go down to the fort with me, where they would be well used and get guns, powder and shot &c, to which he answered, it was far off, and they could not live without buffaloes flesh and that they never would leave their horses, and many other obstacles which I think very just, the chief of which was, they never wanted provisions; he presented me with a handsome bow, arrows and quiver finely ornamented with quills; by his permission I viewed the camp, their tents are pitched close one to another in two regular lines, which formed a broad street, open at both ends; their horses are turned out to grass their legs being fettered, or when wanted immediately are fastened to thongs that are stretched along and fastned to stakes drove into the ground, they have hair halters, buffaloe-skin pads, and stirrups of the same; the horses are fine tractable creatures, of colours as in great Britain, and about 14 hands high with long tails and manes finely plaited; they hunt and kill the buffaloe on them; these natives are dressed in buffaloe-skin nearly in the same manner as the others, but more clean and sprightly; they think little of my tobacco and I think as little of theirs, which is dryed horse dung; they appear to be under proper discipline and obedient to their leader, who orders a party of hors-men evening and morning to reconnoitre, and other parties to bring in provisions; they have other Indians beyond them who are their enemies, who are also called Archithinues, and by what I can learn talks the same language and hath the same customs; they are like the other natives, murthering one another slyly, seed many fine girls and a few boys whom they had taken in war, and a great many dryed scalps they had taken in war, with long black hair, which they and all other Indians displays on long poles whenever they feast and sing &c; they follow the buffaloe from place to place, and that they should not be surprized by the enemy encamps in the open plains, their firing at such times when no woods are nigh is turf and dryed horse dung; their cloathing is finely painted with red oaker, but they do not mark nor paint their bodies; as the buffaloe are black in general, a pye-bald one is held in such esteem, that I am of opinion they worship it: I seed the skin of such an one and by their actions &c I am led into the aforesaid opinion; they eat no kind of flesh, fish or fowl but buffaloe only, for which reason they never will be got down to trade, they boil in stone kettles

and some has brass ones, which they purchase, as also other kinds of
goods from the few Aseenepoet and other tribes that deals with the
English and French, giving them in return beaver and wolves skins
&c; seed 4 asses.

E.2/11

15. Tuesday. wind SE and warm weather, froze a little last night. Our
Women employed dressing Beaver skins for cloathing. About 10
ocloak I was invited to the Archithinue Leader's tent: when by an
Interpreter I told him what I was sent for, & desired of him to allow
some of his Young men to go down to the Fort with me, where they
would be kindly received, and get Guns &c. But he answered, it was
far off, & they could not live without Buffalo flesh; and that they could
not leave their horses &c and many other obstacles, though all might
be got over if they were acquainted with a Canoe; and could eat Fish,
which they never do. The Chief further said they never wanted food, as
they followed the Buffalo and killed them with the Bows and Arrows.
and he was informed the Natives that frequented the Settlements,
were oftentimes Starved on their journey. Such remarks I thought
exceed<ing> true. He made me a Present of a handsome Bow &
Arrows: and in return I gave him a part of each kind of goods I had, as
ordered by Mr Isham's written instructions. I departed & took a view
of the camp. Their tents were pitched close to one Another in two
regular lines, which formed a broad street open at both ends. Their
Horses are turned out to grass, their legs being fettered: and when
wanted, are fastened to lines cut of Buffalo skin, that stretches along
<& is> fastened to stakes drove in the ground. They have hair hal-
ters, Buffalo skin pads, and stirrups of the same. The horses are fine
tractable Animals, about 14 hands high; lively and clean made. The
Natives are good Horsemen, and kill the Buffalo on them. These
Natives are drest much the same as the others; but more clean and
sprightly. They think nothing of my tobacco; & I set as little value
upon their's; which is dryed Horse- dung. They appear to be under
proper discipline, & obedient to their Leader: who orders a party of
Horsemen Evening & morning to reconoitre, & proper parties to
bring in Provisions. They have other Natives Horsemen as Well as
Foot, who are their Enemies: they are also called Archithinue Indians:
& by what I can learn talk the same language, & hath the same customs. They are, like the other Natives murthering one another slyly.
Saw many fine Girls who were Captives; and a great many dried Scalps
with fine long black hair, displayed on poles on, and before, the Leader's tent. They follow the Buffalo from place to place: and that they
should not be surprized by the Enemy, encamp in open plains. Their
fewel is turf, & Horse-dung dryed; their Cloathing <is> finely painted

with red paint, like unto English Ochre: but they do not mark nor paint their bodies. Saw four Asses.

16 October 1754
    B.239/a/40

ye 16 Wednesday fine weather, wind att West, this day we pitcht a Large tent, and smoaked and gave all ye goods as farr as they would hold out there were not one tenth part Enough so I gave Every Leader a Knive and Steel, and the Rest a few Beads, awles, paint, Needle and Rings, as far as they would go, they were all very well pleased, and Every Man gave a side of meat, which I delivered amongst the Ind^s, for they never keep much beforehand, the Earchithinues say they will go with me to ye fort and see ye Govr I Informed them as well as I Could to kill & foxes and save them which they promise very fair so to do, they are mad for guns, Knives, Hatchets &c and have told them there is great plenty of all sorts of goods att the fort.

    E.2/6

16 Wednesd^y fine weather, wind W. women Employed as yesterday; With the Leaders permission I rode out a hunting with 20 of his young Men, they killed 8 Buffalow fine sport, they are so Expert at the Bow and Arrow that with one or two arrows they will drop a Buffalow; as for me I had a sufficient employ to manage my Horse when I came home was invited to the Leaders tent again where were all the Asinepoet Leaders &c, I thought it very curious as they were 4 different Languages amongst us; the Leader gave us directions to pitch away from Him, and that if the Buffalow draws Downwards in the spring He would then see us again, He made me a present of 40 dried tongues, and to some of the Leaders, 2 young Slave Girls.*

    * A.D. 1765 at York Fort gates one of the Girls was Barbarously killed by a home-guard Indian in a fit of jealousy.

    E.2/4

16. Wednesday fine weather wind W. women employed as yesterday, with the leaders permission I rid a hunting with 20 of his young men, they killed 8 buffaloe, fine sport, the horses are trained to the game and the men so expert with the bow and arrow, that they let fly at the animal when on a hard gallop, and with 2 arrows they will kill a buffaloe, as for me I had sufficient employ to manage my horse; when I came home was invited to the leaders tent, where were seated all the leaders of different tribes of Indians. I thought it very curious as there were 4 different languages amongst us, the grand calimuts were smoak'd round and we had orders to pitch away from him next morning, he told me that he loved the great leader who sent me, that I or my countrymen might come again with safety, and said that he would

perhaps see me again at waskesew river in the spring of the year if the buffaloe should take the rout downwards, he offered me two slave girls which I declined accepting, by telling him that perhaps provisions might turn scarce and I would not be able to maintain them, however he gave them to one of my leaders.

E.2/11

1754 Octr 16. Wednesday. Wind West and moderate weather; Women employed as Yesterday. With the Leaders permission, I rode a hunting with twenty of his young men. They killed 8 Buffalo excellent sport. They are so expert that with one, or two, Arrows, they will drop a Buffalo. As for me I had sufficient employ to manage my horse. When I came home I was invited to the Leaders tent again, where were all the Asinepoet Leaders &c. I thought it very curious as there were four different langues among us. The Leader gave orders to pitch away from him, and that we would see him again in the spring, when they came down after the Buffalo. He gave one of the Leaders two young slaves as a present, & 40 Buffalo tongues. they were both Girls.*

* A.D. 1765 One of them was murthered at York Fort by a Home-Native in a fit of jealousy.

17 October 1754

B.239/a/40

ye 17th Thursday fine weather wind att NW^t this day we Expect Ind^s so we travelled none.

E.2/6

1754 october 17 Thursd^y frosty weather, wind NW. 230 tents of Archithinue Indians unpitched and went to the southward, and 17 Tents of Asinepoets unpitched and went to the Northward, and We unpitched and went SWbS 9 miles level Land with ledges of poplars and willows; passed 2 Creeks, little water in them.

E.2/4

17. Thursday frosty weather wind N.W. 320 tents of Archithinues unpitched and went westward, 17 tents of Aseenepoets went northward, and we went S.W.B.S. 9 miles, level land with ledges of poplar and willows, passed 2 creeks but little water in them.

E.2/11

1754 Octr 17th Thursday. wind NW and Frosty weather: 322 tents of Archithinue Natives unpitched & moved Westward; 17 tents of Asinepoet Natives moved Northwards; & We moved SWbW. 9 Miles. Level land, with ledges of poplar & Willows. passed two creeks, but little water in them; and none to be got any where else.

18 October 1754
> B.239/a/40

ye 18 Friday wind att NW^t and fine weather travelled none to day, there Came 17 tents of Esinepoets, severall of ye Earchithinues promised to go with me to ye fort att the spring of the year, and they would get all kinds of ffurrs, that their Country affords.
> E.2/6

18 Frid^y wind NW. & gentle frost; travelled none, Women Employed dressing skins for Cloathing.
> E.2/4

18. Friday wind N.W. and a gentle frost, women employed dressing skins for cloathing.
> E.2/11

18. Friday. wind NW & a gentle frost: Travelled none. The Women employed dressing skins for cloathing &c.

19 October 1754
> B.239/a/40

ye 19 Saturday this day travelled none for it Snowed all ye forenoon afternoon fine Weather wind NW^t this day the Ind^s killed 3 Buffalow and a Hee Bear.
> E.2/6

19 Saturd^y wind NW. with snow at times, travelled none, Women Employed as yesterday.
> E.2/4

19. Saturday wind N.W. with snow at times, women employed as yesterday.
> E.2/11

19. Saturday. Wind NW. with snow at times; Travelled none. Women employed as Yesterday.

20 October 1754
> B.239/a/40

ye 20 Sunday fine weather wind att W^t and frosty nights, this day 230 tents marched to ye Southward, and attickasish and Connawappa* with them, and 17 tents went SWbS° 9 M Levell Land and Ledges of poplars and willows, past 2 Creecks Little water in them.

> * Attickasish and Connawappa, mentioned in Severall places are the 2 Ind^s I fitted out with Captn Hendey.
> E.2/6

20 Sunday wind NW and moderate weather, travelled none, Women making Beaver Coats, Men killed 5 Buffalow, and one black Bear.

E.2/4

20. Sunday fine weather wind N.W. women making beaver coats, men
a hunting, killed 5 buffaloe and one black bear.

E.2/11

20. Sunday. Wind NW and pleasant weather Travelled none. Women
employed making Beaver coats; Men hunting; killed 5 Buffalo, & one
black Bear.

21 October 1754

B.239/a/40

21st Monday wind west and frosty nights, travelled none this day, those
Inds that unpitcht yesterday are Gone to Warr with other Inds of a farther distance.

E.2/6

21 Mondy wind west, and fine weather, travelled none.

E.2/4

21. Monday fine weather wind W. travelled none I asked the men why
they did not go to kill beaver and wolves but they made me little
answer.

E.2/11

21. Monday. Wind West & fine weather, Travelled none. I asked the
men why they did not go to kill Beaver, & Wolves: but they made me
very little Answer.

22 October 1754

B.239/a/40

Octr ye 22d 1754 Tuesday fine weather wind att West, took my depar-
ture from peson Ledge and Steered SWbS 10 M ye Inds killed Some
Beaver, 2 Moose and one Buffuloe, Levell Land and Small Ledges of
Brush poplar and Spruce.

E.2/6

22 Tuesdy fine weather, wind W. took my departure from Archithinue
Creek, and travelled WSW 10 miles, fine level land, with plenty of
Creeks, and poplars. 15 tents pitched away from us NE. the Indians
killed several Beaver, and I killed 3: beaver is here plenty, houses
almost in every pond.

E.2/4

1754 Octr 22. Tuesday. Wind and weather as Yesterday; Travelled 5 Miles
WSW. Level land, with poplars: a great many small Creeks and Ponds,
with plenty of Beaver houses. Indians killed a few; & I killed three. Fifteen tents pitched another way.

E.2/11

22. Tuesday fine weather wind W. travelled 10 miles W.S.W. level land

with poplars; a great many small creeks, and ponds, and plenty of
beaver houses; Indians killed a few, and I killed 3, fifteen tents of different tribes pitched from us.

23 October 1754
B.239/a/40
ye 23^d Wednesday fine weather wind SW^t took my departure from
Nubery Hill and steered WSW^t 14 M, Hills and dales, and Creecks of a
Small Run of water, this day 15 tents pitcht away NE^t, the Ind^s kill severall Beaver and I killed 3 Beaver, there was 6 in ye house, in this part
of ye Country Beaver are plenty being almost in every pond.*

  * here Captn Hendey observes Beaver are plenty, asking the Reason why they did not Lye by and kill more he says that Beaver alone is
not Sufficient to Maintain their familys, therefore are obliged to pitch
from place to place for Larger Beasts such as Moose and Buffaloe, he
also Says notwithstanding they find Sever^ll houses in a day they will
only Break open one or two and Pitch away.
E.2/6
23 Wednesd^y fine weather, wind SW. travelled WSW. 14 miles, level
Land, and ledges of small woods; Indians killed 2 Moose, one Buffalow,
and several Beaver.
E.2/4
23. Wednesday fine weather wind S.W. travelled 14 miles W.S.W. land
&c as yesterday, Killed 2 moose, one buffaloe and only 10 beaver, when
I am certain they might have killed 200, whereas they only kill a few
for cloathing, the creeks and ponds are full of beaver houses.
E.2/11
23. Wednesday. Wind SW and fine weather; Travelled 7 Miles WSW
Land &c as Yesterday. Indians killed two Moose one Buffalo & only ten
Beaver; when I am certain they might have killed 200, if they had
chused, but they only kill a few for cloathing, and for Beaver feasting;
Buffalo being their chief food at present. The Ponds here are surrounded with Beaver houses; & numbers along the Banks of creeks.
the roofs are thin and easily broke into.

24 October 1754
B.239/a/40
ye 24th Thursday fine weather wind NE^t took my departure from
Earchithinue Cove and Steered WSW^t 12 M fine Levell Land with
Ledges of woods, and plains, the Ind^s killed severall Beaver and two
Moose, it freezes Every night, and thaw's again in ye day.
E.2/6
1754 october 24 Thursd^y fine weather, wind NE. it freezes in the night

and thaws in the day, travelled WSW 12 miles, fine level land, plenty of Creeks and Beaver Houses, Indians killed 2 Moose and several Beaver.

    E.2/4

24. Thursday fine weather wind N.E. it freezes in the nights and thaws in the days, travelled 12 miles W.S.W. level land, plenty of creeks and beaver houses, killed 2 moose and a few beaver.

    E.2/11

24. Thursday. Wind NE and fine weather. it freezes in the nights and thaws in the days. Travelled 6 Miles WSW. Level land; Plenty of Creeks, & Beaver houses. Indians killed 2 Moose & a few Beaver.

25 October 1754

    B.239/a/40

Octr ye 25 Friday fine weather wind att SW^t took my departure from Beaver Creeck and steered WSW^t 10 M Land the same, killed severall Beaver & a Buffaloe.

    E.2/6

25 Frid^y fine weather, wind SW. travelled 10 miles WSW. Land the same as yesterday, killed several Beaver, and one Buffalow.

    E.2/4

25. Friday fine weather wind W.S.W. travelled 10 miles W.S.W. land &c as yesterday killed one buffaloe.

    E.2/11

25. Friday. Wind WSW and moderate weather. Travelled 5 Miles WSW Land &c as Yesterday. Indians killed one Buffalo.

26 October 1754

    B.239/a/40

ye 26th Saturday fell large Hail, afternoon fine W^r, wind att W^t. took my departure from Creeck Ledge, and steered WSW^t 9 M, here is plenty of timber very Large, and tall, this day Cross'd Waskesu River, the water on the fall 2 feet deep, the River 10 poles Wide, the Currant Runs Est & Comes from ye westw^d; ye Ind^s killed Severall Beaver, & I killed two.

    E.2/6

26 Saturd^y wind W. and hail at times, took my Departure from Creek ledge, and travelled WSW. 9 miles, Crossed Wykesew River, two feet deep, and 10 poles wide, with large tall timber woods on, Each side, Indians killed several Beaver, the current of this River runs E^t and very deep.

    E.2/4

26. Saturday wind W. and hail at times travelled 9 miles W.S.W. then crossed waskesew river, 2 foot deep and 10 poles wide, killed a few beaver.

E.2/11

1754 Octr 26. Saturday. Wind West and hail at times. Travelled 9 Miles WSW. then crossed Waskesew River 2 feet deep & 10 poles wide. The current runs East Large timber of sorts growing on its banks. Indians killed a few Beaver.

27 October 1754

B.239/a/40

the 27th Sunday fine weather wind WSW^t. took my departure from Labour in vain Creeck and steered WSW 12 M fine Levell Land plenty of timber in Ledges and ponds of water, and swamps betwixt ye Ledges, the Ind^s killed one Buffuloe, & severall Beaver, my partner and I broke open 2 housses and gott nothing.

E.2/6

27 Sunday fine weather, wind WbS. took my Departure from Wykesew River and travelled WSW 12 miles, level Land, Creeks, ponds, Beaver Houses, & ledges of tall and large Birch trees; Indians killed several Beaver, and I killed 2.

E.2/4

27. Sunday fine weather wind W.B.S. travelled 12 miles W.S.W. level land, ledges of large birch, creeks, and ponds, and plenty of beaver houses.

E.2/11

27. Sunday. wind WbS and fine weather; Travelled 6 Miles WSW. Level land; and ledges of large birch, Creeks, ponds, and plenty of Beaver houses.

28 October 1854

B.239/a/40

ye 28th Monday fine weather wind WbS° travelled none, killed severall Beaver, & one Moose.

E.2/6

28 Mond^y fine weather, wind WbS. travelled none; killed several Beaver and one moose.

E.2/4

28. Monday fine weather wind W.B.S. travelled none, killed one moose and a few beaver.

E.2/11

28. Monday. Wind and weather as Yesterday; Travelled none. killed a Moose & a few Beaver.

29 October 1754

B.239/a/40

ye 29th Tuesday fine weather wind NW^t took my departure from
Arsinie Watchee and Steered W^t 10 M fine Levell Land, & tall timber,
& very thick, this day Crossed 2 Creecks.

E.2/6

29 Tuesd^y fine weather, wind NW. took my Departure from muskuty
plains, and travelled W 10 miles; level Land, tall woods, and Creeks: I
have been since the 13th of august in muscuty plains; the Indians calls
the Archithinue Country. by another name, which is Arsinee Warchee
(ie dry Country).

E.2/4

29. Tuesday fine weather wind N.W. left muscuty plains which I have
been in since the 13th of august, and travelled 10 miles W. level land,
tall woods, many creeks, & beaver houses.

E.2/11

29. Tuesday. Wind NW and cold weather left Muscuty plains, Which I
have been in since the 13th August, and travelled 5 Miles West. Level
lands, Tall woods, & plenty of Creeks.

30 October 1754

B.239/a/40

ye 30th Wednesday fine weather wind SW^t took my departure from
Small Moose Creeck & Steered WbN^o 7 M Lands and woods much y^e
same, this day killed 2 Moose and Severall Beaver.

E.2/6

1754 october 30 Wednesd^y fine weather, wind SW. travelled WbN 7
miles, land and woods as yesterday; killed 2 Moose and several Beaver.

E.2/4

1755 Octr 30th Wednesday fine weather wind S.W. travelled W.B.N. 7
miles, land &c as yesterday. killed one moose and a few beaver.

E.2/11

30. Wednesday. Wind SW. and fine weather; Travelled 4 Miles WbN.
Land and Woods as Yesterday. Indians killed 2 Moose and several
Beaver.

31 October 1754

B.239/a/40

31st Thursday wind & weather as before, travelled none, the Ind^s killed
2 Buffaloe, one Moose and severall Beaver.

E.2/6

31 Thursd^y wind and weather, as yesterday, Women drying Beaver
skins, Indians killed one Moose, 2 Buffalow, and several Beaver.

E.2/4

31. Thursday wind &c as yesterday travelled none, women dressing beaver skins for cloathing, killed one moose, 2 buffaloe and a few beaver.

E.2/11

31. Thursday. Wind and weather as Yesterday. Women dressing what Beaver skins they have for cloathing. <NB. This Anthony Hendey was born in the Island of Wight and was in the Year 1748 Outlawed for Smuggling, and in 1750 entered into the Company's Service, the Director not knowing that he was under Sentence of Outlawry. This person whom I knew well was Bold; Enterprizing and Voluntarily offered his Service to go inland with the Natives, and explore the Country, and to endeavour to draw down the different Tribes to the Factory. Before this time None of the Servants at the Factories had ventured to Winter with the Natives. The Accounts of Horsemen being Inland were not credited: He Hendey was misrepresented by those in the Bay who were not acting a just part to the Company, and He perceiving not likely to meet with promotion he had so deservedly merited quitted the Company's Service. Which made one of the Directors observe afterwards "That a valuable Servant oftentimes was not known until lost.>

1 November 1754

B.239/a/40

1754 Novr ye 1st Friday fine weather wind SW^t, we have a white frost every night, and thin Ice, but it is all Consumed by ye middle of ye day, took my departure from Beaver River & steered WbN 10 M fine Ledges of woods, and very tall, killed 2 Moose and severall Beaver, the Earchithinues made a great smoak about a days Journey from us.

E.2/6

Novr 1 Frid^y fine weather, wind SW. we have a gentle frost every night, but is gone by the middle of the day, travelled WbN. 10 miles; level Land, ledges of tall woods, and Creeks full of Beaver Houses; killed 2 Moose, and several Beaver: the Archithinues made a large smoak which appears about a days Journey from us.

E.2/4

Novr 1st Friday fine weather wind S.W. we have a gentle frost in the nights, but it is gone by the middle of the day, travelled 10 miles W.B.N. level land, tall woods and creeks full of beaver houses, killed 2 moose and a few beaver see the Archithinues smoak about a days journey to the N.W. a young man about 22 years old eat hemlocks and died in less than 2 hours after.

E.2/11

1754 Novr 1st Friday. wind SW and moderate weather. We have a gentle frost in the night but is gone by noon. Travelled 5 Miles WbN. Level land, Ledges of tall woods, & Creeks full of Beaver houses: killed Several & 2 Moose. Saw the Archithinue Smoak, about a days Journey off to the NW. A Young man about 22 years old eat a good many Hemlocks & died in less than two hours after. <He eat the above thro' ignorance.>

2 November 1754

B.239/a/40

ye 2^d Saturday wind & weather as yesterday travelled none, being plenty of Beaver, perswaded them to stay killed severall, an accident happened to an Earchithinue Lad who this day Eat of Hemlocks, and died in Less then two hours.

E.2/6

2 Saturd^y wind and weather as yesterday, travelled none; Advised them to stay and kill Beaver, killed a great many; an accident happened to a young Man, who this day eat hemlocks and died in less then two hours.

E.2/4

2. Saturday wind &c as yesterday, travelled none, killed a few beaver.

E.2/11

2: Saturday. Wind and weather as Yesterday; Travelled none. Indians killed a few Beaver.

3 November 1754

B.239/a/40

ye 3^d Sunday wind and weather the same, Lay by killing a Beaver, I killed two.

E.2/6

3 Sunday wind SW. and pleasant weather; Indians killed several Beaver.

E.2/4

3. Sunday pleasant weather wind S.W. employed as yesterday.

E.2/11

3 Sunday. wind SW. and pleasant weather. Indians killed several Beaver.

4 November 1754

B.239/a/40

ye 4th Monday fine weather travelled none, killed severall Beaver.

E.2/6

4 Mond^y wind and weather as yesterday, travelled none; Indians killed several Beaver, and I two.

E.2/4

4. Monday wind &c as yesterday employed as yesterday, beaver very plenty, but the Indians will not kill them, not staying out above 3 hours in a day.

E.2/11

4. Monday. Wind and weather as Yesterday; I went with the men a Beaver killing. They killed a few, & I two: they are numerous hereabouts, but the Indians would not stay above 3 hours from their tents. Dancing, Drumming &c.

5 November 1754

B.239/a/40

ye 5th Tuesday fine weather wind NW^t all Employed killing Beaver, I killed two.

E.2/6

5 Tuesd^y Cold freezing weather, Indians killed a great many Beaver, and I two.

E.2/4

5. Tuesday wind N.W. and cold freezing weather, killed a few beaver, they are very plenty.

E.2/11

5. Tuesday. Wind NW and cold freezing weather. Indians killed a few Beaver, & I two.

6 November 1754

B.239/a/40

ye 6th Wednesday this day fell a great deal of Sleet, and hail, and wind att ye NE^t blowed hard.

E.2/6

Novr 6 Wednesd^y wind N.E. blowing strong with rain and hail. no stirring abroad.

E.2/4

1755 Novr 6th Wednesday a heavy gale wind N.W. with rain and hail, a grand day in feasting dancing &c.

E.2/11

6. Wednesday. wind NE & a Strong gale with Sleet at times. no stirring abroad.

7 November 1754

B.239/a/40

ye 7th Thursday fine weather wind att N^o. took my departure from Squirt Ledge and Steered NW^t 7 M thick Ledges of woods all ye way, this day killed two Moose and Severall Beaver.

E.2/6

7 Thursd^y fine weather, wind N. travelled NW. 7 miles, ledges of woods and Creeks, killed 2 Moose & several Beaver.

E.2/4

7. Thursday moderate weather wind N. travelled 7 miles N.W. ledges of woods and creeks, killed one moose and a few beaver.

E.2/11

1754 Novr 7th Thursday. wind North and fine weather; Travelled 4 Miles NW. Ledges of woods and Creeks. Indians killed 2 Moose & 2 Beaver.

8 November 1754

B.239/a/40

Novr ye 8th Friday Rain and Sleet Till noon then Cleered up Wind NE^t this day killed two waskesw^s and one Buffuloe.

E.2/6

8 Frid^y wind NE. with rain and sleet, travelled none; killed 2 Buffalow & two waskesew's.

E.2/4

8. Friday wind N.E. with rain and sleet at times; killed 2 buffaloe and 2 moose.

E.2/11

8. Friday. Wind NE with Rain Sleet & Snow at times. Travelled none Indians killed 2 Buffalo & 2 Moose.

9 November 1754

B.239/a/40

ye 9th Saturday wind att N^o. took my departure from Bear Cove and Steered N° 9 M, small Brushy plains and Ledges of woods, killed Severall Beaver, and one moose.

E.2/6

9 Saturd^y wind N. and frosty weather, small brushy plains and ledges of woods; travelled N. 9 miles, killed several Beaver, and one Moose.

E.2/4

9. Saturday wind N. and frosty weather, travelled 9 miles N. level brushy land, and here and there a ledge of woods; killed one moose.

E.2/11

9. Saturday Wind North and frosty weather. Travelled 4 Miles North Level brushy land; & here & there a ledge of woods. Indians killed one moose.

10 November 1754

B.239/a/40

ye 10th Sunday fine weather wind NW^t travelled none, killed Severall

Beaver and 3 Waskesw^s Last night it froze so hard, that the plains would bere in Some places.

    E.2/6

10 Sunday wind NW and frosty weather, the Ice in the plains bears; travelled none; killed 3 Waskesew's and several Beaver, Women Employed drying Beaver skins.

    E.2/4

10 @ 11. Sunday & monday frosty weather the wind between the N. and W. travelled none, women dressing shoe leather, killed 3 waskesews and a few beaver, the ponds bears us.

    E.2/11

10. Sunday. Wind NW. and frosty weather. Indians hunting killed 3 Waskesew. Women dressing Beaver skins for cloathing.

11 November 1754

    B.239/a/40

ye 11th Monday fine Weather wind N^o travelled none the Ind^s killed Severall Beaver, and I killed two.

    E.2/6

11 Mond^y fine weather weather, wind N. travelled none, Indians killed several Beaver, and I killed 2, Creeks froze.

    E.2/11

11. Monday. Wind North and fine weather. Indians killed 12 Beaver & I killed 2. The Creeks are froze over, & the ponds will bear a person.

12 November 1754

    B.239/a/40

ye 12th Tuesday fine weather Wind att N^o took my departure from Ice Creeck, and Steered N° 10 M Low grassy Swamps and Ledges of woods, very tall timber, this day killed 2 waskesw^s.

    E.2/6

12 Tuesd^y fine weather, thaws in the day time, wind N, took my departure from Ice Creek, and travelled N. 10 miles; low grassy swamps and Ledges of tall Birch, Juniper and poplar trees; killed 2 Waskesews.

    E.2/4

12. Tuesday fine weather wind N.W. freezes in the nights and thaws in the days, travelled 10 miles N. low, grassy swamps, and ledges of tall birch, Juniper and poplar trees; killed 2 waskesews.

    E.2/11

12. Tuesday. Wind variable and agreeable weather. Thaws in the days, & freezes in the nights. Travelled 5 Miles North. Low Grassy swamps & le<d>ges of Woods, such as Birch, Juniper, & Poplar. Indians killed 2 Waskesew.

13 November 1754
> B.239/a/40

ye 13th Wednesday fine weather wind att N^o travelled none, the Ind^s went to fetch the Meat killed Yesterday.

> E.2/6

13 Wednesd^y fine weather, wind N. travelled none.

> E.2/4

13 @ 14. Wednesday and thursday moderate freezing weather wind N. women making cloathing for cold weather, some familys has not got half enough of skins to cloath them in the cold of the winter, and what surprizes me most, they never go out of their tents but when they want provisions, altho' the beaver and otters are swimming about us; I killed 2 otters.

> E.2/11

1754 Novr 13th Wednesday. Wind North and moderate weather, Travelled none. Women dressing skins for cloathing. Dancing, Conjuring, Drumming, & feasting.

14 November 1754
> B.239/a/40

ye 14 Thursday wind and Weather as before, Laid by, made 4 Beaver Netts, for this 2 Nights past it has froze so hard, that some of ye Beav^r dams will Bare and some will not, the Weather is yet as warm in ye day, that you may Go in ye water and your feet be no Colder, than they are att the fortt in ye summer time

> E.2/6

14 Thursd^y wind and weather as yesterday, froze hard last night; Beaver dams will almost bear, travelled none; Men Employed making Beaver nets; and the Women making Cloathing for cold weather; I killed 2 Otters.

> E.2/11

14. Thursday. Wind & Weather as Yesterday. Women making cloathing for cold weather. Some families have not got half enough of skins for cloathing them on the aproaching Winter: & what surprizes me most, they never go out of their tents but when they want provisions, altho' the Beaver & Otters are swarming about us in the Creeks and swamps, not one went out to day but myself, & I killed two Otters.

15 November 1754
> B.239/a/40

1754 Novr ye 15 Friday fine weather wind att N^o took my departure from Otter Creeck, and Steered S^o 12 M to another Creeck to kill Beaver.

E.2/6

1754 Novr 15 Frid^y wind N. and clear frosty weather, took my Departure from Otter Creek, and travelled W. 12 miles to another Creek to kill Beaver; swampy plains, & woods.

E.2/4

1755 Novr 15th Friday clear frosty weather wind N. travelled 12 miles W. to a creek where are plenty of beaver houses, swampy plains and ledges of woods.

E.2/11

15. Friday. wind North and clear weather. Travelled 6 miles to a creek where there are plenty of Beaver houses.

16 November 1754

B.239/a/40

ye 16th Saturday wind NW^t travelled none, killed severall Beaver.

E.2/6

16 Saturd^y wind and weather as yesterday; travelled none, killed several Beaver.

E.2/4

16 @ 20. Saturday @ Wednesday moderate freezing weather winds from the N.W. to the N. travelled none, men hunting, killed one waskesew, 2 moose and a few beaver, the beaver dams bears; I observe the beaver houses are not so strong built here as those I have seen near the sea-shores; 7 tents of Indians pitched from us to the west-ward.

E.2/11

16. Saturday. Wind North and clear frosty weather. Indians killed several Beaver.

17 November 1754

B.239/a/40

ye 17th Sunday this day 7 tents pitcht farther to ye westward. this day killed some Beaver, 2 Moose, and one waskesu, the frost, the frost has almost gott ye Better of ye warm weather.

E.2/6

17 Sunday wind NW. and Clear weather, the Beaver dams now bears; 7 tents of Indians pitched to the westward; killed 7 Beaver, one Waske-sew, & 2 Moose.

E.2/11

17. Sunday. Wind and weather as Yesterday. Seven tents of Indians pitched W^{t}ward from us & what remained, killed 7 Beaver, one Waske-sew, & 2 Moose the Beaver Dams bear people, which favours us in killing the Beaver.

18 November 1754

B.239/a/40

ye 18th Monday fine weather wind NW^t broke up 2 housses killed no Beaver, killed one waskesu.

E.2/6

18 Mond^y fine weather, wind NW. travelled none, broke open two Houses, but got no Beaver, they had got past our stakes; killed one Waskesew.

E.2/11

1754 Novr 18th Monday. Wind NW. and fine weather. Travelled none broke open two Beaver houses but got none, having got past our stakes. the Beaver houses are not so strong by two thirds of the thickness, as I have seen about York Fort.

19 November 1754

B.239/a/40

ye 19th Tuesday wind as yesterday, Last night froze hard, Lay by killed some Beaver.

E.2/6

19 Tuesd^y wind and weather as yesterday; travelled none, killed several Beaver.

E.2/11

19. Tuesday. Wind and weather as Yesterday. Travelled none. Indians killed a few Beaver. Wild minth grows here in great plenty.

20 November 1754

B.239/a/40

ye 20th Wednesday fine Clear weather wind N^o fell a great deal of snow, killed some Beaver, so we travelled none, Last night it froze so hard, it will bare almost every way, Except ye River.

E.2/6

20 Wednesd^y fine clear weather, wind N. snowed last night, travelled none; killed a great many Beaver: wild minth grows here in great plenty.

E.2/11

20. Wednesday. Wind NNW and clear frosty weather: it snowed a little last night. Travelled none. The Indian Men a beaver hunting: the Women dressing skins for cloathing.

21 November 1754

B.239/a/40

ye 21st Thursday fine frosty weather wind NE^t it begins to freeze hard Every night, and in the day it thaw's but very Little, took my

departure from pepper mint pond, and Steered SE^t 12 M fine plains &
Ledges of wood all ye way, this day killed nothing.

> E.2/6

21 Thursd^y Clear freezing weather, wind NE. took my departure from
minth Creeks, and travelled SE^t 12 miles; plains and ledges of tall
large Birch trees; thaw'd very little to day.

> E.2/4

21. Thursday clear frosty weather wind N.E. travelled 12 miles S.E.
plains and ledges of tall birch trees; thaw'd very little to day.

> E.2/11

21. Thursday. Wind NW and clear frosty weather. Travelled 6 miles SE.
Plains and Ledges of tall Birch trees. Thaws very little to day.

22 November 1754

> B.239/a/40

ye 22^d Friday fine weather wind NW^t travelled none killed severall
Beaver and this day a Large Bear had like to have killed me and y^e
Ind^n man, And I went to ye Hutt* and Laid some great Sticks before,
so that he should not get out in a hurry but he Came out (Just as I
was Going to lay down my Stick) in a great fury, the Ind^n Ran of like a
Lusty fellow, and Left me with my Bow & arrows, to get of as well as I
Could.

> * he means ye Bears den or hole where he Lyes.

> E.2/6

22 Frid^y fine weather, wind N.W. travelled none, killed several Beaver,
one young Man narrowly escaped being tore to peices by a black Bear
that he had wounded but by throwing from him his Beaver Coat which
the Bear tore to peices he got Clear off, this is often done: the Men
went immediately and killed him.

> E.2/4

22 @ 26. Friday @ Tuesday winds variable with warm rainy weather ice
almost gone, employed killing beaver, one young man narrowly
escaped losing his life by a grizzle bear that he had wounded, but by
throwing from him his beaver coat which the bear tore to pieces, he
got clear off, this they always do when closs pursued by it or any other
enraged wounded animal; the men went afterwards and killed him;
the grizzle, brown and red bears are so fierce, that no single native
cares to attack them, and the black bears are so harmless that they
knock them on the head with a hatchet.

> E.2/11

22. Friday. Wind NW and pleasant weather: Travelled none. Indians
killed a few Beaver. One Man narrowly escaped from a Grizzle Bear
that he had wounded, by throwing his Beaver coat from him; which

the Bear tore to pieces. and which the Natives always do when forced
to retreat. The Men & Dogs went out & killed the Bear.

23 November 1754
    B.239/a/40

ye 23^d Saturday fine weather wind att SE^t. Lay by this day, broke open
2 Beaver housses, all of Beaver got away.

    E.2/6

1754 Novr 23 Saturd^y fine weather, wind SE travelled none; Broke open
two Beaver Houses, but got none.

    E.2/11

1754 Novr 23 to 27. Saturday. Sunday Monday & Tuesday Winds from
SE. to South, and Warm weather, with Snow at intervals. The Men
killed a few Beaver; & the Women dressing skins for cloathing. My
Winter rigging is almost in readiness. Drumming, Dancing, & feasting.

24 November 1754
    B.239/a/40

ye 24th Sunday Last night it Rained a smart Shower which melted all
ye snow & Ice away, the Rivers are as open as in the middle of summer, this day fine weather wind S^o took my departure from pine
Creeck & Steered SE^t 12 M, fine Levell Land and nothing but poplar,
and Brush.

    E.2/6

24 Sunday wind S. and rainy weather, travelled none.

25 November 1754
    B.239/a/40

ye 25 Monday fine weather wind att S travelled none this day, killed 2
Beaver & one Moose.

    E.2/6

25 Mond^y wind and weather as yesterday, travelled none.

26 November 1754
    B.239/a/40

ye 26th Tuesday fine warm weather wind att S^o broke open 2 Beaver
housses but killed None

    E.2/6

26 Tuesd^y very warm weather, wind S. Ice and snow all gone, broke
two Beaver Houses open, killed none; killed one Moose.

27 November 1754

   B.239/a/40

yᵉ 27ᵗʰ Wednesday fine weather wind att SWᵗ took my departure from
Sand Stone Creeck & steered Sᵒ 10 M over fine Levell Land & small
Ledges of Brush, killed nothing to day.

   E.2/6

27 Wednesdʸ fine weather, wind SW. travelled SSE. 20 miles to another
Creek to kill Beaver; level land and Ledges of small woods; seed neither Beast nor Bird to day.

   E.2/4

1755 Novʳ 27ᵗʰ Wednesday fine weather wind S.W. travelled 20 miles
S.S.E. and came to another creek where are plenty of beaver houses,
level land and ledges of small woods, seed neither bird nor beast to
day.

   E.2/11

27. Wednesday. Wind SW. and warm weather; Travelled SSE 10 Miles; &
came to another Creek, where there are plenty of Beaver houses. Level land, and Ledges of small woods. Saw neither Beast nor Bird to day.

28 November 1754

   B.239/a/40

yᵉ 28ᵗʰ Thursday wind and Weather as yesterday, very busy in Catching
Beaver, this day broke open 3 housses killed 11 Beaver.

   E.2/6

28 Thursdʸ wind and weather, as yesterday; broke open 3 Houses,
killed 11 Beaver; travelled none.

   E.2/4

28 @ 30. Thursday @ Saturday wind S.W. travelled none, killed a few
beaver, fine pleasant summer weather, killed 6 cats each as large as a
sheep and fine sweet eating, this, and the black bear is the best food I
have yet eat here.

   E.2/11

28 @ 29. Thursday, & Friday. Wind SW and very moderate weather.
Indians employed killing Beaver.

29 November 1754

   B.239/a/40

yᵉ 29ᵗʰ Friday fine weather wind SWᵗ went to yᵉ same beaver housses
killed 6 Beaver More.

   E.2/6

29 Fridʸ fine weather, wind SW. travelled none, killed 6 Beaver, from
the Houses we broke open yesterday.

30 November 1754

    B.239/a/40

ye 30 Saturday wind S^o went to seek for more beaver housses when we see 20 very nigh, killed one Catt.

    E.2/6

30 Saturd^y wind S. and warm weather, Indian Men went to look for Beaver Houses, found 20 very nigh us, killed 6 Cats, the size of a Sheep, and fine eating.

    E.2/11

30 Saturday. Wind SW. and agreeable weather. The Men went to look out for Beaver houses: found 20 very nigh us: killed 6 Cats, each as large as a Sheep and fine eating, like lamb.

1 December 1754

    B.239/a/40

1754 Decr ye 1st Sunday wind as yesterday. killed Severall Beav^r. the weather is very warm, having froze none for 3 Nights past, the Ice on the ponds is not above 3 Inches thick and in Some places is not above one Inch thick.

    E.2/6

Decem^r 1 Sunday fine weather, wind SW. no frost here more than in the middle of summer; killed a great many Beaver, travelled none.

    E.2/4

Decr 1 @ 9. Friday @ Monday winds from the N.W. to N. and blowing snowing freezing weather at times, obliged to pitch our tents in the woods, lay by and killed a few beaver, one moose and a few cats; all the Indians pitched away from us, so that we are now only 12 in number vizt 2 men, 5 women, 4 children and myself, and neither powder nor shot amongst them, so that all depends on mine, which must make me careful in distributing it; myself employed making sleds for the women and one for my horse.

    E.2/11

Decr 1st Sunday. Wind SW no frost here more than in the middle of summer. Indians killed a few Beaver.

2 December 1754

    B.239/a/40

ye 2^d Monday this day travelled none, all Last night it fell small Sleet and Snow, and this Morning ye wind Shifted to ye NEbN^o, and all this day it blowed a meer Hurrican, went a hunting killed 2 Moose.

    E.2/6

2 Mond^y blowed a hurricane of wind, with sleet and snow, which oblidged us to move our tents into the Closs woods.

E.2/11

2. Monday. Wind SW and a Strong gale with Snow & Sleet: Obliged to remove into thick Woods.

3 December 1754
B.239/a/40

ye 3^d Tuesday Cold frosty weather, wind NW^t travelled none, this day killed 4 Beaver, two tents pitched away to the westward, their being plenty of Beaver housses, Bob went with them, now we are twelve in one tent, and the Ind^s has not one Load of powder nor Shott, but what I Give them of my own.

E.2/6

1754 Decr 3^d Tuesd^y Cold freezing weather, wind NW. killed 7 Beaver, Indians pitched to the Westward, so that we are now 12 in number Viz^t myself, two Men, 5 Women, and 4 Children; travelled none.

E.2/11

1754 Decr 3^d @ 4. Tuesday. Wind NW. Frosty weather: it is now very cold: Indians pitched away from us, So that we stand in Number Viz Myself, 2 Men, 5 Women & 4 Children: killed 7 Beaver.

4 December 1754
B.239/a/40

ye 4th Wednesday fine weather wind att NW^t this day killed 7 Beaver.

E.2/6

4 Wednesd^y wind NW. and very cold weather, travelled none, killed 7 Beaver.

5 December 1754
B.239/a/40

ye 5th Thursday Blows hard att N^o with a great drift of snow all day killed one moose.

E.2/6

5 Thursd^y a Continuance of blowing, freezing, snowing and drifting weather; travelled none, killed one Moose.

E.2/11

5. @ 7. Thursday. Wind NW. and <a> Strong gale with freezing, drifting, weather: killed one Moose: My Companions hath neither Powder nor Shot: So that we must use the gun but seldom, as they now depend on me: Women making Shoes of Moose leather: I have as Yet only wore Shoes with the hair on the inside, so moderate hath the weather been.

6 December 1754

B.239/a/40

yᵉ 6ᵗʰ Friday fine Clear weather, wind NWᵗ and very Sharp.

E.2/6

6 Fridʸ a fresh gale with clear freezing weather, wind NW. travelled none; my Companions hath no powder nor shot, so we must use the gun but seldom, as they now depend on me.

7 December 1754

B.239/a/40

yᵉ 7ᵗʰ Saturday fine weather, wind att Nº. travelled none these 4 days past. broke up one beaver house & killed two Beaver.

E.2/6

7 Saturdʸ moderate weather, wind N. travelled none; killed 2 Beaver, put on a Buffalow skin shoe with the hair inwards for cold, until now only wore dressed Moose skin.

8 December 1754

B.239/a/40

Decʳ yᵉ 8ᵗʰ Sunday warm, with the wind att Nº. made 7 Sledges.

E.2/6

8 Sunday moderate weather, wind N. made 7 sleds of Birch tree and one for two Horses.

E.2/11

8 Sunday. Wind North and more moderate, Men employed make Sleds of Birch, for the Women & Horses.

9 December 1754

B.239/a/40

yᵉ 9ᵗʰ Monday fine weather, wind att Sº. killed two Beaver & one Catt. talked with the old Captⁿ abᵗ Every Canoe taking one Earchithinue but he Would give no hearing to such a proposal. I told him Every Indⁿ that would take one Earchithinue you would give them 1 Gⁿ Brandy and 2 Measures of Tobacco and other goods, he att Last Consented to take 2 or 3 if they Come According to promise, which I do Realy believe they will.

E.2/6

9 Mondʸ moderate weather, wind S. froze hard last night, killed 2 Beaver and one Cat.

E.2/11

9. Monday. Wind South and moderate weather. A Strong frost last night: killed 2 Beaver & one Cat.

10 December 1754

B.239/a/40

yᵉ 10ᵗʰ Tuesday fine weather, wind att Sᵒ pitcht 4 M to yᵉ Eastwᵈ fine Levell Land and Ledges of woods, and ponds of water, betwixt which, plenty of moose & Beaver.

E.2/6

10 Tuesdᵞ wind and weather as yesterday. travelled E. 4 miles; level land, Ledges of woods and ponds of water, Came to a Creek, where are plenty of Beaver Houses; seed plenty of Moose, but did not disturb them, bad walking for the Ice will neither bear nor brake down.

E.2/4

10. Tuesday wind N.W. and freezing weather, travelled 4 miles E. level land, ledges of woods, and ponds of water; seed plenty of moose, but did not disturb them, bad walking, the Ice neither bears nor breaks down, so must lay by, my horse not being able to travel.

E.2/11

10. Tuesday. Wind & Weather as Yesterday: Travelled East 4 Miles: Level land; Ledges of woods; & Ponds of Water: Saw plenty of Moose but did not disturb them: bad walking; the ice will neither bear nor break down.

11 December 1754

B.239/a/40

yᵉ 11ᵗʰ Wednesday fine weather wind att Sᵒ no frost for these two nights past, this day killed 2 moose and 5 Beaver.

E.2/6

11 Wednesdᵞ moderate weather, wind S. killed 2 Beaver.

E.2/4

1755 Decʳ 11@ 15ᵗʰ Wednesday @ Sunday warm weather with rain at times, wind southerly, snow and Ice almost gone; killed one moose and a few beaver; waskesews passing and repassing us in large herds.

E.2/11

1754 Decʳ 11ᵗʰ @ 12 Wednesday. Wind South and Thursday Wind North and moderate weather: Broke open several Beaver houses but got none: The Men must look out for Beaver as they have no Ammunition, and I am resolved to take care of mine, neither would it be prudent to expend Ammunition in a Beaver Country.

12 December 1754

B.239/a/40

yᵉ 12ᵗʰ Thursday fine weather wind att Sᵒ broke up 2 housses, no Beaver.

E.2/6

1754 Decr 12 Thursd^y fine weather, wind S. broke open 2 Beaver Houses but got none.

13 December 1754
B.239/a/40

ye 13th Friday wind as Yesterday killed one Beav^r only today.

E.2/6

13 Frid^y wind and weather, as yesterday; killed one Beaver.

E.2/11

13. Friday. Wind North and moderate weather: killed one Beaver.

14 December 1754
B.239/a/40

ye 14th Saturday wind the same and fine weather Lay by this, fell a great deal of Rain, so that it has Left but Little Snow, on the ground.

E.2/6

14 Saturd^y wind S. rained last night and this day, so that it hath left little Ice and snow on the ground; Moose and Waskesew's, are so plenty that they are continually passing and repassing between the Creek and tent, which is not 100 yards distance from one another.

E.2/11

14. Saturday. Wind South; rained all last night and this day, so that it hath left little snow or ice: The Moose and Waskesew passing & repassing in herds, within 200 yards of our tent: The Men beg Ammunition from me but without success.

15 December 1754
B.239/a/40

ye 15th Sunday fine weather wind SW^t took my departure from Amen Creeck & steered NEbN^o 10 M Levell Land & barren, no wood all this day till we Came to ye Ledge where we put up for ye Night.

E.2/6

15 Sunday fine weather, travelled none, wind SW and moderate; killed one Moose.

E.2/11

15. Sunday. Wind SW. and moderate weather: Travelled none: killed one Moose with the Bow and Arrows.

16 December 1754
B.239/a/40

[Decr y^e] 16th Monday fine weather wind SW^t travelled none, killed two Beaver/

E.2/6

16 Mond^y fine weather, wind SW. travelled NEbN. 10 miles, Level land, and ledges of woods; seed plenty of Moose.

E.2/4

16. Monday fine weather wind S.W. travelled 10 miles N.E.B.N. level land and plenty of woods, seed a great number of moose.

E.2/11

16. Monday. Wind SW. & fine weather: Travelled 5 Miles NEbN. Level land, & plenty of woods: Saw a great many Moose.

17 December 1754

B.239/a/40

ye 17th Tuesday wind SWbS° fine weather killed two Beaver

E.2/6

17 Tuesd^y fine weather, wind S.WbS. snow and Ice gone, killed 2 Beaver.

E.2/4

17 @ 18. Tuesday @ Wednesday fine warm weather winds variable from S.W.B.S. to N.W. made 7 pair of snow-shoe frames, there being no birch the way we design to travel.

E.2/11

1754 Decr 17th Tuesday. wind SWbS and fine weather: snow & ice all gone: killed 2 Beaver, and afterwards making Snow-shoes.

18 December 1754

B.239/a/40

ye 18th Wednesday fine weather wind SW^t this day travelled none, made 7 pair of Snow Shoe frames, there being no Birch the way we have to travell.

E.2/6

18 Wednesd^y fine weather, wind SW. made 7 pair snow shoe frames, there being no birch the way we are to travell.

E.2/11

18. Wednesday. Wind NW. and moderate weather; made 7 pairs of Snow-shoes, there being no Birch the way we are to go.

19 December 1754

B.239/a/40

ye 19th Thursday fine weather wind att West, this day pitcht 10 M to ye Eastward, killed one Buffuloe, here the tracks of Buffuloe Moose and Waskesw^s was very plenty; no wood all the days travell but willows

E.2/6

19 Thursd^y fine weather, wind W. took my Departure from snow shoe

ledge, and travelled E. 10 miles, level land & no woods killed one Buffalow.
> E.2/4

19. Thursday fine weather wind W. travelled 10 miles E. level land, no
woods, killed one buffaloe.
> E.2/11

19. Thursday. wind West and fine weather: Travelled 5 Miles East: Level
land, no woods: killed one Buffalo.

20 December 1754
> B.239/a/40

yᵉ 20ᵗʰ Friday wind att West travelled none, this day killed two Waskesu.
> E.2/6

20 Fridʸ wind W. fine weather, travelled ENE 16 miles, Land as yesterday, until night, we put up at a Creek with a small ledge of woods,
seed plenty of Wolves, Moose, and Waskesew's.
> E.2/4

20. Friday fine weather wind W. travelled 16 miles E.N.E. land as yesterday, seed wolves, waskesews, and moose in great herds and droves.
> E.2/11

20 Friday. wind and weather as Yesterday: Travelled 8 Miles ENE. Land
as Yesterday: Saw plenty of Wolves, Moose, and Waskesew.

21 December 1754
> B.239/a/40

yᵉ 21ˢᵗ Saturday fine weather wind NWbWᵗ this day pitcht 16 Miles to
yᵉ Eastward. killed 2 Buffuloe, here wolves are very plenty, saw 4
Beaver housses
> E.2/6

1754 Decʳ 21 Saturdʸ fine weather, wind NWbW. travelled none, killed
two Beaver, and one Waskesew.
> E.2/4

21 @ 22. Saturday @ Sunday fine weather winds N.W.B.N. and S. travelled none, killed 4 beaver.
> E.2/11

21. Saturday. Wind NWbW. and fine weather: Travelled none: killed 2
Beaver & one Waskesew.

22 December 1754
> B.239/a/40

yᵉ 22ᵈ Sunday fine weather wind att Sᵒ killed 2 Beaver.
> E.2/6

22 Sunday fine weather, wind S. travelled none, killed 2 Beaver.

E.2/11

22. Sunday. Wind South: Travelled none: Snowed all day killed 2
Beaver.

23 December 1754
B.239/a/40
ye 23^d Monday fine weather wind SWbS° this day pitcht 14 M EbN°
Crossed a Branch of Waskesu River, the old Man is afraid the
Earchithinues will Come down and kill us but we see none as yet.
E.2/6
23 Mond^y fine weather, wind WbS. took my departure from Wolf
Creek, and travelled EbN. 18 miles, Crossed a branch of Wykesew
River, the old Man is afraid the Archithinues will come and kill us; I
wounded a Buffalow.
E.2/4
23. Monday fine weather wind W.B.S. travelled 18 miles E.B.N. crossed
a branch of waskesew river in the evening; I wounded a buffaloe.
E.2/11
23. Monday. Wind WbS and fine weather: Travelled nine Miles EbN.
Crossed a branch of Waskesew River: in the Evening I wounded a Buffalo.

24 December 1754
B.239/a/40
Decr ye 24th Tuesday fine weather wind att S° Killed one Wolf, this day
went to Look for a Buffuloe that I wounded Yesterday, found him dead
on the top of a Hill where I had a fine View of Arsinie Watchie att a
farr distance it being the Last Sight that I Ever shall have of it this
Year.
E.2/6
24 Tuesd^y fine weather, wind S. we have a little frost in the nights, but
is gone in the day, went to look for the Buffalow I wounded last night,
found him on the top of a hill dead, and I had a fine prospect of Muscuty, or Arsinee Warchee Country, and seed the Archithinues smoak,
this will be the last time I shall see that delightful Country this trip
inland.
E.2/4
24 @ 27. Tuesday @ Friday wind south and west with frosty nights and
warm days, travelled none, found my wounded buffaloe dead on a rising ground, where I had a fine view of the muscuty country, which will
be the last this trip inland; Indians killed 2 waskesews and 2 moose,
wolves are very numerous here: I asked them why they would not kill
them? to which they answered the Archithinues will kill us if we trap

in their country; I then asked them when and where they were to get
the wolves &c to carry to the forts in the spring? to this they made no
answer but laughed one to another: myself trapping wolves.

  E.2/11

1754 Decr 24th Tuesday. wind South and fine weather: Travelled none: I
found my Buffalo lying dead a small distance from our tent. On a ris-
ing ground I had an extensive view of the Muscuty country which will
be the last this trip inland.

25 December 1754

  B.239/a/40

ye 25th Wednesday wind as Yesterday Killed 3 Beaver.

  E.2/6

25 Wednesd^y wind and weather, as yesterday, killed 2 Beaver, Women
brought the Buffalow.

  E.2/11

25. Wednesday. Wind and weather as yesterday: killed 2 Beaver: We
have a frost in the night and partly gone in the day.

26 December 1754

  B.239/a/40

ye 26th Thursday fine weather wind att West, Lay by, went a hunting
Killed 2 Waskesw^s.

  E.2/6

26 Thursd^y fine weather, wind W. travelled none these 3 days past;
killed 2 Waskesew's.

  E.2/11

26. @ 27. Thursday and Friday. Winds Westerly: killed 2 Waskesew & 2
Moose: I set a Wolf trap: I asked the Natives why they did not trap
Wolves; they made Answer that the Archithinue Natives would kill
them, if they trapped in their country: I then asked them when &
where they were to get the Wolves &c to carry down in the spring.
They made no Answer; but laughed one to another.

27 December 1754

  B.239/a/40

ye 27th Friday fine weather wind att West, this day travelled to Look
for Beaver, saw but one House, made 2 p^r Snow Shoe frames, and built
one Wolf trap, Wolves being plenty, I asked the Ind^s why they did not
build traps, they told me it was not their Country, for if the Earchithinues should see us they would kill us all, I told them I would not
believe anything of it unless I see it, att which they were very Angry,

and Ask'd me if I would shoot one of them if I saw him, and I told them not unless they presented for to Shoot att me first.

E.2/6

27 Frid^y fine weather, wind W. made a wolf trap, Indians hunting, killed 2 Moose; the Indians were angry, and said the Archithinues would kill us if we trapped in their Country; I asked the old Man how they were to get Wolves skins to Carry to the Fort; He made me little answer; but am informed by My bedfellow that we shall Trade them from the Archithinues in the spring of the year: for the sake of the Woman, shall take no notice at present.

28 December 1754

B.239/a/40

ye 28th Saturday fine weather wind att SW^t this day pitcht 12 M NEbN fine Levell land, and Small Ledges of Hazell & poplar. this day killed 2 Quiquakahs.

E.2/6

1754 Decr 28 Saturd^y Wind NW. frost and snow, and very Cold weather, took my departure from Buffalow hill, and travelled NEbN. fine level Land, and narrow Ledges of hazel and poplar trees; got a Wolf from my trap I set yesterday, and set two more this evening; if the Indians would build traps, they might get plenty, but they will not hear me.

E.2/4

28 @ 4 Jan^ry 1756 Saturday @ Saturday blowing snowing freezing weather winds from the west to north. travelled 10 miles N.E.B.N. level land and narrow ledges of poplar, alder and hasle trees, was joined by three tents of Indians, lay by all this time; Indians killing moose and waskesews, but very few beaver altho' they are numerous, as are also wolves and foxes, but not one trap have they put up yet; my bedfellow informs me that they were angry with me for speaking so much about traping, and advised me to say no more to them about it, for they would get more wolves and beaver &c from the Archithinues and Aseenepoets than they could carry; I asked her when we would see them again and if they bought the goods every year from them, she said that the Indians that traded at York Fort were supplyed by them, and that we should see them in the spring, but she begged of me to take no notice, otherwise they would kill her, so for ye woman's sake shall take no notice but be quiet; the ice in the ponds 4 inches thick, and the snow on the ground not yet so deep as to wear snow-shoes; for the first time I now wear a pair of buffaloe skin shoes with the hair inside.

E.2/11

28. Saturday. Wind NW with frost and snow & very cold weather: I travelled 5 Miles NEbN. Level land, & narrow ledges of poplar, Alder, &

Hazle trees. got a Wolf in my trap, and set 2 more; the Wolves are numerous. An Indian told me that my tent-mates were angry with me last night for speaking so much concerning trapping, & advised me to say no more about it, for they would get more Wolves, Beaver &c from the Archithinue Natives in the spring, than they can carry.

29 December 1754
B.239/a/40

1754 Decr ye 29 Sunday fine weather Wind att S° travelled none to day killed 3 Beaver, the weather has been so warm to day, that we have gone without any thing over our bodies, and felt no Cold, the Earth is froze a foot or 14 Inches down, and the Ice on the Standing pond of water is froze 4 or 5 Inches thick.

E.2/6

29 Sunday wind and weather as yesterday, travelled none, got 2 wolves from my traps; Indians killed 3 Waskesew's.

E.2/11

29. Sunday. wind and weather as Yesterday. Travelled none: got two Wolves from my traps: Indians killed 2 Moose.

30 December 1754
B.239/a/40

ye 30th Monday Blows hard att SW^t and fine Weath^r this day pitcht our tent 6 Miles further to ye Northward, there being plenty of Beaver housses, Levell Land and Small willows, killed one Buffuloe.

E.2/6

30 Mond^y a Continuance of blowing, freezing, snowing & Drifting weather; got 2 wolves from my traps; travelled NE. 6 miles; level land, Creeks, and willow's; killed one Buffalow.

E.2/11

30 Monday. A Continuance of blowing, snowing & freezing weather: Got 2 Wolves from my traps: Travelled 4 Miles NE: Level land, Creeks, & Willows: killed one Buffalo: I supply them with powder very sparingly, one charge at a time; the bullet we oftentimes get again.

31 December 1754
B.239/a/40

ye 31st Tuesday fine weather wind SW^t killed 2 Beaver.

E.2/6

31 Tuesd^y wind WbN. and hard freezing weather; fine walking; all hands looking out for Beaver Houses, seed but few; killed 2 Beaver.

E.2/11

31. Tuesday. Wind WbN. hard freezing weather: killed 2 Beaver; very numerous hereabout: I did speak again to kill Beaver; but to no purpose.

1 January 1755
    B.239/a/40
Jan^ry ye 1st 1755 Wednesday fine weather wind SWbS travelled none these 2 days past, killed one Beaver & 2 Waskesw^s.
    E.2/6
1755 Jany 1 Wednesd^y frosty weather, with snow at times, wind WbN. killed one Beaver and 2 Waskesews.
    E.2/11
1755 Jany 1st Wednesday. Wind WbN. and freezing weather: Indians killed one Beaver and 2 Waskesew. I wear A Buffalo skin pair of Shoes with the hair inwards.

2 January 1755
    B.239/a/40
ye 2^d Thursday blowed hard att NE^t all this day travelled none killed one Beaver, 3 Ind^s tents Came and pitcht along with us, Bob came along with them
    E.2/6
2 Thursd^y blowed hard at NE. freezes hard, day and night; travelled none, 3 tents of Indians Came and Joined us; killed one Beaver.
    E.2/11
2. Thursday. Wind NE: a strong gale with freezing weather: Three tents of Indians joined us: killed one Beaver.

3 January 1755
    B.239/a/40
ye 3^d Friday fine weather wind att W^t travelled none but went a hunting, and in one plain see near 300 Waskesw^s, there was 5 Ind^s & and my self had all a Shott but killed none.
    E.2/6
3 Frid^y moderate weather, wind W. travelled none, went a hunting with the Men, killed a great many Waskesews; seed above 300 feeding in one plain; the Ice is 4 Inches thick on the ponds, and the ground Covered with snow, but not so deep as to use snow shoes, at night a grand feast &c.
    E.2/11
3. Friday. Wind West and moderate weather: Ice 4 Inches thick on the ponds; and the ground covered with snow, but not so deep as to wear

Snow-shoes: Indians killed 6 Waskesew, Saw above 300 feeding in one plain. I plainly observe all our Traders must be supplyed with Furs from the Archithinue & Asinepoet Natives; as the people that joined us had not Beaver skins to cloath them.

4 January 1755

B.239/a/40

the 4th Saturday wind NE^t blows hard pitcht 10 M NEbN, Levell Land and willows with ponds of water, fell a great deal of Snow.

E.2/6

1755 Jany 4 Saturd^y blowing strong with snow, wind SE. Women brought home the meat killed yesterday, travelled none.

E.2/11

4. Saturday. Wind SE a strong gale with snow. At night we had a grand feast with Drumming, Dancing &c.

5 January 1755

B.239/a/40

Jan^{ry} ye 5th Sunday fine weather wind WbS travelled none, the Ind^s went to kill Beaver, and I went a hunting, killed one Waskesu.

E.2/6

5 Sunday moderate weather, wind WbS. freezes now less or more night and day, took my departure from winter Creek, and travelled NEbN. 10 miles level land and willows; in the Evening came to a Creek and large tall woods

E.2/4

5. Sunday moderate freezing weather wind W.B.N. travelled N.E.B.N. 10 miles level land and willows, in the evening came to a creek and large poplar trees.

E.2/11

5. Sunday. Wind WbN. and moderate weather:

6 January 1755

B.239/a/40

ye 6 Monday fine weather wind att S^o this day killed Severall Beaver.

E.2/6

6 Mond^y snowed all day, wind WbS. travelled none, killed 7 Beaver.

E.2/4

6. Monday blowing snowing weather wind W.B.S. killed 7 beaver.

E.2/11

1755 Jany 6th Monday. Wind WbS: snowed all last night: killed 7 Beaver: Feasting, Dancing, Drumming & Conjuring.

7 January 1755
      B.239/a/40
yᵉ 7ᵗʰ Tuesday fine weather and the wind att South pitcht our tent 12
M NEbNᵒ Levell Land and Brusshy willows. this day killed 2 Waskeswˢ
and 6 Beaver.
      E.2/6
7 Tuesdʸ sharp weather, wind S. took my departure from poplar Creek,
and travelled 12 miles NEbN. level Land with willows, in the evening
came to a Creek where were plenty of Wejacks; killed 2 Waskesews.
      E.2/4
7. Tuesday sharp freezing weather wind S. travelled 12 miles N.E.B.N.
level land and willows, in the evening came to a creek where are plenty of wejacks, killed 2 waskesews.
      E.2/11
7. Tuesday. Wind South and sharp frosty weather: Travelled 6 Miles
NEbN. Level land, & Willows: In the Evening came to a Creek where
were plenty of Wejacks: killed 2 Waskesew.

8 January 1755
      B.239/a/40
yᵉ 8ᵗʰ Wednesday fine weather and the wind SWᵗ Killed severall Beaver.
      E.2/6
8 Wednesdʸ Clear moderate weather, wind W. travelled none, killed
several Beaver.
      E.2/4
8 Wednesday clear moderate weather wind W. Indians killed several beaver.
      E.2/11
8. Wednesday. Wind West, and clear moderate weather: Indians killed
several Beaver.—

9 January 1755
      B.239/a/40
yᵉ 9ᵗʰ Thursday fine weather wind NEᵗ this day pitcht 10 M NEbN Levell Land with Brush & poplar this day 2 tents Came and pitcht along
with us, killed 2 Waskeswˢ and Severall Beaver.
      E.2/6
9 Thursdʸ Closs snowy weather, wind NE. took my departure from
Wejack Creek and travelled 10 miles NEbN. level Land, with ledges of
brush and poplar; killed two Waskesews; in the Evening two tents of
Indians Joined us, we are now a large Gang.
      E.2/4
9 Thursday closs snowing weather wind N.E. travelled 10 miles
N.E.B.N. level land with ledges of brush-wood and poplar; Indians

killed 2 waskesews, in the evening we were joined by two more tents of our trading Indians, they have as few furs as the others that came before.

E.2/11

9. Thursday. Wind NE and snowy weather: Travelled 5 Miles NEbN. Level land with ledges of Brush wood & poplar: Indians killed 2 Waskesew: In the Evening we were joined by 2 more tents of our Traders, they have as few furs as the others.

10 January 1755

B.239/a/40

yᵉ 10ᵗʰ Friday wind att Nᵒ Kill'd one Waskesw & 4 Beaver, I went a hunting, Saw a Large black Bear but I did not Like him, he made a Strong Roaring and Lookt hard att me, he made off and I was not Sorry for it, for their were no Indians nigh me by 6 or 7 M.

E.2/6

10 Fridʸ wind N. and Cold weather, travelled none; Women knitting snow shoes; killed one Moose and 6 Waskesews; I seed a large black Bear, but did not Chuse to be concerned with Him, as none of the Men was with me, He lookt hard at me and went His way, Indians afterwards killed Him.

E.2/4

10 @11. Friday @ Saturday cold freezing weather winds N. and N.W. travelled none, killed 2 beaver; the winter is now set in in good earnest.

E.2/11

10. Friday. wind North and cold weather: Indians killed one moose & 6 Waskesew: Women knitting Snow-shoes.

11 January 1755

B.239/a/40

yᵉ 11ᵗʰ Saturday fine weather wind NWᵗ travelled none this day killed 2 Beaver.

E.2/6

1755 Janʸ 11 Saturdʸ moderate freezing weather, wind N.W. travelled none, killed 2 Beaver; the winter is set in, in earnest.

E.2/11

1755 Janʸ 11ᵗʰ. Saturday. Wind NW. moderate freezing weather with snow: Travelled none: killed 2 Beaver: The winter is set in in good earnest so that we change from leather to Fur cloathing: plenty of Creeks a small distance from where we now are.

12 January 1755
> B.239/a/40

ye 12th Sunday wind as before, this day pitcht our tents 12 M WbS, the Buffuloe & Waskesw^s being Gone that way Levell & willows all the way; this day killed 4 Beaver, and one Buffuloe.
> E.2/6

12 Sund^y wind and weather as yesterday, travelled 12 miles WbS. the Buffalow and Waskesews being gone that way; killed 4 Beaver and one Buffalow; level Land, willows and Creeks.
> E.2/4

1756 Jan^ry 12th Sunday cold weather wind N.W. travelled 12 miles W.B.S. the buffaloe and waskesews being gone this way, killed one buffaloe and 4 beaver, level land, plenty of creeks and beaver houses.
> E.2/11

12. Sunday. Wind and weather as Yesterday. Travelled 6 Miles WbS; The Buffalo & Waskesew being gone that way: Killed one Buffalo & four Beaver: Level land, plenty of Creeks, & Beaver houses.

13 January 1755
> B.239/a/40

1755 Jan^ry ye 13th Monday fine weather wind att West, travelled nor nor killed any thing to day.
> E.2/6

13 Mond^y fine weather, wind W. travelled none smoaking &c.
> E.2/4

13 @ 15. Monday @ Wednesday winds from the W. to N.W. and moderate freezing weather, killed 6 buffaloe and 7 beaver.
> E.2/11

13. @ 15. Monday. Tuesday & Wednesday: Winds Westerly and moderate weather: Travelled none. Indians employed hunting: killed 6 Buffalo; Saw many going Westward.

14 January 1755
> B.239/a/40

ye 14th Tuesday wind and Weather as Yesterday, went to Look for Buffuloe and Beaver housses, see 6 Beaver housses and the tracks of sever^ll Buffuloe & Waskesw^s.
> E.2/6

14 Tuesd^y wind and weather as yesterday, travelled none, went to look for Buffalow and Beaver, found no Beaver Houses, seed Buffalow tracks all going westward.

15 January 1755

  B.239/a/40

yᵉ 15ᵗʰ Wednesday fine weather the wind att Wᵗ this day pitcht 8 M SWᵗ Killed nothing these 2 days.

  E.2/6

15 Wednesdʸ wind NW. travelled none, killed 6 Buffalow.

16 Janaury 1755

  B.239/a/40

yᵉ 16ᵗʰ Thursday wind and weather as Yesterdʸ Killed 6 Beaver & 1 Buffuloe.

  E.2/6

16 Thursdʸ wind and weather as yesterday. travelled 8 miles S.W. killed 6 Beaver and one Buffalow.

  E.2/4

16. Thursday wind N.W. and moderate weather travelled 8 miles S.W. killed 6 beaver and one buffaloe.

  E.2/11

16. Thursday. Wind NW and strong freezing weather: Travelled 4 Miles SW: killed 6 Beaver & one Buffalo.

17 January 1755

  B.239/a/40

yᵉ 17ᵗʰ Friday wind att Wᵗ this day pitcht 10 M to yᵉ westward, here we travell as the Cattle Goes, fell a Little Snow, this part of yᵉ Country is nothing to Compare to York Fort for Cold, having had nothing on my feet but one pair of Buffuloe Shoes, and a thin peice of flannell, the snow is about 6 Inches deep and the Ice about the Same thickness.

  E.2/6

17 Fridʸ blowing freezing weather, wind W. travelled 10 miles S.W. we travell as the Cattle goes, fine level land & no woods worth notice; this part of the Country is not to be Compared to York Fort for cold, have had nothing on my feet yet but one pair Buffalow shoes with the hair inwards, and a thin flannel sock, the snow about 6 Inches deep, and the Ice about the same thickness; the falls on the Creeks not yet frozen over.

  E.2/4

17. Friday blowing freezing weather wind W. travelled S.W. 10 miles after the buffaloe, level land and no woods, the snow 6 inches deep, and the ice about the same thickness.

  E.2/11

17. Friday. Wind West: a Strong gale: Travelled SW. 5 Miles after the Buffalo: Level land, & no Woods. The Snow 6 inches deep & the ice rather thicker.

18 January 1755

B.239/a/40

yᵉ 18ᵗʰ Saturday Blowed hard wind att NEᵗ travelled none, went a hunting killed 3 Buffuloe and 2 Moose.

E.2/6

18 Saturdʸ blowed strong with snow, wind N.E. travelled none, killed 3 Buffalow and 2 Moose, wolves numerous.

E.2/4

18 @ 21. Saturday @ Tuesday winds from the N.E. to N.W. and variable weather. I observe the bad weather is of no continuance, and the cold is nothing like so severe as at York Fort; I have had nothing on my feet yet but a flannel sock and buffalo skin shoe with the hair inwards.

E.2/11

1755 Janʸ 18 @ 21. Saturday. Sunday. Monday & Tuesday. Winds from WNW to NNW and freezing weather, with snow at times: Indians employed killing Moose & Buffalo: Wolves numerous: Every Evening the Natives are employed dancing &c. I have had nothing on my feet as yet but a thin flannel sock, and a Buffalo skin shoe with the hair inwards: My Horse begins to lose flesh.

19 January 1755

B.239/a/40

yᵉ 19ᵗʰ Sunday fine weather wind att West, travelled none went for yᵉ Buffuloe & Moose killed Yesterday.

E.2/6

1755 Janʸ 19 Sunday moderate weather, wind N.W. travelled none, Women went for the meat, killed yesterday.

20 January 1755

B.239/a/40

Janʳʸ yᵉ 20ᵗʰ Monday fine weather wind WbN travelled None, I went a hunting killed a She Buffuloe.

E.2/6

20 Mondʸ moderate weather, wind WbN. travelled none; I killed a Buffalow closs by the tents.

21 January 1755

B.239/a/40

yᵉ 21ˢᵗ Tuesday fine weather wind att West, this day the Indˢ killed 2 Moose.

E.2/6

21 Tuesdʸ moderate weather, wind W. killed 6 Moose, travelled none; my Horse begins to lose his flesh.

22 January 1755
　　B.239/a/40
yᵉ 22ᵈ Wednesday fine weather wind att West. this day pitcht 12 M
NEbNᵒ Level Land, crossed a Branch of Waskesu River, the Indˢ killed
4 Buffuloe.
　　E.2/6
22 Wednesdʸ fine weather, wind W. pitched 12 miles N.E.b.N. level
Land, Crossed a branch of Wykesew River; killed 4 Buffalow.
　　E.2/4
22. Wednesday wind W. and moderate weather travelled 12 miles
N.E.B.N. level land, crossed a branch of waskesew river, killed 4 buffaloe.
　　E.2/11
22. Wednesday. Wind West and moderate weather: Travelled 6 Miles
NEbN: Level Land: crossed a branch of Waskesew River: Indians killed
4 Buffalo.

23 January 1755
　　B.239/a/40
yᵉ 23ᵈ Thursday fine weather wind West, went for the Meat killed Yesterday.
　　E.2/6
23 Thursdʸ moderate weather, wind W. Women brought the meat
killed yesterday.
　　E.2/4
23 @ 27. Thursday @ Monday winds variable from the W.B.S. to the N.
and moderate freezing weather with snow at times; Indians doing little more than feasting on fat buffaloe flesh.
　　E.2/11
23. @ 27. Thursday. Friday. Saturday. Sunday & Monday Winds from
West to North and moderate Weather with Snow at times: Travelled
none: Men feasting, and Women getting Grass for the Horses.

24 January 1755
　　B.239/a/40
yᵉ 24ᵗʰ Friday this day travelled none fine weather spent this day in
feasting.
　　E.2/6
24 Fridʸ moderate weather, wind W.bS. travelled none.

25 January 1755
　　B.239/a/40
yᵉ 25ᵗʰ Saturday fine weather wind SWbS. travelled none the Women
are knitting snow Shoes.

E.2/6

25 Saturd^y moderate weather, wind S.W.b.S. travelled none.

26 January 1755
    B.239/a/40

ye 26th Sunday a fine brease of wind att N^o travelled none, went for
Buffoloe killed Yesterday; I took ab^t 30 lb fatt of one side & hump of
one Buffaloe, to Lay by as a Reserve
    E.2/6

26 Sunday a fresh gale and cold snowy weather, wind N. Women
employed getting grass for the Horses.

27 January 1755
    B.239/a/40

ye 27th Monday fine weather wind att N^o travelled none, made myself
two Juniper Sledges, to hawl my things on, the Ind^s killed 3 Buffuloe.
    E.2/6

27 Mond^y moderate weather, wind N. Men feasting; all the Women
excepting the Cooks &c employed as yesterday.

28 January 1755
    B.239/a/40

the 28th Tuesday fine weather wind NWbN^o this day pitch 14 M to ye N
side of a Branch of Waskesw River, being all barren Land to ye SW^t as
farr as I Cowld see, this Branch is about 8 poles wide, and there is but
Little water, for the Ice Lyes on the Stones.
    E.2/6

28 Tuesd^y moderate weather, wind NW.bN. took my Departure from
Wykesew River branch, and travelled 14 miles WNW. level land, and
ledges of woods, Viz^t Birch, poplar Alder, Juniper and Cherry trees;
killed 3 Buffalow.
    E.2/4

1755 Jan^{ry} 28 Tuesday fine weather wind W. travelled 14 miles W.N.W.
level land and ledges of birch, poplar, juniper, ash, hasle, alder and
cherry trees; killed 3 buffaloe.
    E.2/11

28. Tuesday. Wind NWbN. and fine weather. Travelled 7 Miles WNW:
Level land & ledges of Birch, poplar, Juniper, Alder & Cherry trees:
Indians killed three Buffalo.

29 January 1755
    B.239/a/40

1755 Jan^{ry} ye 29th Wednesday fine weather the wind att S. this day travelled none went for the meat killed Yesterday, all the men making traps, here, being plenty of foxes and Wolves.

E.2/6

1755 Jany 29 Wednesd^y moderate weather, wind N.W. travelled N. 4 miles, came to 2 Creeks that were not yet froze over; killed 2 Moose and 2 Beaver.

E.2/4

29. Wednesday moderate weather wind N.W. travelled 4 miles N. passed 2 creeks that are not yet froze over; my horse loses his flesh; killed 2 moose and 2 beaver.

E.2/11

1755 Jany 29th Wednesday Wind NW. and moderate weather: Travelled 4 Miles North: passed two Creeks that are not frozen over: Indians killed 2 Moose and 2 Beaver.

30 January 1755

B.239/a/40

ye 30th Thursday fine weather wind att NE^t the Indians went to see if they Could see any of the other Ind^s, but Could see None, I wounded one Buffuloe.

E.2/6

30 Thursd^y moderate weather, wind NE. young Men went to look out for Indians, but met with none; I wounded a Buffalow.

E.2/4

30. Thursday fine weather wind N.E. women knitting snow-shoes and geting grass for my horse.

E.2/11

30. Thursday Wind NE and disagreeable weather: The Men went to look out for Indians; but found none: I wounded a Buffalo.

31 January 1755

B.239/a/40

ye 31st Friday fine weather wind att S. this day pitcht 6 Miles to ye N Side of the Branch of Waskesu River, Hills and dales and Ledges of Spruce trees, this day killed one Moose & 2 Buffuloe.

E.2/6

31 Frid^y fine weather, wind S. travelled N. 6 miles hills, dales, and ledges of fir trees; Crossed a branch of Wykesew River, killed one Moose and 2 Buffalow.

E.2/4

31. Friday fine weather wind S. travelled 6 miles N. hills, dales and ledges of fir trees, crossed a branch of waskesew river, killed 2 buffaloe and one moose.

E.2/11

31. Friday. Wind South and warm weather: Travelled 4 Miles North:
Hillocks, Dales, and ledges of Fir-trees: Crossed a branch of Waskesew
river: Indians killed a Moose & two Buffalo.

1 February 1755
B.239/a/40

Feb^{ry} ye 1st Saturday fine weathear wind NW^t went for the meat killed
Yesterday.

E.2/6

Feb^{ry} 1 Saturd^y fine weather, wind NW. Women brought the meat
killed yesterday; travelled none.

E.2/4

Feby 1st @ 3^d Saturday @ Monday fresh gales winds from S.W. to N.W.
with snow at times, Indians feasting and sweating &c, my horse feeds
on willow tops &c, we are joined by a French Leader named Wapenessew* who promises to go with me to the fort, he hath a great sway
amongst the Indians, commands above 20 canoes and is greatly taken
notice of by the French at Basquea house where he hath constantly
frequented; I presented him with a foot of brazile tobacco, a fire steel,
a knife and a little powder and shot.

*This man brings yearly to York Fort 20 canoes, hath the charge
of an Englishman, and is greatly esteemed by the Chief.

E.2/11

Feby 1st Saturday. Wind NW and freezing weather: Preparing Snow-
shoes: I have wore none yet: I made a few Steels for A French Leader
out of an old file.

2 February 1755
B.239/a/40

ye 2^d Sunday fine weather wind att SW^t. all hands Employed making
Sledges, I made 2 Steels, when they Liked them so well that I Could
have got good Custom, but I do not Like so much, for they think I do
nothing but Strive to please the women, which is ye Chiefest thing
that will Encourage the Ind^s to Come to trade.

E.2/6

2 Sunday Closs weather with snow, wind SW. all hands preparing snow
shoes, have wore none yet; I made two fire steels out of an old file, for
a French Leader, who promises to go with me to the Fort, He is a jolly,
stout, good natured Man, and carrys a great command amongst the
Natives; my Bedfellow (who slyly gives me information) informs me He
Commands 20 Canoes, and is much taken notice of by the French.

E.2/11

2. Sunday Wind SW. and close weather: The French Leader named Wappenessew* promises to go with me to the Fort: He hath a great sway among the Natives & is much esteemed by the French: I presented him with a little powder &c. Indians feasting, Smoaking, Dancing &c.

* This Man brings yearly to York Fort 20 Canoes & is greatly esteemed by the Natives and Factors.

3 February 1755

B.239/a/40

ye 3^d Monday Blows hard att NW^t went a hunting see the tracks of Severall Ind^s but no Game.

E.2/6

3 Mond^y blows hard at N.W. travelled none, seed the tracks of several Indians, but no game.

E.2/11

3. Monday. Wind NW a Strong gale with Snow: Indians Sweating &c.

4 February 1755

B.239/a/40

Feb^{ry} ye 4th Tuesday fine weather wind S^o this day pitcht 7 M farther to ye North side of the Branch of Waskesu River, Low Land, the most part Barren, here and there a Ledge of woods.

E.2/6

4 Tuesd^y moderate weather, wind N. pitched N. 7 miles to another branch of Wykesew River, barren land to the SW. as far as I could see, this branch is 8 poles wide, and shoal water, open in several places; the Horses feeds on willow tops, and spruce, like unto a Moose.

E.2/4

1756 Feby 4th Tuesday moderate weather wind N. travelled 7 miles N. to a branch of waskesew river, it is 8 poles wide, shoal water and open in many places; the land to the S.W. is quite barren as far as I can see.

E.2/11

4. Tuesday. Wind North and moderate weather: Travelled 4 Miles North to a branch of Waskesew river, this branch is 8 poles wide & shoal water & open places: The Horses feed on Willow-tops: the land SW is quite barren as far as I can see.

5 February 1755

B.239/a/40

ye 5th Wednesday Good weather Wind NW^t killed 2 moose & 2 Beaver, Cross'd 2 Small Creeks, where the water has not been froze over this Winter.

E.2/6

1755 Feby 5 Wednesd^y moderate weather, wind S. travelled none, all hands trapping Foxes and Wolves.

E.2/4

5 @ 9. Wednesday @ Sunday winds S. and S.W. and clear sharp weather, all hands trapping wolves and foxes, killed 2 moose and one buffaloe, dined and smoaked with the French leader.

E.2/11

5 @ 9. Wednesday. Thursday. Friday. Saturday. & Sunday. Wind from South to West and moderate weather: All hands trapping Foxes: I walked in Snow-shoes for the first time this winter: in the Evening Smoaked and feasted with the French Leader.

6 February 1755

B.239/a/40

ye 6th Thursday wind as before, went for the meat killed Yesterday.

E.2/6

6 Thursd^y wind and weather as yesterday, travelled none, all hands hunting and trapping, good luck, wolves & Foxes plenty, killed 4 Moose and 2 Buffalow; gave the French Leader (named Wapenessew)* two charges of powder & 2 ball; Walked in snow shoes for the first time, this winter.

*This Man brings yearly to York Fort 20 Canoes, He hath the Charge of an Englishman, and is greatly Esteemed by ye Chief.

7 February 1755

B.239/a/40

ye 7th Friday fine weather wind SW^t. the Ind^s killed 2 Moose and a Buffuloe.

E.2/6

7 Frid^y wind S. and moderate weather, all hands employed as yesterday, killed 2 Moose and one Buffalow.

8 February 1755

B.239/a/40

ye 8th Saturday wind as Yesterday went for the meat.

E.2/6

8 Saturd^y wind SW. and moderate weather, Men trapping, and Women brought the meat.

9 February 1755

B.239/a/40

ye 9th Sunday fine weather wind att S° Lay by.

E.2/6

9 Sunday moderate weather, wind SW employed as before.

10 February 1755

B.239/a/40

ye 10th Monday wind as before, this day pitcht 8 M NW^t from the Branch, fine Levell Land and tall woods, this day Came 4 Ind^n men brought ye news of 30 Earchithinues, & 7 of our Ind^s were killed, and that they were going to Warr again, for they Came away to Acquaint all the Ind^s of it, I have Some Reason to think it is true, because I see the Skulps of some Earthidinues, that they killed the Year before.

E.2/6

10 Mond^y wind and weather as yesterday, took my Departure from Wykesew River branch, and travelled 8 miles NW. level Land and tall woods; met 4 Indian Men who told us that the far distant Archithinues had killed 30 nigh Archithinues, and 7 of our Indians, and that they were going to war again, and so left us.

E.2/4

10. Monday wind SW and warm weather, travelled 8 miles N.W. level land and tall woods, all hands walked in snow-shoes for the first time, spoke with 4 men who told us that the far distant Archithinues had killed 30 nigh Archithinues and 7 of our Indians, and that they were going to war again, and so left us.

E.2/11

10. Monday. Wind SW and moderate weather: Travelled 4 Miles NW. Level land & tall woods: Spoke with 4 Indian Men who told us that the far distant Archithinue Natives had killed 30 of the nigh ones & 7 of our Indians.

11 February 1755

B.239/a/40

ye 11th Tuesday fine weather wind att S^o travelled none, the Ind^s made Severall Sleds, and I made myself one.

E.2/6

11 Tuesd^y wind S and a fresh gale with snow and drift at times; travelled none.

E.2/4

11. Tuesday wind S. and a fresh gale with drift and snow, travelled none.

E.2/11

1755 Feby 11th @ 27th Tuesday the eleventh to the 27th Employed Travelling and sometimes laying by killing Buffalo, Moose &c in a pleasant & plentiful country, our Course towards the NE: We were joined by different tribes of Natives, who yearly visited our Settlements, they brought with them Several Archithinue Women & Children Captives, with many Scalps quite green: We are Now at Archithinue lake, about one mile broad and a good days journey in length; with tall woods on both sides, mostly Pines, the largest I have yet seen.

12 February 1755
B.239/a/40

1755 Feb^ry ye 12th Wednesday fine weather wind att S^o pitcht 10 M SE^t thick Ledges of woods and Brushy plains, I killed 2 Moose.
E.2/6

12 Wednesd^y moderate weather wind S. travelled SE. 10 miles; thick ledges of woods and brushy plains; killed 2 Moose; and 4 Buffallow.
E.2/4

12. Wednesday moderate weather wind S. travelled 10 miles S.E. thick ledges of woods and brushy plains, killed 2 buffaloe.

13 February 1755
B.239/a/40

ye 13th Thursday fine weather wind SE^t travelled none went for the Meat killed Yesterday.
E.2/6

1755 Feby 13 Thursd^y moderate weather, wind SW travelled none.
E.2/4

13. Thursday wind S.W. travelled none, moderate weather.

14 February 1755
B.239/a/40

ye 14th Friday fine Weather Wind West, this day pitcht 10 M SE^t, here is very tall woods, and Levell Land, past by 2 Running Creecks of water, we Crossed the other Ind^s tracks, the Ind^s killed 3 Moose and three Buffuloe.
E.2/6

14 Frid^y moderate weather, wind W. travelled 10 miles SE. lofty woods and level Land, Crossed the tracks of several Indians; but we are not afraid, for by their marks on the sticks, and other signals in their way, they are known to be Friends; killed 3 Moose and 2 Buffalow.
E.2/4

14. Friday moderate weather wind W. travelled 10 miles S.E. level land and lofty woods, killed 3 buffaloe.

15 February 1755
>B.239/a/40

ye 15th Saturday fine weather wind att S^o made severall Sleds to day went for the meat killed Yesterday.
>E.2/6

15 Saturd^y moderate weather, wind S. travelled none; Women brought the meat killed yesterday.
>E.2/4

1756 Feby 15 @ 16th Saturday @ Sunday moderate weather wind S. & S.W. feasting, sweating and dancing &c; here are the largest pines I have yet seen, fit for ships masts.

16 February 1755
>B.239/a/40

ye 16th Sunday wind att SW^t and fine weather travelled none.
>E.2/6

16 Sunday wind S.W. and fine weather, travelled none, thawed a little on the leeward side the tent; a fine Country.

17 February 1755
>B.239/a/40

ye 17th Monday wind and Weather as Yesterday, pitcht 12 M SEbS, here is ye Largest pine I have Yett Seen, fitt for masts of Larges Ships.
>E.2/6

17 Mond^y wind and weather as yesterday. travelled 12 miles S.E.b.S. level Land with Ledges of the largest pine trees I have yet seen, fit for Ships masts.
>E.2/4

17. Monday wind S.W. and moderate weather, travelled 12 miles S.E.B.S. level land with ledges of woods.

18 February 1755
>B.239/a/40

ye 18th Tuesday fine warm Weather wind att SWbS. this day killed 2 Moose and 3 Beaver.
>E.2/6

18 Tuesd^y moderate weather, wind SWbS. travelled none, killed 3 Moose and 2 Buffalow.
>E.2/4

18 @ 19. Tuesday @ Wednesday variable weather, winds S.W.B.S. & S.W. travelled none, killed 3 moose and 2 buffaloe, a fine plentyfull country; thaws in the middle of the day.

19 February 1755
  B.239/a/40
Feb^ry ye 19th Wednesday fine weather wind SW^t travelled none, the Ind^s are Employed fitting of Sleds.
  E.2/6
19 Wednesd^y wind SW and a fresh gale with snow. travelled none, Women brought the meat killed yesterday.

20 February 1755
  B.239/a/40
ye 20th Thursday wind as before, this day pitcht 16 M NE^t to ye far-thesst Branch of the River, Levell Land and Ledges of pine and Birch, killed 2 Moose and Buffaloe.
  E.2/6
20 Thursd^y wind and weather as yesterday, travelled 16 miles NE. to the northernmost branch of Wykesew River, level Land with ledges of pine and birch trees, killed 2 Moose and one Buffalow.
  E.2/4
20. Thursday snowy weather wind S.W. travelled 16 miles N.E. to the N. branch of waskesew river, level land with ledges of large pine and birch trees; killed one buffaloe and 2 moose.

21 February 1755
  B.239/a/40
ye 21st Friday fine weather, wind att NW^t this day pitcht 17 M NE^t Lev-ell Land and thick woods, this day 2 Indian tents was pitch beside us, brought 3 Earchithinues they had taken in Warr, and 3 Scalps.
  E.2/6
21 Frid^y wind WbN. and fine weather, travelled none.
  E.2/4
21. Friday fine weather wind W.B.N. travelled none.

22 February 1755
  B.239/a/40
ye 22^d Saturday fine weather wind WbN^o travelled none to day.
  E.2/6
1755 Feby 22 Saturd^y moderate weather, wind NW. travelled 17 miles N.E. level land, and thick woods; two tents of Indians came to us, brought 4 Archithinue Women, and 4 scalps they had taken at war.
  E.2/4
22. Saturday moderate weather wind N.W. travelled 17 miles N.E. level land and thick woods, two tents of Indians came to us, brought 4 Archithinue slave girls.*

* Anno Domini 1765 one of them was murthered at York Fort gates by a home Indian in a fit of jealousy.

23 February 1755
B.239/a/40
ye 23^d Sunday wind as before, this day pitcht 15 M NE^t Levell Land and fine Woods all ye way, Killed one Moose.
E.2/6
23 Sunday wind and weather as yesterday. travelled 15 miles NE. level Land and fine woods, killed several Moose.
E.2/4
23. Sunday moderate weather wind W. travelled 15 miles N.E. level land and fine woods; killed several moose.

24 February 1755
B.239/a/40
ye 24th Monday wind and weather the same, Lay by, ye Ind^s Employed in fitting of Sleds travelled 20 M NE^t two tents of Ind^s Came to us;
E.2/6
24 Mond^y thawing weather, wind W. travelled none, two tents of Indians came to us I smoakt with their Leader, they had not been at war, but killing Beaver, they have a great Many skins.
E.2/4
24. Monday thawing weather wind W. travelled none; two tents of Indians came to us, smoaked with the leader, who said he always traded at Churchill.

25 February 1755
B.239/a/40
ye 25th Tuesday fine weather wind SW^t. pitcht 17 M NEbE^t hills & dales & thick woods, this day Came 7 tents of Ind^s to us brought 6 Earchithinues to us alive and the Scalps of 4 more.
<ye 27 Thursday fine weather wind West>
E.2/6
25 Tuesd^y fine weather, wind SW travelled 17 miles N.E.b.N. the Land hills, dales and tall woods.
E.2/4
1756 Feby 25th Tuesday fine weather wind SW. travelled 17 miles N.E.B.N. hills dales and tall woods.

26 February 1755
B.239/a/40
1755 Feb^ry ye 26th Wednesday fine weather wind as before this day pitcht 20 M NEbE^t the Land hills & dales and tall woods.

E.2/6

26 Wednesd^y wind and weather, as yesterday. travelled 20 miles NEbE, Land as yesterday, came 7 tents of Indians, brought 2 Archithinue Boys and 5 girls. and 4 scalps they had taken at war.

E.2/4

26. Wednesday wind & weather as yesterday travelled 20 miles N.E.B.E. land as yesterday, came to 7 tents of Indians, brought from war two Archithinue boys, 3 girls and 4 scalps.

27 February 1755

B.239/a/40

ye 27th Thursday fine weather wind W^t pitcht 15 M NE^t ye Land the same, this day pitcht our tents in Earchithinue Sokahegan, it is a mile wide and 16 M in Length.

E.2/6

27 Thursd^y moderate weather, wind W. Land as before, Came to Archithinue Lake, one mile, wide & 16 miles long, tall woods on both sides.

E.2/4

27. Thursday moderate weather wind W. travelled 8 miles N.E.B.E. land as before, came to Archithinue lake, one mile wide and a days journey in length, and tall woods on both sides.

28 February 1755

B.239/a/40

ye 28th Friday fine Weather wind NE^t travelled none, the Ind^s killed two Moose and three Buffuloe.

E.2/6

28 Frid^y Closs snowy weather, wind NE. travelled none.

E.2/4

28 @ March 1st Friday @ Saturday winds variable between the W. and N.E. with snow at times, feasting &c, the scalps were displayed on long poles round the tents and the Captives, boys and girls, were given away to one another; they offered me a boy and girl which I refused, one of the Captive girls aged about 17 years was knocked on the head with a hatchet by the mans wife to whom she belonged, no notice was taken as such game is common amongst them; killed 2 moose and 3 buffaloe.

E.2/11

28. Friday. Wind West and moderate weather: Travelled 4 Miles NEbE then put up to feast &c. The Scalps were displayed on long poles round the tents; & the Captives, Boys & Girls, were given away as pre-

sents to one another. They presented to me a Boy & Girl; which I declined accepting of in as modest a manner as possible.

1 March 1755
B.239/a/40
March ye 1st 1755 Saturday fine weather wind SW^t. Lay by went for the meat killed Yesterday.
E.2/6
March 1 Saturd^y wind SW. and sharp weather, travelled none, killed 3 Buffalow and 2 Moose; the scalps were displayed on long poles round the tents, they offered me a Slave Boy and Girl which I refused; they appear to be kind enough to them, especially the Men.
E.2/11
March 1st Saturday. Wind NW and Sharp weather: killed 3 Buffalo & 2 Moose: A Captive Girl aged about 17 years was knocked on the head with a Tomahauk by a Man's wife in a fit of jealousy: No notice was taken as such game is common amongst them: the unfortunate Girl had been presented to the Murtherer's husband yesterday.

2 March 1755
B.239/a/40
ye 2^d Sunday wind as Yesterday, pitcht 20 M NEbE^t Levell Land and tall woods all ye way, Crossed 2 Creecks.
E.2/6
1755 March 2 Sunday moderate weather, wind SW. travelled 20 miles NEbE level land, and tall woods, Crossed two Creeks.
E.2/4
2. Sunday wind S.E. and moderate weather, travelled 20 miles N.E.B.E. level land and lofty woods, passed 2 creeks.
E.2/11
2 @ 3. Sunday & Monday. Winds in the SE. quarter and moderate weather: Travelled 20 Miles towards the NE: Level land; tall woods; passed two Creeks and crossed another branch of Waskesew river.

3 March 1755
B.239/a/40
ye 3^d Monday wind the same, travelled 20 M NE^t here we Came to a Large Creeck or Branch of Waskesu River, Levell Land and thick Woods all the way have killed nothing these 2 days past.
E.2/6
3 Mond^y wind and weather as yesterday. travelled 20 miles N.E. level Land, and thick woods, came to a Large Creek which the Indians tells me is a branch of Wykesew River.

E.2/4

3. Monday wind &c as yesterday travelled 20 miles N.E. level land and thick woods, came to another branch of waskesew river.

4 March 1755

B.239/a/40

ye 4th Tuesday fine weather wind NW^t travelled on the, the water Runs over the Ice, so that our Sleds Rather Swam then hawled, on the Ice, for 15 M the banks are high, and tall woods, we killed nothing to day.

E.2/6

4 Tuesd^y fine weather, wind N.W. travelled 15 miles NE. on the River, the water running on the Ice in places; high banks and tall woods.

E.2/4

4. Tuesday fine weather wind N.W. travelled 15 miles N.E. on the river, the water running on the ice, high banks and lofty woods.

E.2/11

4. Tuesday. Wind NW and moderate weather: Travelled 7 Miles NE on the river: the Water running over the ice in places: High banks of tall woods.

5 March 1755

B.239/a/40

March ye 5th Wednesday fine weather wind SW^t we travelled on the River 10 M here we see to Leave our goods and go to hunt, for we Can get nothing here.

E.2/6

5 Wednesd^y fine weather, wind SW, thaws much, travelled on the River NE. 10 miles, our sleds rather floated then hauled; the River & banks as yesterday.

E.2/4

5. Wednesday fine weather wind S.W. travelled 15 miles N.E. on the river, it thaws so much that our sleds are in the water all the way; banks as yesterday.

E.2/11

5. Wednesday. Wind SW and warm weather: Travelled 5 Miles NE on the river: it thaws very much; our Sleds in the water most part of the way: the banks as Yesterday.

6 March 1755

B.239/a/40

ye 6th Thursday fine weather wind SW^t made all ready to go a hunting, but they have neither powder nor shott, so that all are att me for to give them some, I told them it was my own and that all this winter my

Ammunition had killed provisions for 30 Ind^s and that I would give them none.

E.2/6

6 Thursd^y fine weather, wind SW. the Indians Employed securing their furs on stages; in order to go a hunting, nothing to be got here, or at least not sufficient to maintain such a large body of people.

E.2/4

6 @ April 22^d Thursday @ Tuesday winds from the S. to N.W. the weather for the most part moderate, and when we had blowing weather it was of no continuance; by the middle of april the snow all gone and creeks and ponds broke open, as this place is a rendezvous for the Indians to build their canoes and buy their goods from the Aseenepoets, which they have done notwithstanding I have done my endeavour to get the Aseenepoets down with their goods, I am only able to get 12 canoes of them more than what yearly visits York Fort and Churchill; they are a great many of them building canoes here, half of whom trades with the French at Baskquea house, and the other French houses; we have been employed, the young men in geting provisions, and the old men in building canoes, which are now finished, and only waits the breaking up of the river.

E.2/11

6. Thursday. Wind & Weather as Yesterday: Employed securing their Furs from Water, in order to hunt, Game being scarce here.

7 March 1755

B.239/a/40

ye 7th Friday fine weather wind NW^t, all the Ind^s pitcht for to get provisions, asked me why I would not Go with them, I told them I would stay here and hunt for myself, so one of the young Men told me he would stay with me, and go a hunting.

E.2/6

7 Frid^y fine weather, wind NW. all the Natives unpitched and went different ways in search of food; myself and Family, Viz^t 3 Men and 9 Women and Children, are resolved to stay here if we can get any food; before the Natives went away I was plagued with them begging my powder and shot; I gave to the French Leader and other Leaders what I could spare, and they all promised to come and build Canoes, and go with me to York Fort.

E.2/11

1755 March 7th Friday. Wind NW and fine weather: Indians pitched different ways in search of food: Myself and Tent mates are to continue here if we can procure food: We are twelve in number; three men,

Nine women & Children: What Ammunition I had I gave to those I
hope will join me, and proceed to York Fort in May next.

8 March 1755
> **B.239/a/40**

y[e] 8th Saturday fine weather wind att NW[t] this day went a hunting,
and the Indian he being acquainted with the Country and a very Good
hunter, gave him my gun and I took to My Bow & Arrows, and being
But a Learner they gave me good Encouragem[t] to Learn, they are all
all Employed in fitting their Bows and Arrows, this day we killed one
Bufflow & wounded another, so we have plenty for we are but 8 in family, 6 Women and 2 Men.
> **E.2/6**

March 8 Saturd[y] wind NW. and hard freezing weather, with snow,
repairing our snow shoes, and sleds; my Horse is very thin, but his
worst times are past for this season.
> **E.2/11**

8. Saturday. Wind NW and hard freezing weather: Men & Women
repairing Snow Shoes and Sleds: My Horse is now very lean.

9 March 1755
> **B.239/a/40**

y[e] 9th Sunday fine weather wind att S[o] went for the Bufflow, and killed
one Moose
> **E.2/6**

9 Sunday fine weather, wind S. went a hunting, killed one Buffalow
and one Moose.
> **E.2/11**

9. @ 12. Sunday. Monday. Tuesday. Wednesday. Winds Variable: Men employed hunting, killed several Moose: We live well the provisions being good.

10 March 1755
> **B.239/a/40**

1755 March y[e] 10th Monday fine weather wind att N[o] this day made 2
pair of snow Shoes, my partner went a hunting killed one Moose.
> **E.2/6**

10 Mond[y] Closs weather wind N. went a hunting, killed a Moose,
women brought the meat.

11 March 1755
> **B.239/a/40**

y[e] 11th Tuesday fine hott weather wind att S[o] went for y[e] Moose my
partner killed Yesterday.

E.2/6

11 Tuesd^y warm weather, wind S. killed a Moose, we go on very well, my two Companions are good Men.

12 March 1755
B.239/a/40

ye 12th Wednesday wind as before, the women are Employed in Knitting our Snow Shoes.

E.2/6

12 Wednesd^y wind and weather as yesterday. Women brought the meat.

13 March 1755
B.239/a/40

ye 13th Thursday fine weather wind W^t this day Came 2 Ind^s brought severall Beaver Skins, to trade powder and Shott, I told them they all trade with french, and they gave them Little or nothing for their goods, they said that was true and that if I would give them a Little for their Skins, they would go See the Govr and Carry all their goods, I gave Each 2 Loads of powder, and shott and told them to take Care of their Goods, and Carry them to ye fortt, where there are plenty of sorts.

E.2/6

13 Thursd^y fine weather, wind W. two young Indian Men in the French interest, brought me 12 Beaver skins to trade for powder and shot; I told them they trade with the French, who gives them little or nothing for their furs, they said that was truth, I gave them 3 Charges of powder and ball, and told them to take care of their furs and go with me to the Fort where they would get powder &c and be kindly used, they promised that they would.

E.2/11

13. Thursday. Wind West and moderate weather: Two Young Natives in the french interest brought 12 Beaver skins to trade with me for Ammunition; I gave them a little & told them to go down with me to York Fort with their furs, where they would receive more goods for them in barter, than they did from the French: They gave me fair promises.

14 March 1755
B.239/a/40

ye 14th Friday fine weather wind att West, this day and all Last night a violent Pain in my head, so that I Can hardly see out of my Eyes, a great Cold with it, and att present very much out of order;

E.2/6

14 Frid.^y fine weather, wind W. very much out of order with a pain in my head.

E.2/11

1755 March 14 @ 16th Friday. Saturday. & Sunday. Wind from South to West and variable weather: Indians hunting, very good success: Myself hath been out of order with a Head-ack: Several Indians came begging powder but I gave them none; as I have only two pound weight remaining.

15 March 1755

     B.239/a/40

March ye 15th Saturday fine weather and the wind SW^t this day much the same as yesterday, very much out of order.

     E.2/6

15 Saturd.^y fine weather, wind SW. it thaws very much, still out of order.

16 March 1755

     B.239/a/40

ye 16th Sunday this day very much out of order, came one Indian for more powder, and Shott, I gave him none, for in Short have not above one Measure and one half for my Self, and that when I grow better, intend to take care to kill provisions for myself and family.

     E.2/6

1755 March 16 Sunday moderate weather, wind W. one Indian came for powder, gave Him none, as I have but 1½ lb left; still out of order.

17 March 1755

     B.239/a/40

ye 17th Monday fine weather wind att S^o this day I and my partner went a hunting, killed nothing, see the tracks of severall Shee Buffuloe, which had been disturbed by the Ind^s that hunts to the Northward of us.

     E.2/6

17 Mond.^y fine weather, wind S. something better, went a hunting with my Companions, and seed several tracks of Buffalow, but they had been disturbed by the Natives who hunts to the Northward of us.

     E.2/11

17. Monday. Wind South and warm weather: freezes in the nights and thaws in the days. I went a hunting with my Companions; killed nothing: plenty of Buffalo tracks, but they have been disturbed by the Natives who hunt to the Northward of us.

18 March 1755
> B.239/a/40

yᵉ 18ᵗʰ Tuesday the wind NWᵗ and very hott, this day Came ten tents and pitcht by us, in order to build Canues, went a hunting see severall Waskeswˢ being Little wind & the snow hard, Could not get a nigh them.
> E.2/6

18 Tuesdʸ warm weather, wind SW. went a hunting, seed several Waskesews, but could not come nigh them the snow so hard makes a noise under our snow shoes; 10 tents came to us and pitched, in order to build Canoes.
> E.2/11

18. Tuesday. Wind SW and warm weather: I went a hunting with my Companions; Saw many Waskesew but could not come at them; the Snow so hard makes a noise under our Snowshoes: Ten tents came & pitched along side of us in order to build Canoes.

19 March 1755
> B.239/a/40

yᵉ 19ᵗʰ Wednesday fine weather Wind SWᵗ, hott Sultry Weather the almost all Melted away, being none to Speak off.
> E.2/6

19 Wednesdʸ fine weather, wind SW. old Men making gunnels for Canoes, and young Men went a hunting, not yet returned.
> E.2/11

19. @ 20. Wednesday & Thursday. Winds form South to SW. and warm weather: Snow almost dissolved. The Aged Men making Gunwales for Canoes, & the Young Men hunting, & not yet returned.

20 March 1755
> B.239/a/40

yᵉ 20 Thursday fine weather wind SWᵗ this day went and made severall Gunnels, of our Canoes, the Rest went a hunting and are not Returned.
> E.2/6

20 Thursdʸ wind SW. and hot weather, thaw'd greatly snow almost gone.

21 March 1755
> B.239/a/40

yᵉ 21ˢᵗ Friday SWᵗ we pitcht our tent to yᵉ other side of yᵉ River. Came two tents of Indˢ and pitcht along with us.

E.2/6

21 Frid^y wind SW. and moderate weather, pitched our tents on the
other side the River, water running over the Ice; two tents of Natives
came to build Canoes.

E.2/11

1755 March 21st Friday. Wind & Weather as before: Pitched our tents on
the other side the River, Water running over the ice.

22 March 1755

B.239/a/40

1755 March ye 22^d Saturday the weather much the same, & wind NE^t
Last night and this day it Rained and Snowed very thick.

E.2/6

22 Saturd^y wind NE. and Closs sleety wet weather.

E.2/11

22. @ 25. Saturday. Sunday. Monday. Tuesday. Winds from West to NW
and very cold weather, with Snow at intervals; no Walking abroad: All
hands preparing Wood &c for building Canoes: The Asinepoet Natives
are building Canoes below us.

23 March 1755

B.239/a/40

ye 23^d Sunday the weather much the same, as has been these 2 nights
and 2 days past never Ceased Snowing, so that now we have more
snow upon the Ground, then we have had this winter, the Ind^s are daily att me for powder, and shott, so that I am forced to hide it and
show them the Empty bags.

E.2/6

23 Sund^y wind NE and wery bad weather, no walking abroad; Indians
continually plaguing me for powder.

24 March 1755

B.239/a/40

ye 24th Monday this day we are all busy in getting the wood Ready for
to Build our Canoes, the Ind^s are daily Coming here to build their
Canues, the Esinepoets are farther down the River, there are a great
many of them promised to to the fortt, for many Years (has not been).

E.2/6

24 Mond^y fine weather, wind NW. hunters returned, having killed 6
Waskesews, Natives dayly coming in.

25 March 1755
> B.239/a/40

yᵉ 25ᵗʰ Tuesday fine Weather wind NWᵗ went for 6 Waskeswˢ which the Indˢ killed Yesterday, a deal of snow on the ground.
> E.2/6

1755 March 25 Tuesdʸ fine weather, wind NW. all hands getting wood ready for Canoes building; the Asinepoets are below us building Canoes, some of them has not been at the Fort these many years past.

26 March 1755
> B.239/a/40

yᵉ 26ᵗʰ Wednesday fine weather wind att Wᵗ all hands busy in Getting things Ready to build Canoes, this Evening they had a Skeem for to Get my powder & Shott, but it would not take they told me the Earchithinues would be here and kill me, if I did not give them powder & Shott for to kill them, I told them I was not afraid of yᵉ Earchithinues, & that I would give them None.
> E.2/6

26 Wednesdʸ fine weather, wind W. all hands Employed as yesterday.
> E.2/11

26. to April 7ᵗʰ Wednesday. Thursday. Friday. Saturday. Sunday. Monday. Tuesday. Wednesday. Thursday. Friday. Saturday. Sunday. Monday. Winds Westerly, And Warm thawing Weather: All hands building Canoes & hunting: pretty good Success: Every Evening Feasting &c.

27 March 1755
> B.239/a/40

March yᵉ 27ᵗʰ Thursday fine weather wind att SWᵗ all hands att work on their Canues.
> E.2/6

27 Thursdʸ fine weather, wind SW. River Ice blowed up in several places; busy making Canoes.

28 March 1755
> B.239/a/40

yᵉ 28th Friday wind att Sᵒ, building Canues.
> E.2/6

28 Fridʸ wind S. and warm weather, Employed as yesterday.

29 March 1755
> B.239/a/40

yᵉ 29ᵗʰ Saturday fine weather wind att Sᵒ severall men are gone a hunting, the Rest about Canues.

E.2/6

29 Saturd^y fine weather, wind S. gave away my Horse to an Indian who is to return him in case I should return.

30 March 1755

B.239/a/40

ye 30th Sunday fine weather wind NW^t the Ind^s are all Employed about their Canues, I went to Shenap for a hatchet I Lent him when he went up the River a hunting, he said he would not give it me. I said but Little to him for he is Like a Child, and would Not be Long Considering for to knock me on the Head, for I know not what.

E.2/6

30 Sunday fine weather, wind NW. some a hunting, and the others building Canoes; killed 2 Buffalow, and 4 Moose.

31 March 1755

B.239/a/40

ye 31st Monday fine weather wind att S° all about their Canues this day we parted the tent, shenap took the tent Cloth and said it was his, and that he was Master of it, I told him my hatchet & Gun was not his but Mine, when he told Me I should not have it till Attickasish & Connawappa was Come, that in 4 days they would be here.

E.2/6

31 Mond^y warm weather, wind S. Women brought the meat, the Men brought some to me; busy building Canoes.

1 April 1755

B.239/a/40

Ap^ll ye 1st Tuesday fine weather wind SW^t some gone a hunting, the Rest about Canoes, killed 2 Buffuloe & 4 Moose, gave my Man 4 Loads of powder and Shott, to go & hunt for Me, not Returned.

E.2/6

April 1 Tuesd^y fine weather, wind SW. Employed as yesterday.

2 April 1755

B.239/a/40

1755 Aprill ye 2^d Wednesday wind as before, my Indian Returned, brought me some Buffuloe flesh, the Rest about their Canues.

E.2/6

2 Wednesd^y fine weather, wind SW. Indians brought me some meat.

3 April 1755

    B.239/a/40

ye 3^d Thursday Fine weather wind SW^t all hands about their Canues.

    E.2/6

3 Thursd^y wind and weather as yesterday, all hands busy building Canoes.

4 April 1755

    B.239/a/40

ye 4th Friday fine weather wind SbW^t severall of ye Ind^s are gone a hunting, and as for Shenap and his Lame Lye, they are all angry but I Cannot help it, and the Ind^s all told Me, if I saw him or his Son, not to say anything to them (the old Man is Like a Child, and the son a prowd fool.

    E.2/6

4 Frid^y fine weather, wind SbW. some hunting and some building Canoes.

5 April 1755

    B.239/a/40

ye 5th Saturday fine weather wind SW^t all about their Canues, this day the Large Creeck on the West Shore broke up.

    E.2/6

1755 April 5 fine weather, wind SW. Hunters returned, brought 6 Waske-sews; a Creek broke up a little way above our tents, which has over-flowed the River.

6 April 1755

    B.239/a/40

ye 6th Sunday wind as before the Men gone a hunting waskesw^s, and their dog with them they run down 3.

    E.2/6

6 Sunday fine weather, wind SW. feasting and smoaking.

7 April 1755

    B.239/a/40

ye 7th Monday fine weather wind att West, this Evening thunder and hail, all about Canues.

    E.2/6

7 Mond^y wind W, thunder and hail, no working abroad.

8 April 1755
      B.239/a/40
yᵉ 8ᵗʰ Tuesday Wind SWᵗ this day all hands are a Smoaking tobacco, they have saved till now 6 fathom, they Smoak one fathom a night, and they Sing and are as Merry, as if they had one Hogshead of Brandy.
      E.2/6
8 Tuesdʸ wind SW. and moderate weather. building Canoes, in the Evening smoaking, dancing and singing, and are as merry as if we had a Hogshead of brandy.
      E.2/11
8. Tuesday. Wind SW and pleasant weather: last evening We had thunder & hail accompanyed with a NW. Wind: Men Employed as formerly: I gave my Horse to an old man who is to return him in case I should return again to this plentiful Country. Dancing, Drumming &c, and all good humoured.

9 April 1755
      B.239/a/40
Aprill yᵉ 9ᵗʰ Wednesday fine weather wind NWᵗ all about their Canoes, and this day Shenap told the Man that I tent with, he would go away to yᵉ fort and Leave Me behind, I told him I would not go with him.
      E.2/6
9 Wednesdʸ fine weather, wind W. busy building Canoes.
      E.2/11
1755 April 9. @ 12. Wednesday. Thursday. Friday and Saturday. Winds in the SW. quarter and agreeable weather: All hands employed building Canoes and in the Evening Smoaking the Grand Calimut &c: Several Asinepoet Indians pitched their tents a small distance below us; and in the Evening smoaked with me and promised not to trade with the French at Basquea settlement, but accompany me to York Fort.

10 April 1755
      B.239/a/40
yᵉ 10ᵗʰ Thursday fine weather wind att Sᵒ this day all hands Smoakt it, and I went & Smoakt with them.
      E.2/6
10 Thursdʸ fine weather, wind S. smoaking &c.

11 April 1755
      B.239/a/40
yᵉ 11ᵗʰ Friday wind as before, all Employed abᵗ their Canues, and this day their broke up a Large hole in yᵉ River opposite to our tents and Expect it all to break up daily.

E.2/6
11 Frid^y fine weather, wind S. all hands building Canoes.

12 April 1755
B.239/a/40
ye 12th Saturday fine weather wind SW^t, all hands are gone a hunting, killed 2 Large black Bears, and one Buffuloe.
E.2/6
12 Saturd^y wind SW and fine weather, young Men hunting & not yet returned; several Asinepoet Leaders came and smoaked with me, and in the evening returned to their tents, about 6 miles below us.

13 April 1755
B.239/a/40
ye 13th Sunday fine weather wind NE^t all Employed about their Canoes, the Men went out killed one Moose Close to our tents.
E.2/6
13 Sunday fine weather, wind NE. Hunters returned, having killed 10 Buffalow and two black Bears.
E.2/11
13. Sunday. Wind NE and close weather: Hunters killed ten Buffalo's, & two Black Bears.

14 April 1755
B.239/a/40
ye 14 Monday fine weather Wind SW^t Still about Canoes.
E.2/6
14 Mond^y fine weather, wind SW. Women brought the meat; busy about Canoes.
E.2/11
14 @ 16. Monday @ Wednesday. Winds Southerly and pleasant weather: Busy building Canoes &c.

15 April 1755
B.239/a/40
ye 15th Tuesday wind as before, the Ind^s Came from hunting, still very Busy ab^t Canoes.
E.2/6
15 Tuesd^y wind and weather as yesterday, all hands feasting, dancing, drumming and singing.

16 April 1755
B.239/a/40

ye 16th Wednesday fine weather wind S^o this day my partner and I went a hunting ab^t 30 M NW^t, we travelled hard here is nothing to be got nigh where we are making our Canues, killed nothing so Went to Sleep for we had nothing to Eat.

E.2/6

1755 april 16 Wednesd^y fine weather, wind S. busy building Canoes.

17 April 1755
B.239/a/40

1755 Aprill ye 17th Thursday fine weather wind NE^t this morning see 4 Swans, my partner went to get a Shott att them killed two, and I was Standing att a distance, I saw a moose Coming Right to me I was to Leeward of him, but had no Gun, but it being so nigh that I with my bow & arrow prickt him thro' the throat and with another Arrow in his broad side, so that he soon Lay down, my partner Come with his 2 Swans , and I was a Skinning My Moose, now we have plenty of provisions, and a great way to our tent, this Evening we went about 10 M on our Journey homewards.

E.2/6

17 Thursd^y moderate weather, wind SW. killed a Moose with my Bow and arrows, and the Indians killed a great many.

E.2/11

17. Thursday. Wind NW and moderate weather: I killed a Mouse with my Bow and Arrows, & the Natives killed a great many.

18 April 1755
B.239/a/40

ye 18th Friday fine weather wind NW^t got to our tent Loaded with fatt Moose flesh.,

E.2/6

18 Frid^y fine weather, wind NW. Women gone for the meat and not yet returned; seed a great many swans.

E.2/11

18. Friday. Wind SW and fine weather: Saw several Flocks of Swans flying towards the NE.

19 April 1755
B.239/a/40

ye 19th Saturday wind SW^t and fine Weather, all hands are killing their dogs & Eating them.

E.2/6

19 Saturd^y fine weather, wind SW. snow all gone. Women returned with the meat, Men getting the birch rind for our Canoes.

E.2/11

19. Saturday. Wind WSW. and warm weather: Snow all gone: Men collecting Birch-Rind for Canoes.

20 April 1755

B.239/a/40

ye 20th Sunday wind as before All hands att work on their Canues.

E.2/6

20 Sunday wind and weather as yesterday, each tent killed 2 Dogs, and had a grand feast, with dancing and Conjuring, I am not yet so much of an Indian as to relish Dogs flesh, especially when I have good Buffalow &c to eat.

E.2/11

1755 April 20. Sunday. Wind and Weather as Yesterday: Each Tent killed two Dogs and had a Grand feast; I must take not<ice> they do not Skin the Animal but scrape it and Roast <it> over a fire, two Young Men keeping turning it; for no Women hath any concern, not even to be present: the old men Conjuring &c.

21 April 1755

B.239/a/40

ye 21st Monday fine weather wind W^t this day Came Connawappa to our tents, being the first time I have seen him Since the fall of ye year, he when went away he Left his Wife, Bob and An Earchithinue Girl for me to keep, he has made an Exceeding Good use of his time having gave his and Bobs Gun away, and all his powder & Shott, he said he had Eat nothing for 2 days, I told him I had nothing for to Eat myself, when he went to his own tent I gave him Some dryed Meat, and 4 Loads of Shott.

E.2/6

21 Mond^y fine weather, wind W. busy about Canoes.

E.2/11

21. Monday. Wind West and pleasant weather: All hands preparing our Canoes.

22 April 1755

B.239/a/40

ye 22^d Tuesday fine weather wind SW^t all very Busy about their Canues.

E.2/6

22 Tuesd^y fine weather, wind SW. musketoes bites sharp, and by the warmness of the I suppose we shall have plenty.

E.2/11

22. Tuesday. Wind SW. and agreeable weather: the Musquitoes are plenty and sting severely.

23 April 1755

B.239/a/40

ye 23^d Wednesday fine weather wind att S^o went a hunting killed 6 Swans, the Ice in the River so Loose, and all broke up in holes, as that it is very dangerous to go on it, the snow almost gone, and all the Creecks are Running very Clear, and we are Likely to have a good Season of Muskeeteers.

E.2/6

23 Wednesd^y wind S. and rain at times, last night I acquainted the Leaders that my flag would be flying to day, and the reason for so doing, as well as I was Capable, so they followed my example, and the day was spent in feasting &c, in Honour of St George; and to crown the day, the River broke open; several white and gray Geese, and Swans flying to day.

E.2/4

23. Wednesday wind S. and rain at times displayed my flag in honour of St. George as did all the other Leaders both in ye English and French interest, and had a grand feast with dancing &c and to conclude all, the river broke open.

E.2/11

23. Wednesday. Wind SW and Rain at times: Displayed my Flag in Honour of St George; and the Leaders did the same, after acquainting them and explaining my reason: In the Afternoon the ice in the River broke up: a great many Geese and Swans were seen flying to the Northward: In the Evening we had a grand feast with Dancing, Drumming, Talking &c.

24 April 1755

B.239/a/40

ye 24th Thursday fine weather wind S^o my partner and I went a hunting, I killed one Swan with my Bow & Arrow.

E.2/6

1755 April 24 Thursd^y fine weather, wind S. busy about Canoes, killed a swan with my Bow and arrows.

E.2/4

1756 April 24 @ 27th Thursday @ Sunday very warm weather wind S.

musketoes plenty, and bites sharp, a great many gray geese and swans flying; all hands employed packing up furs in proper bundles for the canoes, a great may Aseenepoets that goes to no settlements whatever pitched away towards the muscuty country after the buffaloe.

E.2/11

24. Thursday. Wind South. Busy about Canoes: killed A Swan with my Bow & Arrow; they are plenty.

25 April 1755

B.239/a/40

ye 25th Friday fine Weather wind NE^t all hands are making Ready for to Sail, killed 4 Swans and Returned to our tents, and the River (to my great Joy) was quite broke up, and all ye Ice Gone.

E.2/6

25 Frid^y fine weather, wind NE. Ice driving in ye River.

E.2/11

1755 April 25 Friday Wind NE and cold disagreeable weather: Ice driving down the river Finished the Canoes and preparing to set out for York Fort.

26 April 1755

B.239/a/40

ye 26th Saturday fine weather wind att W^t making all ready to Sail to Morrow, for the Ind^s are all in a Starving Condition.

E.2/6

26 Saturd^y fine weather, wind W. packing the furs in proper bundles for stowing in the Canoes which are ready.

E.2/11

26. Saturday. Wind West and moderate weather: Busy packing the Furs in proper bundles for Stowing in the Canoes.

27 April 1755

B.239/a/40

ye 27th Sunday fine weather wind att S^o this day sailed 20 Canoes, and I Embarked on board a new Ship and help (by ye help of God) to Sail to York Fort; we padled this day NEbN^o 24 M.

E.2/6

27 Sunday warm weather, wind S. musketoes plenty and bites without Mercy, they are worse than cold weather.

E.2/11

27. Sunday. Wind South and warm weather: Musketoes plenty and sting without mercy.

28 April 1755

    B.239/a/40

1755 Aprill ye 28th Monday fine weather wind NW^t this day padled 30 M.

    E.2/6

28 Mond^y fine weather, wind NW. Embarked on board our Canoes, and paddled down the River 54 miles, in Company with 20 Canoes Asinepoet Indians; the river Large and wide with many Islands.

    E.2/4

28. Monday fine weather wind N.W. imbarked on board my canoe and paddled down the river 54 miles, 50 canoes in company; the river large, deep and wide, and a great many Islands, and the banks high and tall woods.

    E.2/11

28. Monday. Wind NW and pleasant weather: Embarked on board my Canoe, and paddled down the river 34 Miles, in company with 20 Canoes of Asinepoet Natives: the River large, with several Islands, and high banks, and tall woods.

29 April 1755

    B.239/a/40

ye 29th Tuesday fine weather wind att S^o this day we padled 50 M, the water deep and the River is Large and wide in the middle is full of Islands.

    E.2/6

29 Tuesd^y fine weather, wind S. paddled 50 miles Down the River, deep water this time of the year not one fall to be seen, tho' the Men informs me that this river is almost dry in the middle of summer and full of falls.

    E.2/4

29. Tuesday fine weather wind S. paddled 50 miles down the river, deep water and not one fall to be seen, but I am informed it is almost dry in the summer and full of falls.

    E.2/11

29. Tuesday. Wind South and pleasant weather: paddled 30 Miles down the river: deep water & not one Cataract to be seen; tho' I am informed it is almost dry in the summer, and full of small Cataracts.

30 April 1755

    B.239/a/40

ye 30th Wednesday wind as before. this day padled 30 M here we Came to where Attickasish and ye Ind^s were making their Canoes, all in a Starving Condition.

E.2/6

30 Wednesd^y wind and weather as yesterday. paddled down the River 30 miles, when we came to Attickosish and a great many Indians, who had not yet finished their Canoes.

E.2/4

30. Wednesday wind &c as yesterday, paddled 30 miles down the river, then came to Attickosish and several Indians who had not yet finished their canoes, the water falls a little, high banks and lofty woods, we are joined by 20 canoes of Indians.

E.2/11

1755 April 30 Wednesday. Wind & weather as Yesterday: paddled 20 Miles down the river then came to Attickosish my Guide and a great number of Natives, who hath not yet finished their Canoes.

1 May 1755

B.239/a/40

May ye 1st Thursday wind as before, this day padled 40 M past severall small Creecks and 30 Islands and 3 Small falls, the water deep and the Land high and small woods, here 20 tents of Indians were making Canues, no Buffuloe this way nor moose, so that we are obliged to kill our dogs and think them a very Good Shift, Course this day SEbE^t.

E.2/6

May 1 Thursd^y fine weather, wind S. paddled 40 miles; high banks, a great many Islands, the water falls a little; Course SEbE. Joined by 20 Canoes.

E.2/4

May 1st Thursday fine weather wind S. paddled 40 miles down the river.

E.2/11

May 1st Thursday. Wind South and pleasant weather: paddled 30 miles down the river: High banks: a great many Islands, and lofty woods: the Water hath fallen a little: we are joined by 20 more canoes.

2 May 1755

B.239/a/40

ye 2^d Friday very fine weather wind att S^o this day padled 30 M SEbS^o the River is full of small Islands, but the Water Continues very deep.

E.2/6

2 Frid^y wind and weather as yesterday. paddled 30 miles SEbS.

E.2/4

2^d Friday wind &c as yesterday paddled 3 miles down the river. water falls fast; banks &c as before.

E.2/11

2. Friday. wind and weather as Yesterday: paddled 3 miles down the river.

3 May 1755
B.239/a/40

May ye 3^d Saturday wind as before, this day padled 60 M, the water is still very deep and the River wide.

E.2/6

1755 May 3 Saturd^y wind S and pleasant weather, paddled 50 miles down the river, very broad, and many Islands.

E.2/4

3. Saturday pleasant weather wind S. paddled 50 miles down the river, very wide, large Islands, banks high, and lofty woods, the chief of which is birch.

E.2/11

3. Saturday. Wind South and pleasant weather: paddled 30 miles down the river: it is very Large and many Islands, with lofty well-grown woods.

4 May 1755
B.239/a/40

ye 4th Sunday fine weather wind att N^o this day padled 60 M SEbE^t this day past Severall Islands, and to day killed 4 Waskesw^s & 2 Buffuloes.

E.2/6

4 Sunday wind N. and moderate weather, paddled 60 miles, SEbE. killed 4 Waskesews and 2 Buffalow.

E.2/4

1756 May 4th Sunday fine weather wind N. paddled 60 miles S.E.B.E. killed 4 waskesews and 2 buffaloe.

E.2/11

4. Sunday. wind North and close weather: paddled 40 miles SEbE: killed 4 Waskesew & 2 Buffalos.

5 May 1755
B.239/a/40

ye 5th Monday fine weather Wind att S^o. this day we padled 40 M fine deep Water, past 14 Islands, the River Runs NNE^t and NEbN^o.

E.2/6

5 Mond^y fine weather, wind S. paddled 40 miles NNE & NEbN. River broad, deep, and many Islands.

E.2/4

5. Monday fine weather, wind S. paddled 40 miles N.N.E. and N.E.B.N. river large and deep water.

E.2/11

5. Monday. Wind South and fine weather: paddled 20 miles NNE & NEbN: the River very wide & deep water.

6 May 1755

B.239/a/40

ye 6th Tuesday this day had a Large shower of Rain, cleared up by noon then fine Weather, Wind att S^o this day padled 50 M, fine Levell Land and the River deep.

E.2/6

6 Tuesd^y wind S. and rain at times, paddled 50 miles, expecting to see the Archithinues dayly; low banks.

E.2/4

6. Tuesday wind S. with rain at times, paddled 50 miles E. expecting to see the Archithinues dayly, river large and high banks.

E.2/11

6. Tuesday. Wind South with Rain at times: Paddled 30 Miles: We expect to see the Archithinue natives.

7 May 1755

B.239/a/40

ye 7th Wednesday fine weather wind att SE^t this day padled 40 M NEbN^o the River Large and wide, and the Water deep past Severall Islands.

E.2/6

7 Wednesd^y fine weather, wind SE. paddled 40 miles, the River broad and many Islands, provisions turning scarce: Course NEbN.

E.2/4

7. Wednesday fine weather wind S.E. paddled 40 miles N.E.B.E. the river as yesterday.

E.2/11

1755 May 7th @ 8. Wednesday and Thursday Winds variable: Paddled 66 miles down the river: Provisions begin to be scarce.

8 May 1755

B.239/a/40

ye 8th Thursday fine weather wind att SW^t this day we padled 36 M NE^t the River Continues much ye Same, have nothing to Eat but dogs.

E.2/6

8 Thursd^y wind SW. and fine weather, paddled 36 miles NE. the River looks much the same.

E.2/4

8. Thursday wind N.W. and fine weather, paddled 36 miles N.E. provisions grows scarce.

9 May 1755

B.239/a/40

ye 9th Friday fine weather wind att N^o this day padled 50 M the River is very wide, and deep water, past severall Islands.

E.2/6

9 Frid^y wind N. and moderate weather, paddled 50 miles, River much the same.

E.2/4

9. Friday moderate weather wind N. paddled 40 miles N.N.E. the river as before.

E.2/11

9. Friday. Wind North and moderate weather: paddled 30 miles NEbN down the river.

10 May 1755

B.239/a/40

ye 10th Saturday fine Weather, wind att West. this day padled 40 M, NNE^t the River deep and the Land High, this day killed one Buffuloe.

E.2/6

10 Saturd^y fine weather, wind W. paddled 40 miles NNE; the River deep and the banks high. killed one Buffalow.

E.2/4

10. Saturday fine weather wind W. paddled 50 miles N.E.B.N. the river deep and the banks high; killed one buffaloe.

E.2/11

10. Saturday. Wind West and pleasant weather: paddled 40 miles NNE: the river deep and the banks high: Indians killed a Buffalo.

11 May 1755

B.239/a/40

1755 May ye 11th Sunday the wind att S^o this day padled 30 M the River much the same, and nothing to Eat.

E.2/6

11 Sunday fine weather, wind S. paddled 30 miles, the River much the same, little or nothing to eat.

E.2/4

11. Sunday fine weather wind S. paddled 30 miles N.N.E. river as yesterday.

E.2/11

11. Sunday. Wind South and agreeable weather: paddled 30 miles NNE: River as Yesterday.

12 May 1755

B.239/a/40

yᵉ 12ᵗʰ Monday fine weather wind att Sᵒ this day padled 10 M NEbNᵒ came to us the Earchithinues, 100 tents, and all in a starving Condition, they called me to their tents but they have Little or no Victuals, and they told me that in 2 or 3 days time that we should have plenty of provisions.

E.2/6

12 Mondʸ fine weather, wind S. paddled 10 miles NEbN. then came to 100 tents of Archithinues, the Leader invited me to the tent and gave me plenty of Buffalow's flesh; Indians traded with them their old hatchets &c, for above 500 Wolves, I could not perswade them to go to the Fort.

E.2/4

12. Monday wind &c as yesterday paddled 10 miles N.E.B.N. then came to 100 tents of Archithinues, their leader invited me to his tent, and gave me plenty of buffaloe flesh; our Indians traded a great many wolves &c from them for old hatchets, guns, knives &c; I could not perswade them to go to the fort.

E.2/11

12. Monday. Wind and Weather as Yesterday: paddled 10 miles EbN. then came to one hundred tents of Archithinue Natives. Their Leader invited me to his tent, and gave me plenty of Buffalo flesh: our Indians bought a great many Wolves from them, for old axes &c. I could not perswade them to go to the Fort.

13 May 1755

B.239/a/40

yᵉ 13ᵗʰ Tuesday fine weather wind NWᵗ this day padled 50 M, the Indˢ went a hunting, see severall Buffuloe killed 4.

E.2/6

1755 May 13 Tuesdʸ fine weather, wind NW. paddled 50 miles, killed 4 Buffalow, seed a great many along the banks.

E.2/4

1756 May 13ᵗʰ Tuesday fine weather wind N.W. paddled 50 miles N.N.E. killed 4 buffaloe, seed a great many feeding along the banks.

E.2/11

13. Tuesday. Wind NW and agreeable weather: paddled 30 Miles: killed 4 Buffalo, a great number grazing along the Banks: The Archithinue Natives were mounted on good Horses.

14 May 1755

B.239/a/40

yᵉ 14ᵗʰ Wednesday fine weather wind NEᵗ this day padled 15 M and went a hunting, and killed 20 Buffuloe.

E.2/6

14 Wednesdʸ fine weather, wind NE. paddled 15 miles, then killed 20 Buffalow closs to the River side.

E.2/4

14. Wednesday fine weather wind N.E. paddled 15 miles N.E.B.N. killed 20 buffaloe.

E.2/11

1755 May 14ᵗʰ Wednesday Wind NE and close weather paddled 15 miles; then killed 20 Buffalo grazing along the river side.

15 May 1755

B.239/a/40

yᵉ 15ᵗʰ Thursday fine weather wind SWᵗ the Indians are all Employed in drying of Meat and Making Ruhigan. and this day the Earchithinues Came and pitcht their tents on the other Side of the River, the Men Swam their Horses across the River, and Went a hunting killed 10 Buffuloe, and this day I dried my Meat, that I got Yesterday and to day, and now I think I am in as Good form for to Sail as the Best of them; the Earchithinues told Me they would go and See the Govʳ and I told them he would give them powder, Shott &c, which they mightily admired att, they are 127 tents of them.

E.2/6

15 Thursdʸ fine weather, wind SW. paddled none, killed a great many Buffalow, busy drying meat; 127 Tents of Archithinues came to us, I bought 30 Wolves from them and the Indians bought a great many, which proves what my Bedfellow formerly told me concerning the Indians, getting the most part of their furs from the Archithinues; they told me I would soon see the Leader, and Gang of Archithinues that I was with in the fall in muscuty Country; I did all in my power to get some of them down to the Fort, but all in vain, and altho' the Indians promised to the chief of York fort, to do their endeavour to bring them down, they never opened their mouths, and I have reason to think they are rather a stoppage, for if they could be brought down to trade, the others would be obliged to trap their own furs, which at present two thirds of them does not: I seed 50 Archithinues swim their Horses across the River, they look more like Europians than Indians, they shared 10 Buffalow amongst the Indians.

E.2/4

15. Thursday fine weather wind S.W. paddled none, killed a great many buffaloe, women busy drying meat, 127 tents of Archithinues came to us, I bought 30 wolves skins from them, and the trading Indians bought a great many skins of sorts, which proves what my bedfellow formerly told me concerning the traders geting the most part of their furs from the Archithinue and Aseenepoet Indians, they told me I would soon see the leader and gang of their countrymen that I was with in the fall in the muscuty country; I did my endeavour to get some of them down to the fort but all in vain, and altho' the traders promised to the chief of York Fort to talk to them strongly on that subject they scarcely opened their mouths, and have great reason to think they are rather a stoppage, for if the Archithinues and Aseenepoets could be brought down to trade, the others then would be obliged to trap their own furs, which at present two thirds of them does not; the Archithinues swimmed their horses across the river, they look more like Europians than Indians, they shared 20 buffaloe amongst our Indians; we have neither hatchet nor knife left, having sold all for furs.

E.2/11

15. Thursday. Wind SW and very warm weather: paddled none: killed a great number of Buffalos: Indian Women & Children employed drying meat: One hundred & twenty-seven tents of Archithinue Natives came to us: I bought 30 Wolves skins from them, and the Indians purchased great numbers of Wolves, Beaver & Foxes &c which proves what the Woman formerly told me, concerning the Natives getting part of their Furs from the Archithinue Indians. They told me that I should soon see their Leader: I did my Endeavour to get some of them down to the Fort; but all in vain: And altho' the Indians promised the Chief Factor at York Fort to talk to them strongly on that Subject, they never opened their mouths; and I have great reason to believe that they are a stoppage: for if they could be brought down to trade, the others would be obliged to trap their own Furs; which at present two-thirds of them do not. These brave Natives swimmed their Horses across the river; they look more like to Europeans than Indians. They shared amongst us 10 Buffalos.

16 May 1755

B.239/a/40

ye 16th Friday fine Clear weather, & Blows hard att SW^t this day padled 30 M NbE^t and on the River Sides the bloody Ind^s were tented, the Leader Came and took me to their tents, where there was dancing, drumming and Singing; he treated Me with a pipe of his tobacco, and then his Wife Brought some fatt & berries mixt together and the belly of a buffuloe, which is very fine Eating, and he told Me he would go to ye fortt and Gett powder & Shott, Knives, Guns &c, I told them there were plenty of all Sorts of Goods, they are More Like English than Indians, have Great plenty of fine horsses.

> **E.2/6**
> 16 Frid^y Clear blowing weather, wind NW. paddled 30 miles NbE. when we came to 30 tents of Archithinues, I talked to them as I did to the others but all to the same purpose, they were very kind, and had the finest Horses I have yet seen here.

> **E.2/4**
> 1756 May 16th Friday clear blowing weather wind N.W. paddled 30 miles N.B.E. then came to 30 tents of Archithinues, I talked and smoaked with them but all to no purpose, the Indians got furs from them on credit, they have the finest horses I have yet seen here and are very kind to me.

> **E.2/11**
> 1755 May 16th Friday wind NW and clear blowing weather: Paddled 30 miles NBE when we came to 30 tents of Archithinue Natives: I talked with them as I did with the others; but all to no purpose: Our Indians traded a great many Furs from them: They have the finest Horses I have yet seen here, and are very kind people.

17 May 1755

> **B.239/a/40**
> ye 17th Saturday fine weather wind NE^t here the Earchithinues Joined the bloody Ind^s, I went & Smoak'd with them till my head was Sore: this day padled NNE^t 22 M.

> **E.2/6**
> 1755 May 17 Saturd^y fine weather, wind NE. paddled none; Ten Tents of Bloody Indians Joined the Archithinues, 5 Canoes of them are going to the Fort with me; Invited to the Archithinue tents, to a feast where was dancing, drumming, and singing after the same manner as the other Indians does.

> **E.2/4**
> 17. Saturday fine weather wind N.E. paddled none, 10 tents of mirthco or bloody Indians joined the Archithinues, 5 canoes of them are going to York Fort with me; I was invited to the Archithinues tents, where were feasting, smoking, singing, dancing and drumming.

> **E.2/11**
> 17. Saturday. Wind NE and close weather. Paddled none: Ten tents of Eagle Indians joined the Archithinue Indians: Five Canoes of them are going to the Fort with me: They are a Tribe of the Asinepoet Nation;

and like them use the Horses for carrying the baggage & not to ride on: I was invited to the Archithinue tents, where were feasting &c much in the same manner as our Indians practise.

18 May 1755
B.239/a/40
yᵉ 18 Sunday fine weather wind SEᵗ this day the Indˢ padled 20 M and then went a hunting and killed 4 Buffuloe.
E.2/6
18 Sunday fine weather, wind SE. paddled 42 miles NE. the River broad, deep, and many Islands, the banks low with small woods, Vizᵗ Birch, Hazle, poplar, and fir trees, a pleasant Country; killed 4 Buffalow.
E.2/4
18. Sunday fine weather wind S.E. paddled 42 miles N.E. the river broad and deep with many Islands, the banks low with small woods vizᵗ birch, poplar, hasel and fir; killed 4 buffaloe, they are numerous about the river sides.
E.2/11
18. Sunday. Wind SE. and fine weather. paddled 22 miles NE: the river broad & deep with many Islands: the banks low and small woods, Viz. Birch, Hazle, poplar & Fir: killed four Buffalo; they are numerous about the river sides

19 May 1755
B.239/a/40
yᵉ 19ᵗʰ Monday wind SEᵗ this day padled 56 M NEbNᵒ deep water past Severall Islands.
E.2/6
19 Mondʸ wind NE. and closs weather, paddled 56 miles, River as before; Course NEbN.
E.2/4
19. Monday closs weather wind N.E. paddled 56 miles N.E.B.N. a fine spacious river.
E.2/11
19. Monday. Wind NE and close weather. paddled 20 miles NEbE: River as before; Musketoes plenty.

20 May 1755
B.239/a/40
yᵉ 20ᵗʰ Tuesday wind SEᵗ this day padled 40 Miles, and then went a hunting, killed 2 Bufflow the Water Much the same.

E.2/6

20 Tuesd^y wind SE. paddled 40 miles; River much the same; hot weather, and plenty of musketoes.

E.2/4

20. Tuesday fine weather wind S.E. paddled 40 miles N.E.B.E. the river as yesterday.

E.2/11

1755 May 20th Tuesday. Wind NE and close weather: paddled 36 miles NEbN. a noble spacious river.

21 May 1755

B.239/a/40

1755 May ye 21st Wednesday fine weather Wind SE^t this day saw the Earchithinues again, but they have neither victuals nor goods, and Cannot padle, so we shall proceed to Morrow for the fort, As fast as we Can, here is 60 Canoes designed for the fort if ye french does not stop them.

E.2/6

21 Wednesd^y fine weather, wind SE. paddled none, Came to us the old Archithinue Leader, that I seed in the fall in muscuty plains, with 70 tents of His Countrymen; I smoaked with Him. and did all in my powr to get some of His young Men down with me to the Fort, His objections were Viz^t they could not paddle; and that there were plenty of Buffalow all the year through in muscuty plains; they had not many Wolves, the Pegogomaw Indians, who were gone before us to the Fort had got them from them; We are now above 60 Canoes and there are scarcely a Gun, hatchet, or knife amongst us, having Traded them with the Archithinues for Wolves.

E.2/4

21. Wednesday fine weather wind S.E. paddled none, came to us the Archithinue leader that I seed in the muscuty country with 70 tents of his countrymen, I endeavoured all I could to get some of them down to the fort with me but all to no purpose, they had few furs, having traded them with the pegogamaw Indians, who are gone to the English and French.

E.2/11

21. Wednesday. wind SE and moderate weather: paddled none: Seventy tents of Archithinue Natives came to us, headed by the same Leader that I saw in the Muscuty Country: I used my utmost endeavours to get a few of his Young men to the Fort; but to no purpose: They had very few Wolves or Furs of any kind, having traded them before with the Pegogamaw Indians, who are gone to the Fort: We are above 60 Canoes and there are scarce a Gun, Kettle, Hatchet or Knife amongst us, having traded them with the Archithinue Natives.

22 May 1755

> B.239/a/40

ye 22^d Thursday fine weather wind NE^t this day padled 60 M N^o & NbW^t Barren Land and plenty of Buffuloe, this day fired the Last of my powder and Shott, killed Severall Buffuloe & one Moose.

> E.2/6

1755 May 22 Thursd^y fine weather, wind SE. paddled 60 miles N. & NbW. the River broad, deep, and no Islands, the Indians informs me that Wyke-sew River is dry in several places in the summer; but at present it is the finest River I have yet seen; killed 4 Buffalow; this morning I gave away the last of my powder; I shall see no more buffalow this voyage.

> E.2/4

22. Thursday fine weather wind S.E. paddled 60 miles N. and N.B.W. the river broad, deep and no Islands, it appears to me to be a fine river, but the Indians says it's almost dry every summer, killed 4 buffaloe; this morning I gave away the last of my powder and shot.

> E.2/11

22. Thursday. wind SE and moderate weather: Paddled 30 miles North & NbW: the River broad, deep and no Islands: It appears to me at present to be a fine river but the Indians tell me that it is almost dry in the middle of Summer: The Young Men killed 4 Buffalo this morning & I gave away the remains of my Powder and shot. <NB. Anthony Hendey <<the writer of this Journal>> was from York Fort on the 21st day of Novr S^o 59 W^t Dist 810 Miles.>

23 May 1755

> B.239/a/40

ye 23^d Friday very Little wind att SE^t and fine weather, this day we padled 40 M then we Came to a french House where was 5 french Men, the Govr Came with his hatt in his hand, and followed a great deal of Bowing and Scraping, put neither he understood me, nor I him, he treated me with 2 Glasses Brandy and half a Bisket, this Evening he gave the Ind^s 2 Gallons Brandy, for to get them for to trade, but he got but very Little trade.

> E.2/6

23 Frid^y fine weather, wind SE. paddled 40 miles, then came to a French House, where were 6 Men, the Master invited me in to supper but we had no Bread until we were done, then He presented me with half of a biscuit, and a dram of French brandy; He said that He was informed by the Master of Basquea House that I passed by there in the fall.

> E.2/4

23. Friday fine weather wind S.E. paddled 40 miles N.E. then came to a french house where were 6 men, the master invited me to supper but

we had no bread untill we were done, then he presented me with half
a biscuit and a dram of french brandy, and told me that this house is
subordinate to basquea, and that he heard of my being there last fall.

E.2/11

1755 May 23^d Friday. Wind SE. and pleasant regular weather: Paddled
20 miles NE, then came to a French Trading House where were 6 Men:
the Master invited me to supper, but we had no bread until we were
done; then He presented me with half a biscuit and a dram of French
Brandy, and told me that this House was subordinate to Basquea and
they heard of my passing by last Autumn.

24 May 1755

B.239/a/40

May ye 24th Saturday fine weather wind SE^t Lay by, this day breakfasted, Dined and Sup'd with the french, he asked me Many Questions, but I told him I know nothing but Come to see the Ind^n Country.

E.2/6

24 Saturd^y wind and weather as yesterday, paddled none breakfasted,
dined, and supped with the French; He gave the Natives 10 Gallons of
brandy mixed half with water, and traded Martins, Cased Cats, good
parchment Beaver, refusing Wolves, and Coat Beaver. This House is
subordinate to Basquea House.

E.2/4

24 @ 25. Saturday and Sunday wind S.E. and rain at times the master
gave the natives 10 gallons of adulterated brandy and has traded from
them above 1000 of the finest skins, refusing wolves, bears & dressed
beaver skins in coat, as also skins that are in any manner damaged or
are not in season; I cannot get them to proceed, it's surprizing to
observe what great influence the French hath over the natives.

E.2/11

24. Saturday. Wind and weather as Yesterday: The Natives received
from the Master ten Gallons of Brandy half adulterated with water;
and when intoxicated they traded Cased Cats, Martens & good parchment Beaver skins, refusing Wolves & dressed Beaver: In short He
received from the Natives nothing but what were prime Winter Furs.

25 May 1755

B.239/a/40

ye 25th Sunday this day and all Last Night there fell a great deal of
Rain, with thunder & Lightning, in the Evening Cleared up, wind from
the SE^t to ye NE^t.

E.2/6

25 Sunday wind SE and moderate weather, rained hard last night, I could not get the Indians away so am forced to stay here to day; I am Certain He hath got 1000 of the richest skins.

E.2/11

25. Sunday. Wind SE. and moderate weather: Rained hard last night; I could not get the Natives away to day: It is surprizing to observe what an influence the French have over the Natives; I am certain he hath got above 1000 of the richest Skins

26 May 1755

B.239/a/40

ye 26th Monday fine weather wind NE^t padled 47 M NEbN^o Low Land and tall woods with deep water.

E.2/6

26 Mond^y fine weather, wind NEbN. paddled 47 miles NEbN. the River broad and fine wood on the banks.

E.2/4

26. Monday fine moderate weather wind N.E.B.N. paddled 47 miles N.E.B.N. the river broad and lofty woods.

E.2/11

26. Monday. Wind NEbN and fine weather: Paddled 47 Miles NEbN. the River broad and lofty woods.

27 May 1755

B.239/a/40

ye 27th Tuesday fine weather wind SW^t padled 70 M NEbN^o neither fish nor flesh for these 3 Days past.

E.2/6

1755 May 27 Tuesd^y fine weather, wind SW. paddled 70 miles NEbN. low banks, tall woods, and deep water.

E.2/4

1756 May 27th Tuesday fine weather wind S.W. paddled 70 miles N.E. deep water, low banks and lofty woods.

E.2/11

27. Tuesday. Wind SW. and warm sultry weather. Paddled 70 miles NE: Low banks, Tall woods, and deep water.

28 May 1755

B.239/a/40

ye 28th Wednesday a great deal of Rain & thunder and Lightning, wind NW^t padled 24 M, then Came to a Creeck, plenty of fish.

E.2/6

28 Wednesd^y wind NW. with thunder lightning & rain, paddled 24
miles, then came to a Creek caught plenty of Fish.

E.2/4

28. Wednesday wind N.W. with rain, thunder and lightning, paddled 24
miles E.N.E. then came to a creek where we angled plenty of pike fish.

E.2/11

28. Wednesday. Wind NW with Rain, Thunder and Lightning. Paddled
24 Miles ENE. then came to a Creek where We angled plenty of Fish
which were acceptable.

29 May 1755

B.239/a/40

ye 29th Thursday fine Weather wind att S° this day padled EbS° 60 M,
then we Came to Another french fort, Called Paskeway Yay, here was 3
french Men, 2 of them I see in this fall.

E.2/6

29 Thursd^y fine weather, wind S. paddled 60 miles EbS. then came to
the French House I passed in the fall, there were a Master and 9 Men,
He said nothing to me worth notice; but was very kind, He gave the
Indians 10 gallons of adulterated brandy, and they are now drunk.

E.2/4

29. Thursday fine weather wind S. paddled 60 miles E.B.S. then came
to basquea house* which is the same I passed in the fall on our arrival
the master came to the bank side, and in a genteel manner invited
me in, which I readily accepted, he entered into discourse with me
about indifferent subjects, but took no notice why I came inland, he
gave the Indians brandy and they are now drunk.

*This house is about 26 feet long, 12 foot wide, 9 feet high to the
ridge, having a sloaping roof, the walls log upon log, the top covered with
birch rind, it is divided into three appartments, one for trading goods,
and where the Master lives; one for the men; and one for the furs &c.

E.2/11

29. Thursday. Wind South and sultry weather. Paddled 60 miles, then
came to the French House I passed last Autumn; there were a Master
and 9 Men. On our arrival they gave the Natives ten Gallons of Brandy
adulterated, and they are now drunk. The Master invited me in to sup
with him, and was very kind: He is dressed very Genteel, but the men
wear nothing but thin drawers, and striped cotton shirts ruffled at the
hands and breast. This House has been long a place of Trade belonging to the French, and named Basquea. It is 26 feet long; 12 feet wide;
9 feet high to the ridge; having a Sloping roof; the Walls Log on Log;
the top covered with Birch-rind, fastned together with Willows, and

divided into three Apartments: One for Trading-goods, one for Furs, and the third they dwell in.

30 May 1755

    B.239/a/40

ye 30th Friday wind att S^o the Ind^s are busy talking &c.

    E.2/6

30 Frid^y wind south and very warm weather, forced to lye by, Indians drinking, talking, and trading with the French, and I Traded 5 cased Cats for powder & shot, breakfasted &c with the Master of the House, seed their stock of furs a brave parcel of fine cased Cats, Martins. and parchment Beaver, they have no Brazile Tobacco, but white tobacco like unto our English role; the Master was well dressed, and the Men wore nothing but thin drawers, and striped cotton shirts ruffled at hand and breast, they all talk the Language as well as the Natives themselves, and has a command over the Natives, notwithstanding the Natives tells us otherwise; in a fortnight the Master, 5 Men, and some Indians were going to their Chief Fort with the furs, and they arrive at this House again in the fall, and if they fall short which is sometimes the case, they then steal the goods, and with the help of Indians hawls all to this House in the winter.

    E.2/4

30 Friday warm weather, wind S. obliged to lie by, could not get the natives away, they have traded the most valuable furs, I breakfasted with the master and he showed me his stock of furs, a brave parcel of cassed cats, martins and parchment beaver; their birch rine canoes will carry as much as a long-boat and draws little water and are so light that two men can carry one of them with ease some miles, they are made in the same form and slight like the small ones, only they have a thin board runs along the bottom on the inside, and can sail them when going before the wind; the Frenchmen are masters of all the Indian languages & have greatly the advantage of us, and if they had brazile tobacco which they have not would entirely cut our trade off, they have white tobacco made up in roles of about 12 Hw^t, the master desired me to bring or send him some brazile tobacco and a quart or pint japanned drinking mug; he was dressed very genteel yesterday, but to day he is dressed like the natives excepting his white ruffled shirt, silk handkerchief tied round his head and laced hat; his men wears ruffled striped cotten shirts and a silk handkerchief round their heads, and in every other respect are like the natives.

    E.2/11

30. Friday. Wind South and very warm weather: The Indians drank so <much I> could not get them away; nor was I capable to prevent

them from trading their prime Furs. I breakfasted with the French
Master, and he shewed me the stock of Furs Viz. A brave parcel of
Cased Cats, Martens, and parchment Beaver. Their Birch-rind Canoes
will carry as much as an India Ships Long-boat, and draws little water;
and so light that two men can carry one several miles with ease: they
are made in the same form and slight materials as the small ones;
only a thin board runs along their bottom; and <they> can sail them
when before the wind, but not else. The French talk several Languages to perfection: They have the advantage of us in every shape,
and if they had Brazile tobacco, which they have not, would entirely
cut off our trade. They have white tobacco made up in Rolls of 12 Hw^t
each. The Master desired me to bring or send him a peice of Brazile
tobacco, & a quart, or pint, jappanned drinking mug.

31 May 1755
    B.239/a/40
May ye 31st Saturday fine weather wind SbW^t padled none the Ind^s are
Mending their Can^s.
    E.2/6
1755 May 31 Saturd^y wind SbW. and fine weather, oblidged to lye by, for
the Indians would not paddle to day, breakfasted &c with the French
Master, He begged the favour of me to bring or send Him one quart
and one pint black-Jack, & some Black tobacco.
    E.2/4
31. Saturday wind S.B.W. and fine weather, the Indians would not paddle, they have kept a continual trading, and I believe many would
trade all the furs and pelts they have if they could perswade them to
take their heavy goods, breakfasted &c with the master, he said that
he was going with the furs to one of their chief settlements as soon as
he received the furs from the upper house, which would be in a few
days hence.
    E.2/11
31. Saturday. Wind SbW. and warm sultry weather. The Indians would not
set out: they have kept a continual trading with the French; and I beleive
many would <trade> all if they could perswade the French to take their
heavy Furs. Breakfasted &c with the Master: He said he was going with
the Furs to one of the Chief settlements, as soon as he received the Furs
from the upper house, which would be in a few days hence.

1 June 1755
    B.239/a/40
June ye 1st Sunday Blowed hard and fell a Great deal of Rain in the
Evening fine weather Wind NE^t.

E.2/6
June 1 Sunday blowed strong, wind NE. could not paddle; breakfasted
&c with the French Master, He was daily expecting down the Cargo of
furs from the upper House.

E.2/4
June 1st Sunday blowed strong wind N.E. could not paddle, breakfasted &c with the master, several Aseenepoets distributed their heavy
furs and pelts that the French would not take, among our Indians,
with directions for what to trade them for.

E.2/11
June 1st Sunday. Wind NE and a strong gale: could not paddle: Breakfasted with the Master: Several Asinepoet Natives distributed their
heavy Furs and Pelts, that the French have refused, amongst our Indians with directions what to trade them for.

2 June 1755
B.239/a/40
ye 2d Monday fine weather wind att So this day we padled 70 M ENEt
and NEbNo deep water all the way, Land Low & tall woods.

E.2/6
2 Mondy fine weather, wind S. paddled 70 miles ENE & NEbN deep
water, Low banks, and tall woods.

E.2/4
2. Monday fine weather wind S. paddled 70 miles E.N.E. & N.E.B.N.
deep water, low banks and tall woods.

E.2/11
2. Monday. Wind South and fine weather: paddled 70 miles ENE &
NEbN. deep water, low banks, and tall woods.

3 June 1755
B.239/a/40
ye 3d Tuesday fine weather wind NEt this day padled 60 M NEbNo
padled through Monoko Sogahegan.

E.2/6
3 Tuesdy fine weather, wind NE. paddled 60 miles NEbN paddled
through Monoko Lake.

E.2/4
3. Tuesday fine weather wind N.E. paddled 60 miles N.E.B.N. and
entered monoco lake called by the Frenchmen Frenchmans lake, and
by the nakawawuck or bungee Indians little sea.

E.2/11
3. Tuesday. Wind NE and disagreeable weather: paddled none: Mustered my Gang total 70 Canoes.

4 June 1755

    B.239/a/40

ye 4th Wednesday a hard gale of wind att NEbN^o so that we Can paddle none, in the Evening Clear weather & Little wind.

    E.2/6

4 Wednesd^y a strong gale wind NEbN. paddled none, muster'd my Gang, total 70 Canoes.

    E.2/4

4. Wednesday a strong gale wind N.E.B.N. paddled none, mustered my gang after parting with the Churchill Natives, found it to be 70 canoes.

    E.2/11

4. Wednesday. Wind NE and cold weather; Paddled 60 miles NEbN. and entered Christianaux Lake.

5 June 1755

    B.239/a/40

ye 5th Thursday fine weather wind SW^t this day padled NEbN^o 40 M padled across the pond and Carried our Cannues &c over three points of Land for there is no Water in the River.

    E.2/6

5 Thursd^y fine weather, wind SW. paddled 40 miles NEbN. sometimes in Lakes and sometimes in Rivers, carryed our Canoes over 3 points of Land.

    E.2/4

5. Thursday fine weather wind S.W. paddled 40 miles N.E.B.N. sometimes in lakes, and sometimes in rivers, carryed our canoes over 3 points of land; the freshes in the rivers abating.

    E.2/11

5. Thursday. Wind SW and fine weather: paddled 40 miles NEbN. sometimes in Lakes and sometimes in Rivers: Carried our Canoes over three points of land

6 June 1755

    B.239/a/40

June ye 6th Friday wind NW^t this day padled and hawled our Cannoes 20 M killed Severall Jack and Carp with our paddles.

    E.2/6

6 Frid^y wind NW and a fresh gale, paddled & hawled our Canoes 20 miles, shoal water, and stones.

    E.2/4

6. Friday a fresh gale wind N.W. paddled and hawled our canoes 20 miles N.N.E. and N.E. shoal water and stones.

E.2/11

6. Friday. Wind NW and a strong gale of Wind; paddled & dragged our Canoes 20 Miles: Shoal Water & stones.

7 June 1755

B.239/a/40

ye 7th Saturday fine weather Wind S^o this day padled 40 M NNE^t and NbE^t being scarce Water to Swim our Cannoes, and the River full of Stones.

E.2/6

7 Saturd^y fine weather, wind SW paddled 40 miles NNE and NbE. scarce water to swim our Canoes, and full of stones killed several Large pike and Carp with our paddles &c.

E.2/4

7. Saturday fine weather wind S.W. paddled 40 miles N.N.E. & N.B.E. just water for our canoes, killed several large pike and carp with our paddles.

E.2/11

1755 June 7th Saturday. Wind NW and agreeable cold weather: Paddled 40 miles NNE & NBE barely depth of water for our Canoes: killed several large Pike and Carp with our paddles.

8 June 1755

B.239/a/40

ye 8th Sunday this day all hands fishing, for there is nothing to get Except a Duck or a Goose, and but few of them, fine Weather Wind SW^t.

E.2/6

8 Sunday fine weather, wind SW. paddled none, killed plenty of fine large fish of different kinds.

E.2/4

8. Sunday fine weather wind SW. lay by a fishing.

E.2/11

8. Sunday. Wind SW. and fine weather: paddled none: killed plenty of fish.

9 June 1755

B.239/a/40

ye 9th Monday this day fell a great deal of Rain wind NE^t this day padled 50 M in ye River.

E.2/6

1755 June 9 Mond^y wind NE. and rain all day, paddled 50 miles, down the River, good water, pleasant banks, with fine large lofty woods.

E.2/4

9. Monday wind N.E. and rain at times, paddled 50 miles down the river.

E.2/11

9. Monday Wind NE and rain all day; Paddled 50 miles down the River: Good Water, pleasant banks, with large lofty woods.

10 June 1755

B.239/a/40

ye 10th Tuesday small rain till Evening then fine weather, Wind att South, padled None to day.

E.2/6

10 Tuesd^y small rain wind S. paddled none, all hands fishing, plenty of pike, shads, Carp, & Merthy.

E.2/4

1756 June 10th Tuesday small rain wind S. lay by a fishing, caught plenty of pike, tickomeg, carp, shads, perch, merthy and suckers.

E.2/11

10. Tuesday. Wind South and small rain paddled none: all hands employed killing Fish Viz. Carp, Guyniad, & Pike, also a few Shads, Burbot & perch: the fish eats insipidly without Salt; my stock being expended.

11 June 1755

B.239/a/40

ye 11th Wednesday fine Weather Wind SW^t this day padled to Mukekemen Sogohigan.

E.2/6

11 Wednesd^y fine weather, wind SW. paddled to Mekekeman Lake; Caught several sturgeon with our fishgigs.

E.2/4

11. Wednesday fine weather wind S. paddled to mekekiman lake, caught several sturgeon with our fish-gigs.

E.2/11

11. Wednesday. Wind South and warm weather: Paddled to Mekekeman Lake: Caught several Sturgeon with our Fish-gigs; good food.

12 June 1755

B.239/a/40

ye 12th Thursday fine weather and the Wind att South, this day padled half way through the pond.

E.2/6

12 Thursd^y fine weather, wind S. paddled half way through the Lake, a great many woody Islands in it, lay on one.

E.2/4

12. Thursday fine weather wind S. paddled half way through the lake, and lay all night on one of its woody Islands.

E.2/11

12. Thursday. Wind South and warm Sultry weather. paddled halfway through the Lake and came to a small Island where we put up for the night.

13 June 1755

B.239/a/40

ye 13th Friday wind att NE^t, this day Came to the River or Creeck.

E.2/6

13 Frid^y wind NE. and Closs weather, paddled through the Lake, and came to a small River.

E.2/4

13. Friday wind N.E. and foggy weather, paddled through the lake and came at a small river.

E.2/11

1755 June 13th Friday. Wind NE and close weather, paddled across the Lake and came to a small river, there put up for the night.

14 June 1755

B.239/a/40

ye 14th Saturday fine weather & wind S° this day padled thro' the Creeck and thro' Attick Sogohigan.

E.2/6

14 Saturd^y fine weather, wind S. paddled down the River, and came to Deer Lake.

E.2/4

14. Saturday wind E. and fine weather, paddled down the river and came to deer lake.

E.2/11

14. Saturday. Winds variable and pleasant weather: paddled down the river and came to Deer Lake.

15 June 1755

B.239/a/40

June ye 15th Sunday fine weather wind att N°, this day 4 Cannoes past by us, told me the Govr was alive and well, and that Mr Skrimsher was dead.

E.2/6

15 Sunday fine weather, wind N. paddled through Deer Lake, and came to steel River, here met 4 Canoes who had been at the Fort, informed

me of the Death of Mr Saml Skrimpshewr, second in Command at York
Fort; and the Governor and all the Men were well; went and found my
tobacco safe, that I left here in the fall, and we all smoaked and drank
out 2 Rundlets of Brandy, that the Indians had brought from the Fort.

    E.2/4

15. Sunday fine weather wind N. paddled through deer lake and came
to steel river, here met with 4 canoes who had been at the fort, they
informed me of the death of Mr Skrimpshew second in command at
York Fort, and that the Governor and all the men were well, went and
found one fathom of brazile tobacco I left here last summer, with
which we smoaked, and are as happy as Princes.

    E.2/11

15. Sunday Wind North and fine weather: Paddled through Deer Lake
and came to Steel river: here met with 4 Canoes who had been at the
Fort, and who informed me of the death of Mr Skrimsheur, second in
Command at York Fort; and that the Governor & all the men were
well. Went & found my tobacco safe that I left here last Autumn: We
smoaked and drank out two Runlets of Brandy that the Natives had
brought from the fort.

16 June 1755

    B.239/a/40

ye 16 Monday fine weather wind West, this day padled thro' the River.

    E.2/6

16 Mond^y wind W. paddled down the River, good water.

    E.2/4

16 @ 23. Monday @ Monday winds variable in the E^tn hank, after paddling down the river, sometimes in good water, and sometimes
obliged to hawl and carry our canoes &c over shoals, arrived at York
Fort at the head of 70 canoes of different tribes of Indians.

    Course from YF to Basquea house on keskechewan river south 54
Degrees West & Dist 535 M. From YF to his greatest distance inland
south 63 D. W. Dist 1130 M.

    E.2/11

16. @ 20 Monday @ Friday Winds Westerly and pleasant weather.
Sometimes had good Water and sometimes dragged our Canoes; had
several Canoes damaged: when on the 20th day of this month of june
we arrived at the fort, where we were kindly received.

17 June 1755

    B.239/a/40

ye 17th Tuesday fell a great deal of Rain untill Evening, then fine
weather, wind NE^t. padled thro' the Islands of Shebastock

E.2/6

17 Tuesd^y pleasant weather wind W paddled down the River, passed several Islands, and falls.

18 June 1755
B.239/a/40

ye 18th Wednesday fine weather wind SW^t this day Carried our things over 7 falls.

E.2/6

1755 June 18 Wednesd^y wind SW. and rain at times, paddled and sometimes carryed our Canoes &c, the falls are so troublesome.

19 June 1755
B.239/a/40

ye 19 Thursday fine weather wind SE^t. this day padled thro' falls & betwixt Rocks, very dangerous Stove my Canue, and Severall of the Ind^s Stove theirs, one broke in the middle.

E.2/6

19 Thursd^y fine weather, wind SE. paddled, carryed, and hawled our Canoes, several broke and mine greatly damaged.

20 June 1755
B.239/a/40

ye 20th Friday fine weather wind att West padled and Carried our things over 6 falls.

E.2/6

20 Frid^y fine weather, wind W. mended our Canoes, and set out, the River as yesterday, several Canoes damaged.

21 June 1755
B.239/a/40

June ye 21 Saturday fine weather wind SE^t padled from Lock fall to pine Reach, mett Severall Gangs of Ind^s.

E.2/6

21 Saturd^y wind SE. and fine weather, paddled to pine reach, met several Gangs of Indians, that were come from ye Fort.

22 June 1755
B.239/a/40

ye 22^d Sunday fine weather Wind NE^t. padled down steel River into Hayes River, and then down Hayes River to the 20 M Creeck, the Shores Lined with Ice.

E.2/6

22 Sunday fine weather, wind NE. paddled down steel River into Hayse River to 20 mile Creek, shores lined with Ice, a strange alteration in so short a time.

23 June 1755

B.239/a/40

ye 23^d Monday fine weather, wind Veriable from SW^t to E^t. Sett out, this att the Head of 46 Cannues (12 More will be att the fort Shortly) and att 10 Gott to the fort.

E.2/6

23 Mond^y fine weather, wind SE. paddled down the River, and got to York Fort at 10 o clock A.M. at the head of 65 Canoes, there were 70 but 5 were broke to pieces on the falls of steel River, and the Goods put into other Canoes.

Corrected Course from York Fort to Basquea House on Keskachewan River South 54 Degrees West, Distance 535.

Corrected Course from York Fort to the greatest distance He was inland South 63 Degrees 13 minutes West 1130 miles.

Notes and Remarks
appended to the B.239/a/40 journal

This Finished Captn Hendey's Journey and beg Leave, & beg Leave to observe some Remarks on the foresaid Journal, and what he observes to me of ye Country.

Captn Hendey was gone from the fort one year; by his observations & accounts he gives me, he underwent not a little hardship, in particular att times travelling some days, and not a drop of sweet water to be had, yet he proceeded on his Journey with a Resolution suitable to ye design he was sent upon, & att Last arrived att the Earchithinue Country, where says he they are more Like English than Indians, having plenty of fine horsses of all Colours, are very Dexterous in Rideing, & managing ye Same. When they go a hunting they mount their horsses and Ride after ye Bufflow, moose or waskesw^s & with their Bows & arrows kill ye Beastes as they ride along; their Bridles & sadles are made of ye strips of Buffuloe or moose hides, with stirrups, Crupper &c of ye same, & ride ye same as in other parts, these horsses are of great Service to them in Carrying or hawling of goods, for altho' they have no Carts, yet they have a contrivance which answers the same Effect, which is Sleds, having a pole fixed on Each Side the head of the Sled, which hangs by a back band on Each side the horse (the same as Shafts to a cart) by which they Hawl good Loads: when these Ind^s wants to Cross Rivers or Rivulets, they swim their horsses, but the other Ind^s he tells me have another method, which is having some moose or Bufflow parchment Skins these are sowed together, then 2 Long poles is Led along Each Side for a Gunnell, and willows bent and tied in for the Ribbs, which keeps the skins out; when Crossed the River they unty the Gunnels & Ribbs & Role the skins up, so Carry them till they come to another River.

[3 July: "16 falls, where we was obliged to Carry our Canoes"]
Here says Captn Hendey was ye most difficulty in his travell, being
obliged to hawl and Carry their Cannues &c the Chief part of ye way,
the Quantity of stones was Ruff to their feet, Caused his Legs to Swell
that once He thought he would not be able to proceed, but finding
the Road Better & the swelling abating, he proceeded on his Journey,
he also observes a Ledge of Rocks, and stones which Runs across
Country which makes it unnavigable for any Vessell proceeding up
Country, more than small Cannues, and those with much difficulty, as
observed by Experience.

July ye 31st ["they all promised to go with me to the fort"] These
Esenepoets are very Numerous have plenty of Goods in their Country,
kill but Little and that they Carry to the french, these has the knowledge & art of making and using Cannues, using such Formerly (that is
to say) before the year 1733 they used to frequent York Fort to trade,
but that year in Returning back, the North River Esenipoets and them
had a battle up steel River, by which ye Captn & most of his Men were
killed, and have not been att any of ye fortts since, they were very
Civill to Captn Hendey, mightily pleased att his Coming to See them,
and did promise to go to the fort with him in ye Spring of ye Year, but
the Reason they did not shall be observed hereafter, he observes there
are upwards of 50 tents of these Esinepoets, which may be Computed
att 400 Ind^s or more which knows ye nature of Cannues, and plenty of
Goods in their Country;

Augst ye 3^d ["fine Levell Land . . ."] Now Captn Hendey arrives
in a fine pleasant Country, with plenty of provisions, here says he is
plenty of fruit of severall Sorts, such as plums, Damsons, Cherrys,
Nutts, fillberds, and Rasberries. &c but tho' all these Rarities and a
pleasant Country, yet was not so to him, being scarce of good sweet
water, which made it quite unpleasant, being obliged to travell hard,
sometimes 2 or 3 days before they Could Reach where small springs of
good Water was to be had, ye water att other places being Either Salt
or Stinking so no drinking of it att many of these salt ponds, or
Lakes, there is upon the shores Large Lumps of had Candid Salted,
which he tasted of and Caused a purging.

[26 August: "one of the Ind^s brought me a Snake"] the Snake
Skin as well as all other of ye Captains Curiosities I have sent home.

[14 October: "we mett the Earchithinue men on horse back"]
Here was what Captn Hendey after a 114 days travelling thro' great
hardships and difficultys arrived att (vizt) the Earchithinues; where
ascending up a high hill he had the prospect of a Camp of upwards of
200 tents, these Ind^s were as much overjoyed to see him, as the
Esenipoets were, made very much of him, he the Captn in Return

made their King, then the officers & Soldiers a present of such Commodities as he had. they all promised faithfully to come to the fort,
being in want of ammunition, Guns, hatchets &c as to paint and
tobacco they made but slight of saying they have Enough of their own
better (tho' att the same time sad stuff) these are quite different to
all other Ind^s in Regard to their Customs, manners, Behaviour &c
there are as much discipline observed as in some other parts of y^e
world, their Monarch or King is obliged by all he is seated att times
on the throne where he gives out orders to his officers for his Men to
do so and so, no Sooner the word is past but Directly Each man or
Soldier performs his part According as ordered with a willing Chear-
full Behaviour, some on ye paroll, others Rideing round the borders of
their Country, to see if any Enemies are att hand, this is done twice a
day, and some times oftner, Just as their King has Intelligence of an
Enemy: their Enemies are the other Earchithinues, which are at a further distance, which the former warrs with are not so fair a Complex-
ion nor yet ye Qualitys the former are Endued with. These are more
Numerous, have nothing but Bows, and are no more then ye former,
Except a few the English Earchithinues gets of our Ind^s, was they
brought to trade and had guns, these near or English Earchithinues
(as Captn Hendey calls them) wowld soon overpower their Enemys
and by that means Leave More att Ease as those forregn Earchithinues are frequently Coming down upon the English Earchithinues
(I call them English Earchithinues, to distinguish them from the others) I observe in Captn Hendeys Acc^t their is upwards of 250 tents of
English Earchithinues, and Esenepoets, besides the Bloody Ind^s which
are Numerous, and differs Little from ye Esinepoets, that might be
brought to trade.

But the misfortune is the English Earchithinues has not y^e
knowledge of padling in cannues, nor Even knows not how to make
such, they Rideing Chiefly; two of them was 2 or 3 days Sitting in a
Cannue, other Ind^s padling, but being afraid turned back neither, did
those Ind^s Encourage them, that I sent in Care of Captn Hendey, by
reason if they were brought to trade it would deprive them of Getting
Goods of the English Earchithinues, Which att present they do for ½
the value they gett such of us, but also be obliged to hunt and gett
goods themselves, which att present they are Loth to do, while they
can have them att such a Cheap Rate of ye aforesaid English Earchithinues.

NOTWITHSTANDING all this Captn Hendey told the King, and all the
Earchithinues to gett goods, and he would go see the governor, and
Return again with more presents, and Conduct them to the fort
where they might trade themselves, being great plenty of sundry

Goods, they as well as the Esinepoets and Bloody Ind^s promised so to
do, told Captn Hendey to be as good as his word, and to bring two
More of his country Men (they said their Country Men for they
Looked upon Captn Hendey as their Country man) for in truth they
had a great deal more Love & Respect for him then our Ind^s had, they
being Jealous, Captn Hendey should succeed), and gett them to trade,
as before observed.

ACCORDING to this Capt Hendeys Acc^t I fitted him out again with
proper assistance, of goods, on the 27th of June 1755, and Willm Grover
comp^y apprentice, hiring an Ind^n which Captn Hendey had by wintering and hunting with, for to assist in Learning and showing the
Earchithinues the art of Cannues, this Man (says Capt Hendey) is the
most beloved by ye Ind^s, a down Right Civill Man and one (says Captn
Hendey that will succeed therein; the Man I gave a Small present to
Talkt to him, found him fitt ye purpose, and promised him a further
Reward if he succeeded therein, that is in Aiding & assisting Captn
Hendey and Grover, in Learning and Showing the English Earchi-
thinues how to paddle & make Cannues) he promised faithfully so to
do.

Captn Hendey further says, that he does Really believe if English
were to go in Land for 2 or 3 years would not only bring the Esinepoets,
to trade, but also the English Earchithinues, which would be a great
Addition in trade, having plenty of goods in their Country.

Certainly for By so doing opens a new trade, and might in a few
years have twice the Cannues that now Comes, and Consequently double the trade.

In my Humble Opinion a Method their is, which would not only
Confirm the above, but cause the present Ind^s to be more Industrious
in getting of Goods. (That is)

Supposing severall men were sent inland Each for the first
time, to be fitted out att ye Comp^{ys} Charge, in goods Requisite for
there Mentenance for one year, afterwards Each Man to Support
himself (ie) that is What ffurrs or other Commodities he Gott to
trade such att ye fortt for Merchandize Goods, not Exceeding the
value of his furrs, first Knowing the price of such Merchandize Goods
they are to pay for, next the price of Each Sort of Furrs per peice or
pound to be Rated att in money for the said Merchandize goods, in
so dealing and in ca[xxx] any furrs more then he takes up in goods,
to be sold by ye Company, for the said person, the Comp^y to have Per
C^{wt} for such sum or Sums of money, the furrs Sold for as the said
Company shall think Reasonable, Besides what wages the Comp^y
thinks proper to Allow Each Man per Annum (ie) the french allowing
Each Man Per Annum so Much the Goods they deal for/ The Afore-

mentioned proceeding would be the only Means to Root ye french
out, and therefore Recover the trade they have so Long Enjoyed by
Encroaching upon the Borders of our Country, neither is there any
fear of their Rising by persons being sent in Land, when Captn
Hendey observes he and 2 more Could have took Either of their
hutts, and startled them to See one Man, much More if severall were
sent. This I mentioned to My officers who thought it proper to be
mentioned to Your Hon^{rs}.

I mentioned before of sending Captn Hendey a Second time, but
all these my Endeavours, (which we had brought to such a Height and
please God Captn Hendey had proceeded would have (its my humble
opinion) have succeeded next season) were att once frustrated, by an
Unforeseen Accident, for on July ye 2^d See a Cannue Coming down
the River, which to my great Surprize was Captn Hendey who
Returned with all his things and Grover who was not Capable of proceeding, being quite Jaded before he got a 100 Miles from the fortt,
this was a great disappointment in our proceedings, Captn Hendey
being no Less Concerned then Myself being disappointed of an Undertaking he had so Good a prospect of success in.

THIS put a stop to ye undertaking for this season for the Ind^s
when they see Captn Hendey Return with Willm Grover, who would
have persuaded Captn Hendey to put Grover on Shore and Lett him
take his time in getting to ye fort, being Sorry that the Captn should
Leave them, But the Captn told them if any Accident befell his Companion he must Answer for it to his Country Men, therefore the Ind^s
all proceeded on their Journey, by which having got so far, and so
many days padle of, it was too Late for Captn Hendey to Gett up to
them, before they would Seperate that he might not see them all the
Year, therefore be of no Signification of going by himself. But please
God he Continues in health, he is willing to proceed the Next season
by himself, and Ind^s, or with 2 or 3 More.

[17 January: "nothing to Compare to York Fort for Cold"] here
Captn Hendey Observes the Moderate Climate they were in, where
says he I wore but one Buffuloe shoe and a peice of flannell on Each
foot, this Buffaloe shoe (its to be observed) had the Hair on which is
Equivolent to A Good Sock, But yet att the fort we are obliged to wear
3 or 4 Good Soacks on Each foot for several Months.

[2 February: "Strive to please the women"] Here the Captn is in
a merry mode, Yet I Cannot say he is in ye wrong in one shape, that is
to please the Ladys so farr as not to Create a Misunderstanding
between Man & Wife; in such a Case the men are pleased, you have a
Modest Regard for them. I Can but own if I had been in Captn
Hendey's place, when the King of the Earchithinues offerred him his

Daughter in Marriage (and I a single man as he was) would have
Embraced ye proposal, which would have Created a firm friendship,
and wowld have been A great help in Engaging them to trade.

[10 February: "our Ind^s . . . were going to Warr again"] in asking
Captn Hendey Concerning their Warring he says 20 young Men went
with ye English Earchithinues to war against the other Earchithinues,
7 of our Ind^s he says was killed, the rest was not Returned when he
Came away in ye spring, which therefore makes them Imagine they
they are all killed, it's a Common Rule when any is killed on Either
Side to Skulp them; (that is) taking the Skin from the forehead, to
the pole of the Neck off, with the Hair on the Skin; this they tie upon
a Long stick and Carry before them, when Return from Warr, as a
mark of their Abilities &c this way of Sulping is done when the person
is alive. Sometimes, having a Esinepoet Captn who has used this place
many years, who was Served so, made his Escape by the Assistence of
another Indian, I observed the Hair never Grows on that part afterwards, tho' I knew the said Indian 20 Years.

[8 March: "the Indian he being acquainted with the Country"]
this is the Indian I mentioned before as a proper person to be with
Captn Hendey, yet I can but observe Captn Hendey was in the wrong
to part with his Gun in a Strange Country, by himself and before he
had tryed the Behaviour of this Indian, Howsomever the Man proved
to be An honest Man & a good friend.

[13 March: "I told them they all trade with the french"] Here he
hints of ye Ind^s trading with ye French, which they Cannot deny; this is
no More then what I always Understood, therefore No Wonder they
bring so Little goods to us, there is Certainly a Good Reason for there
so doing, the great distance they are of from the ffortt, and no
English Settlements in Land, obliges them to trade with the french,
as they Cannot Carry a Sufficient Quantity of ammunition &c such a
distance from the fort to Supply them, for the year a plain proof of
which, Notwithstanding I supplyed Captn Hendey well with Ammunition, he was obliged to trade for a Little powder of the french, on his
Road down to bring him to ye fort, not but that if the English was Inland about 500 Mile, ye Ind^s would Come sooner 200 Mile to them
then 100 to the french, by reason they would Gett Considerable More
for their Goods, Enough of this having before observed upon the same
head, of which I was Informed, and which is partly true by the Acc^t of
Captn Hendey.

Having examined or att Least proposed questions to Captn
Hendey of what I had been Informed of the Country, and of what I had
att times observed to your Hon^rs, found all Such Remarks to vary but
Little from the truth.

[30 March: "Not be Long Considering for to knock me on the Head"] here Captn Hendey observes the danger he was In on Acc^t of the old Man & his Son, which Caused him to be Cautious how he discoursed with them howsomever he was danted att their Behaviour, the Chief part of the Ind^s being his friends.

[17 April: "I with my bow & Arrow"] Now Captn Hendey begins to Show his dexterity by being among Ind^s who took a delight in Shewing him the use of the Bow & Arrow by which Means he is as near able to Maintain himself by the Bow & Arrow as the best of them, as may be Seen by his killing Moose, Swans &c.

[27 April: "I Embarked on board a new Ship"] now he Embarks for York Fort with a Chearfulness after So Meny Months travelling about the Country, and Notwithstanding their padling about 40, 50 or 60 Miles a day before a strong Current it was the 23^d of June before he arrived att the fort, and

[16 May: "the Leader . . . told me he would go to ye fortt and Gett . . . all sorts of Goods"] if the Indians Could have Come on horse back they would not have hesitated upon it, but that is unpracticable, and

[21 May: "here is 60 Canoes designed for the fort if ye french does not stop them"] 58 of the 60 Cannues Came to ye fort altho' but thinly gooded.

[23 May: "we Came to a french House"] Here the Captain Gets to the french, Leaving all those Bloody Esinepoets and Earchithinues, but 2 days padle of which Certainly must trade with the french, as they Can Ride so farr, tho' Captn Hendey observes they had but Little goods att present, But promised to Get goods Another Season ag^t his Return as before observed.

IN DISCOURSING with Captn Hendey he tells me of a Skeam the Earchithinues have to deceive their Enemys, which is:

They make a Round Spott about 14 Inches Over, or Just Room for a mans body, they then take the Duff off, and Lay it carefully on one Side, they then digg a hole down under the Solid Ground, 5 feet deep and about 5 feet over, being also Round taking Care to Lett none of the dirt drop near the place, but Carry it in their Coats a Considerable distance of, when done they take small sticks and Lay Across, then Cover over with the Above peice of Duff, then much of this is to Deceive their Enemy, that none shall know where they Hide.

He also observes in the English Earchithinue Country their are plenty of horsses, Goats very Large, and turkees plenty and full as Large as in England.

Up Navigable River which opens into steel River, and below pine Reach, as per draught; Captn Hendey observes Cannues such as the french has, might go from the fort up to the Lake, where a Settlement Might be Erected, which is but a small distance from the french, and where the Ind^s told him if a Settlement there all the Ind^s would Come to the English, & not go to the french; by his draught it seems Likely being a branch or River of Deep Water, free from Windings; butt up port Nelson Captn Hendey thinks unpracticable, being very Intricate, full of Showles, falls &c.

Month & day	Miles	Course	Remarks
	583		
July 24	6	W^t	
25	27	SWbW^t	from the French fort to the peatago River
26	28	d^o	
27	2	(SWbW^t) (SWbS^o)	
28	26	d^o	
29	24	SW^t	
30	22	d^o	
31	26	WSW^t	
Augt 1st	24	SWbS^o	
2	20	d^o	
3	21	d^o	
4	20	NW^t	
5	22	W^t	
7	24	SW^t	from where Left Canoes to Mermans Lake,
9	6	W^t	
	14	WbS^o	from Mermans Lake to salt plain
10	4	WbN^o	from salt plain to plentifull plain
11	22	WSW^t	from plentifull Plain to Burnt hill
12	15	WSW^t	from Burnt hill to cherry plain
15	17	W^t	from Cherry plain to horse plain
16	15	WbN^o	from horse plain to hair plain
17	17	NW^t	from Hair plain to Link Spaw
19	20	WNW^t	from Link Spaw to Yealage pond
20	15	N^o	from Yealage pond to Wapuse Copeto
22	14	NW^t	from Wapuse Copeto to Shenap's plain
23	25	W^t	from Shenap's plain to poston plain
24	12	WbN^o	from poston plain to Earchithinue C^k
25	20	W^t	from Earchithinue C^k to Low life point
	1095		

26	17	WbN^o	from Low Life point to Shad Creeck
27	16	d^o	from Shad Creeck to Bear Valley
30	20	NW^t	from Bear Valley to Lawrence Bosom
31	14	d^o	from Lawrence Bosom to Beaver Creeck
S[ept] 1st	10	NWbN^o	from Beaver Creeck to St Caterns hill
3	14	NW^t	from St Caterns hill to Swan pond
4	12	d^o	from Swan pond to Jamon Creek
5	14	W^t	from Jamon Creeck to Sandy hill
6	10	WSW^t	from Sandy hill to Wood Creek
7	12	d^o	from Wood Creek to Squasish plain
8	10	d^o	from Squasish plain to Connawappa C^k
9	10	d^o	from Connawappa C^k to Buffalo plain
11	15	WNW^t	from buffalo plain to Maidenhead
12	24	d^o	from Maidenhead to frog pond
13	10	NW^t	from frogg pond to Barren plain
15	14	WNW^t	from Barren plain to snake pond
16	12	NW^t	from Snake pond to Cunekan Creek
19	14	d^o	from Cunekan C^k to Esinepoet hill
20	12	SW^t	from Esinepoet hill to horse pond
21	14	SWbS	from Horse pond to toad pond
24	10	d^o	from toad pond to Magpy plain
25	10	W^t	from Magpie plain to thrush ledge
26	11	WbN	from thrush ledge to Grasshopper plain
27	14	d^o	from Grasshopper plain to Constenak R^r
30	15	WSW^t	from Constenak R^r to W^e horse plain
O[ct] 2	14	SW^t	from White horse plain to Accident C[^{k}]
3	12	WSW^t	from Accident Creeck to Skunk pond
5	12	d^o	from Scunk Pond to Beaver Creek
	1457		
Octr 6	15	SW^t	from Beaver Creeck to flint Hill
8	14	d^o	from flint Hill to Mowld Hill
9	11	SWbW^t	from Mowld Hill to Seakip pond
11	14	d^o	from Seakip pond to Waskesu River
12	16	d^o	from Waskesu R^r to Earchithinue hill
13	15	d^o	from Earchithinue Hill to Hayes plain
14	4	d^o	Here Mett y^e Earchithinues &c.
	1546		

The above is a Remark of y^e Course and Miles &c the Captn Steered, which by a Computation he makes out to be 1546 Miles from York Fort to y^e English Earchithinue Country.

Maps

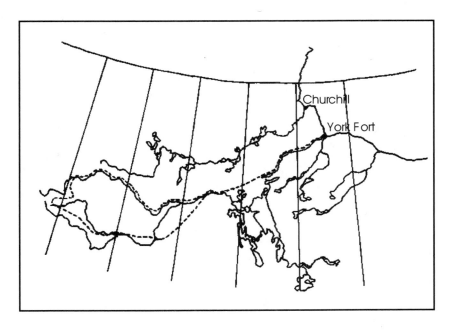

Churchill

York Fort

LINE MAP

This map shows Henday's route as traced by Richard Ruggles, the foremost historian of Hudson's Bay Company cartography (*The Historical Atlas of Canada*, plate 58). Ruggles based the route on Clifford Wilson's endorsement of Morton's and MacGregor's deductions. In his history and catalogue of HBC maps, Ruggles states that quite possibly Henday "was the first European to sight the Rocky Mountains front from Canadian [*sic*] territory" (*A Country So Interesting*, 38), yet his verbal description of the route places Henday no farther west than Olds, Alberta, a location which is at variance with the route as mapped and too far east for a glimpse of the Rockies.

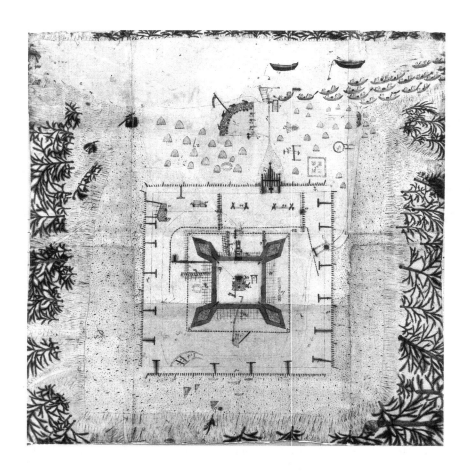

HBCA G.2/5
James Isham, "Plan of York Fort," undated.
Isham is thought to have drawn this map of York's old site on the north bank of the Hayes River, downstream from the present site. A brigade of canoes arrives to trade, led by a hatted winterer. The plan shows a landing dock, Native tents, the gated pallisade and ground cleared to prevent an ambush of the fort.

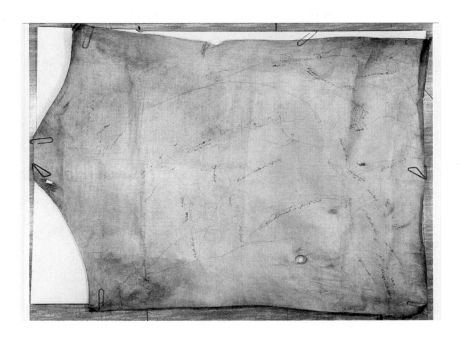

HBCA G.2/8
Moses Norton, "Draught of the Northern Parts
of Hudson's Bay . . . " 1760.
This map shows routes and landmarks described (and probably drawn)
by Matonabbee and Idotlyazee, two leaders who traded at Churchill.
Features of this map include the "middle track" up the Hayes River,
the Saskatchewan River with three French houses, a Beaver River, a
"Beaver Mount" and "Ye track to Henday's tent."

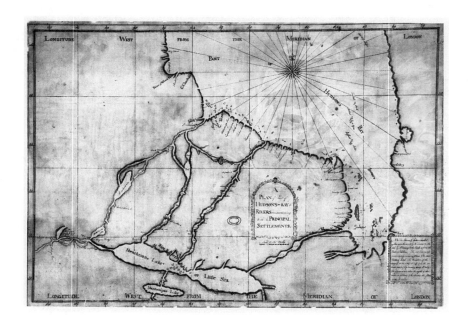

HBCA G.2/15

Andrew Graham, "A Plan of Part of Hudson's-Bay & Rivers, communicating with the Principal Settlements," 1772.

This map shows the extent of the Bayside factors' knowledge of the interior before the explorations of Hearne and Cocking. It is a valuable record of the three "tracks" (upper, middle and lower) leading from York Fort to the Saskatchewan River and Lake Winnipeg ("Frenchman's Lake or Little Sea").

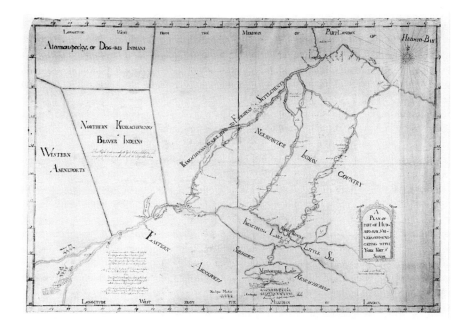

HBCA G.2/17
Andrew Graham, "A Plan of part of Hudson's-Bay & Rivers,
communicating with York Fort and Severn," 1774.
Drawn after Cocking's return from his year inland, this map repeats
the three canoe routes from York Fort, and traces the Saskatchewan
River as far west as the Eagle Hills. Tribal territories are assigned to
new Native groups trading at the Bay.

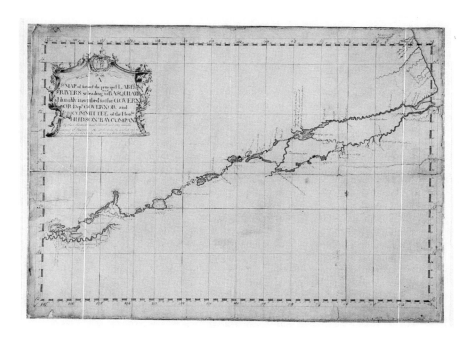

HBCA G.1/20
**Samuel Hearne, "A Map of some of the principal Lakes River's
&c leading from YF to Basquiaw," [1775].**

Hearne kept not only journals but this cartographic record of his two
winters inland from York Fort (1773-75). The map shows the river
routes in great detail (the shape of lakes, the direction of river flow,
the number of rapids and portages), as well as furnishing the Native
names of certain features.

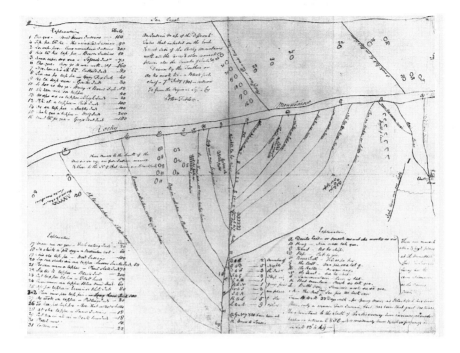

HBCA G.1/25

Peter Fidler, "An Indian map of the Different Tribes that inhabit on the East & west side of the Rocky Mountains . . . Drawn by the Feathers or ac ko mok ki—a Blackfoot chief . . . " 1801.

This map, well known for its representation of the Missouri River and its tributaries, is remarkable also for its location and designation of western Native groups during the period of early contact. Fidler calls these small groups "Tribes," but few of the names listed on the map are the large linguistically based categories familiar to anthropologists.

Notes to the Texts

Codes Used in Notes to the Texts

T = Textual Notes and Cross-references
P = Contemporary Hudson's Bay Company Maps and Plans
    HBCA G. 2/8, Norton, "Draught," 1760
    HBCA G.2/15, Graham, "Plan of Hudson's-Bay . . . " 1772
    HBCA G.2/17, Graham, "Plan of Hudson's-Bay . . . " 1774
    HBCA G.1/20, Hearne, "Map of some of the principal Lakes Rivers . . . " [1775]
    HBCA G.1/25, Ackomokki, "An Indian Map of the Different Tribes . . . " 1801
C = Contemporary Hudson's Bay Company Records and Correspondence
    HBCA A.6/8-10, London Committee letters outward, 1752-77
    HBCA A.11/114-15, York Fort letters inward, 1752-72
    HBCA B.239/a/37-66, York Fort post journals, 1753-72
    HBCA B.198/a/9, Severn House post journal, 1767-68
W = Winterers' Journals
    HBCA B.239/a/43, Smith, journal, 1756-57
    HBCA B.239/a/45, Smith, journal, 1757-58
    HBCA B.239/a/56, Pink, journal, 1766-67
    HBCA B.239/a/58, Pink, journal, 1767-68
    HBCA B.239/a/61, Pink, journal, 1768-69
    HBCA B.239/a/63, Pink, journal, 1769-70
    HBCA B.239/a/64, Tomison, journal, 1768-69
    HBCA B.239/a/69, Cocking, journal, 1772-73
    HBCA B.239/a/72, Cocking, journal, 1774-75
    HBCA B.239/d/44, York Fort Account Book, 1754
    HBCA B. 49/a/1, Hearne, journal, 1774-55
M = Hudson's Bay Company Memoirs
    HBCA E.2/1, Isham, "Observations on Hudson's Bay," 1743
    Robson, *Account of Six Years Residence in Hudson's-Bay,* 1752

HBCA E.2/6, E.2/4, E.2.5, E.2/9, E.2/11, E.2/12, Graham, "Observations on Hudson's Bay," 1767-92
Umfreville, *The Present State of Hudson's Bay*, 1790
H = Commentary on Henday's Year Inland
　　Burpee, "York Factory to the Blackfeet Country," 1907
　　Burpee SWS, *The Search for the Western Sea*, 1908
　　Isbister, correspondence with J. B. Tyrrell, 1909
　　Tyrrell, introduction to *The Journals of Hearne and Turnor*, 1934
　　Morton, *The History of the Canadian West to 1871*, 1931/1973
　　Mandelbaum, *The Plains Cree*, 1942/1979
　　MacGregor, *Behold the Shining Mountains*, 1954
　　Rich, *The History of the Hudson's Bay Company 1670-1870*, 1967
　　Morse, *Fur Trade Canoe Routes of Canada*, 1969/1971
　　Ray, *Indians in the Fur Trade*, 1974
　　Williams, "The Puzzle of Anthony Henday's Journal," 1987
　　Russell, *Eighteenth-Century Western Cree and their Neighbours*, 1991

Complete bibliographical citations are given in the List of Sources.

Notes to the Texts

Instructions

C   YF post journal (Isham): "att noon all the traders went away with whom Anthony Hendy who is a hearty Man, and very fond & willing to Go inland, I therefore procured a trusty home Ind^n, and a Lad with a Leading Ind^n, who has Lived Long with the Earchithinues, I have therefore According to Orders fitted out the Said Anthony Hendy, with the aforesaid Ind^s, and sent them with the Keschachewan Indians to ye Earchithinues, in order to bring to trade next summer &c a Copy of his Instructions are herein Inclosed in this packet." (HBCA B.239/a/37, 26 June 1754)

C   James Isham, "Instructions to Anth^y Hendy Dated att York Fort, Feby ye 19th 1754":

1st You are to proceed with the Wheel and Guides, up Hays'^{s} River, untill you Come to the Enterance of Steel River, which open's into Hays'^{s} River, on the NW^t Side, from which place you are to proceed up Steel River, by wheel and Compass, till such time you Come to a branch that open's into Nelson River; Do not be misled by the Indians, but observe truely whether you think such a branch is Likely for the Natives to pass with Cannus &c because you will meet with a sort of branch or two, as I have been Inform^d that does not reach Nelson River, the true branch being the track the Indians comes down &c: when you have enter'd Nelson River, if you observe any thing perticular mark it Down, and then Steer your Course Down Nelson River and so to the Fort./

2^d Every three or four mile Examine what Depth of water, up Steel River, the branch and Nelson &: and mark it Down in the Colum of your wast book as near as possable./

3^d Observe the wedth at Defferent Distances as you proceed up, also the Currant, taking perticular care to be exact in showing the points, Islands, Bluffs, woods, Barren Lands, Creeks, Lakes or branches as you proceed, that they may answer truly with the Distances as measured p^r Wheel, also minding your Cou'se from point to point or Bluff, by Compass./

4th Take perticular notice of the falls, what Depth, water above and below &c the natives Informing me some are perdigious high; also if any Remarkuble point, tree, or bluff; Enquire of the natives the name of Such, if none, give Such a name and Remark it in your wast Book./

5th Every Evening you put up, observe while your guides are making a Hutt, if any trees, Shrubs &: grows that Does not near the fort, wheather in bud or otherwise, and if any possability try the Soil at each place, Reserving a Little in a peice of paper, marking upon the paper the Day of ye month./

6th When the Indians has done the Hutt, be sure to try the Depth of water and Currant, by which you have an opportunity of trying for fish, also Remark what game you Kill, and sett gins &c:

7th Be sure to be upon your Journey by 6° in the morning, Saying [   ] y^e sett out at 6°, took my Departure from _____ Steering my Course as p^r wheel and compass & giving the place a name if already none, where you Last put up./

8th As you proceed observe the winds and weather, Every two hour's, and Remark in your wast Book;—Converse with the guides as much as you can, that you attain the Language; that you may be Qualified the better to undertake a Journey hereafter./

9th When you Enter into Nelson River out of the branch that Leads into Steel River, take perticular notice wheather that is the upper or Lower fork, and the name the Indians tells you, that I may Know if they Inform a me wright (I Knowing the Indians name for such./

10th If the guide say's the fork, may be a Day or two higher up Nelson River from the above Enterance, then if your Health and Necessarys will allow, proceed up to the said fork, but no higher at Pres^t, but if the fork should be at the said Enterance or Lower Down, then proceed to the fort as in the first Instructions./

11th And Lastly, be sure to be very Exact in your acc^t taking time.—I observed before sett out by 6° and put by 4 afternoon, Sooner or Later, as oppertunity and Conveniency for a Lodging will allow, I Computing by what I have been Inform^d

your Journey to be from the fort, round and Down Nelson ab^t 300 miles, which at 15 mile Pr Day, will be twenty Dayes, which may be allowed 30 Days, on acc^t of bad weather and sometimes perhaps travel Less or more, but in my opinion you will find it far short of 200 M.—be Resolute in your proceedings. and you need Doubt of Encouragem^t from

Your Freind

James Isham

Vera copia

[endorsed] YF 1754 A Copie of Instructions to Anth^y Hendey
Dated at York Fort Feby ye 19th 1754''

(HBCA A.II/II4)

C   YF Account Book (Isham): "Gave for Journeys att times and Sent By Anth^y Hendey to present to foreign Indians &c^a

	N^o&c^a	quantity	Bear^r
files	N^o	3	3
Guns Long		3	42
powder	lb	24	24
Shot Brist		48	12
L. E^t In^da		48	12
tobacco Brz^l		26½	35⅓
Roll		16	16
Steels	N^o	24	6
Awles		64	8
Needles Q^g		100	8⅓
paint	lb	1½	24
Beads China) Red & White)	lb	2	12
Black b^y C^n		2	12
White		2	12
L^g r^d white		6	[ ]
Small		3	6
Blew		3	6
Feathers		3	1½
Knives Jack	N^o	48	12
L^g Roach		48	12
Brandy	G^n	7	28
Blankets	N^o	2	14
Cloth red	Y^d	8	24
Hatch^ts M.	N^o	4	4
Ice Chess^ls		2	2
Hatts Laced		3	12

. . . Men's Debts . . . Anth^y Henday . . .		$\mathcal{L}$	s	D
To Blankets	2 N^o	16		0
To Cloth white	¾ Y^d	4		10½
To Flannel	4 Y^{ds}	6		0
To Stockings Knitt	1 P^r	3		0
To Tobacco Vir^g L^t	28 lb	14		0
To D^o English Roll	8 lb	8		0
To Sugar Brown	13 lb	9		9
To pipes	8 Doz^n	2		8

(HBCA B.239/d/44)

M   Isham: "[The Earchithinues] have no trade with any Nation as Yet . . . why may not peace be made up between these [stone] Indians and those Earchethinues I can see no Difficulty why itt shou'd not, the method Lying so plain and op'n to be Done;—2 men is Suffitient for such an undertaking y^t is to go with some trusty S^o Indian, in the fall or Summer, to the Earchithinue Country, taking with them some trifles to give to the Natives, when Done with the S^o Indians to thier Country tell the spring, Keeping as near as possable to the Earchethinue Country the mean while to see none molest's or Disturbs them tell the Spring, then proceed again to the Earchethinues, using them Civily, with promise of many such fine Goods &c if they will Come with them to the fort to trade, with a Great many more of such Like Inducements y^t is Requir'd in Such casses, by which I do not Doubt but the trade y^t might be gain'd by that Country wou'd be Equivolent with York fort trade in a Small time." (HBCA E.2/1. f. 72r, p. 135)

26 June 1754

T mss   B.239/a/40: the long title is written on folio 1v, and the first entry begins at the top of folio 2r; the year, month and day are normally written in the upper left margin beside new entries; subsequent entries on the same page are marked by the day, and occasionally the month; the note follows the entry for 1 July 1754.

T mss   E.2/6: the long title appears at the top of the page, followed by the first entry; "*paddled*" or "pad*dled*" corrected over erasure ("d" to "dd" in each case), *passim*.

T mss   E.2/4: the long title is given as a paragraph in "A Small Account of the Archithinue Indians"; the passage in angled brackets to the words "to trade" is added in the unknown copyist's hand in paler ink; the phrase "in . . . Century" is a later addition in black ink in Andrew Graham's hand; the years recorded in this ms are 1755 and 1756; catchwords appear at the foot of each page.

T mss E.2/11: in the long title, "y" in "Journey" is flourished to cover an erasure; a double ruled line in red ink is drawn under the title; the first of three marginal notes is written to the left of the title, the second and third to the left of the first entry; catchwords indicate entries which run on to the following page.

W Smith: "We took our Departure from York fort, and in 4 days Reached Steal river, seed two tents of Ind^s. Stayed there two days, the wind blowing hard att NW^t." (HBCA B.239/a/43, 23 August 1756)

W Smith: "June ye 30 in the year of 1757 we tuck our daperter from the factory and thasdey ye 30 we leay at the big stone and fridey ye 1 we lea in Stell rever and seatedy 2 day we lea in Stell rever a litel be yand the crick" (HBCA B.239/a/45, 30 June-2 July 1757)

W Cocking: "At Noon I took my departure from York Fort in the Latitude of 57°00' N. . . . Courses Distance &c as Pr Log. . . . NB my Courses and distances very incorrect for these Canoes have such a motion in paddling the Compass was never still, and I find it impossible to heave the Log at present." (HBCA B.239/a/69, 27, 29 June 1772)

M Robson: "YORK-FORT stands above high-water mark, about eighty yards from Hayes's-river, and four miles from the sea. It is built with logs of white fir eight or nine inches square, which are laid one upon another. In the summer the water beats between the logs, keeping the timber continually damp; and in the winter the white frost gets through, which being thawed by the heat of the stoves, has the same effect." (30)

M Graham: "YORK-FORT (Peine-si-wi-che-wan Whis-ki-heg-gan) lies nearly in the 57th degree of north latitude and 93rd west longitude from London. . . . This fort is situated on an island form'd by the Rivers Nelson (Po-ko-thi-co-hoe Se-pee) and Hayes (Pe-ne-si-wi-che-wan Se-pee) on the north shore of the latter about five miles from its influx into the sea. The land on the shore is low, the water ebb some miles owing <to> the long flats which run off the river Hayes, is full of sands and shoals dry at half ebb, the channel difficult . . . indeed, the shoalness of the river seems to be our greatest security from a foreign enemy." (HBCA E.2/9. f. 108r, p. 209)

H Russell: "Henday went inland with a group of, apparently, Pegogamaw Cree whose core area was between the branches of

the Saskatchewan River. . . . his main goal was to 'bring the
earchithinues to a Trade.' . . . Henday's group, like most of the
trading Indians from the Saskatchewan River area, avoided the
hazards of Lake Winnipeg and circled north by way of Cross
Lake, Minago River and Moose Lake to the Saskatchewan
River." (94)

27 June 1754

T mss E.2/11: the note appears in the margin to the left of this entry,
       signed Andrew Graham.
P   Graham, "Plan" 1774: Steel River marked "Shoals and Falls,
       often dragging and carrying canoes and goods"; tributary from
       NW marked "here is the R. called Shepastic" (HBCA G.2/17)
C   Isham to the HBC London Committee: "I went Last Year . . . as
       high up as a place called Steel River which is upwards of 52
       Miles from the Fort, where I was not a little surprized to find
       the alteration of that distance from the Fort, the Climate more
       moderate, [in April] the Trees out in full bud; and some in
       Leaf . . . the Main River is narrow, a very Strong Current at the
       Enterance of Steel River which empties into Hayes's River for
       two Miles up Steel River its very intricate turnings with high
       broken banks and Narrow." (HBCA A.11/114, 6 August 1754)
W   Hearne: "Steel River at this Part tends nearly SSW and NNE—
       the Mouth of which is about 60 Miles from the Fort, and Hays
       River from the Mouth of Steel River nearly South-West." (HBCA
       B.49/a/1, 26 June 1774)
M   Robson: "When the season approached for going abroad, I
       mentioned to the governor a design I had long entertained of
       travelling up the country, not only to confirm what I had
       heard, but to make new discoveries. This brought on dismal
       tales of the difficulties to be encountered in such an expedi-
       tion: and when I talked of going up the rivers, I was told of stu-
       pendous heaps of ice and dreadful waterfalls, which would not
       only obstruct my passage, but endanger my life." (21)
M   Umfreville: "The face of the country is low and marshy, and a
       little distance off, seems to present to the eye a fine prospect
       of tall pines and junipers; but upon a nearer approach you
       find yourself most egregiously deceived. The pine [conifer-
       ous] trees, which are of different kinds, are but small; near
       the seacoasts they generally run knotty, and are unfit to be
       used in the structure of good buildings. . . . But on leaving
       the marshy ground, and retiring inland to the southward, the
       trees are of a more stately growth . . . Here the climate is

much more temperate than at York Fort and Churchill Settlement." (26-27)

H   Isbister: "Your [Tyrrell's] very interesting letter to me of the 13th ulto—safe to hand the other day, and it's something new to me, the way and Names of places Mr Anthony traveled up from YF . . . but I do not understand how he would have to travel on Steel River it runing S.East, Ah peth te sepee, up to God's Lake, Cree Munto sa ka e can, I would say that he came up they Hayes to Foxes River, Cree Mak se we sepee." (Thomas Fisher Library, Tyrrell-Isbister correspondence, 21 April 1909)

H   Tyrrell: "Hayes river as then understood meant the river southward from York Fort for a distance of fifty-six miles to 'The Forks', above which it was applied to the larger South East branch of the river, while the South West branch was called Steel River." (99)

H   Morse: "in the days when it was used as a fur trade route . . . the name, Hayes, applied only to the sixty miles below where the present Gods River flows in. From here upstream to the junction with the Fox River, it used to be the Steel River; and the steep portion between Knee Lake and the Fox junction was known appropriately as the Hill River." (36)

28 June 1754

T mss B.239/a/40: the note follows the entry for 1 July 1754.

T mss E.2/11: the note is written at the foot of the page in red ink.

T xref B.239/a/40 and E.2/11 notes: cf E.2/6 and E.2/4 notes, 29 June 1754.

29 June 1754

T mss E.2/6: the note follows this entry; E.2/4: the note follows the entry for 1 July 1754; E.2/11: hyphen of "Pine-Reach" in ms.

T xref E.2/6 and E.2/4: cf B.239/a/40 and E.2/11, 28 June 1754.

1 July 1754

T mss E.2/4: a sum of mileages is pencilled beside the entry at the foot of each page until folio 49v (5 November 1754): these figures are not contemporary with the ms, but antedate microfilming in November 1952.

W   Pink: "this Day j Came to the first of the Carrying plases Likewise Came over Seven of them." (HBCA B.239/a/58, 7 July 1767)

W   Cocking: "As I am unacquainted with the method of steering a Canoe am always obliged to track, could not stop to set a reach of the River, indeed the Indians complain that I hinder

them by making the small remarks I do." (HBCA B.239/a/69, 30
June 1772)

M Graham: "The canoes are 18 feet long, 18 Inches deep, and 2
feet broad, and sharp at both ends, the gunnels are willows
about the substance of a walking cane, the timbers &c one
quarter inch thick and close together, being rounding at bottom, and turned up a little at head and stern, & covered on
the outside with birch rind, and lined with thin shavings of
wood on the inside; the seams are stuffed with turpentine to
make it water tight . . . they are very tottery vessels, an
Indian cannot manage them standing upright . . . the canoe
paddles are 6 feet long, one half of which is the wash . . . the
women commonly sits in the stern and manages the canoe,
the goods and children are stowed in the middle, and the
man in the fore part . . . the reason the women steers is to
give the men liberty to fire at the deer &c . . . when the
stream runs strong against them, the man tracks and the
woman steers the canoe, and when carrying over falls and
shoals, which they often do, the men always carries the
canoe." (HBCA E.2/4. f. 29r, p. 51)

2 July 1754

T mss E.2/11: hyphen of "Stony-Banks" in ms.
C Anthony Henday to James Isham:
               Dated at Desolation fall July the 2^d 1754
Hon^d Sir
Having an Oppertunity of Sending a line or two by these Indians, this is to acqu^t you the River we are now in is Nothing but
Falls, Rocks, and Islands, We are Obliged to Carry the Cannoes
and things over most of them, and have been obliged so <to>
do ever since we left the River that goes into the North River
which is about 60 Miles a bove where we crost the Island, We
are all in good health at present, for We made a good Dinner
on the Roots of Rushes such as the Cooper use about His
Cask^s, having nothing else to eat for two Days but two Jack,
but we are to see a place to Morrow Where we shall take them
up with Our hands. Sir I hope Your Honour will excuse my
Ashureance, Sir I remain Your Obedient Servant, and will
endeavour to Discharge the trust Laid on me.
       Anthony Henday
(HBCA A.11/114)

W Pink: "Met a Bodey of Sinn<a>poits Consisting of 8 Caneus
the ware all Gowing down to Yorke Forte to Trade thare Fores j

Gave them a foot of tobacoo to Smoke." (HBCA B.239/a/58, 17 July 1767)

W Cocking: "all the Natives in general are afraid of Writings as being above their Comprehension." (HBCA B.239/a/69, 4 March 1773)

M Isham: "It's a Very uncertain place for the English mens Living in these parts, we Living sometimes Like princes, and other times Like beggars, not a morcel of fresh provisions to put into our mouth's by which itt may be say[d] itt's Either a feast or a famine." (HBCA E.2/1. f. 72v, p. 136)

M Graham: "The Company's Servants lives like Princes, seldom a week passes but they have fresh provisions of different kinds, and the Factors and Officers lives in so grand a manner beyond description: this living, with the healthfulness of the Climate, the easy labour, and regular command induces the generality of us to continue many years in Hudson's-Bay." (HBCA E.2/4. f. 77v, p. 148)

M Umfreville: "The provisions allowed the servants are, taken altogether, but of the middling kind . . . Great quantities of venison and geese are salted for the use of the Factories during the spring and fall of the year. This provision will sometimes remain three or four years in the casks unopened; after which it becomes so completely putrified, rancid, and devoid of taste, that a person might as well expect nutriment from the shavings in a carpenter's shop." (117)

3 July 1754

T mss B.239/a/40: the note follows the entry for 6 July 1754.

T mss E.2/11: "are" pencilled above "is."

P Hearne, "Map" [1775]: shows the Grass River route: "Pe-gog-a-mee River" is indicated as a tributary of Steel River flowing from S. (HBCA G.1/20)

C see Isham, "Remarks" (HBCA B.239/a/40)

W Pink: "Heare j find that the Shoares are all Nothing but Stones and Rocks and the River fool of Falles and Small jlands." (HBCA B.239/a/58, 12 July 1767)

W Hearne: "The water ware so shoal this day as not to admit of either us or the Ind[ns] to sit in the Cannoes, but ware oblig'd to walk alongside of them and hand them clear of Stones &c, by which means we Drag'd and carried, in all about 10 Miles, in the way Cross't 2 Carrying Places one of which ware at least a Mile long—at Night we Put up at the branch wher Fox River & the Pe-gog-a-may River Joins and Emptys themselves into Steel

River. The Pe-gog-a-may River I destinguish by that Name on
account of the Pe-gog-a-may Indians always comeing that way,
when they visit YF it is also the way M[r] Cocking went inland in
the Year 1772.—and is the Westernmost Track Mention'd in
Isaac Batt[s] Draft [map] The Woods near this part are mostly
Pine, and the Banks of the Rivers Steep, high, and Stoney."
(HBCA B.49/a/1, 2 July 1774)

H   Burpee: "Hendry's course lay up the Hayes river to what was
then called Attick-Sagohan or Deer Lake, now known as Knee
Lake. . . . From Knee Lake it becomes for a time a little more
difficult to follow Hendry's movements. The natural supposition would be that he followed the afterwards familiar route by
way of Oxford lake, Echimamish river and the Playgreen lakes
to Lake Winnipeg; and this supposition gains support from the
fact that he presently mentions a lake which he calls Christianaux—one of the old French names for Lake Winnipeg. His
distances, however, put such a theory out of court; and even if
that were not the case, his description of Christianaux lake
cannot be made to fit Winnipeg. . . . It happens, however, that
between Knee and Oxford lakes and Cross lake on the Nelson
lies a considerable extent of country that has never been
explored; or rather it was supposed that it had never been
explored. . . . In the summer of 1906, however, . . . Mr Banel, a
missionary, . . . discovered about midway an unmapped lake, so
large he had been lost upon it for three days. The lake was
described as being about a day's journey from Oxford lake. . . .
It is morally certain that [Henday] never saw Lake Winnipeg
on either his outward or his return journey." (308-9, 316)

H   Isbister: "the Lake called Cree or Cristeneau I do not know
May this not be ke-nis-te-noo, meaning, the 3rd Lake, which is
between Oxford & Deers Lake. I hard of Indians talk of the
aboave Named." (Thomas Fisher Library. Tyrrell-Isbister correspondence, 2 April 1909)

H   Rich: "Henday and his companions went by the route which he
had already travelled on foot, up the Hayes to the Fox River;
then, however, they took the southern branch of the Fox and
so, by a route which subsequently dropped out of use, and
which is difficult to check from his Journal, across from the
Hayes River to the Nelson, to Cross Lake and so up to Moose
Lake on the Lower Saskatchewan." (1: 630-33)

H   Morse: "The *main* canoe route between Cumberland House
and York Factory via Lake Winnipeg . . . did not come regularly
into use until after Cumberland House was established [in

1774]. . . . The 'Middle Track' was the canoe route principally used by Indian middlemen coming and going between York Factory and the Saskatchewan River, prior to the establishment of Cumberland House. From below The Pas on the Saskatchewan, this route passed down the Summerberry River and up into Moose Lake; crossing a low divide it went down the Minago River to Cross Lake on the Nelson. From the east end of Cross Lake the 'Middle Track' branched, one route passing north-east directly to Utik (Deer) Lake and down the Bigstone and Fox Rivers to the Hayes. Henday and Cocking used this route on their way west [reversing the direction of this downstream sequence]." (44-46, original emphasis)

6 July 1754

T mss E.2/4: "*and entered*" written over erasure.

T mss E.2/11: hyphens in "Pike-Reach" and "Attick-Sagohan" in ms; "Deek Lake" corrected in E.2/11, 7 July 1754.

P   Graham, "Plan" 1772 and 1774 (HBCA G.2/15 and G.17): "Deer Lake" marked on both maps.

W   Pink: "one Carrying plases this Day j Came out into the first Leakes that thare is a Gowing up in Land it is Called a,Teack,we,Sock,a,ha,Can Roning to the N.E. or Rather to the E.N.E., as <neare as> j Can tell in my Sityation for j has Nothing for to Go By j has None Boock that Can Give me aney inStrucktions in aney thing of that kind." (HBCA B.239/a/58, 13 July 1767)

W   Cocking: "Paddling in fine Water for the most part and entered the Deer Lake. Lay at one of the Islands. Indians say this Lake is well stored with Fish, but see no Fowl except a few Gulls." (HBCA B.239/a/69, 9 July 1772)

M   Graham: "Keneshu, the Pike or Jack-Fish, Are frequent in the Lakes, Rivers and Creeks; are caught both with Nets and Hooks, are esteemed good eating, and weigh about twelve pounds at farthest. It would be unnecessary to describe It, as the Learned Pennant has already employed his pen that way in the British Zoology." (HBCA E.2/9. f. 47r, p. 87)

H   Isbister: "it seems that Foxes River falls into Deers River and comes into Hayes River below the first fall from York call^d the Rock . . . which is the rout that was used to a voide the Nelson, in Coming up by Cross Lake in olden times not that waters from Cross Lake flow into deers lake—but by making cross Land portages from Lake to Lake &c." (Thomas Fisher Library, Tyrrell-Isbister correspondence, 11 September 1909)

7 July 1754

T mss E.2/11: hyphen in "Three-Beacon" in ms; "Deer Lake" noted in
the right margin in Graham's hand.

8 July 1754

T mss E.2/6: "*entr*ance" written over erasure.

C   Jean-Baptiste Proux to James Isham:
           le 8 de juiette Saute au pa 1754
           Monsieur,
           je pran la liberté de vous se [xxx]pt ligne pour vous faire
ahsur[ance] de no nous velle qui son bonne dieu mersi je soite
que la votre en soi de mme de la miene monsieur le porteure de
letre si vous vous lé bien lui donné se que je va vous mandé monsieur si ses votre plaisir de man voire 5 brase de tabac et puis 1
pere de soullie double et pui 1 bele boite dun fair blan et puis 1
violon et de corde tan que vous pou[vés] pour le peyeman vous
me le manderé je vous lanverré par bonne mai le p[r]intan
prauchin [et] vous me fairé bien plesire par que janné basin
monsieur si juubli quel que chause vous me fairé bien plesire
monsieur je vous pri de mescuse par que je sui for présé monsieur je fini je sui votr[e] tré af[fectueux] Serviteu[r]
           janbapteste proux négaussian au pa
           [endorsed] A Monsieur KK/monsieur le Conmandant du
for de la bé d'unson
           [folded and sealed with five red wax seals]
           Saute au pas 8^(th) July 1754
           Trans: of a Letter from a low Ignorant fellow
           Sir,
           I take the liberty of <u>writing</u> you these lines to let you
know of our news, which are good God be praised I wish that
Yours may be the Same as mine.—Sir ~~the bearer of this letter~~
If you will <please> to give the bearer what I am going to ask
you Sir, If it is Your good pleasure to Send me 5 brase of
Tobacco and then a pair of double shoes and then a fine tin
box and then a fiddle and Strings as many as you can, Sir, as to
the payment You'll let me Know it I shall send it to you by good
hand the next Spring, you will do me a good deal of pleasure
because I am in want Sir If I forget Some thing you will do me
a good deal of pleasure Sir I desire you to excuse me because I
am in haste, Sir I finish I am your very affectionate Servant
           John Baptist P—
           Trader or negotiating
           at the Pas

[translation made at York Fort, underlining and strikeout in ms]

York Fort July the 8th 1754

To John Baptist

prove of Guison

S^r

By the Bearrer I recd a Letter from You, which being wrote bad Could not make it out by what I understand, you want a Confedericy, also some instruments &c which I have not also a pipe to be mended but the Bearer had no such thing

As I do not know your Intention I cannot give a derect Answare to Your letter

I rest,

Sir Yours Unknown

James Isham

[endorsed] A Copie of a Letter from Monsiure Jean Baptiste, to Governor Isham with Govr Isham^s Answare 1754

(HBCA A.11/114, 8 July 1754)

9 July 1754

C Anthony Henday to James Isham:

To the Honble James Isham, Governor in Cheif at York Fort: Theese/

Hon^d Sir—

Having an Oppertunity to let Your Hon^r know that We are got near 300 Miles up this Country, and the Indians last Night inform'd Me that we should see a French Factory in 3 Days more, and that We must go by it, before We can go their Country I dont very well like it, having nothing to Satisfye Them on what account I am going up the Country, and Very possably they may suspect Me to be a Spy, but I will Face them with a good Countinance let it be how it will, for as I am gone thus Farr, if it please God, Will see the Farthest end of all Their Country, as I can if the French do not stop Me, as I don't doubt but they will be very Inquisitive about it I shall say nothing at all to them (if they cannot talk English,) and then I will give them a Civil lye. We are all in good health, and Feed on good Moose and Swans for two Days past it having Rain'd and blow'd hard all the Time. I wish Your Hon^r Health, and if the French should shoot me, I have nothing to lay to Your Hon^{rs} Charge.

Sir I remain Your

Dutiful Servant

Anthony

Dated July the 9th 1754
Minissco River
Apetty Tuskey
(HBCA A.11/114, 9 July 1754)

M   Graham: "Servant's Contract. . . . During my being in the said
[Hudson's Bay] Company's Service , I will, with the utmost
hazard and peril of my Life, in my station, with Courage and
Fidelity, maintain and defend the said Company's Factory and
Factories, Territories, Rights, Priviledges, Goods & Properties,
against all Enemies whatsoever, either foreign or of our own
Country; and to the utmost of my Power will cause the same to
be maintained and defended by all others, According to the
duty of my service. And I will in all things submit myself to the
Commands & Discipline of the Governor or Commander in
Chief for the said Company, and all other my superior officers,
by his Directions." (HBCA E.2/6. ff. 43v-44r, pp. 85-86)

10 July 1754

T xref B.239/a/40: cf B.239/a/40 note to the entry for 20 July 1754.

P   Graham, "Plan" 1772 and 1774 (HBCA G.2/15 and G.2/17): the
second lake is marked as "Pimochicomou Lake" on both maps.

W   Cocking: "Passed two Carrying Places and paddling in fine
Water for the most part. At Noon entered a Lake called Pim-
mochicomow Sackaeagan. See several fish jumping up, but
being cloudy could not see to Spear any. Many Rocky Islands
producing small Wood." (HBCA B.239/a/69, 11 July 1772)

H   Morton: "Henday . . . was taken by the Indians along one of
their customary water-routes to the Saskatchewan. He
ascended the Hayes to the Fox River. By its southern branch,
our Leaf River, he came to the portage leading to the expansion of the Nelson River known as Cross Lake, his Nelson
Pond." (245)

11 July 1754

T mss B.239/a/40: the note follows the entry for 16 July 1754; E.2/11:
"way" added above the line, over a caret.

12 July 1754

M   Isham, "Discourses on Different Subjects [conversation of two
Indians]:
    B. what will you Drink
        Kaquan Cuttaminaquau
    A. a Little punch & to Sleep

B. I'll make you Drink
    Enkotarpartin
A. Very well we must gett up as soon as Day Light
    ha ha'oco, shashie, wappun Cuttawiniskow
B. Come itt's Day Gett up
    Ecco shashie wappun weniskaw
A. my head ach's with drinking Last nigh't
    Entestaquan wache minnaqutt tobiscoak
B. to walk out you will be well
    Cuttamurrawashing permotau . . .

These Natives are given, very much to Quarrell[s] when in Liquor
having Known two Brothers when in Liquor to Quarrell after
such a manner, that they have Bitt one anoth[s] nose, Ears, and
finger's off; Biting being Common with them when in Liquor . . .
they also are Very Sulky and sullen, and if at any time one has a
Resentment against another, they never show itt, tell the Spuri-
tious Liquor's work's in their Brains, then they Speak their mind
freely." (E.2/1. ff. 39r-39v, 58r, pp. 69-70, 107)

M   Robson: "They are fond of the taste of brandy, and of being
    intoxicated with it; esteeming it an honour to be drunk, and
    striving who shall continue so longest: indeed this is a corrup-
    tion not of their own growth, but introduced among them by
    the folly and villany of Europeans." (50)

M   Graham: "They are a very extraordinary set of People when
    drunk, for Liquor usually makes Europeans merry, but when an
    Indian drinks too much he recollects his departed Friends and
    Relations and Laments their Deaths very pathetically with
    tears. . . . They are much given to Quarrelling and Fighting on
    these occasions, and conscious of ill effects that may ensue;
    they have the prudence frequently before they begin to drink
    to Order the Women and Children to remove the Guns, Bayo-
    nets and other offensive weapons out of the Tent and hide
    them in the Woods; but as they cannot part with their
    Teeth . . . sometimes they come off with the loss of an Ear or
    joint of a Finger." (HBCA E.2/9. f. 62v, p. 118)

H   MacGregor: "This is the first time that Henday mentions any
    drinking on the part of his Indians. Undoubtedly, a drink would
    help to take their minds off the pouring rain. He does not indi-
    cate in his remarks that they drank to excess." (42)

13 July 1754

P   Graham, "Plan" 1774: the river marked as "Sequashu River"
    and "Pine R." with a tributary from SW marked

"Keskatchewan R." (HBCA G.2/17)

C   YF post journal (Isham): "att noon 29 Canoes of Missinipy and Esinipoet Indians Came to trade, the said Leaders of which Seldom used to be less then 40 or 50 Canoes, they Complain very Much of the death of Ind[s], which is the occasion of many Going to Warr, and the Great Scarcity of Beaver; By those Ind[s] I Rec[d] a Letter from Anthony Hendy who was well and in a pleasant Country on the 2[d] Instant, where says he, we have plenty of the Roots of Rushes which they Lived upon for 2 days, but are in Hopes of better food Soon." (HBCA B.239/a/37, 13 July 1754)

W   Cocking: "Proceeded in the Morning passing over the Carrying Place, and entered what they called Minihague Sepy or Spruce River, Good Water at present between the Falls but a very strong Current in most places." (HBCA B.239/a/69, 20 July 1772)

14 July 1754

C   James Isham to Anthony Henday:

York Fort Sunday July 14: 1754

Anthony,

I received Yours and am glad to hear You are all well, as we are at present, and hope by the receipt of this will be got into a plentifuler Country then when You last Wrote, there was a French man coming to the Fort, but light of a Misfortune to break his Cannoe therefore did not Come, but sent me a letter; Monssure wants a Correspondance I sent him an Answare by the Young Captain Tribe who saye he'll be down with You and the Indians next Summer.

By eny Indians that You see Coming for the Fort send Me a line of Your Welfare and a Small Account of your Country,

I have had very few Indians down, 60 Cannoes less then last Year, they tell me there is but few, and them gone to Warr, this You will know if Truth, and you You see eny going upon such and Errand, perswade them from it.

I hope by Your means good Success in promoting the Company[s] Trade, by Exorting the Indians to live peaceably, and encouraging them to get goods, Espetialy Beaver, and above all besure to bring as many Cannoes of Earchethinues You can to Trade, of their Own Furrs, and for their Own Use,

I Conclude wishing You Health and Success, and am
Your Faithful Friend and welwisher
James Isham

All Friends give thier Love to You.
(HBCA A.11/114, 14 July 1754)

15 July 1754

W   Smith: "[The Frenchmen] Came up to us Att night, and Ind[s]
with them one of which was a Capt[n] of Yours belonging to York
Fort, he told me he had not been down these 3 or 4 years, We
Gave them what things We had." (HBCA B.239/a/43, 17 November 1756)

W   Tomison: "the Indians a Cungring and dancing fore <the>
traders to come. . . . in the evening Smoakt with the men, two
Susanewa Indians Came for Some tobacco, they told me that
there is above 100 tents waiting for the traders for there
Suply." (HBCA B.239/a/64, 16-17 October 1769)

W   Hearne: "I must needs say that it gave me no little uneasiness
to see so many fine fellows of Indians and their Families not only
Cloath'd with the Canadians goods finely ornimented, but ware
also furnish'd with every other Necessary artical, and seem'd not
to be in want of any thing. Not the least appearance of the Companys Trading goods among them, Except a few guns and Hatch-
etts, the latter of which the Canadians brings but few and sell
them Dear." (HBCA B.49/a/1, 23 July 1774)

16 July 1754

T mss E.2/11: "Tuesday" added above the line.

P   Graham, "Plan" 1774: the entrance to "Auteatewan Lake" is
marked "Swamp, Dragg'd Canoes 4 Miles." (HBCA G.2/17)

W   Cocking: "Passed three Carrying Places and several Shoals
entering a Lake called Ooteatowen Sackaeagan . . . a fresh
Gale clear Weather. Paddling in the Lake (a great Swell, verry
dangerous Paddling) and came to a Noted fishing place for
Jack Perch and other Fish, called Apeasooapahsoo; So named
because it is a Narrow between two Points. Here laid up a
Reserve of Tobacco. No Success in Angling." (HBCA B.239/a/69,
22-23 July 1772)

H   Burpee: "For some reason he makes no special mention of
Cross lake, but says that he . . . paddled up a river. This river is
given in Cocking's journal as the Minahage or Pine river—the
Minago of our modern maps. Ascending [Minago River,
Hendry] came to a large lake, which he calls Othenume, and
Cocking, Oteatowan Sockoegan; evidently Moose Lake. Both
Hendry's and Cocking's descriptions agree with recent
accounts of Moose lake." (309)

H   Isbister: "I do not know, or even heard, of Inland boats, coming up from Foxes River & through to cross Lake Cree Pe-me-che-ca-maw, only Indians with Canoes, <by> making Cross Land portages. . . . there is thoes two Lakes. of Moose Lake. I cannt get the sound to be certain or correct 1st oteatawan, may not this be it, oo-teeth-ta-wan. meaning, there staying Lake, 2nd othenume, oo-the-nu-we sa-ca-he-can <wind from Lake> . . . I never was up to Moose Lake or to Grand Rapids but I have a Son who started with survayors that were going down to churchill & york . . . one party went to the Paw & started from there down to split Lake [the "lower track"] . . . but I think that they will be too fare south East of Moose Lake they may come across the <2> aboave Lakes North of the Sask.—Riv they are reported to be back <and will let you know> on the latter end of April." (Thomas Fisher Library, Tyrrell-Isbister correspondence, 2 April 1909)

H   Morton: "At the western end of [Cross Lake] he entered the Minago, his Minishco river, and portaged from its upper waters into 'Othenum' (the Oo-tea-towen or Mesha, i.e. Mooswa Lake of Matthew Cocking), our Moose Lake. Its outlet brought him into the Summerberry branch of the Saskatchewan. This he ascended, reaching the French Fort Paskoyac on 22nd July." (245)

20 July 1754

T mss B.239/a/40: the note follows this entry in ms.

T mss E.2/11: "& paddled on" added above the line, over a caret; "Nelson R" noted in Graham's hand to the right of this entry.

P   Graham, "Plan" 1774: the river marked "Kepehagan River, here Sturgeon plenty" (HBCA G.2/17)

W   Cocking: "Entered a Small River called Kippaeagan Sepy or Shut up River. Here the Natives have a Stage built across on which they stand to Spear Sturgeon, stopping the Passage with long sticks stuck in the Ground a small space asunder, supported at top by the Stage; before these they have other small sticks stuck in the ground, about a foot asunder unsupported at top, the Sturgeon swimming against these shake them which directs the Indians where to strike. This River also abounds with abundance of Tickameg and other fish. Put up here, Saskachiwan River in sight bore WSW a quarter Mile distant." (HBCA B.239/a/69, 23 July 1772)

M   Isham: "Of sorts of fishes in these parts . . . this part abounding with plenty of fish, as Jack, & pike, of a Large size . . .

being some 4 foot in Length, &c:—Sturgeon I have seen 7 foot
4 inches from the tail to the head, these are Catch't, by the
Natives in Wair's,—made after the same manner as in other
parts . . . Mer'thy (as the Natives styles itt,) are a fish [burbot]
Resembles an Eal in taste, they are muddy fish and skin's.
Tickomegg [whitefish] which is Like a herring is also Very
Numerious, Catching with a Setting net, in the Summer season, when they come from the sea into the Rivers to spawn,
some hundreds, and with a sean [seine] some thousands at
one haw'l, they are a Very soft fish but good Eating, we preserve y^m with salting as also Jack pike trout & perch for the
winter time,—perch here is the same as in England, Carp and
tench very plenty, silver trout and Sammon trout Very Numerious, and Large." (HBCA E.2/2: ff. 27v - 28r, pp. 220-21)

21 July 1754
P   Graham, "Plan" 1774 : the river marked "Keskachewan River"
     (HBCA G.2/17)
P   Hearne, "Map" [1775]: "Keiscatchewan R^r" and "Basquiau"
     (HBCA G.1/20)
H   Burpee: "Paddling up a river emptying into Moose lake,
     Hendry finally reached the Saskatchewan, or Keiskatchewan as
     he spells it, and the following day came to a French house, Fort
     'Basquea,' at the mouth of the Pasquia river." (309)
H   Isbister: "Mr Anthony traveled up from YF to the Kei-
     siskatchewan, meaning in Cree, swift-stream, or current, which
     is the proper name." (Thomas Fisher Library. Tyrrell-Isbister
     correspondence, 21 April 1909)

22 July 1754
T mss B.239/a/40: the note follows this entry.
T mss E.2/6: "French" written over erasure.
T mss E.2/4: "*were* very kind" written over erasure.
T mss E.2/11: "S" pencilled before "W"; "on" follows "I was going
       inland" but is crossed out; the note on Attickasish, signed by
       Andrew Graham, is placed in the left margin and appears to
       have been added at the same time as marginal notes beside the
       entries for 26 and 27 June 1754.
T xref B.239/a/40: cf E.2/6: 23 July 1754, E.2/4 and E.2/11: 29 May 1755.
C   Isham, instructions to Smith and Waggoner: "As it is Warr with
       the French, be Ca<u>tious how You enter Their Hutts or Con-
       verse with Them, if They seem to Threaten stand upon Your
       Guard, & keep Close to the Indians, who I have Charged (if the

French offer to Mollest or Interrupt Your Pass<a>ge) to Stand by You and Assist in Killing or takeing Your Enemyes, but if They are quiet and do not Offer any Violence then proceed." (HBCA A.11/115, 20 August 1756)

W   Smith: "the french Men that was in our Company All winter always told us he would Certainly kill us but the Ind^s said if they did or offer'd to do any harm to us they would kill them all." (HBCA B.239/a/43, 9 February 1757)

W   Pink: "Came out in to the Large River Whare the Ruen<e>s of the to Ould French Houses are standing the Calles this River His,sis,Scho,Gi,one. . . . j Now find by those people and by thinges that j See heare that the people of Canada are neare hand j has Seen heare bouth Cloth, and hats, & kittles, & Blankets, and Tobacoo, Shurtes and all Such like things. that those people has Got from them . . . j heare that thare are Som of the French men that formely lived heare at those houses, in Companey with them." (HBCA B.239/a/58, 23-24 July 1767)

W   Pink: "this Day we Came to the Lower house whare the people of Mountreale ware Staying but heare now is Onely one English man Staying heare Exspecting of Canewes up in the fall of the Yeare with Goods." (HBCA B.239/a/63, 23 July 1769)

W   Cocking: "paddling all day and came to the place called Basquio. A fishing Place here at a small River for Tickameg which the Indians kill with hand Nets. . . . We put up a little beyond this place, where We met with a Basquio Indian his wife & Child, He tells me that he was often the Canadian Pedler's Tentmate killing Moose for them in the Winter: By the help of a little Liquor We prevailed with him to accompany us; and he promises to use his endeavours to induce his Countrymen to accompany us on our return to the Fort." (HBCA B.239/a/69, 31 July 1772)

W   Hearne: "came to Basquiau which is entirely bare of all kind of woods. where the house formally stood is all over with willows &c and not the least bit of the Building standing or Remaining except Part of the Fire Place." (HBCA B.49/a/1, 19 August 1774)

M   Robson: "the Company . . . had not taken care to check the incroachments of the French, who are daily increasing and extending their Fur-trade within land to the south-westward and westward of the bay, among the lakes and near the sources of the several rivers upon which the Company have made settlements. . . . The Company have for eighty years slept at the edge of a frozen sea; they have shewn no curiosity to penetrate farther themselves, and have exerted all their art and power to

crush that spirit in others. They have kept the language of the
natives, and all that might be gained by a familiar and friendly
intercourse with them, as much as possible, a secret to their
own servants; and the invaluable treasures of this extensive
country a profound secret to Great Britain.'' (1-2, 6)

H   Burpee: "This place, now known as The Pas, was a notable spot
throughout the entire period of the fur trade, from the days of
La Vérendrye down. The elder La Vérendrye, so far as his journals and letters show, was never on the Saskatchewan, but one
of his sons built Fort Bourbon on the shores of Cedar Lake,
about 1748, and ascended the river as far as the forks, somewhere below which he built Fort Poskoyac. . . . [In 1753] Saint-
Luc de la Corne . . . is said to have built Fort Poskoyac—Fort
Poskoyac the second—on the lower Saskatchewan." (309)

H   Tyrrell: "The name means a narrow place between steep or
high banks. For a long distance above it the banks are rather
low and muddy, and for an equally long distance below it the
stream flows through a vast reedy marsh, teeming with water
fowl, and with hardly any well defined banks at all. Here on
both sides of the river is an extensive gravel plain which furnished beautiful dry camping grounds in the middle of the
watery wilderness." (109)

23 July 1754

T mss   E.2/6: the note follows the entry for 27 July 1754.

T xref   E.2/6: cf B.239/a/40, 22 July 1754, E.2/4 and E.2/11, 29 May 1755.

C   Henday to Isham: "I don't doubt but that [the French] will be
very Inquisitive . . . I shall say nothing at all to them (if they
cannot talk English,) and then I will give them a Civil lye."
(HBCA A.11/114, 9 July 1754)

C   YF General Letter (Isham to the HBC London Committee):
"Joseph Smith, and Joseph Waggoner . . . see to the Number of
20 french Men who used them Extreamly Civill (the Expression
of the Chieff French man Says Joseph Smith:) what if the King
of England and the French King are att warrs together, that is
no Raison why we Should; so Lett us be friends." (HBCA
A.11/115, 18 August 1757)

W   Tomison: "passed by to the Westward a french Trader, with 10
french servants & 14 Indians in 6 large Canoes full of goods, he
came into our tent and smoaked his pipe but did not speak to
me altho' I spoke to him in the Keskachewan Indian language;
I asked one of his men who could talk English, where they were
going? he said towards Basquea, I asked him where he learned

English, he said he had been a prisoner last warr in New York."
(HBCA E.2/6, 2 October 1767)

M   Isham: "[The Natives] first Strips the skin of then cutt Each
     joint of heaving nothing away . . . they then take some poles,
     on which they hang the meet, making a good fire under, which
     is Kep't turning, tell itt's thoroughly Dry^d which will be a bout
     4 Day's . . . this meet when Dry'd they take and pound, or beat
     between two Stones, till some of itt is as small as Dust, which
     they styl (Ruhiggan) being Dry^d so much that their is Little
     moisture in itt;—when pounded they putt itt into a bag and
     will Keep for several Years, the Bones they also pound small
     and Boil them over a moderate fire to Reserve the fatt . . . Pim-
     megan as the Natives styles itt, is some of the Ruhiggan fatt
     and Cranberries mix^d up togeather, and Reckon'd by some Very
     good food by the English as well as Natives." (HBCA E.2/I. ff.
     17r-18r, pp. 199-201)

M   Graham: "The French who had formerly 2 trading houses on
     the . . . Keskachewan river carried to Canada 6 or 8 large
     canoes full of the richest furrs, which they got from our trad-
     ing Indians, and the Assenepoets; the last of whom told me
     in the year 1762 when the French quitted their Settlements,
     that if we would come and settle on Keskachewan river, they
     would bring their Countrymen to us, who would bring plenty
     of martins and beaver. These Natives hindered the French
     from burning Basquea house, in hopes that we would come
     and settle there; The Canadians being now returned again
     the number of Aseenepoets has decreased from 54 to 18
     canoes these two years past at York fort." (HBCA E.2/5. ff.
     11r-11v, pp. 15-16)

H   Burpee: "the conversation was probably in French." (SWS 120)
H   Rich: "[Henday] was able to speak French." (637)
H   Williams: "One wonder[s] about [Henday's] origins and past.
     Dr Jennifer Brown has pointed out to me that Henday's name
     could be of French origin, and that there is a river-mouth town
     named Hendaye on France's Biscay coast. . . . The Company
     records throw no light on this." (53-54)

24 July 1754

T mss E.2/11: hyphen of "Birch-trees" in ms.
P   Graham, "Plan" 1774: two lakes S of "Keskachewan River"
       marked "Shohonan Lake" and "Manesquanan Lake";
       "Peatagon R." drawn as a tributary flowing from S. (HBCA
       G.2/17)

P   Hearne, "Map" [1775]: a "fishing ware" marked upstream from "Basquiau." (HBCA G.1/20)

W   Pink: "this day j Came By a Smal River on the No Side of this, Roning from out of a Large Leake whare j Came to our Famelyes Last Yeare." (HBCA B.239/a/58, 28 July 1767)

W   Cocking: "We proceeded up a Branch near where we lay to hunt . . . high Land appeared at a distance like a Cloud called Basquio Hills; . . . we met with an Indian Leader with ten Canoes; He is laying here waiting for his Son, who with one Canoe only is down at York Fort.—Pleading Poverty I gave him a small supply of Tobacco and Ammunition. He denied having traded with the Pedlers saying that he and his Gang had killed but few Furrs in the Winter: but the Pedlers Goods amongst them contradicted his assertion, and he has only sent his Son down to the Fort for such things as he could not be supplied with by them." (HBCA B.239/a/69, 1 and 4 August 1772, second passage marked by a fist ☞)

W   Hearne: "In the Evening we Returned up the River to the Small Creek about 2 Miles above Basquiau where we lay alnight, by the side of a Fishing ware, which abounded with fish of several kinds, many of which we Caught, namely, Pike, Sturgeon, Carp, Tittemeg, Perch, and Burbutt." (HBCA B.49/a/1, 19 August 1774)

H   Burpee: "[Hendry's] course lay for a few miles up the Saskatchewan; . . . then he left the river and paddled . . . across a lake . . . This could only be Saskeram lake. . . . I am informed by Mr. D. B. Dowling, of the Geological Survey, to whom I am indebted for a great deal of assistance in tracing Hendry's course after he left the main Saskatchewan, that in periods of high water a channel might easily be found from Saskeram lake to the Carrot river." (315)

H   Tyrrell: "The French trading houses were probably in the angle between [the Pasquia River] and the Saskatchewan river. The creek two miles above would be Carrot River." (111)

H   Morton: "Henday's party proceeded six miles up the Saskatchewan. They then avoided the long sweep of the river to the north with its strong adverse current by entering the Birch River, and so to the still water of Saskeram Lake. Here the Indians must have found signs that their families were up the valley of the Carrot River. Turning back they ascended that stream to its shoals, where they abandoned their canoes." (245-46)

H   Russell: "Henday's group travelled up the Carrot River

tributary [of the Saskatchewan River] where they abandoned their canoes, probably near modern Red Earth Reserve." (94)

27 July 1754

T mss E.2/11: "Wind" added above the line, over a caret.

W   Smith: "We did not go far in a day by Reason their familys was with them, and they have So many dogs they Cannot go farr." (HBCA B.239/a/43, 8 May 1757)

W   Pink: "this Day we Came to the plase w<h>are our Famelyes ware Tenting a bout four dayes a Gown, not haveing aney thing to Live upon, So they Mooved away Something forder in Land to the W,N,W for hunting, So j Stayed none here, for al thare ware Tenting heare 16 Tents of indaines, Some ware Staying for thare frends that ware Gone to the Factory to Trade." (HBCA B.239/a/58, 10 August 1767)

W   Cocking: "The Natives I am with all rejoice greatly that the toile in their passage up from the Fort is ended: . . . rendered more so by the swarms of Musketos that plagued us with very little intermission all the way; at the Carrying Places especially, these Vermin were very troublesome, the dress we were obliged to wear affording us but little defence against them." (HBCA B.239/a/69, 12 August 1772)

M   Graham: "As the chase and making of Utensils are the sole care of the men, so all the drudgery and domestic duty is performed by the women. They pitch and unpitch the tent, cut fire-wood, dress the victuals, and when the Man comes home, they take off his socks and shoes, hanging them up to dry, fill his pipe and light it, and give him a drink. After he has smooked a while he orders them to go for the beast he has killed. The women also catch fish, Hares, fetch all the water used in the tent, knit the Snow-shoes, and make the cloaths. They esteem it very indecent to step over a man's legs, or even to pull off their Socks or Shoes before them; but always go out of the tent, and then bring them in order to dry them in their bosom, or hold them at the fire, never hanging them up: but their feet being very hard they have very seldom occasion to dry their things. <I mean in the Winter season.>" (HBCA E.2/12, p. 301)

H   Russell: "When Henday accompanied him inland, [Attickosish] and his group met their families on the upper Carrot River, very close to the Red Deer River [of Manitoba] where Cocking was later to meet Pegogamaw Cree. It is not known if these families had canoes down the Saskatchewan with the flotillas going to the Bay or if they had walked there later in the summer." (145)

29 July 1754

T mss B.239/a/40: the note follows the entry for 31 July 1754.

T mss E.2/11: "a" follows "berries the size of" but is crossed out.

T xref all texts: cf E.2/6 and E.2/4: 17 August 1754.

W Pink: "Heare the Contrey is covered thinly with Small popler and Wilde pease and Tares Some Rasbearyes and a Great maney other Sortes of Bearyes that j Neaver See in England." (HBCA B.239/a/63, 13 August 1769)

W Cocking: "travelling through a hilly short Grass Country, a few small sticks and Ponds in places well stored with Ducks, abundance of what I called stone Currants which the Natives call Tuckquahaminanah [autumn berry], but no Rasberry Shrubs. We pitched on the edge of the Barren Ground." (HBCA B.239/a/69, 25 August 1772)

W Hearne: "tho the men went ahunting each Day they did not kill anything. Dureing the whole time we had nothing to Eat except Berries, which when eaten in so large a quantity as to stop hunger are of such an astringent quality (Espessually to Strangers) that me and my 2 men ware much desorder'd by them, at the same time hunger oblig'd us to have recorse to a still greater quantity let the Consiquence Prove as it may. . . . The Berrys chiefly consist of Cherreys, Rasberys, Black Currans and hipps." (HBCA B.49/a/1, 11 and 19 August 1774)

M Isham: "Of Berries there is several sorts here not Known in England, Severall of which I cou'd gett no acc^t of. . . . Thier is no oak or ash growing Downe by the sea shore but in Land a Considerable Distance great Quantity's, as also Ceder, pears, Plum's, Cherry's wild &c." (HBCA E.2/1. ff. 91r-91v, pp. 174-74 [*sic*])

M Graham: "There are several . . . species of Berries growing near the Coast: Such as the As-he-me-nuck or Crow Berries: Outa-me-nack or Dew Berries: Wus-is-kim-me-nack or Cranberries; Pe-thay-me-nack or Partridge Berries; Ne-keek-o-menack or Willow Berries; Ske-shick-a-menack or Strawberries: Sha-po-me-nack or Goose Berries: Man-too-me-nuck or black Currants: A-theek-i-me-nack or red Currants: Kaw-kaw-i-me-nuck or Juniper Berries; Very far In-land is a small kind of Nuts, and black Cherries, together with a species of Currants similar to those imported into England from the Meditarenian, yet are not quite so sweet." (HBCA E.2/9. f. 52v, p. 98)

H   MacGregor: "These obviously were not black currants. Neither
        were they cherries. They must have been berries new to Hen-
        day. They must have been saskatoons. . . . Henday's Indians
        were now reaching the country about forty miles south and
        east of Tisdale. They were near the Muscuty Plains—the land of
        plenty . . . There have been many plants known as 'tares'. I am
        certain that Henday referred to peavine and vetch. The party
        had definitely reached the parklands." (47-48)

30 July 1754

M   Graham: "Moosu. The Elk or Moose [moose] are never found
        on the sea-coasts, but are very numerous in land; they are not
        migratory like the Deer but will continue in one plain through-
        out the Year providing there is food sufficient; <when young>
        the legs are so long that they are obliged to bend the knees for
        the mouth to touch the grass which is their common food in
        summer, as the Birch willow and white moss are in winter.
        They are much larger than the Deer and require more dexter-
        ity to kill them, as they are of a more shy nature. It is uncom-
        mon for the Indians to bring any of the meat green to the Fac-
        torys the distance being very great but we receive a little of it
        dried in the summer. The nose is esteemed a great delicacy,
        several of them are brought in frozen in the winter season as a
        present to the Factor. They have two young at a birth, and
        bring them borth in the month of May. The Skins make buff
        leather and sell in England for four or five Shillings each."
        (HBCA E.2/9. f. 8r, p. 9)

31 July 1754

T mss   E.2/11: "but" and "two" added above the line, over carets; the
        Cree words for the French post written in enlarged letters.
C   see Isham, "Remarks" (B.239/a/40)
W   Pink: "jn the Morning j Sent a Way by an Jndaine Man a Mea-
        sure of Tobacoo to a Bodey of Jndaines Consisting of Forteen
        Tents for Encouradgment for them To Catch what Furrs They
        Could" (HBCA B.239/a/58, 1 October 1767)
W   Pink: "this Day we Hareed of a Bodey of Sinnapoits Consisting
        of one Hundred and fiftey Tents a Great Nomber that Never Se
        the Forte the Cannot paddle j sent Tobacoo to them for them
        to Smoke all" (HBCA B.239/a/63, 26 August 1769)
W   Tomison: "Smoakt with the men and gave them all the encour-
        agement I possable Could to Come down and trade at Your
        Hon^rs forts, they make many fair promises while Smoaking but

after soon forget. . . . I travled to the northward about 40 miles to some Indians with tobacco and to endeavour to get them down to trad, they mead many fair promises but as they ar so nigh to the trading house and a people of no creaded there is but little hope." (HBCA B.239/a/64, 22 August 1769 and 13-24 April 1770)

W Cocking: "All the Natives I have seen and heard from promise to go down <to> the Forts with all their Furrs; but they are such Notorious Liers they are little to be depended on; So that I fear the Pedlers will intercept much of the Companys Trade; and as Franceway is so near many of the Assinnee Poet Indians who are unacquainted with Canoes will go to him by Land." (HBCA B.239/a/69, 10 February 1773)

M Isham: "the Sinnepoets and other Indians Going to warr with [the Earchithinues], is a hinderance to their Coming to the English Setlements to trade, and I have Enquir'^{d} whether or not itt was not unpossable, if peace was Concluded betw'n them and other Nations, by which was the English to Per'u up the Country, that way, as the french has Done otherway's, I can not think but itt wou'd turn to Great advantage to our Merchants of England." (HBCA E.2/1. f. 71v, p. 134)

M Robson: "[The Indians] smoke brazil-tobacco mixed with a peculiar herb, of which both sexes and all ages are fond to excess. They have even stated entertainments of smoaking; on which occasion a pipe is produced, ornamented with feathers of various kinds. . . . This ornamented pipe is what I suppose the French call the calumet of peace. The Indians generally travel with one, which they offer to any party of a different nation that they happen to meet with; and their accepting it, and smoaking with them, are considered as an exchange of peace and friendship." (48)

M Graham: "The assenipoet Indians inhabits a fine pleasant country abounding with plenty of Buffaloe, Moose and Waskesews &c . . . they are a brave, lively, warlike people, and not so slothfull as the other Indians; they talk a different language, and their manners and customs greatly differ from the others; their country is above 600 miles from the Company's Settlements inland to the southwest [of Hudson Bay]; they are very numerous and are divided into tribes, two of whom trades yearly at York Fort & Prince of Wales's Fort: I cannot say whether all of them understand padling in canoes, but those that comes to the above Forts are very expert in manag<e>ing them; . . . we know little of their language more than the names of goods we trade in . . . in the year 1765 when Chief Factor at York Fort I sent an Englishman with them who says they are a numerous brave people, and they used him with such kindness that encouraged him to go again; before his going people were of opinion that they were a morose, surly people, and that it would be dangerous to send an Englishman with them." (HBCA E.2/4. ff. 34r-34v, pp. 61-62)

M   Umfreville: "Assinnee Poetuc. This nation is thus named by the [Nehethewas], which signifies in their language, the Stone Indians. In the maps of North America, where the residence of these incognita is said to be, a nation of Indians is marked down, called the Assinneboils; and this is the name by which the Canadian French, still continue to call them. . . . The nation under description is a detached tribe from the Naudawissees on the river Mississippi, mentioned in Carver's Travels, who anciently separated from the general stock, on account of some intestine commotion. At present these tribes are declared enemies to each other; yet their language, from the best information, has undergone no material alteration. The Assinee Poetuc are pretty numerous, and are scattered over a great extent of country. They bring many peltries to the traders, and are a principal support to the commerce." (195-96)

H   MacGregor: "This, apparently, was [Henday's] first meeting with the Assiniboines. He had now entered the country which they inhabited in north-eastern Saskatchewan. This tribe, otherwise known as the Stoneys, eventually were pushed back to the western side of the prairies. . . . Their favorite home, or hunting grounds, whichever you wish, appears to have been the Eagle Hills. . . . Some days later, on September 5th to be exact, and near the modern Village of Carruthers, he met some of them again, only this time he calls them the Eagle Indians." (55-56, 78)

1 August 1754

T mss E.2/6: "*The* Country . . . at pres*ent in*" written over erasure.

T xref E.2/6, E.2/4, E.2/11: cf. E.2/6, 21 September 1754.

W   Cocking: "The Country within about a mile from the [Saskatchewan] river (where small wood chiefly Spruce grows) hilly, producing short Grass in general except in the Vallies about a foot high; low Willows and Ponds in places, abundance of vermin Holes; the Soils a fine black Mould. . . . Indians say there are plenty of Buffalo here in Winter, which is confirmed by the quantity of Dung on the Ground." (B.239/a/69, 14-15 August 1772)

H Morton: "Henday's party continued in a general south-westerly direction, now over hills and through dales, now in light woods and along tall 'ledges' of trees, and many a happy hunt there was of red deer and moose. It was a land of plenty . . . It was all to Henday's liking." (246)

2 August 1754
T xref B.239/a/40, E.2/6 and E.2/4: cf. E.2/11, 5 August 1754
M Graham: "Stag. Waskesews [elk] These are not so large as [moose] yet considerably exceed the Deer both in he<i>ghth and size; the horns are lofty having few branches or rather processes (being very small) and those on the back part have no flat surface, but are round like the handles of knives. They are never seen on this side the great Lakes, but inhabit more to the Southward in a warm climate where they have grass for food all the year: They are very fat, but the meat is extraordinary coarse though otherwise good eating. The natural colour of the hair is red, but as they grow old it changes to a dirty brown. The feet are very small. They have two young at a time about the beginning of May." (HBCA E.2/9. f. 8v, p. 10)

3 August 1754
C see Isham, "Remarks" (B.239/a/40)
W Cocking: "The Natives call this part Pusquatinow from its being the termination of the woody Country." (HBCA B.239/a/69, 7 August 1772)
H MacGregor: "Henday's party would be in the general vicinity of Watson, Saskatchewan. . . . At last he was very near the Muscuty Plains." (59)

5 August 1754
T xref E.2/11: cf. B.239/a/40, E.2/6 and E.2/4, 2 August 1754.

7 August 1754
T mss E.2/11: the "m" of "Calm" flourished to cover an erasure.

8 August 1754
W Tomison: "Wind N.W. and squally W. with rain at times, the Indians a feasting Druming and dancing as they offten do when bad weather or want provisions." (HBCA B.239/a/64, 30 September 1769)
W Cocking: "The Natives are very delatory in proceeding; their

whole delight being in indolently sitting Smooking or Feasting.
Yesterday I received invitation to no less than ten of their
Feasts; some Berries dressed up with fat, others Meat Blood
&c. . . . This day the Natives pitched a very large Tent. A large
stick was set up in the midst, round this a Leader danced with
six others he making several attempts to thrust a wooden dart
like a skewer into the stick; at length he entered it into a hole
previously made beforehand, the Men Singing & Drumming
and the Women Dancing, every one being dressed in their best
apparel." (HBCA B.239/a/69, 19 August and 22 September 1772)

M   Isham: "They have perticular Days they make feasts of which is
     at a time when several tribes meets togeather, at such a time
     one treats another tell all their provender is gone, Eating from
     morning to night,—and itt's to be observ'^d he who Keeps the
     feast obliges Every one to Eat what is alotted him, and not to
     make waste, or to give any of his Companions any." (HBCA
     E.2/I. f. 49v, p. 90)

M   Robson: "At their feasts and merry meetings, when they are
     disposed to dance, the company join hands and shuffle round
     the musician, who sits upon the ground, and beats a kind of
     drum, the dismal sound of which he accompanies with a more
     dismal tone of voice." (52)

M   Graham: "Their Feasts are very extraordinary, being celebrated
     when they have plenty of Provisions and not instituted in hon-
     our of any remarkable Events, Person or Day. . . . Being come
     to the hospitable Tent; the Men all sit in a ring round the fire,
     next behind sit the Married Women, and the third ring the
     young Women and Children. The Victuals are all laid on a
     clean skin before the Host . . . every Person must eat what he
     gets; none is to remain or be carried away: notwithstanding
     they are great Gluttons they are often put to it to devour this
     quota; sometimes they get up, beat their sides and jump to
     shake it down, and very often they have another person to eat
     it for them. After this the Men strike up a drum and the mar-
     ried Women dance. Then they sit down and Silence reigns
     again, while some of the Old Men make Orations on different
     subjects. . . . everyone departs when he thinks proper, without
     taking any leave." (HBCA E.2/9. ff. 67v-68r, pp. 128-29)

9 August 1754

W   Pink: "heare i find on this South Side of the Maine River the
     Contrey Quite Oapen But Veary hilley Most parte of it, Some
     Lardge Standing Waters are heare found as Salte as the Water

is at Sea and all Round the Shoures is Laying Something Like Salt, one would think it was Snow at a Distance." (HBCA B.239/a/61, 18 October 1768)

W Cocking: "We pitched on the side of a Lake or rather Pond of Water, a disagreable bitterish salt taste; Salt laying on the Surface an Inch thick <Christaline> (a specimen of which I have preserved) and on the shore to a considerable distance like rime in a frosty morning." (HBCA B.239/a/69, 6 October 1772)

M Graham: "Sackhigan. Lakes are very numerous inland; some of fresh water, and others salt or brackish, are well stored with fish; and empty themselves either immediately, or by an outlet, into the Rivers which flow down to the sea. Some of our people who have been up the Country, affirm, that on the Banks of the salt water lakes, the salt is laid in large quantities and looks like snow; some of them made use of the water, but its cathartick quality obliged them to reject." (HBCA E.2/9. f. 4v, p. 2)

H MacGregor: "By now the party was reaching the region of the alkalai lakes close to Humboldt." (62)

12 August 1754

T mss E.2/6: "*tr*avelled" written over erasure.

W Pink: "Heare j find Verry little Green wood Standing for Some Yeares a Gone heare was <a large> fire wich Bournt the Chief of it up, So that it is now nothing but Berryes and tares some peaes and hearbes, weades, and Such Like thinges, the Chief, no Sweat Grace for Cattle." (HBCA B.239/a/58, 18 August 1767)

W Pink: "this Day an Jndaine Man a bout Four M<i>ldes to the windwarde of whare we put up, Set Fire to Grasey Open Contrey, and By the winds Blowing a Stronge Gale & the Grass Being Longe it Soon Bournt its way Down to the Tents, But being allreadey Darke and Seeing the Fire neare hand we did not Now which way to Ron to Save our things and our Seveles, So we Set fire to the Grass to the windward of the Tents and as Soon as it was Bournt a Little way of, then we Carryed our things on thare as Fast as we Could, But before we Could Get all thare the Tents ware Sevrill Bournt, and Four Wemen ware Bournt to Death and Sevrill others hands and Feate Deasparley Bournt." (HBCA B.239/a/61, 1 October 1768)

M Graham: "The Asp [aspen], Ash, and Hazle with several other kinds of wood are in the interior part of the Country, as we are informed; but can give no particular account of either. . . . Muscoshee. Several Species of Grass grow in this Country: but

as I am unacquainted with their proper Names, I shall only
mention their distinguishing Characters. In the Plains a long
coarse wire grass is produced. In dry soils a fine sweet Grass.
The Marshes produce another kind which is made into Hay for
Fodder for the Cattle during the long Winter. Here is also Rye
Grass, it has an Ear but does not fill; and a Rush." (HBCA E.2/9.
ff. 5IV, 53r, pp. 96, 99)

H   Morton: "The two lakes passed on 12th August on a south-
south-westerly course may be Dead and Gertrude lakes northwest of Humboldt. On the following day they were out on the
Muscuty, the buffalo grass plains in a region of salt lakes."
(246)

13 August 1754

W   Tomison: "on the West side the lake [Lake Winnipeg] is the
Muscuty Country where the Archithinues & Aseenepoet Indians Inhabits" (HBCA E.2/6, 6 June 1768)

W   Cocking: "travelling through a hilly short Grass Country . . .
We pitched on the edge of the Barren Ground; see several Buffelo feeding about one one-half mile distant, Indians killed ten
some with Guns & others with Bows, hunting on Horseback."
(HBCA B.239/a/69, 25 August 1772)

M   Isham: "Earchithinues . . . I never see, at the fort, Excep't a
Slave, which was Brought Downe by the Southw^d Indians,—their
Country Lyes on the back of this Land, and to the westward of
Churchill River, where the Spaniards frequents those seas, at the
same time does not traffick with y^t nation,—I have heard from
the mouth of the said Slave Conserning that Country, by which I
understood itt was situated much as York Fort Hays'^{s} River, with
a fine Navagable River than op'ns into the sea, and great plenty
of the best and finest of fur's, which is their Chiefest Commod-
ity's." (HBCA E.2/I. f. 7IV, p. 134)

H   Ray: "The Upland Indians included both Assiniboine and
Cree. . . . The other trading parties that arrived at the post
were fewer in number and generally came from much greater
distances. . . . Muscotay was a geographic term referring in
this instance to the grasslands between the forks of the
Saskatchewan River." (53-55)

H   Russell: "Isham's reference to two locales for the Archithinue
suggests he is conflating the Athapaskan groups with groups
from the northern plains. Further, his reference to the Spanish
suggest[s] he is specifically speaking of the Snake and their
allies who were obtaining goods from the Spanish." (189, 191)

15 August 1754

T mss E.2/11: "several" repeated in ms.

M   Isham: "Mus,tuce: a Cow or horse . . . Murs,tuce: a Bufflow" (HBCA E.2/1. ff. 13r-13v, pp. 17-18)

M   Graham: "Buffalows are as large as the North British horned Cattle, have short thick horns, black curling hair, hump between the shoulders and a bushy tail. They inhabit the Country to the Southward beyond Christianaux Lake wander about in large herds, feeding on the grass. The meat is much esteemed by the Natives who prefer it to any other kind of food. I have seen some of the tongues which were very large, but being dried in the smoak and kept a considerable time, I cannot say they were very agreable. The Archithinue Indians kill great Numbers, sometimes by running them down on Horseback and killing them with bow and arrows, but mostly by driving them into an enclosure or pound where they stab them with spears or shoot them with arrows." (HBCA E.2/9. f. 8v, p. 10)

H   MacGregor: "[Henday was] somewhere near Viscount, Saskatchewan." (65)

16 August 1754

W   Pink: "j Heare by thes Jndaines that to the South and SWwarde of whare we are now, thare is plentey of Beaver and Woulves, Neare hand, But being allwayes in Feare of the Jndaines Called Kene,pick,we,e,thyn,na,wo[ck] is the Reason that the Jndaines Dos not Gow aftor them, the Contrey Quite Open and those Jndaines Southwarde having all horses is the Reason the Jndaines that j am With are in Fear of them." (HBCA B.239/a/63, 18 September 1769)

W   Cocking: "Hunters see several strange Horses up the Branch on the other side; they are all in general afraid, supposing them to belong to the Snake Indians with whom they are always at variance." (HBCA B.239/a/69, 24 August 1772)

M   Umfreville: "That there are European traders settled among the Indians from the other side of the continent is without a doubt. I myself have seen horses with Roman capitals burnt in their flanks with a hot iron. I likewise once saw a hanger [sword] with Spanish words engraved on the blade." (178)

17 August 1754

T xref E.2/6 and E.2/4: cf all texts, 29 July 1754.

C   Isham to Jacobs: "By Anthony Henday who is gone in Land, and at this time is amongst the Pegogamy and Earchethinue

Indians I hope Good success, he is gone for the Winter, and to
Return next summer, please God he is well; my Chief View in
this is not only to Exhort and Encourage the Indians to come
to Trade, but to bring the Earchithinues to a Trade, who are
very Numerous." (HBCA B.239/b/11, 17 August 1754)

M   Graham: "Wapuss. Rabbets . . . in Summer they are brown like
British Rabbets but begin the change in October and before
Christmas are quite white yet this colour does not continue
more than half the length of the hair that part next the pelt
having a strong blue tinge and in trying to pluck the furr off
the pelt it will separe just at the juncture of the two colours.
This is found to be the American Hare from Mr Pennant."
(HBCA E.2/9. f. 12r, p. 17)

H   Morton: "they appear to have crossed the ridge, Henday's
Large Hill, which limits the horizon east of Saskatoon to about
six miles." (246)

H   MacGregor: "The great hills of the prairie and parklands . . .
are rarely more than four hundred feet above the surrounding
country, but . . . the sight of the hills, . . . their dark, blue mys-
tery, fills one with an inexplicable longing." (116)

18 August 1754

W   Cocking: "An Indian Lad . . . had the misfortune to have his
thigh bone broke by a fall from his Horse; they brought him to
my tent and I bandaged splinters round it, previously bathing
the part with Oppodeldoch [liniment]; but I have little
prospect of a Cure, wanting a proper Apperatus and besides
having but little skill in these matters." (HBCA B.239/a/69, 14
October 1772)

M   Isham: "The Natives in these parts are of an incredeable strong
Constitution both men and women . . . I Never Coud be
inform^d, of more y^n 2 Remedies they have for any wound, which
is, water and turpintine, they washing the wound Clean and
applying this Bolsome, by which they most and End [usually]
Recover, they Likewise use fatt sometimes, tho' Nature is Very
favourable to them;—and as for any Sickness or any Distemper
Inwardly, they have no other Remedy for such then Sweeting
itt off." (HBCA E.2/1, ff. 60r-60v, pp. 111-12)

M   Graham: "There are many Doctors amongst [the Indians], and
are held in great esteem, and they are of opinion that Physick is
not acquired by learning and study, but that the knowledge is
hereditary, and that no one can be a Doctor but the Son of a
Doctor, or else be made one by the Chief who is looked on by

them to be a very great Doctor; these Doctors comes to the
Forts well gooded, as they are well paid by their patients; they
don't trap their own furs; besides their own medicines they buy
a parcel from the Chief, such as sugar-candy, boiled prunes, car-
raway seed, salves, and ointments, made up of deers fat, and
bees-wax coloured with different paints; all of which are put in
small gallypots; the liquids are quite simple, and contained in
small vials: all which medicines are put up in a red trunk with a
common print, which is, his diploma." (HBCA E.2/4, f. 23v, p. 40)

21 August 1754

T mss E.2/6: "Wednesday" written over erasure.

W Pink: "This day we Came Down to the Side off a Large River
Called the Same as the Maine River Rones from the S,E, in to
the Maine River . . . this Day we Made Rafts of wood and
Crossed the River and Swom our Horses." (HBCA B.239/a/63,
9-10 September 1769)

W Cocking: "came to a branch of Saskachiwan River where we
pitched. About fifty yards wide a strong Current; It abounds
with plenty of Small Fish . . . We <all> crossed the Branch in
temporary Canoes covered with parchment, and pitched on
the other side." (HBCA B.239/a/69, 22-23 August 1772)

M Graham: "When they cross small rivers and have no canoes.
they make floats of wood, tieing them with the small fibres of
the roots of trees, and with the help of a padle or oar they get
safe across, never knowing any native to be drowned by the
above floats or out of a canoe; but I have known several
Englishmen lose their lives by attempting to manage their
canoes." (HBCA E.2/4. f. 25v, p. 44)

H Burpee: "[Hendry] crossed the South Saskatchewan somewhere about Clark Crossing, north of Saskatoon, and three
days later reached the North Saskatchewan." (315)

H Morton: "They . . . reached the South Saskatchewan near
Clarkboro . . . or more probably farther north at Osler Crossing. In Henday's manuscript the name of the river must have
been difficult to decipher. Isham's version [B.239/a/40] makes
it Wapesekcopet (seepee, river): the other two [*sic*] have it
Wapesue and Wapesew. The original must have been Waskesew
or Red Deer . . . The two later versions of the Journal have
notes [11 October 1754] at Henday's crossing of our Red Deer
River in Alberta . . . This is of great importance in determining
the several branches of the Waskesew River referred to in the
Journal." (246)

H   MacGregor: "[Henday's party crossed] the South Saskatch-
      ewan River, five or six miles below the heart of the present City
      of Saskatoon . . . Henday was probably the first white man to
      see this river this far up. The French . . . may have ranged this
      far from their fort [Fort à la Corne], but, if they did, they have
      left no record." (67)

H   Russell: "The group crossed the South Saskatchewan on open
      prairie north of Saskatoon and crossed to the Elbow of the
      North Saskatchewan and on to the Battlefords area." (95)

23 August 1754

C   Jacobs to Isham: "I wish, Anthony Henday may meet with the
      success You expect, hope he Will encourage the Indians to
      come and Trade, but Sir, pardon my freedom in saying, am of
      Opinion those Earchethinue Indians will never be brought to
      Trade at either of theese Factorys (I say, never) my reason
      stands Good, they being a very Timerous People, and make no
      use of Canoes, nay, nor won't be perswaded to Venture in one,
      besides the Indians which trades Yearly with t[hem] get great
      Quantity of Furrs (Catt in particular) from the above said
      Earchethinues, and Trade from them for Our Goods, and may
      probably be the reason for their not encourageing them to
      come Down to Trade, by which means the Indians keep the
      Benefit of that Trade amongst them Selves." (HBCA B.239/b/11,
      23 August 1754)

24 August 1754

T mss E.2/11: "Miles" added above the line, over a caret.

W   Cocking: "Several Indians have been tenting on these Hills for-
      merly, Stones laying in circular forms in many places which
      had been placed round the Eves of their Tents; the Natives tell
      me the Yachithinnee Indians. Obliged to use Buffelo dung for
      fewel. . . . This day I found in a Yachithinnee tent place part of
      an Earthen Vessel in which they dress their Victuals. It
      appeared to have been of the form of an Earthen Pan." (HBCA
      B.239/a/69, 5 and 7 October 1772)

H   Burpee: "As far as one can judge [Henday] reached the North
      Saskatchewan at the Elbow . . . about midway between Prince
      Albert and Battleford. He did not cross the river, but continued
      his way to the westward, following its banks, to a point some-
      where in the neighbourhood of the site of Battleford." (315)

H   Morton: "From the South Saskatchewan Henday passed over
      an almost waterless prairie to the Elbow of the north branch of

the Saskatchewan. He calls the river here the Sachown River, probably from the Ojibway *seeguong*, spring. It was the river he was to come down by in the spring." (247)

H   MacGregor: "the North Saskatchewan River . . . Henday first saw this river about the mouth of Eaglehill Creek, which is some ten miles upstream from the Ceepee Bridge, north-west of Saskatoon. His description of the river fits perfectly, for in the fall it is about two furlongs wide and it is full of sandy islands." (71)

27 August 1754

H   MacGregor: "Undoubtedly their camp would be on one of the branches of Cooper Creek." (75)

31 August 1754

P   Graham, "Plan" 1774: "Sakatow Hills" and "Eagle Hills" are marked, the second with a "Buffalo Pound"; a dotted line indicates Cocking's overland route: "NB The dots from the Place of Mr Cocking's disembarcation to where he Embark'd show his Journey in the Winter. From York Fort to Pomochicimo Lake, & Keskatchewan River to the Buffalo Pound is Mr Cocking's Path with the Indians in the Years 1772 and 1773. This is the NE. part of the Archithinue Country, where the Keskachewans resort after Bufalo, & to trade with the Archithinue Indians." (HBCA G.2/17)

H   Morton: "Passing over some of the spurs of the Eagle Hills, Henday's party directed its course along the southern edge of the wooded valley of the Battle River. . . . The three creeks passed in the first week of September must be so many tributaries of the Battle [River]." (247)

H   MacGregor: "Henday camped on Cutknife Creek, two or three miles north of Cutknife Hill, and not far from the scene of the battle [Poundmaker vs. the Canadian militia, 3 May 1885]." (82)

1 September 1754

C   Isham, instructions to Smith and Waggoner: "take perticular Care not to be too Bussy with the Indians Wives, so as to Create a misunderstanding, the contrary may by Your Own Ruin, and a great detriment to the Design your sent upon." (HBCA A.11/114, 20 August 1756)

M   Isham: "the women are for the most part short and thick, and not so Lively as the men when they are turn'd 20 Years; But very frisky when young &c. . . . Maidens are Very rare to be

found at 13 or 14 Years, and I believe m'y Safely say none at 15
Years, fine Ladies &c. . . . the women [are] good Breeder's, and
the Grey mair is ye best horse most an End [generally] with
them as well as other Nations that is more polite." (HBCA E.2/1.
ff. 51r, 60r, pp. 93, 111)

M   Graham: "The Company permit no European Women to be
brought within their territories, and forbid any Indians to be har-
boured in the Settlements: but nevertheless an obliging Nymph
now and then pays the Officers a visit in their apartments unless
the Governor (who keeps a Girl himself) is of an ill natured disposition and forbids it." (HBCA E.2/9. f. 113r, p. 219)

H   Morton: "Incidentally, on more than one occasion where there
was difficulty, this lady, whom Henday describes in his Journal
as his bedfellow, contributed to the success of his voyage by
keeping him well informed of what the Indians about him were
saying and proposing. As connections of the kind were prohib-
ited in the service, Isham eliminated all reference to her in the
official copy of Henday's Journal forwarded to the Governor
and Committee." (244)

H   MacGregor: "Going about with the men all day, Henday was a
great chief, but at night he came home to this young squaw
and asked her advice. She counselled him and cherished him,
and next morning sent him forth fresh to face the day's problems. So, for nearly a year, this laughing girl of the plains and
this eager young man from a far country shared each other's
hardship and happiness." (55)

H   Rich: "[Henday's] interest in the Indians and their families,
and their acceptance of him, was undoubtedly facilitated by
the fact that by this time he had settled down with what he
described as his 'bed-fellow' from among the Indians with
whom he was travelling. She performed all the normal functions of a squaw for him, and very greatly assisted his
journey. . . . she does not appear in the official copy of Henday's Journal . . . but he could not have lived and travelled as
an Indian, nor, in all probability, could he have gained acceptance as he did, without her help." (1: 633)

H   Russell: "It seems only to have been a portion of the families
of some of the trading Indians who rendezvoused in the east.
Surprisingly, in none of the inland journals is there any mention of groups of families waiting at other rendezvous along
the river. Yet, the numbers of families at these rendezvous were
not large and could not have represented all the trading Indians from the entire Saskatchewan River." (145)

4 September 1754
C   James Isham to Anthony Henday:
               York Fort Septr 4th 1754
Anthony Henday
I rec'd Yours of July the 9th; and hope theese will come safe,
and find You in good health, as we all are at present Captain
Spurrel of the Prince Rupert is now with us, which I doubt not
but will be pleasing to the Indians to hear. You seem fearful of
passing the French Follow Your Instructions in such a Case, I
do not Imagine they will Intercept You, I am tould Bob has
seen the French who used Him well, I hope health and success
will attend You, be sure to Keep in Friendship with Attick-
os<is>h; I have sent You a Roll of Tobacco, and a Quire Paper
by the Bearer, You say You live on Moose and Swans, an
Earchithinue that is Hear, tells me there is Wild Goats Nutts
Apples &c in thier Country, I desire You will be particular in
Your Journal, I wish You health, and hope to see You at the
head of many Earchithinues, and forreign Indians, next Summer, from Your loving
        Friend, and Servt
           James Isham/
[endorsed] YF 1754 Copys of Letters To & from Anthony Henday on a Journey in Land
(HBCA A.11/114, 4 September 1754)

5 September 1754
T xref B.239/a/40: cf E.2/6, E.2/4 and E.2/11, 6 September 1754.
M   Isham: "Discourses upon Different Subjects [conversation
     between an Englishman and an Indian]:
     E.   where will the most geese be or weyweys
          tanta Kuttahurrawock, mechet Wawewuck A'komick
     A.   Over the River . . . har'k don't you here wey weys
          A'komick . . . maw, nema, naw. Kepathtum, wawewuck . . .
     E.   the weywey's are comming this way, Call
          pimmathow wawewuck, tapo'ss . . .
     A.   how many geese have you Kill^d, to day
          tantarto wawewuck, anoach Kesichkkaw, kenippahaw'
     E.   twenty and nine
          shaw'k, tartoshop neshu, tenna
     A.   why you are a good hunter, hay!
          mawna sucky naharshaway Chee' . . .
Thier is Seven sorts of geese, as first the white geese, which
[the Indians] style (wappawawewuck) which the english Call's

weywey's, these has only Black feathers in their tail and wings Reg Leg[d]—the Ganders has a little Reddish feathers upon the head, and smells of mus'k, the geese being white headed and no musky smell." (HBCA E.2/1. ff. 35v-36r, 74v-75r, pp. 62-63, 140-41)

6 September 1772

T mss E.2/4: "*bloody*" written over erasure.

T mss E.2/11: "es" of "does" crossed out in pencil; "Since 1755 . . . at the factory" is written in paler ink and seems to be a later addition to the main text.

T xref E.2/6, E.2/4 and E.2/11: cf. B.239/a/40, 5 September 1754.

C   Isham to the HBC London Committee: "Have had five Cannoes of those Bloody Indians Henday formerly Mention[d] made the Chief a Present, who Promised to bring many the next Year, and have Order'd in such Case further Encouragement." (HBCA A.11/115, 16 September 1758)

M   Isham: "There is the Eagl[d] Ey'd Indians which I never see, but are Sensible they are the same Nation as the sinepoats, or stone Indians, speaking the same Language, Sinepoets their name Derives from the stony Country they live in." (HBCA E.2/2. f. 42v, p. 250)

M   Graham: "The assenipoet Indians . . . one of the tribes that comes to York Fort does not cover their private parts, even their women are but careless in that respect, but are now more decent owing to the advice given them by the Factors, who always does or at lest should use them with the greatest kindness, as they can well live without coming down to trade; when at the Forts they always tent by themselves." (HBCA E.2/4. f. 34v, p. 62)

M   Graham: "A view of the various Nations & their Tribes which contribute towards the Fur-trade in Hudson's Bay. Nation . . . Assinepoet . . . Tribes . . . Mei kis sew [eagle] . . . " (HBCA E.2/9, f. 84r, p. 61)

H   Rich: "As Henday turned away west and south-west from the course of the North Branch on 5th September (somewhere in the region of the modern Battleford) he met a band of Eagle Indians, remarkable for the fact that the men went entirely naked; they had never previously traded with any European but he persuaded them to hunt furs and to take them down to the Bay." (634)

H   Russell: "At first sight it is puzzling why the group is called the Eagle Indians in one place and the Bloody Indians in another. . . . The confusion may have been caused by the differences in the 'th' and the 'y' Cree dialects. In 'th' dialect, blood is pronounced *mithko* but in 'y' dialect it is *mihko*. In both dialects, eagle is *mikisew*. Persons familiar with the 'th' dialect [spoken at the Bay forts], but not the 'y' dialect to the west, may well have thought *mihko* (Plains Cree 'blood') was simply a variant of the general Cree word *mikisew*. . . . Henday's comment that the Bloody Indian men were naked gives important information on the distribution of these Assiniboin and identifies them as being the Southern Assinipoets . . . a group of Assiniboin stretching from the Branches of the Saskatchewan south . . . all had one element in common which was different from all groups east and north of them including other Assiniboin: their manner of dress. . . . the Northern Assiniboin were similar to their Cree neighbours while the Southern Assiniboin resembled the Plains groups to the west and south." (184)

8 September 1754

T mss E.2/4: "*W.S.W.*" written over erasure.

C YF post journal (Isham): "We have Entertained John Plum Smith 5 Years att 20℔ per Annum, Peter Vincent Sailor 5 Y^rs att 8℔ Pr Annum, Willm Monk, Thos Cook & Isaac Batt Lab^rs for 5 years Each att 10℔ Pr Annum . . . also And^w Graham, 5 years att 15℔ Pr Annum . . . All which have Signed Contracts Accordingly. . . . Anth^y Hendey who is now inland, two or three years Longer with Encouragement." (HBCA A.11/114, 8 September 1754)

C see note, E.2/11, 31 October 1754.

M Graham: "Servant's Contracts":

I A. B. of ___ aged ___ years . . . do hereby Covenant and agree to, and with the Governor and Company of Adventurers of England, Trading into Hudson's Bay and their Successors to serve them for the Term of five Years, to commence from the time I shall arrive at Hudson's-Bay: at ___ ℔ per Annum until I shall be discharged from the Factory, and if I intend to return at the limitted time to give notice to the said Committee unless sooner recalled by them, and to . . . perform such Labour and work, and obey such commands as the Governor in Hudson's-Bay, or chief Factor there, shall impose upon me. . . . And in case I the said A. B. shall make any breach or default of or in Performance of all, or any the aforesaid Covenants, Agreements, or Things, Then I and my Executors and Administrators will not only forfeit and lose all Wages, Salary and Monies, as by Virtue of this Contract, or Otherwise, shall be due to me, or them, from the said Governor & Company or their Successors,

which I do hereby enable them to detain to their own Use & Benefit; But also I and my Executors and Administrators will, for every such breach or Default, also forfeit to the said Governor and Company the sum of ___ of lawful Money of England, over and above all Damages that may arise, or happen to them, by reason or means of such Breach or Default. In Witness whereof I have hereunto set my Hand and Seal this ___ Day of ___ in the Year of our Lord God 1768.   A. B.
>Sealed and Delivered in the
>Presence of Us;
>>A. C.
>>T. M."

(HBCA E.2/6, ff. 43v-44v, pp. 85-87)

M   Umfreville: "Each servant signs a contract on his entrance into the service, but he is not allowed to have a copy of it, for fear the secrets of the Company should gain admittance into the world. . . . The chief employments of the inferior servants in the settlements, is carrying logs of wood, walking in snowshoes, sledging the snow out of the Factory avenues, and hunting; and notwithstanding the inconveniences . . . , after a person has been a few years in the service, he generally imbibes a love for the country, unless discouraged by the bad usage of his superiors." (113, 118-19)

10 September 1754

W   Cocking: "A plentiful Country of Provision, for an Indian need only mount his Horse taking his Gun or Bow, and in a short time return with his Horse Loaded also supplying his Neighbours: indeed they are very kind this way to each other, every one being entitled to a share of a Beast who goes for it." (HBCA B.239/a/69, 29 September 1772)

M   Isham, "Discourses on Different Subjects [conversation between an Indian and an Englishman]:
>A. I'll bring some deer if I Kill any
>   Enkopeshuwuck, attick, nippahau't—
>A. What is your Loving bitt
>   Kaquan, Kuttawachetogan
>E. the tongues
>   Uttethin<n>ue . . . "

(HBCA E.2/1. f. 37r, p. 65)

M   Graham: "The Country beyond the Lakes is so well stocked with various kinds of Animals, that the Indians can indulge their Indolence and never be in want of Food . . . they kill ani-

mals &c sometimes out of wantonness, alledging the more
they destroy the more plentiful they grow . . . frugality and prudence in this respect are not amongst the Virtues of these
Natives, though to be impartial, it is just to mention that the
reason of a Conduct so unaccountable to Englishmen, may
proceed from the difficulty that would arise from conveying a
Stock of Provisions from place to place in their migratory way
of Life: We ought therefore not to be rash in our Censures. . . .
After having travelled as far as they chuse they make a mark
for the Women to put up at that place, and then every Man
takes a different rout in search of game . . . when they kill any
thing large as Deer, Buffalo, Elk &c. the Man only takes out
the tongue, heart or what is his favourite piece leaving the car-
case for the Women to fetch." (HBCA E.2/9. ff. 62r, 71r, pp. 117,
135)

11 September 1754

H   MacGregor: "Henday . . . travelled by easy stages over the
delightful parklands north of Freemont and Neilburg. He
wound down into the coulee which drains Manito Lake, and on
September 11th strode over that imaginary line that later was
to become the Alberta-Saskatchewan border. Eventually he
crossed the Battle River about six miles north and four miles
west of Wainwright." (87)

13 September 1754

W   Smith: "came to twentey teantes of the Sineapoils and ther
was a pound the mead to kill the boffler in and that day
wandey ther was 67 cam in at onese and thasdey the 3 we lea by
and fridey the 4 we smocked it with all the Sineapoites and
gave tham backer and other thinges as we hade and Seatedy
the 5 we lea by and ther was feisting with the Sineapoits"
(HBCA B.239/a/45, 2-5 November 1757)

W   Cocking: "This day spent . . . in singing their Buffelo Pound
Songs. . . . Buffelo at present but scarce. . . . Male Buffelo only
to be had at present; this often happens, these the Natives do
not approve being poor all the Year except in the first part of
the Summer. . . . Two Tents of our Company seperated from us
going Northerly, at present four Tents." (HBCA B.239/a/69, 3
and 7 and 9-10 October 1772)

H   MacGregor: "By 1890 the immense herds of Henday's time had
been reduced to a mere handful. The earth of the Wainwright
Buffalo Park that had trembled to the trample of stampeeding

[*sic*] hoofs was stilled . . . Then in 1908, in box-cars, penned like pigs, the pitiful remnant of the buffalo returned to the fenced remnant of their old haunts. The old days, the days that had lasted 10,000 years, were gone, because fence and plow now ruled this land." (100-1)

H   Rich: "Henday's gifts were not literary, and the first English description of a buffalo hunt does nothing to impress upon the reader the stupendous wealth which confronted him. The comparatively easy living which he had enjoyed since striking the Saskatchewan had probably dulled his appreciation of even the coarser pleasures which the buffalo brought, and it is only from later descriptions that it is possible to imagine the plenty, and the slaughter, among which Henday moved." (1: 634)

15 September 1754

T mss   E.2/6: "*their*" written over erasure.

C   see Isham, "Remarks" (B.239/a/40)

W   Smith: "mondey the 3 we lea by and ther came to hus four teans of indens and we lea at the Side of a grat Lak as the call monito Lak it is in the Baren grownd" (HBCA B.239/a/45, 3 October 1757)

W   Pink: "this Day we put up by a Large Leake Called Minnato Cockhagan it Rones in to a Small River that Rons to the North warde and in to the Main River, Round this Lardge leake Euse to be a Noated plase for Bofflow But hear is None, Nor we has Not Seen Now Beast this Fourteen Dayes a Gone, So that we are Greatly in want of provisions for we has Nothing to Eate but Now and then a Rabit that the Jnda<i>nes Kills with the Bow and a Row . . . this Day the Jndaines that ware with me Mooved Some one way Some a Nother for Traping. . . . we are now Busy a Trapping." (HBCA B.239/a/63, 22 and 26 and 30 September 1769)

W   Cocking: "I see two Snakes this day each about a yard long; harmless, Indians handling them and putting them in their Breasts." (HBCA B.239/a/69, 25 August 1772)

M   Graham: "Snakes are found in various species In Land beyond the Lakes: but none are found <within> a great distance of the Forts. I have seen the stuffed skins brought down by the Natives; and found some of them to measure above six feet. Indian name of this Reptile is Kinepuck." (HBCA E.2/9. f. 46r, p. 85)

H   Morton: "On September 15th [Henday's party] was in sight of a large lake (Manito Lake) beyond which it reached the Battle River." (247).

H MacGregor: "The lake which Henday passed on September 15th was Baxter Lake." (101)

16 September 1754

H Burpee: "[Henday] came to a small river which he calls Chacutenah, presumably Sounding Creek." (315)

H Morton: "the Battle River, Henday's Countenack, the river of the Nootinitoowuk, the people who fight one another." (247)

H MacGregor: "Henday and his Indians spent two days camping in the majestic valley of the Battle River a few miles north of Wainwright." (106)

17 September 1754

T xref all texts cf E.2/6, E.2/4 and E.2/11, 22 November 1754.

W Tomison: "two young men got very much wounded by a grizzled Bear, one of them is so much bite through the body that he is not expected to live." (HBCA B.239/a/64, 19 May 1770)

M Isham: "Black bear's thier is a pretty many and some Very Large, Espitially ye Grizel bears which will Seize a man if Come in his way having Known an Indian tore in a Sad manner with one, they are Extrodinary good food, and Very fatt in the winter, they have 2 and 3 at a Litter Gendering in may & Breeding June, and July, as the Natives say's which I can not Readily blieve,—they have holes or Caves in the ground, or under the snow, where they Live all winter . . . by Sucking thier paw's, and are fattest at y^t time, in the Summer they Live upon Berries and Grass." (HBCA E.2/2. ff. 24r-225r, pp. 213-15)

M Graham: "Brown and Grizzle Bears are found up the Country harbouring amongst the Buffalo's on which they prey are very large and fierce, especially if wounded, frequently tearing the adversary to pieces, for which reason no single person dare attack them, unless in a thick wood. It is customary on hearing of one of these Bears being near for several of the Men to go in Company to kill him, and coming up to him the Dogs are set on to annoy and engage him, until the Men shoot him dead. Notwithstanding these Indians ride upon good Horses yet several are destroyed in these encounters every year. This is named Meshe Muskqua." (HBCA E.2/9. f. 13r, p. 19)

19 September 1754

H MacGregor: "Henday's Crees . . . camped somewhere on Grattan Creek, a mile or so west of the hamlet of Hawkins." (108)

20 September 1754

W   Pink: "This Day was a bad day with me, for j had Got me a
    horse to Cary my thinges, thinking that j Should Get it alonge
    without being Troblesom to the Jndaines for the think a Great
    deal of Carriing aney thing for an English man un less he pay
    them well for it, so i put all my things that j had upon this
    Horse Excepet parte of the pouder that j Carryed, So an Indain
    man Says to me this, as I has Nothink to Carry Shall j Leade
    your hors for you yes Sayes j So he toock hym in his hand But
    to my Troble & Vexshation for as he was Crossing a Crick
    whare the Bankes ware Steep so the hors for the want of some
    Care of the man Sliped down in to the Crick and thare lye So
    longe that all my thinges ware wet." (HBCA B.239/a/58, 7
    August 1767)

W   Tomison: "the Indians returned with Several very fine horses
    from 13 to 14 hands high, they are of different Coulers the
    Same as in England." (B.239/a/64, 29 October 1769)

M   Graham: "The Natives far inland beyond the Lakes have a fine
    breed of Horses of various colours as in Europe but as none are
    ever brought down to the Factories, I cannot say much con-
    cerning them. . . . <Horses are so numerous Inland that M^r
    William Tomison who commands Cumberland & Hudson Hous-
    es trades with different Tribes of Equestrian Indians to the
    Amount of five hundred in one Gang. The Horses are Small in
    Size, clean made, and very nimble. They are mostly Grey col-
    ered, Mr Tomison writes me that He built a Stable for One
    Horse and provided Grass for the Winter Season, but the Ani-
    mal soon died not agreeing with good usage.>" (HBCA E.2/9.
    ff. 14v, 35v, pp. 22, 64)

M   Umfreville: "Many of the men shew more affection for their
    horses than for their wives. The horses bred here are variously
    coloured, like our English horses, and about the size of those
    found in the north of Scotland and the Scottish isles. . . . Many
    broils and animosities among the natives, originate from a
    desire of being in possession of these animals. One party gen-
    erally commences hostilities by stealing the horses of their
    adversaries, and they in turn retaliate; so that at length a
    mutual resentment takes place, and war becomes absolutely
    necessary." (189)

H   MacGregor: "How pleased Henday's squaw must have been that
    her great chief owned the only horse in the band. Moreover, he
    had bought it not to ride, but to relieve her of the burden of car-
    rying his tent and his supplies. How fortunate she was." (109)

21 September 1754

T xref E.2/6: cf. E.2/6, 1 August 1754, E.2/11, 22 September 1754 and E.2/4, 23 September 1754.

M   Umfreville: "[If we consider the inland plains and the coast of Hudson Bay] the two countries will admit of no comparison: one is temperate and healthy; the land is dry, pleasant, and fertile in spontaneous productions, and the animal creation is various and excellent for the support of man: in it, a person who could live retired, might pass his days with ease, content, and felicity, and if he did not enjoy an uninterrupted state of health, it would not be the fault of the air he lived in. On the other hand, the lower country is one endless bog . . . The whole country furnishes but one quadruped fit for the support of man; and the Europeans are accursed with an afflicting epidemical disorder, which they very emphatically term . . . 'The Country Distemper.' " (157)

23 September 1754

T mss E.2/4: "I cannot describe . . . I am now in" underlined in pencil, as are references to the weather in following entries.

T xref E.2/4: cf. E.2/6 and E.2/11, 1 August 1754.

24 September 1754

T xref E.2/6 and E.2/11: cf. E.2/4, 25 September 1754.

M   Graham: "Pau-pas-tuow. The Woodpecker. . . . There is [a] species of Woodpeckers . . . with a blooming crimson Crown; these are In-Land to the Southward. the skins of the Heads are used by the Trading Indians to ornament the Calimut." (HBCA E.2/9. ff. 38r, 39v, pp. 67, 70)

25 September 1754

T xref E.2/4: cf. E.2/6 and E.2/11, 24 September 1754.

26 September 1754

T xref B.239/a/40: cf. E.2/6, E.2/4 and E.2/11, 28 September 1754.

27 September 1754

W   Cocking: "A smook seen this day the way We are intended to go; as they are uncertain whether it is made by Friends or Foes some young Men are going off tomorrow to Reconnoitre, I have sent a present of Tobacco to be smooked if they are friends. . . . Ten tents of Assinnee Poet Indians came to us. they inform us that they left several tents of Yachithinnee Indian

Friends two days journey beyond Manito Sackaeagan and
twelve from hence." (HBCA B.239/a/69, 27 August and 18
September 1772)

28 September 1754
T xref E.2/6, E.2/4, E.2/11: cf. B.239/a/40: 26 September 1754.

1 October 1754

W   Cocking: "One of the [Yeachithinnee] Leaders is fully
acquainted with the Assinee Poet Indian tongue, so that we
shall be able to understand each other, my Leader also being
acquainted with that tongue.—Those Natives are called Powe-
stick Athinnewock or Water-fall Indians. The People I am with
inform me there are four Nations more which go under the
name of Yeachithinnee Indians with whom they are in friendship. Viz^t Mithcoo-Athinneewock or Blood Indians: Koskiketew
Watheessituck, or black-foot Indians; Pigonew Athinneewock
or muddy Water Indians and Sussewuck or woody Country Indians. Their Enemies also go under the general Name of Yeachithinnee Indians, four Nations. Kanapickathinnawock or
Snake Indians; Wah-tee or Vault Indians; Kuttunnayewuck; and
Nah-puck Ustiquanock, or flat-Head Indians so called they tell
me from their forheads being very flat." (HBCA B.239/a/69, 1
December 1772)

M   Graham: "Archithinue Nation. These Indians possess an extensive Country beyond that of the Asinepoets to the Southward
and Westward; they have plenty of Buffalo, and never eat
Beaver or Fish; have no water carriage, and know nothing
about managing a Canoe; some Englishmen have been sent
amongst them to induce them to come down to the Forts, but
they answered, that, they lived very well; know not how to manage a Canoe, nor were willing to undergo the inconveniences
of such a journey: however one or two have had the curiosity to
come to York Fort but never repeated the visit. Those who live
on the frontiers of the Asinepoets Country abide in tents, but
as wood is scarce they carry the poles about with them, and
use the dung of the Buffalo for firing. They cultivate a wild
species of Tobacco which they are fond of smoaking; They are
expert hunters, and procure many Furrs which they exchange
at a dear rate with the Keiskatchewans for Guns, hatchets, and
other goods. There are others far more to the Southward who
live in little houses made of logs and as their habitations are
fixed they cultivate the wild rice and corn in little spots of

ground, but unhappily for them they frequently fall a prey to the wanton unprovoked slaughter not only of the Keiskatch-ewans and Asinepoets, but also of a neighbouring Tribe wh<ose Native barbarity is equally destructive to the Earchithinues.> We have advice of other Nations beyond these, but as they contribute nothing towards the Trade of Hudson's Bay, and the accounts are very imperfect and dissatisfactory, I shall say nothing more about them." (HBCA E.2/9. ff. 82v-83r, pp. 158-59)

M   Umfreville: "Fall Indians. This nation is thus named by us, and by the Nehethawa Indians, from their inhabiting a country on the Southern branch of the river, where the rapids are frequent. As they are not very numerous, and have a harsh, gutteral language peculiar to themselves, I am induced to think they are a tribe that has detached itself from some distant nation, with which we are not as yet acquainted. . . . The Susee Indians. Though this nation have a language intirely to themselves, and which no others can learn, they are very few in number, being no more than a small tribe which has separated from the main body, and now harbour in some country about the Stony Mountain, where they keep to themselves, for not many have as yet appeared at any of the trading houses. . . . The Blackfoot, Paegan, and Blood Indians. These Indians, though divided into the above three tribes, are all one nation, speak the same language, and abide by the same laws and customs. For what reason they are thus denominated, I have not been able to discover, but they go by no other name among the Nehethawas. They are the most numerous and powerful nation we are acquainted with; and by living on the borders of the enemies country, are the principal barrier to prevent their incursions." (197-98, 200)

H   Burpee: "It would be impossible to identify the tribe with any degree of certainty were it not that Cocking supplies the key . . . 'This tribe is named Powestic-Athinuewuck (ie) Waterfall Indians . . . ' The Archithinue Indians whom Hendry visited . . . were, therefore, Blackfeet." (316)

H   Morton: "Continuing south-westward, Henday reached the Earchithinues (here the Bloods) somewhere west of the present Balermo." (247)

H   Rich: "about sixty miles (by his reckoning) short of the Red Deer River of Alberta, [Henday] made serious contact with the Archithinues, a term applied to the four equestrian tribes, the Gros Ventres, the Blackfeet, Bloods and Peigans (the last two

being sub-groups of the Blackfeet). Seven tents of the Bloods
came to Henday's camp . . . Henday travelled on . . . in a south-
west-by-westerly direction until . . . he had reached a point
somewhere west of the present town of Balermo. Here he met
the main body of the Blackfeet, assembled under their Great
Leader." (1: 635)

H   Ray: " 'Archithinue,' was a Cree word that was applied to the
Blackfoot and Gros Ventre." (55)

H   Russell: "This anglicized Cree term, often written as
Archithinue, was applied to all groups of western Indians who
were neither Cree nor Assiniboin. It was often translated as
'Slave', hence our Great and Lesser Slave lakes. On the
prairies, it could refer to any or all of the Blackfoot, Peigan,
Blood, Sarcee, or Gros Ventre. Since neither Henday nor his
employers ever used the term in a more specific sense, it is not
possible to identify the various groups which he met although
it is commonly assumed they were members of the Blackfoot
Nation." (94)

2 October 1754

M   Graham: "Mathetick. Wild Goats [pronghorn antelope] are
found in the Southern Country. their horns are black and vary
in shape from the English or Welch Goats, for besides the
branches which turn down laterally they have another part,
which projects over the crown of the head." (HBCA E.2/9. f. 14v,
p. 22)

3 October 1754

T mss E.2/11: "trees *I have*" written over erasure.

T xref E.2/6 and E.2/4: cf. E.2/4, 15 October 1754.

H   MacGregor: "These two creeks . . . were Hastings Creek and
the Battle River . . . about eleven miles south and a mile west
of Heisler." (125)

5 October 1754

T xref B.239/a/40: cf. E.2/6, E.2/4 and E.2/11, 11 October 1754.

M   Graham: "Several Englishmen who have <been> travelling all
the Year with the Upland Indians, Inform me they have seen
veins of Iron-Ore long and broad on the surface of the Ground;
but as they were illiterate people no great stress can be laid on
their information." (HBCA E.2/9. f.55v, p. 104)

7 October 1754

M   Graham: "Flint Stones are found in small pieces amongst the sand on the shores of Rivers, but not so pure as those Received from England. Chakesigahan so called." (HBCA E.2/9. f. 54v, p. 102)

H   MacGregor: "That night [Henday and his companions] camped two or three miles north and east of the Town of Stettler. . . . This ridge of fine flint stone has given me more mental torment than most of Henday's diary. . . . While the snow covered the ground . . . I read and re-read the diary, ever anxious for spring to come, so as to get out and prove how simple it would be to follow Henday. . . . If I . . . could finally hit on this flint ridge, I would feel pretty certain I was on the right track. . . . There are no out-croppings of rock within seventy-five miles of this spot. . . . This, then, must have been merely a gravelly ridge. These are frequent in this part of the country, although the ridges are not of very great extent. . . . One can find an assortment of field stones and pebbles on them. The particular one on which Henday camped must have had more flinty pebbles than the majority of them." (133-34)

11 October 1754

T mss   B.239/a/40, E.2/6 and E.2/11: the note follows the entry for 12 October 1754.

T mss   E.2/4: the note follows this entry (misnumbered 12 October 1754).

T xref   E.2/6, E.2/4 and E.2/11: cf. B.239/a/40, 5 October 1754.

H   Burpee: "after an uneventful journey over the Great Plain, [Hendry] crossed the Waskesew. It is pretty safe to assume that this was the Red Deer [River of Alberta], and that the place where Hendry crossed was a little above Knee Hills Creek. This conclusion is based upon a careful comparison of his distances and directions and his description of the country, all three pointing to the place indicated. Curiously enough Waskesew means Red Deer, but this in itself has no particular significance, as there have been innumerable Deer rivers throughout the West. . . . [re Graham's note:] Undoubtedly the Red Deer and the Saskatchewan are all one river, but Hendry has already crossed the South Saskatchewan and seen the North Saskatchewan. Why did he not name them Keskatchew or Waskasew?" (315-16)

H   Morton: "On 11th October, on a general south-westerly course came to the Waskesew River, our Red Deer River of Alberta,

one of the upper waters of the South Saskatchewan, and then
bearing the same name as it did. His Journal indicates that at
this point the course of the river was 'NWt and SE' and that he
crossed it at its south-easterly course. He was, therefore, at the
point about three miles west of the present Nevis." (247)

H   MacGregor: "The Red Deer River [of Alberta] was crossed . . .
about ten miles downstream from the Content Bridge. His
description of the stones of an iron colour would fit this place,
as well as veins of iron running along the surface of the
ground. This is a very common phenomenon almost anywhere
in this stretch of the Red Deer River." (139)

H   Russell: "[From] the Battlefords area . . . they struck southwest along the Battle River until, on 14 October, they finally
reached the Archithinue camp near Red Deer, Alberta." (95)

13 October 1754

T mss E.2/11: "*variable*" and "Archith*in*ue" added above the line, over
carets.

14 October 1754

T mss B.239/a/40: this entry runs over two pages; the note appears at
the foot of the first page, after the line "fatt Buffaloes flesh,
and after that we had."

C   see Isham, "Remarks" (B.239/a/40)

W   Cocking: "A general smooking with the Yeachithinnee Indians;
also presented the Leaders and principal Men with Tobacco,
Ammunition and other Goods as far as prudence would allow.
At the same time (by the mouth of my Leader) I did endeavour
to perswade two of them to accompany me on my return to the
Fort, where I promised they should meet with the kindest
treatment, and be greatly favoured.—I cannot pretend to take
more with me at present than two, these People being entirely
unacquainted with Canoes. . . . The Tobacco they use is of their
own planting, which I cannot say has an agreable flavour. I
have preserved a specimen.—Their Cloathing is much the
same as the Indians that come to the Forts . . . These People
are much more cleanly in their cloathing and food than those I
am with . . . A General Smoak again with our Yeachithinnee
Friends, and enforced my former desire, that two of them
should accompany me on my return to the Fort; but notwithstanding all I could say, promising they should be greatly
rewarded; they were all unwilling, alledging they were unwilling to leave their Families and feared a scarcity of Provision."

(HBCA B.239/a/69, 3 and 5 and 15 December 1772)

H   Mandelbaum: "It is well to note that the compelling grip exerted by the [fur] trade upon the Cree did not hold true for other peoples. The several men that the Hudson's Bay Company sent into the plains to induce tribes there to come to the posts, were not entirely successful. The plains dwellers proffered a variety of excuses to Kelsey and Henday, the upshot of them all being simply that they did not want to trap beaver for the English." (29)

H   MacGregor: "The site of this momentous event was between the present city of Red Deer and Pine Lake. . . . Henday was the first white man anywhere to meet any member of the Blackfoot Confederacy. On this visit he met the branch known as the Blood tribe. . . . It is too bad that we cannot be sure of the exact location of this great camp. In ten years no trace would remain of it. It is possible that other camps were made on the same spot as the varying fortunes of the Indians carried them to and fro across Alberta." (147, 166)

H   Russell: "Henday in 1754 and Cocking in 1772 indicate a long term alliance between the Blackfoot Confederacy and the Cree and Assiniboin and their union against a common enemy, the Snake and their allies. However, in the inland journals kept by Joseph Smith [1756-58] and William Pink in the 1760s, there is information regarding the Archithinue which is difficult to interpret. . . . It is possible that relations were briefly severed between the Cree and the Blackfoot Nation groups in 1768/9, though this would seem to be unlikely. Pink had said that the enmity had been long-lasting yet his journal reflects amiable relations between the Cree and Assiniboin and the Blackfoot groups during the winter of 1769/70. . . . likely, Pink is referring to the other members of the Blackfoot Confederacy, the Sarcee and the Gros Ventre. . . . There is nothing to suggest chronic hostility between the Cree and Assiniboin on the one hand, and the Blackfoot Nation on the other." (196-99)

15 October 1754

T mss   E.2/11: "A.M." written after "10 ocloak" then crossed out; "exceed*ing*" and "& is" added above the line, over carets; "are" crossed out and replaced by "Cloathing *is*"

T xref   E.2/6, E.2/4 and E.2/11: cf. B.239/a/40: Isham, "Notes and Remarks"; E.2/4: cf E.2/6 and E.2/4, 3 October 1754

W   Cocking: "This day I see what the Indians say is a Yachithinnee Indian's Tobacco Plantation.—A small plot of ground about an hundred yards long and five wide, sheltered to the Northward by the Ledge, and to the Southward by a ridge of high ground, there appeared to have been several fires upon it, burnt wood laying in many places which the natives tells me had been done in the Spring to prepare the Ground for planting." (HBCA B.239/a/69, 19 October 1772)

M   Graham: "The Mule is found Inland amongst the Tribes of . . . Equestrian Indians. Mr William Tomison informed me that neither he or the Indians pay attention to the Mules, they preferring the Horses; both are numerous." (HBCA E.2/12. p. 38)

H   MacGregor: "It seems highly improbable that these were true asses or donkeys. The explanation may be that they were mules stolen from the Spaniards or the Americans and moved this far west and north into the continent by having been stolen four or five times." (162)

16 October 1754
T mss E.2/6, E.2/11: the note follows this entry.

17 October 1754
H   MacGregor: "I cannot explain the discrepancy between the previous reference to two hundred tents and this reference to 322. One or other is in error, and it may be the smaller figure. Henday, in first writing up his diary early in the visit, estimated them as two hundred tents. By the end of his visit he had had time to count them, and they could well have amounted to 322." (165)

18 October 1754
H   Burpee: "After taking leave of the hospitable Blackfeet, Hendry travelled in a leisurely fashion, first to the westward, crossing Knee Hills Creek; then north-west to a point near the present line of the Calgary and Edmonton railway, about 51°50′ N. This was his farthest point to the westward." (318)

H   MacGregor: "Henday's party travelled over the country some ten miles east of Innisfail and crossed the uppermost tributaries of Three Hills Creek. Then they went up over the hills, where, if the weather had been fine, they would have got their first glorious view of the mountains. . . . Why is it that Henday's Journal does not refer to his first sight of the mountains? Could it be that the copyist, in his ignorance, did not see fit to clutter up the version sent to England with unnecessary descriptions of scenery? It must be that. . . . What must Henday have thought as here on top of the hill some ten miles east of Innisfail the mountains burst upon his view? . . . On foot and by canoe Henday had travelled fourteen hundred miles for this view. It was worth every paddle stroke, every step. Here, for the first time in history, a white man beheld the great blue barrier of the Rocky Mountains eighty miles away . . . Cold and clear, icy and blue, this great jagged wall occupied the whole horizon. What a privilege to see them; and Henday was the first of all white men to do so." (167-68)

H   Williams: "Henday's journal throughout is a 'nose-to-the-ground' document; he mentions rivers, lakes and hills as he comes to them. if we delete Graham's editorial interpolations, then the journal rarely speculates or mentions any natural feature other than those immediately confronting Henday. Difficult to believe though it may be to a modern observer, it is quite conceivable that Henday, whose references to the prairies across which he was travelling were fleeting enough, never thought it worth while to describe the mountain range he could see many miles farther west." (56)

20 October 1754

T mss B.239/a/40: the note follows the entry for 21 October 1754.

W   Cocking: "We are preparing to proceed, when we shall seperate for the Winter Season. This day was spent in feasting on Berries (which are going out of Season) and a farewell smooking. The Leader gave a Wippetanassowin or throwing away of things, this they commonly do every Year. On this occasion all the Men and Women were invited, the Leaders grand Pipe-Stem being exposed to view, and several speeches made. Two Looking Glasses with several other triffles were presented, these were to be given to the ground to induce it to favour them with plenty of Furrs and Provision; they have a notion that these gifts have a great effect, and when anything happens contrary to their desires, they commonly use this method to appease the ill Damon. When sick especially they are very foolish this way, throwing away many things; also presenting to others as payment for singing their God Songs, so that if the sick Person recovers he is a poor wretched creature, having scarce any thing to cover his Nakedness." (HBCA B.239/a/69, 2 October 1772)

M   Graham: "In the summer season when food is plenty, vizt deer, fish, and fowl, [the Indians] live together in great numbers, but in the winter never above two or three families lives

together, and when food is scarce to be got, they separate,
each family taking a different route in search of food, and
almost every winter melancholy accidents happens from their
not meeting with game, sickness, the mans gun breaking, and
many more unforeseen misfortunes." (HBCA E.2/4. f. 21v,
p. 36)

21 October 1754
T xref E.2/4 and E.2/11: cf. E.2/11, 27 December 1754.

W Smith: "tusdey the 22 we lea by and the was Smocking and all
the Sineapils Cried and the cauees of ther cring was be caues
the was a go ing to ware" (HBCA B.239/a/45, 22 November 1757)

W Pink: "this Day Came and put up heare a Bodey of Jndaines
Consisting of 20 Tents With the Leading jndaine Called
Wap,pe,nas,sue and Sevrill others the has Bin at war with, the
Jndaines Called Kee,ne,pick,e,thin,a,wock these Jndaines
Came Doun upon ours, with thare horses, and Likewise Sevrill
Gones that the had But the Cannot S<h>ote well yet this is
the Firs time that <the> See Gons with them Natives we now
Not whare the Get them, for the Catch No Fores, our jndaines
Say that the Cary Deare Sinnares to the South ward and Trad
With Some p<e>ople thare But the Dos not Now ho, the has
Killed one of our Jndaines and Wounded Three. But our
jndaines Killed 80 of them." (HBCA B.239/a/63, 1 April 1770)

W Tomison: "in the evening two YF Leaders and 10 young men
Came with two Ware pipe Stams, they Smoakt all night and
talked strongly to the old <men> to leat the young men go
with them to ware; I lighted the Factory pipe Stame and talked
to them not to go to ware, but Come and trade at Your Hon^rs
forts, they mea[d] very little answer." (HBCA B.239/a/64, 24
January 1770)

M Isham: "[After smoking, one man will say,] 'O'h', itt's very
hard, itt's very hard; (sham cry) the Earchithinnues Came and
Kill'^d severall of our Country man wherefore I will Go to
warr;—will you go with me, (meaning his fellow sufferers.) we
do not want to Kill them but they are alway's Comming against
us What do yo say to itt. speaking to the factor,—who per-
swades them from itt as much as possable, and Desires them
to make peace with those natives, But they Seldom Regard
Such advice, therefore to warr they go the following year,
Killing men, but Chiefly women and Child^n tak'n the oppurtunity when men are out a hunting not having the h<e>art to
face them, &c." (HBCA E.2/1. ff. 55v-56r, pp. 102-3)

M   Robson: "the several tribes of natives hinder each other, by their wars, from hunting to advantage, and coming to the English factories: whereas, if the English had settlements among them, and took pains to civilize and endear them, they would apply themselves to hunting in the proper seasons, and bring all their furs to the English factories; which would put an effectual stop to the incroachments of the French." (8)

M   Graham: "As for the failure of York Fort trade, I am certain does not proceed so much from the return of the Canadians, but from considerable numbers of Keskachewan Indians harbouring and strolling among the Archithinue and Asinepoet Indians for the sake of good living. This game they call going to war, which is an annual excuse the leaders gives to the York Fort Factors for the young men not coming down. To break them of this pernicious practice requires the utmost efforts of a York Fort Factor." (HBCA E.2/5. f. 16v, p. 26)

M   Umfreville: "On the other, or western side of the Stony Mountain are many nations of Indians, utterly unknown to us, except y Indian information, which we cannot enough rely on to justify us in advancing for facts, what may, perchance, be founded in error and misrepresentation. All I can say for certainty is, that a principal nation of these Indians is known to us by the name of the Snake Indians. That all the other Indians we have received an account of go to war against them every summer." (176-77)

23 October 1754

T mss   B.239/a/40: the note follows the entry for 24 October 1754.
T xref   all texts: cf E.2/4, 13-14 November.

M   Isham: "Itt's a Little strange the Breed of these beaver Does not Deminish greatly Considering the many thousands that is Kill^d of a Year [near Hudson's Bay] . . . they are Very Large with the wester'n Indian's, having seen some as Large as an ornairy Calves skin, and to the Northw'^{d} they are very small . . . they are Extrodinary good Eating if young and the tail which is of a Differant taste from the other part of ye body, I think is the finest Eating in the Country . . . upon this tail they Carry sticks and trees of a great bigness, in the water swiming to their housses with such.—It's Very Curious to see the Nature of these Amphibious Creatures, are indued with;—they have a house they build mostly by creeks or Rivilets, the strength & Curiousness, of which house woud puzle a good workman to do the Like." (HBCA E.2/2. ff. 9v-10v, pp. 186-88)

M   Graham: "The Beaver . . . build their houses . . . in the form of an Oven-crown, and composed of willows, poplars, stones, and mud intermixed. Near the sea-coast they are two feet thick, to resist the intensity of the cold, but farthar to the southward they decrease in thickness and strength; accommodating their habitation to the nature of the climate in which they reside. What a demonstration is this of the wisdom of goodness of God, who furnishes even the brute creation with instincts and strength to supply its wants!" (HBCA E.2/9. ff. 5r-5v, pp. 3-4)

H   MacGregor: "I believe it possible that [Henday's party] may have camped on the little lake immediately west of the Town of Innisfail." (174)

26 October 1754

H   Morton: "On 24th October [*sic*] Henday's diminished party crossed the Red River [*sic*] once more—at a point where the river flowed eastward—and drifted in a north-westerly direction into the country east of the Clearwater River . . . Here, within sight of the Rockies, in a bush country with many creeks—a fine country for beaver—the party spent two months gathering furs, though often forced to move out into the open prairie to hunt buffalo for provisions." (248)

H   MacGregor: "We are almost tempted to say that the small band of Crees with which Henday was travelling went into their homelands in the forests west of Red Deer. But to say this would be treading on thin ice. This really was not the homeland of the Crees. It belonged to the Blackfeet. The Crees should have been much further north and east." (171)

27 October 1754

W   Pink: "Bad Trav<i>ling the Contrey Being heare Very foll Swomps and Large ponds or Standing Waterss." (HBCA B.239/a/58, 28 September 1767)

29 October 1754

T xref B.239/a/40: cf. all texts: 24 December 1754.

W   Pink: "we are now Tenting by a Very Noated plase off this Contrey it is Called Mous,wa,Chee [Moose Hills] it is a high Hill Coaverd with woods Neare the Maine River Noated for Mous Deare and Mortones." (HBCA B.239/a/58, 26 February 1768)

W   Pink: "we put up By the Side of a Hill Called MickeCue wachee [Eagle Hills], heare the Contrey is Covered with wood Except for out to the Southwarde a Noated Plase for Red Deare and

Mouse and some Bofflow." (HBCA B.239/a/63, 24 September 1769)

W   Cocking: "travelling along the River, pitched at a Creek called Mehisew Sepisish or Eagle Creek. here we met with fifty tents of Indians with several Leaders many of them Beaver Indians. . . . We proceeded all in Company; our Course West and Distance twelve Miles leaving the River. We came to some high land called Mekisew Wachy or Eagle Hill where We pitched. Poplar and Birch about four Inches Diameter in places but mostly very small. Plenty of low Nut trees & Berry Shrubs. plenty of Moose & Waskesew at other times but at present scarce, several Ponds well stored with Ducks and some Grey Geese. . . . We seperated the Beaver & other Indians going Westerly others S.W." (HBCA B.239/a/69, 4, 6 and 9 September 1772)

W   Cocking: "We seperated, part going Westerly towards Manito-Sakehagan & Assine Wache." (HBCA E.2/6 abstract of B.239/a/69, 9 September 1772)

M   Graham: "Wachee. Mountains are not met with any where near the sea-shore and are very rare Inland." (HBCA E.2/9. f. 4v, p. 2)

H   Williams: "If Henday really meant the Rocky Mountains by this [reference to Arsinie Watchee], then the entry makes no sense. It is very doubtful whether he was even within sight of the Rockies at this time, and for the next three weeks he was drifting in a westerly direction, nearer the mountains, not away from them." (56)

31 October 1754

T mss E.2/11: Henday's biographical notice is written on a separate page (folio 21v) followed by two blank pages (folios 22r and 22v); the journal resumes on folio 23r as indicated by a note after the 31 October entry.

P   Graham, "Plan" 1774: "Northern Keskachewans or Beaver Indians: These People trade annually at York & Churchill Forts, and receive a Part of their Furs in Barter with the Dog-Rib Indians." (HBCA G.2/17)

W   Pink: "in the Evening pitched by the Side of a River Called a,Misk,o, Cepee, a Noated River for Beaver Some Yeares a Gone But being So Ofton honted that thare is but Few now, Roning <to the> N,E, . . . pitched by the Sid<e> of a Nother River Called a Misk o Cepee Roning from the W,N,W in to this one that we has been Traveling up by till Now . . . heare j find Beaver very plentey the Contrey heare Beaing fool of Small

Rivers or Cricks and Standing Waters, the Land Coeavered with woods Bofflow Likewise plentey, But very wilde to what the are in the Oapen Contrey. it is not Often that Maney of those indaines Comes in Land so far as this <this way>, Except the are for Wars." (HBCA B.239/a/58, 19 October and 5 and 13 November 1767)

M   Umfreville: "It may be argued by the abettors of the Company, (if they have any) that after the period of the apprentice's indentures is expired, he has an opportunity of rising in their service, if by good behaviour he has merited so much favour; that from his apprenticeship, he may be made a writer at 15*l.* per year, from thence be raised to an assistant at 25*l.* per year, after a second at 40*l.* per year; and from thence to the exalted station of a Governor, at 150*l.* per year. To this I would reply, that I am enabled to say, from the eleven years service which I passed through in their employ, that the prospect of ascending this important ladder is very faint indeed. . . . Such is the usual progress of the servitude of their apprentices; and so little is the probability of the young men reaping any advantage of it." (122-23)

H   Russell: "The Beaver River is the main southern tributary, actually the upper reach, of the Churchill River and approaches within 60 km. of the North Saskatchewan River just west of the Alberta border. Many, if not most, of the Beaver Cree travelled to the Bay not by the Churchill River but by way of the Saskatchewan River. . . . It is clear, from their use of the Saskatchewan to travel to the Bay, that the Beaver Cree were not located solely on the Beaver River. Instead, they were found each spring at canoe-building sites on the North Saskatchewan and were probably wintering in the area between the North Saskatchewan and upper Beaver River from the Thickwood Hills west to Moosehills Lake and probably even to the Beaver Hills in central Alberta. . . . It seems probable that the term 'Keskachewan' was bestowed by English at the Bay on a group who were known locally as the Beaver Cree." (149-51)

1 November 1754

T mss   E.2/11: "He eat . . . ignorance" may be a later addition to the main text.

T xref E.2/4 and E.2/11: cf. B.239/a/40 and E.2/6, 2 November 1754.

W   Cocking: "In the Evening an Assinnee Poet Young fellow shot Himself in the Lungs and died soon after, the Occasion very trif-fling. this deed was nearly the death of two others, his Friends,

who intended to stab themselves, but were prevented by some
bystanders. These People I am told are very foolish this way, the
Women as well as Men being guilty of Suicide on meer Childish
Accounts." (HBCA B.239/a/69, 23 December 1772)

2 November 1754
T xref B.239/a/40 and E.2/6: cf. E.2/4 and E.2/11, 1 November 1754.

9 November 1754
T mss B.239/a/40: "*took my de*parture" written over erasure; the
erased lines between the 8 and 9 November entries read "took
my Departure from Beaver river and Steered WbN . . . fine
Ledges of woods and very tall,"

12 November 1754
T mss E.2/11: "d" of "ledges" added above the line.
H   MacGregor: "the party was somewhere up in the Stauffer coun-
try." (178)

13 November 1754
M   Isham: "The men pretends to be great Conjurer's, tho' Know
nothing of any such artifice, and all I Cou'd make of itt, is Very
Eronious and purely Design'd to frighten' the women and Children,—I think I never was so full of mirth, then once in Seeing
their Conjuring & Dancing, when in Liquor . . . if an Indians is
sick or out of order, they go to singing and Conjuring which
they have a notion will make them well,—they have also a Con-
ceited notion, some things the Sick Keep's is the occation of
their Sickness, which if put a side Cures them; (this is when
their Conjuring won't take Effec't, they pretend to Show a
hundred other tricks, which is Really not worth the observing
[*sic*]." (HBCA E.2/1. ff. 61v-62v, pp. 114-16)
M   Robson: "[The Indians] make pretensions to divination; for the
exercise of which they form a square close tent, by laying skins
upon four sticks cut green from the tree, peeled, and fixed per-
pendicularly in the ground. Into this they enter, staying two or
three hours; in which time many future events, they say, are
made known to them. Some of our people are weak enough to
give credit to this prophetic spirit." (49)
M   Graham: "Juglers or Conjurers are very numerous amongst
them. These are generally Men who are good Hunters and have
a Family. Some of them are very clever at it, they are supposed
to have Intelligence with the Evil Spirit, and by that means can

procure any thing to be done for the Good or Injury of others,
foretell Events pacify the malignant Spirit when he plagues
them with misfortunes, and recover the Sick. . . . The People in
general are so extremely superstitious; that they will give any
thing they have to these Conjurers, in fear of their conjuring
them, or their Relations to death: by this means the Imposter
often receives considerable presents." (HBCA E.2/9, ff. 67v-68r,
pp. 128-29)

M   Umfreville: "Some of the curious performers of deception will
pretend to lay eggs, and swallow wooden pipe stems, as large
as walking sticks. They will tell you very seriously, that they are
able to make rum, tobacco, cloth, &c. but whenever we put
their dexterity to the trial, we always discovered the deception.
We took care always not to let them know that we had done so,
for fear of lowering them in the esteem of their credulous followers, which would have been very mortifying to the inge-
nious performer." (194)

14 November 1754
W   Pink: "j Smoked a Measure of tobacoo With the Jndaines that
ware in Companey with me for Encuragement for them to Trap
& Catch What Furrs they Could, and Not for to Gow to Warr
with the Other Natives." (HBCA B.239/a/58, 30 September 1767)

W   Tomison: "Some a traping, and the rest a making Snowshoe
freams, ther is plainty of martins to be Caught her, but most of
the young men ar very indolent in traping." (HBCA B.239/a/64,
6 December 1769)

M   Isham: "Otter's are . . . harbouring mostly in holes on the side
of Creek's and Lake's, where fish are, being their Chiefest pray,
they are not Eat by the natives, and are the Size, shape and
make as in other parts." (HBCA E.2/2. f. 24r, p. 213)

H   Russell: "Although the journals of the inland HBC employees
are invaluable for even the brief hints they give of the daily life
of the western Cree, there are several biases in the journals
which must be kept in mind. First, none of the journals cover
the entire year. . . . Secondly, the way of life reflected in the
journals was not necessarily applicable to all inland Cree. The
HBC men were sent inland with Indian leaders who were
involved with the fur trade and who were committed to either
trapping furs themselves or obtaining them from other
groups. . . . Yet . . . only a small part of the inland Indians were
involved, in any one year, with the trade." (92)

16-20 November 1754
T xref E.2/4: cf. E.2/11, 18 November 1754.

18 November 1754
T xref E.2/11: cf. E.2/4, 16-20 November 1754.

21 November 1754
H   Burpee: "November 21st Hendry reached his farthest point to the westward. According to a note by Andrew Graham, he was on this day in latitude 59°, 810 miles from York Fort. Latitude 59° crosses Peace River and Lake Athabaska, and by no process of reasoning can it be supposed that Hendry ever got anything like as far north as this. Even though his courses were entirely wrong, his descriptions of the country through which he travelled make it impossible to suppose that he was at any time north of the North Saskatchewan. Graham's latitude is quite out of the question. His estimated distance from York Factory is almost equally unreliable. Checking Hendry's distances and directions with the safe test of the character of the country through which he travelled, it is pretty safe to say that on November 21st he was in about latitude 51°50′ longitude 113°50′. Since leaving York Fort he had travelled, by his own reckoning, in the neighbourhood of 1250 miles, and if his position on November 21st was as above indicated, he would be at his turning-point 945 miles from York as the crow flies." (SWS 131-32)

H   Rich: "Henday reached his farthest point westwards on 21st November, when he was about in latitude 51°50′ North and longitude 114° West. He was almost certainly within sight of the Rockies, though his Journal does not mention the fact." (636)

22 November 1754
T mss B.239/a/40: the note follows this entry.

22-26 November 1754
T mss E.2/4: "*ice*" written over erasure.

30 November 1754
C   Graham to the HBC London Committee: "thirty-four Canoes of Indians . . . gave a fine help out being well gooded both in Quality & Quantity amongst which a large Parcell of Split Cats which they Purchase from the Western Archithinues two of whom came with them. I shewed them how to Case [to skin] &

Stretch them, & they promised to bring them so & tell their
Countrymen." (HBCA A.11/115, 26 August 1772)

M   Isham: "Catt's [lynx] are a feirce Creature to Look at, and
about as big as a small sheep, thier Skin's are the finest and
softest furr in the Country, they are also—Numerious, they
style these (peshue) they Live Chiefly upon Rabbitts and par-
tridges, tho Kill Deer some times . . . they are a Spotted skin, a
head and Ear's Like unto a tame Catt, but a Scutt Like a Rab-
bitt,—they are Eat by the Natives and wou'd also by the
English if they can gett them, being Reckon'd as sweet and as
fine Eating as any Lamb, the flesh being white smooth grain'd
and the fatt firm." (HBCA E.2/2. ff. 7v-8v, pp. 182-84)

2 December 1754

W   Pink: "Mooved to the N,W warde, the Snow now is vearey Deape
upon the Land, veary few Woulves to be Catcht Sow now we are
Mooving a Way for a Hammock of Bourc<h> woodes that we
Came By in the fall of the Yeare, for Makeing of our Sledges a
Snow Shoe Frames." (HBCA B.239/a/61, 18 December 1768)

W   Cocking: "Indians are some of them intended to pitch from
this place in a few days,—intended to proceed back to Mekisew
Wachy fearing the Cold will be intence here, wood being thin."
(HBCA B.239/a/69, 6 November 1772)

H   MacGregor: "In general, during that winter, Henday travelled
west from Innisfail until he was on the north side of the Red
Deer River. Then he worked up into the country along Raven
Creek and Stauffer Creek, and then over towards the Clearwa-
ter River, although apparently they did not reach this river.
They wandered around in the forest between there and
Medicine River, finally, about Christmas time, crossing the
main stream of the Medicine near Eckville. From there they
passed over the hills west of Sylvan Lake, wound round its
north-west end, and trapped in the valley of the Blindman
[River] between the Town of Bentley and those inspiring three
Medicine Lodge Hills." (193-94)

H   Russell: "all the evidence indicates that by 1740, or at least
1754, the Cree were far beyond the border of the grasslands and
their trading expeditions were carried out from bases in the far
west. . . . Henday met small Cree groups scattered . . . along
the Saskatchewan as far as the Edmonton area with no hint
that this was a recent occupation." (151-52)

5-7 December 1754

T mss E.2/11: "a" added above the line, over a caret.

7 December 1754

T xref E.2/6: cf. E.2/11, 1 January 1755, B.239/a/40 and E.2/6, 17 January 1755, E.2/11, 18-21 January 1755.

M Isham: "I . . . think itt not Inconvenient to observe the English Dress in these Norther'n parts.—I can not say but we can make a tollerable shift to go in our English Dress that is a coat waist-coat & shirt &c in the Summer, for abou't 4 month's, But the other Eight Long tedious months, Necessity obliges us to appear in another fashion . . . appearing more Like Beasts than men, with the hairy Cloathing we wear, and Notwithstanding all this warm Cloathing, the penetrating Cold has it's Effect that men freezes . . . I do not Doub't in Land 4 or 5 Hundred miles, but itt must be a fine Country, and the Climate quit Differ^t to what it tis by the Sea shore,—having seen Severall Indians that has not Known what snow shoes was, they not having snow above 3 inches Deep all winter." (HBCA E.2/1. ff. 73r-73v, 89v, pp. 137-38, 170)

M Graham: "We make a shift to wear our English dress in summer, but in winter we wear a beaver toggy [garment] that reaches the calf of the leg, under which a cloth waistcoat lined with flannel, a pair of beaver mittens lined with blanketing or duffle, the fir side outwards for the conveniency of holding to the face in sharp weather, a pair leather breeches lined with flannel, a cloth cap . . . a pair of cloth stockings . . . under which are a pair of yarn stockings without feet, three or four socks of blanket or duffle on each foot, and a pair of deer or moose skin shoes . . . a powder horn, shot pouch, gun, hatchet, skipatogan [tinder pouch] hanging at his belt, the partridge bag on his back, and a pair of snow shoes on his feet, one so rigged and fitted out is a compleat traveller and hunter." (HBCA E.2/4. f. 78r, p. 149)

9 December 1754

T mss B.239/a/40: "Would" written over erasure.

17 December 1754

M Isham: "their snow shoes are of Different form's and sizes, some being 7 and 8 foot Long, a small Comfort for a man to Carry upon his feet Severall months up to the Knees in Snow,—thier is round toe^d shoes which runs to a sharpe point at the Hee'l, and about 18 inches over in the middle, all of one peice being before turn'd by the fire and water 14 and 16 foot in Length,—Galley shoes are in two peices Narrow at the top and turns up a Little, and sharpe at the Hee'l, another which is round toed, and hee'l is what Children wears, which they Styl' (musquatum).'' (HBCA E.2/2. ff. 4v-5v, pp. 176-78)

M   Graham: "neither English nor Indian can walk without [snow shoes] in the winter the snow is so very deep: I have myself walked 30 miles of English measurement in one day; for please to observe the snow is not wet and clogy as in warmer Climates, but is as drie as powder and sifts through the netting of the shoe every time the foot is lifted.'' (HBCA E.2/4. ff.28v-29r, pp. 50-51)

24 December 1754

T xref all texts: cf. B.239/a/40, 29 October 1754.

W   Cocking: "We proceeded, our Course about N.N.E. and Distance six miles . . . leaving Mekisew Wachy and travelling over barren Ground. small plots of Wood in places. We crossed one of the Branches of Saskatchiwan River . . . The Indians say this place is the termination of the barren ground to the Northward.'' (HBCA B.239/a/69, 19 and 22 January 1773)

M   Graham: "Mountains are not met with nigh the sea-coast [Hudson Bay], and none have been discovered by the Company's Servants who hath travelled far inland to the distance of 1200 Miles WSW from York Fort.'' (HBCA E.2/12. p. 4)

H   Morton: "After the return journey was begun on a general eastward course, on 23rd December Henday crossed a branch of the Waskesew River (probably our Blindman River). The next day, from a high knoll he bade farewell to the Rocky Mountains under their Cree name . . . Arsinie Watchie.'' (248)

H   MacGregor: "[From] the Medicine River near Eckville, . . . Henday had his last view of . . . the Rocky Mountains. . . . Only a few times all winter had he seen them, because he was travelling in relatively flat country where, except on rare occasions, timber shut off his view of them. . . . So, by himself, Henday . . . look[ed for the last time] at these inscrutable mountains. What a trip this had been—first white man to pass all the way across the Muscuty Plains, first to see Indians with horses, first to meet the regal Blackfeet, and first to see the Shining Mountains. His cup was full. His throat was full, and his eyes too.'' (196-98)

27 December 1754

T xref B.239/a/40 and E.2/6: cf. E.2/4 and E.2/11, 28 December 1754.

W Pink: "we being now to Trap for Woulves for the are very plenty
heare in this Open Contrey the Jndaines are Staying onley to
or three Tents to Geather now. . . . the Jndaines heare Now
Constantley Keep garde in the night time for Fear of the other
jndaines Called Yearchethynnewock and Cenepick we ethynewock for Feare they Should Come up on them all on a Suden in
the night time." (HBCA B.239/a/61, 22 October 1768)

W Pink: "this Day j Sent Tobacoo a Bodey of ye archethynnawock
Called Mithquothanawock for Encouradgement for the Snare
Woulves for the Trap None . . . Now these Black footted
Jndaines are a Snaring of Woulves the fence is in a pese of
Land of a Bout one hundred and fiftey Fathom Round on one
Side the Leave open a Bout a Fathem for the Woulves to Gow
in at, a Bofflow heare is Cot to pesses and Laide all a Bout in
the in Side thare is Ten holes left Open Round this fence and
thare the put up Snares Made of Leather Thonges." (HBCA
B.239/a/63, 13 December 1769 and 17 January 1770)

W Tomison: "I Smoakt with the men and told them to pitch away
a Beaver hunting, they made me no answer for some time but
at last they told me it were a Long <winter> and that they
would See the Asinepoites Indians in the Spring and that they
would trade furs with them, these Indians for the most part ar
very indolent and delight in nothing but gaming and
Smoaking . . . Several Indians Sett out for the trading houses
with what furs they had traded with the asinepoites, few of
these Indians ever trap there owne furs." (HBCA B.239/a/64, 1
November 1769, 2-3 February 1770)

H Mandelbaum: "When the English finally ousted the French,
trade from York Factory to the interior developed rapidly. From
then on the Cree and Assiniboin became important middlemen, trading between the people of the hinterland and the
English. These middlemen probably trapped during the
winter. . . . This group certainly lived on the plains only a part
of the year, but later found the plains life so congenial that
they severed all connections with the woodlands. The transi-
tion from forest to plains was not accomplished all at once."
(31)

H Russell: "Henday's journal indicates that the Cree, for some
time, had been coming to the Red Deer area to trade with the
Archithinue. . . . However, there are references which might
suggest that the Cree were interlopers in what was Blackfoot

country from their own lands to the northeast . . . [and were]
fearful of attacks by the Archithinue. . . . although furs were
available, his tentmates told him . . . that they would be killed
if they trapped in Archithinue country. However, these statements are contradicted by others and his comments must be
placed in context. . . . It is not surprising that his tent mates
were apprehensive of danger, whether real or not. They were on
the edge of Cree territory and open to attacks not from their
Archithinue allies, the Blackfoot Confederacy, but rather their
common enemies who were also called Archithinue. That hunting furs was forbidden because they were in Archithinue territory is contradicted by all the other evidence in Henday's
account. . . . Clearly, Henday's group was simply reluctant to
hunt in mid-winter as were the groups described by all later
observers." (95)

28 December 1754
T xref E.2/4: cf. B.239/a/40, E.2/6 and E.2/11, 27 December 1754.
T xref E.2/11: cf. B.239/a/40, E.2/6, E.2/4, 23 December 1754.
M   Isham: "Discourses on Different Subjects [conversation
       between two Indians]:
       A. It's a Drifty snowy Day & Cold
           narspitch, pewan, uma Keshickaw. Kissen wawach
       B. 20 martins freind this is well
           neshutenna wappastan uma murthawashing Coshake
       A. the Quiquahatch has Eat four & broke many trap's, here is
           his track where he is just gone
           Yo'shashie navo mitsutt, Quiquahaku, mechit mawka,
           wunahiggan, pekopatum, mawny ota' anoach mattahaw
       B. make a trap for him & I will sett my Gun
           wunnahiggan worshatit, neder enparskasiggan,
           enksockatan
       A. Come we will sett some snares
           Ecco nawquaquan, kopucatawow, nemattau wappathau . . .
       Wolvereen's, or Quequahatches (alias) murtastuss are also
       Very Numerious—they are ruff Coated and short Leg'd, Very
       strong for their bigness,—being not higher the a fox, but
       thicker and more Like a Badcher, they are very Glomsay
       [clumsy] and Slow footed . . . of all the beast's in the Country,
       thier is none so much of an Enemy to the Indians, as these
       Creatures are; by breaking their stages op'n and getting all
       their provender away . . . I have Known them when catch't in a
       trap by the thigh to break the bone, and then Naw themselves

out and march of with 3 Leg's,—thier black or browne with a white Circle round their back's, they never Change their Colour,—they are Catch't in Log traps Chiefly, and are Eat by the natives tho not by the English, they are Very strong Rank food." (HBCA E.2/I. f. 39v, p. 70; E.2/2. ff. 7r-7v, pp. 181-82)

30 December 1754

H   Rich: "The first Englishman, in all probability the first white man, to see the buffalo hunt, does nothing to rouse the imagination. He does, however, make it clear that the hunt was with bows and arrows only, ammunition being scarce and costly, and so he reveals the possibilities of the frantic waste of the great wealth of the buffalo which later came when the hunt was made with guns . . . For even with bows and arrows, and hunting for their own immediate subsistence, the Indians killed great numbers, 'only taking what they choosed to carry.' " (I: 634-35)

H   Ray: "One of the reasons the Parkland Indians preferred to hunt bison was that it could easily be taken with their traditional weapons. Moose and red deer, on the other hand, were usually killed with guns . . . An expenditure of ammunition that could not be reclaimed was consequently required. In contrast, when the bow was employed, the arrow could be retrieved, or one could be made without trade. With these considerations in mind, the Parkland hunters often neglected other game when bison herds were nearby. Anthony Henday noted this in 1754." (77-78)

I January 1755

T xref E.2/II: cf E.2/6, 7 December 1754, B.239/a/40 and E.2/6, 17 January 1755.

7 January 1755

M   Graham: "Wejack, or the Brown—Pole-cat [fisher]. These creatures harbour inland, they are not prolific breeding only once a year . . . Their Skins are of little value. The Natives never eat the flesh but when necessity urges them." (HBCA E.2/I2. p. I2)

II January 1755

T mss B.239/a/40: "2" written over another figure now indecipherable; E.2/II: "*with snow*" written over erasure.

17 January 1755

T xref B.239/a/40 and E.2/6: cf E.2/6, 7 December 1754, E.2/11, 1 January 1755 and E.2/11, 18-21 January 1755.

C   see Isham, "Remarks" (B.239/a/40)

W   Pink: "the Contrey heare is Quite Oeapen Boffellow plentey So
        now we are jntending for Traping for Woelves and foxes for
        Beaver heare is None." (HBCA B.239/a/58, 30 December 1767)

W   Cocking: "We proceeded at eight in the morning and put up at
        three in the afternoon, Young Men hunting as we go. . . . Our
        Course very uncertain. I found it inconvenient to use the Com-
        pass in travelling, so was obliged to set our Course as well as I
        could by the Natives direction in the morning, which I find
        very incorrect scarcely two of them agreeing in one direction."
        (HBCA B.239/a/69, 14 August 1772)

M   Isham: "The Natives are Seldom at a Loss in their travelling,
        no part being Difficult for them to find, tho never was in some
        parts of their Country in thier Lives,—yet will steer by the sun,
        or, moon,—or by notching the Bark's of the trees to see which
        side is the thickest; wch is always the S^o or warm side." (HBCA
        E.2/1. f. 65r, p.121)

M   Robson: "The natives talk of two moons as the shortest time in
        which they perform their journies to the factories: but it is to
        be considered, that they are an improvident and lazy people, hav-
        ing no concern but the subsistence of the present day; and that
        they are perpetually wandering out of the way to hunt for provi-
        sions, and loitering when they have procured them. This, togeth-
        er with the obstructions they must unavoidably meet with in
        travelling a pathless country, will easily account for the length
        of time they mention, without supposing that they come from
        places at several hundred miles distance, and that the conti-
        nent is of such a prodigious extent to the westward." (29)

H   Morton: "Henday's party now drifted, trapping as it went, in a
        general north-easterly direction towards the North Saskatch-
        ewan." (248)

18-21 January 1755

T xref E.2/4 and E.2/11: cf. E.2/6, 7 December 1754, E.2/11, 1 January
        1755, B.239/a/40 and E.2/6, 17 January 1755.

22 January 1755

H   Morton: "The branches of the Waskesew River passed on 22nd
        January and 20th February were the upper streams of the Bat-
        tle River." (248)

28 January 1755
T mss E.2/6: "*Birch*" written over erasure.
T mss E.2/11: the phrase "killed three buffalo" cut when the ms was bound.

1-3 February 1755
T mss E.2/4: the note follows this entry.
T xref E.2/4: cf. E.2/6, 6 February 1754 and E.2/11, 2 February 1754.

2 February 1755
T mss E.2/11: the note is written in the lower margin under the line "great sway . . . is much."
T xref E.2/11: cf. E.2/6, 6 February 1755 and E.2/4, 1-3 February 1754.
C see Isham, "Remarks" (B.239/a/40)
C Graham to the HBC London Committee: "Wappenasew . . . is a Person of Prime Consideration with the Natives, & his Influence is very extensive, he came to York Fort in 1755 & continued with us until two Years ago, when the Canadians who have great need of his Assistance to promote their Trade & protect their Persons, tried every means to attach him to their Service, & they have succeeded, He lives in their House all the Winter, dines at Table with the Master, & his family are Cloathed with Cloth, & no favour is refused. In return he induces the Indians to resort thither, he Convoys the large Canoes up & down to Michillimackinac & in great Measure Prevents the numerous Tribes through which they are obliged to pass from molesting them." (HBCA A.11/115, 26 August 1772)
W Smith: "the men came from the freansh but the had no pouder leaft for the Lorst too of ther conues and the boret Sum backer but it was veary bad." (HBCA B.239/a/45, 26 December 1757)
W Tomison: "I seed many Jndians but could not perswade them to keep their Furrs until the spring and go down to the Forts; whenever they Collected a few Furrs they went to . . . the Canadians, and am certain what Furrs goes down to Severn & Albany is Collected from different Indians, and were it not for Brazile tobacco, very few would come; they told me they had no Occasion to go down when they could get goods so nigh hand." (HBCA E.2/6, 16 May 1768)
W Cocking: "I smooked with the Assinnee Poet Strangers, and advised them to be diligent in trapping Furrs and to go down to the Company's Forts, most of them being Strangers; but they were seemingly unwilling, saying they were unacquainted with the method of Building Canoes and Paddling: however

their Furrs were sent by Friends that were to be traded at the
Forts." (HBCA B.239/a/69, 19 September 1772, passage marked
by a fist ☞)

M   Isham: "A Captn or Cheif Comes with a gang of Indians, in this
Gang they Divide they Divide [*sic*] themselves into Severall
tents or hutts, where their is an ancient man, belonging to
Each family, who is officers under the Cheif (alias) Uka maw."
(HBCA E.2/1. f. 53r, p. 97)

M   Graham: "They are Indians who are made and stiled Captains
or Leaders by the Chief; such persons must be endued with the
following qualifications vizt A good hunter, a great talker, and
conjurer, 10 or 20 young men under his direction, from 2 to 7
wives and a good many children, such an one is greatly
esteemed by the Factors. . . . those Captains hath no command
over the Indians they only consult him in affairs, as going on
parties to hunt, to war, to trade &c. but he is without power to
enforce what he would effect; they are intirely free, every man
being master of his own family; all he can do is only by the
esteem which the people have for him, that lessened his
authority is gone." (HBCA E.2/4. f. 19v, p. 32)

4 February 1755

H   MacGregor: "By the end of January Henday had worked up
past Forshee and Rimbey, to the headwaters of the Blindman
River near Bluffton. He spent most of February in the area
between there and Battle and Pigeon Lakes." (199)

6 February 1755

T mss E.2/6: the note follows the entry for 12 February 1755.
T xref E.2/6: cf. E.2/4, 1-3 February 1754 and E.2/11, 2 February 1755.

7 February 1755

T mss B.239/a/40: "*Friday fine*" written over erasure.

10 February 1755

T mss E.2/11: the last line of the entry "nigh ones . . . our Indians"
cut when the ms was bound

C   see Isham, "Remarks" (B.239/a/40)

W   Pink: "Yesterday night, Dyed an Jndaine Man So the Stay to
Day the Bearying of hym, all theare Tolck is Now a bout War,
the Say that this is the Reason of it, that is jf a ney porson dyes
With Sickness or is Killed a Mongst them the Must Gow to war
With the Other Natives Called Ye,artch,a thyne,a, Wock and

Kill as Maney as the Can of them and then the Say that the are
Eavning with them for the Dearth of thare Frend or Frends."
(HBCA B.239/a/58, 26 September 1767)

W   Cocking: "I find it is the professed intent of most of the
Natives to go to War next Year. They own these Expeditions
cause them to undergo great hardships and besides are distressed for want of Ammunition and Tobacco for two Years
after; but the Loss of their Friends seems to be above all difficulties." (HBCA B.239/a/69, 28 March 1773)

M   Graham: "In War a mutual resentment against their Enemies,
forms the Union for perpetrating their revenge: Personal
courage, Patience under hardships, and the knowledge of the
manners and Country of their Adversaries, are the Qualifications sought for in the choice of a Leader. They follow him
with fidelity and execute his projects with Alacrity: But their
obedience does not follow from any right in the Leader to
Command but what is founded on his merit, the affections of
his followers, and the desire of subduing their Antagonists.
These actuate every breast and cements the union, which in
civilized Nations is effected by subordination to the Laws of
Government. . . . They travel with their families to the confines
of their adversaries Country; they then have a dance and conjuring feast; the old Men are left to provide for the Women and
Children whilst the young people pursue their journey. Their
attacts [*sic*] are all by stratagem surprize and ambush: in
Europe it is thought brave, honourable, and valiant to face the
foe in open field, and even to approach the mouth of a Cannon; but in America where their is no emulation of place or
dignity for a reward, they are the more esteemed, as they have
circumvented the enemy with the greater cunning; accounting
it a disgrace to loose their friends in an open engagement."
(HBCA E.2/9. ff. 71r, 72r-72v, pp. 135, 137-38)

M   Umfreville: "In their war excursions, the old men, women and
children stay behind in a place of safety; while the younger
part of the tribe cautiously approach the confines of their enemy's country. During their approach they make no fires, for
fear of their adversaries discovering the smoke; and they travel
more in the night than the day, that the darkness may favour
their attack. When the encampment of the enemy is discovered, they lie in ambush for the remainder of that day, and
when they suppose all wrapt up in sleep, the slaughter is began
with a ferocity that Indian fury could alone inspire. Men, wom-
en and children all fall promiscuously to satiate the warrior's

revenge, and compensate the loss of deceased friends; none are spared but young girls, who are taken captive and sold to the Canadian Traders, and become thereby more happy than their slaughtered parents had ever been." (187-88)

H MacGregor: "Who these different tribes were that Henday mentions is a little hard to make out. I think some of them would be other branches of the Cree tribe, although it may be that he was referring to some Assiniboines. It might even be that he meant the Sarcees . . . In any event, these people had fought the Blackfeet very recently, for the scalps were still fresh." (204)

11-27 February 1755
T xref E.2/11: cf. B.239/a/40, 21 and 25 February 1755, and E.2/11, 22 February 1755

20 February 1755
H Morton: "The branches of the Waskesew River passed on 22nd January and 20th February were the upper streams of the Battle River." (248)

22 February 1755
T mss E.2/4: the note, in Graham's hand, follows the entry for 24 February 1754.

27 February 1755
T mss B.239/a/40: an entry for 27 February 1755 ("Thursday fine weather wind West") was begun after the entry for 25 February 1755 and then crossed out.

H Burpee: "[Hendry turned] north-east again to a long, narrow lake which he calls Archithinue Lake, and which appears to have been present Devils Pine Lake. It was now the end of February, 1755, and a few days later Hendry, having travelled north-east from Devils Pine Lake, reached the Red Deer once more, many miles above the point where he had crossed five months before." (318)

H Morton: "His Earchithinue Sokohegan (Blackfoot Lake) of 27th February would be Saunders Lake, ten miles north-west of Wetaskiwin." (248)

H MacGregor: "Henday had now reached the long narrow depression occupied by a chain of lakes starting with Saunders Lake near Leduc and running through Ord Lake and then one or two other small lakes to the south of that, and, finally, ending

in Coal Lake. Two hundred years ago the water in these lakes
would have been almost a mile wide. . . . There is no alternative to this lake. This must be what Henday referred to as
Archithinue Lake." (211)

28 February-1 March 1755

M   Isham: "Jelioussey that—thing that Ranges so much in all
      parts of the world, is Likewise very much amongst these
      Natives, and will be reven'g^d of their antagonist some time or
      another, and oftn' will be the Death of such that has offended
      them . . . Notwithstanding thier Jeliousy they will take wives,
      put them of, and take them or other's again at their pleasure."
      (HBCA E.2/1. ff. 59v-60r, pp. 110-11)

M   Graham: "These Indians are no Strangers to the passion of
      Love and Friendship; but there seems not that tenderness in
      either as appears in Europeans when under the influence of
      those affections, tho' perhaps the American is not less sincere
      in his professions: the Manners of politer Nations have taught
      them to express their Sentiments not only by words but by ges-
      tures, which add much force to the Idea intended to be raised:
      but the Indian who has not those Arts and Blandishments to
      set off his declarations, appears to an Englishman morose,
      insensible and much on the reserve." (HBCA E.2/9. f. 60r, p. 113)

6 March-22 April 1755

W   Smith: "thasdey the 5 we moved and came to the plaes wear we
      made oure conoues fridey the 6 we want to gate our borsh
      rine" (HBCA B.239/a/45, 5-6 April 1758)

W   Pink: "Now we are Continnyly a heareing of Jndaines all Most
      Ev<e>ry Day; Som a Gowing to one plase and Some to a
      Nother to Bilding thare Canewes and Some a Comeing hither,
      and now j am Continyly a Sending of Tobacoo to Jndaines for
      Encouradgment for Them to Carry thare Fors Down to Yorke
      Forte and Not for to Give them to the people that Comes from
      Mountreale." (HBCA B.239/a/63, 11 March 1770)

W   Cocking: "I find the Natives consider an Englishman's going
      with them, as a Person sent to Collect Furrs, and not as an
      encouragement to them to trap &c. from the Company's Ser-
      vants who come with them Inland trading the chief part of the
      Goods they were furnished with at the Forts: and notwithstand-
      ing all I can say to the contrary, will hardly believe but I shall
      also collect Furrs in their Season." (HBCA B.239/a/69, 23
      August 1772)

M   Isham: "I once or twice see them fitting, and making one of
      these Vessels, they making a frame of the bigness the Vessel is
      to be, which Done they fix ye Rhyne, having a good fire on Each
      side, for to make the Rhyn pliant,—they then take 2 pieces of
      the full Length and fix fast on each side of the Gunnels, they
      then Lay 3 Lath's or thin pieces on the Bottom, three or 4
      Double, then fix the Ribs upon them, and with the heat of the
      fire turn the Rhyn to the side or gunnel, making them all fast,
      building them to a sharpe at Each end, which turn's up, and
      round bottom^d,—the women then Comes and sow's the Rhyn
      to the Gunnels or sides, the Ribs Closing in between,—having
      4 thaw'ts one at Each End 2 almost in the midle, Leaving
      Vacancy for one to Sitt between Each thaw't, when the women
      has Done Sowing; they Launch her out of the Dock or frame,
      turn her up and pitch the Seam's, which is occationd by Cut-
      ting slits in the Rhyn to round itt,—this pitch is turpentine,
      they gett from the trees; which they style (peque) which some
      mixes up with fatt, others chaw's itt in their mouth's to make
      itt pliant, and this is the method I see, they making them
      mostly in Land, not being Berch within 60 or 8 miles of the
      Sea shore." (HBCA E.2/2. ff. 5v-6v, pp. 178-80)
M   Graham: "In the month of March the foreign or upland Indians
      assemble on the banks of a particular River agreed upon by com-
      mon consent before they seperated for the winter. Here they
      build their Canoes which are compleated very soon after the
      River breaks up." (HBCA E.2/9. f. 84v, p. 162; cf. Umfreville 56-57)
H   Burpee: "[Hendry] journeyed downstream on the ice [Red
      Deer River of Alberta] for a few miles, and then he and his
      Indians set to work to build canoes and gather provisions for
      the long trip back to Hudson Bay." (318)
H   Morton: "As he mentions a large creek on the western shore, it
      was probably at the confluence of the Sturgeon and the
      Saskatchewan, at the lower end of the present Saskatchewan
      Settlement. . . . Henday's description of the branch of the
      Waskesew River by which he descended tallies with the North
      Saskatchewan below Edmonton. . . . As the Indians of the
      South Saskatchewan, which runs out into the prairies, were
      not trappers and were unfamiliar with the use of the canoe,
      that route is out of the question." (248)
H   MacGregor: "There is no doubt in my mind that Henday and
      his Indians were now camping near the mouth of the Sturgeon
      [River] . . . this was the rendezvous of which the North West
      Company and the Hudson's Bay Company had heard so much,

when, in 1795, fifty years later, they established Forts Augustus
and Edmonton. Henday . . . was back now to the great water
highway across the continent." (215)

13 March 1755
C   see Isham, "Remarks" (B.239/a/40)

17 March 1755
T mss E.2/11: "Mouse" for "moose."

25 March 1755
T mss E.2/6: "*getting*" written over erasure.

29 March 1755
T mss E.2/6: "*Indian who*" written over erasure.

30 March 1755
C   see Isham, "Remarks" (B.239/a/40)

4 April 1755
M   Isham: "I find good usage and civility agrees well with these
Natives,—if they grow obstobilious [unyielding and rebellious],
a Little Correction, then sweatning makes them pliant.—they
are Cunning and sly to the Last Degree, the more you give, the
more they Crave,—the generality of them are Loth to part with
any thing they have, if at any time they give they Expec't Double Satisfaction." (HBCA E.2/1. f. 52v, p. 96)

8 April 1755
W   Smith: "the 18 the made a Large teant for Smocking and the
hade one fadem of backer and wandey the 19 and thasdey the
20 and than had done Smocking" (HBCA B.239/a/45, 18-20 April
1758)

15 April 1755
T mss E.2/6: "*drumm*ing written over erasure.

17 April 1755
M   Isham: "Swans we have great and small, a fine Noble Lofty bird
swimming in the water.—seeing morning and Evening some Hundreds at a time . . . [they] are Very shy, thier is no Killing them
but as they fly by when setting in a stand. they are Larger then
the English swans and fatter, . . . a Young swan is Reckon'd

tolerable good Eating; (as for my part shall always prefer a (pickle'd) round weywey before them)." (HBCA E.2/1. f. 86v, p. 164)

H   MacGregor: "Henday, the alert and adaptable white man, had achieved the supreme accomplishment. No longer was he the blundering tenderfoot. Here in the land of the Indians he had killed a moose, a most difficult thing to do at any time, and he had killed it with a bow and arrows." (222)

20 April 1755

T mss E.2/11: "not*ice*" added on the line, "it" added above the line, over a caret.

W   Smith: "We did not go far in a day by Reason their familys was with them, and they have So many dogs they Cannot go farr." (HBCA B.239/a/43, 8 May 1757)

W   Tomison: "above 40 Ind⁵ Came for buffloes flesh, they are so Starved that they are eating there dogs, the reason is that they have Sold their guns to the asinepoite Indians, a good gun 36 Beaver half wore from 25 to 30 Beaver, they are now endeavouring to pound the buffloe but have not yet Succeded nor will without the help of the asinepoite Indians." (HBCA B.239/a/64, 31 December 1769)

23 April 1755

M   Isham: "I have observ^d the Indians or natives in these Northr'n parts have no Regard or Distinction of Days! sundays and work-days being all alike to them,—observes the Christians Keeping the Sabbath day, which they stile a Reading Day, by Reason of the men's not being at their weekly work on that Day, also Christmass Day, New years Day, & St. G. day, which they stile the Englishmans feast, &c." (HBCA E.2/1. f. 49v, p.90)

M   Graham: "Those Natives who harbour near the settlements and observe the customs of Europeans have given names to particular days, and as they do not know the motives for the observance of them nothing could be happier than their epithets. . . . St George's day is named Uckimow Kishikow or the Chief, or Great Man's day." (HBCA E.2/12. p. 282)

27 April 1755

T xref B.239/a/40 and E.2/6: cf. E.2/4 and E.2/11, 28 April 1755.

C   see Isham, "Remarks" (B.239/a/40)

W   Smith: "Sundey the 14 Sum of tham weant in to ther conues and mondey the 15 we all want in to thar coneues and the rever

wear we made our cone[ue] the [called] it Sickteacon rever and
at night we put up at the Lake as the call Soon Lak and it was
not brock up . . . fridey the 26 we moved and want NbE over the
Lak and we lea in the rever" (HBCA B.239/a/45, 14-26 May 1758)

H   MacGregor: "The women, children and old men were left at
home. Many an old man waved to the departing canoes and
thought sadly of the great days when he was young and had
ambition enough to go on this great adventure. . . . There was
one comely young squaw . . . who laughed little that evening
after the canoes had vanished around the bend . . . She was to
be the first of a long line of Alberta squaws whose white man
had loved and left them. . . . Who knows her subsequent history? When the smallpox epidemic of 1781 swept through the
Cree camps, did it carry off a squaw old and haggard at forty-
five years, the mother of many Indian children and one fair
haired boy?" (236-37)

28 April 1755

T xref E.2/4 and E.2/11: cf B.239/a/40 and E.2/6, 27 April 1755.

H   Burpee: "[Hendry] followed the Red Deer to its junction
with the South Saskatchewan, and the latter to the Forks."
(318)

H   MacGregor: "the party travelled to the mouth of Saddlelake
Creek and here [Henday] met Attickasish, his guide, and a
number of other natives who were making canoes . . . These
Crees would be those living in the lake country around Good-
fish and Whitefish Lakes. This would be the natural point at
which they would reach the Saskatchewan." (246)

12 May 1755

C   YF post journal (Graham): "busy dealing with the Natives they
are poorly gooded and what furs they have brought are the
refuse of the Canadian Pedlars however as it is in vain to make
bad worse I am giving great encouragement and streatching
every nerve to break their connection with them." (HBCA
B239/a/66, 22 June 1772)

W   Pink: "this Day Came and pitched on the South Side of this
Maine River Opisite us a Bodey of Jndaines Consisting of a
Hundred Tents thos people that j am with Call them
Yeartch,athen,a,wock. . . . those people Called Ye,artch,a,thyn,
ne,Wock and those that J am with Some Yeares a Gow ware
Most times at warr with one a Nother But Now the has
<made> an a Greement one with a Nother that the <will> be

<both as one> now, and will <not> Gow to warr one with a
Nother a Gaine, as Soon as j Come up a Gaine to those people
the <are> to Gow a way up inland for to acquaint the Rest of
thare Contrey people of this and Like wise for to Trap an Catch
what Fores thay Can. and Give to thoes people that j am with
Called Ne,hithe,<ny,>thyne,wock. Yearch, e,thyn,na,wock Cannot paddle in a Canew. . . . this Day J went with about Twenty
of those Jndain men up after the Jndaines Called
Ye,artch,e,thyn,na,wock and Made frends with them and gave
them what few Triflyng Things j had that was a knife or to and
Beades and Told them that the Nead not be in feare of those
Jndaines that j was with for the w^d not Middle with them. J
find that those are Difrent from them that j See at the Plase of
Bilding of our Canewes the Cannot paddle Nor kill but few Fors
upon the aCcount of those being at war with them. Most times
and not Jn Couradging them to Do it." (HBCA B.239/a/58, 2-3
and 14 May 1767)

W   Tomison: "the Indians a trading with the asinepoiets old Ket-
      tles hatchets and knives for buffaloe fatt." (HBCA B.239/a/64,
      29 May 1770)

M   Graham: "Archithinue Nation. These Indians . . . are expert
      Wolf-hunters and kill great numbers, which they exchange at a
      dear rate with the Keiskatchewans for Guns, Hatchets, and
      other goods. As the Archithinue Natives are possessed of fine
      Horses which they ride on and manage with amazing dexterity,
      in the month of march they draw from their pleasant country
      towards the NE as far as their Horses can permit; where they
      are met by our traders, and where several of the Company's
      Servants have seen above three hundred brave men mounted
      on light Horses of various Colors, but the Grey color by far pre-
      vails." (HBCA E.2/12. p. 349)

H   Mandelbaum: "[The Cree] were well adapted to the demands
      of a trapper's existence, [b]eing aboriginally a hunting people
      dispersed in small groups over a wide territory . . . Secondly,
      they were a canoe-using people and so were readily able to uti-
      lize the network of waterways in their terrain to transport the
      raw materials to the posts. This trait influenced their later sta-
      tus as middlemen. Their early introduction to the ways of the
      whites and ability to travel by canoe, gave them a great advan-
      tage over the more distant people who lacked both the early
      start and the technique of water transport. For the Cree could
      reach out into far lands and, armed with guns, repel the previ-
      ous inhabitants." (30)

H   MacGregor: "At this Blackfoot camp Henday's eyes were finally opened to a phase of the trade that no one at York Factory had realized. This was that many of the furs which the Crees took down to the Bay were trapped by the Blackfeet. The Crees were only middlemen, making a good profit . . . Now Henday found that his Crees had been lying all the time. Someone had spoken with a forked tongue." (259-60)

H   Rich: "The Assiniboines and Crees who came to York were, when [Henday's] Journal is pointedly analysed, the 'factors' of those who refused to come. . . . Old Axes, guns, knives, powder and shot—all were traded, and Henday grasped and reported the fact that this intermediate trade in European goods was an added argument for direct contact between the Company and the hunting Indians, whether they were Blackfeet or Assiniboines. . . . it becomes obvious that Henday's contribution to the logical argument for penetration to the interior was as important as his contribution to the knowledge of routes and methods for such penetration." (1: 639-40)

H   Ray: "through the use of force the various Assiniboine and Cree bands increasingly took over control of the inland trade of York Factory. . . . Those that occasionally did make the voyage such as the Shussuanna, Blood, and Archithinue, always arrived in company with the Assiniboine and Cree, suggesting that perhaps they were not permitted to do so without the escort of the latter groups. . . . By 1740 the use of horses had spread northward . . . This development, along with an increasingly grassland orientation which became characteristic of such groups as the Blood and Blackfoot, meant that many bands of these tribes no longer would have been able to make the journey to the Bay, since they abandoned the use of canoes." (59-60)

15 May 1755

T mss E.2/6: "*stop*page" written over erasure.

M   Isham, "Discourses on Different Subjects [conversation between two Indians]:

    B. will you go along with me in the spring
           Kowichewow na neder Sekonoak

    A. Yes
           Skeamon

    B. Don't Lie
           Ecco weder Kedasque

    A. I won't Lie, I'll come in Eagle moon, or Grey goose moon

nemaweder Kedasque mekushaobesum enkotuckashin,
Esko neder nish koobesum
B.   farewell freind tell I see you againe
W'hatcheer Cosha'ke Errekoak mena wappamow
A.   farewell Live Long
w'hatche'r sucky athethu &c. . . .

These Natives are not Very numerious Considering the Vast
track of Land, they have to Range in, we having Seldom comming Yearly to the head factory to trade more y^n 250 Cannoes,
one Year with another, which contains 550 Ind^s bringing in
some Cannoes three Indians, besides their Goods, so y^t I compute thier is Comes Yearly to all the English setlements in
these parts, or belonging to the Hudsons Bay Company a'bout
1200 Indians;—being nigh as many Comes to the head fort of
trade as Goes to all the other Setlements.'' (HBCA E.2/1. ff. 41r,
57v, pp. 73, 106)

M   Graham: "When several Tents or families meet to go to War, or
to the Factories to Trade; They choose a Leader, but it is only a
voluntary Obedience: every one is at liberty to leave him when
he pleases, and the notion of a Commander is quite obliterated
when the voyage is over. . . . They follow him down to Trade at
the Settlements, and stile him Uckimow (that is a great Man,
Chief or Master) but he is obliged to secure their attendance
by promises and rewards; as the regard paid to his abilities is
too weak a nature to purchase Subjection. . . . During the voyage each Leader is canvassing with all imaginable art and
earnestness for people to join his gang, and influences some by
presents, others by promises; for the more Canoes under his
command the greater he appears at the Factory." (HBCA E.2/9.
ff. 70v-71r, pp. 134-35)

16 May 1755
T mss B.239/a/40: "*than*" written over erasure.

21 May 1755
W   Cocking: "The Natives all in general own that when they Trade
with the Pedlers; they are always distressed for want of Ammunition and Tobacco the greatest part of the year after; but the
opportunity of being supplied at home, besides Liquor is a
temptation they cannot Resist. As to their Promises they are
never to be depended on; and if they were given much more
Goods than usual at the Forts, it would not prevent their Trading with the Pedlers. Gratitude for any Favours recieved being

a Virtue the Natives are all in general unacquainted with. . . .
Sent a present of Tobacco to each Leader below remonstrating
against their going to the Pedlers, and telling them of their
ingratitude for the Favours they always receive at the Forts."
(HBCA B.239/a/69, 25 April and 2 May 1773)

M   Graham: "The Canadian Traders being returned to the lakes
and rivers above us are now carrying on trade with more vigour
than when they were under a French Government . . . making
settlements inland . . . would not encrease the Furr trade one
skin, excepting they [the Hudson's Bay Company] could get
the Archithinue Indians and Asseenepoet Indians to come to
trade at Basquea on Keskachewan river, then the Indians that
yearly visits York Fort & Churchill fort would be obliged to trap
their own Furrs which 20 Canoes out of 400 that Yearly comes
to the above Forts does not do; my two main reasons for saying
that inland houses would not be advantageous is, first when
the Natives found they could be supplyed so nigh, they never
would come down to the lower Forts; my next reason is, there
are not Natives sufficient to raise the trade 2000 Skins more
than is Yearly sent home from all their Honours Settlements in
the Bay without the two aforementioned tribes or more properly nations." (HBCA E.2/6. ff. 42v-43r, pp. 83-84)

H   Morton: "Beyond the Elbow [Henday's brigade] were met by
the Blackfeet (Bloods) whom Henday had seen, and by the
Assiniboins of the Eagle Hills, and traded their 'Wolves, Bears
and Foxes'—all furs of the open plains." (249)

22 May 1755

T mss   E.2/11: the note is written in the lower margin following this
entry; "the writer of this journal" written above the line, over
a caret; "*810*" written over erasure.

23 May 1755

C   see Isham, "Remarks" (B.239/a/40)

C   Isham, "French trade for one Canoe": "Foxes 160, Beaver
Parch^t 840, Catts 400, Beaver in Coat 343, Martin Skin 3000,
[total] 4743 made Beaver." (HBCA A.11/115, 20 June 1759)

C   YF post journal (Graham): "I wish sincerely that York Fort may
enlarge her Trade am certain great numbers of Young Fellows
lay up the Country strolling about amongst the Archithinnees
and will not look after Furrs to come down with, this and this
alone they call going to War I had one Archithinnee Man down
here this Summer He told me that He was not afraid of the

Trading Indians and said they were more obliged to Him & his
Countrymen than he was to them. He told me Furrs especially
Wolves were plentifull and that the Trading Indians might get
them and bring them down to the Fort, He was surprized to see
what Tobacco, Powder and Shot &c they carry away, when his
Countrymen give them 40 or 50 Wolves for an old Gun or Kettle,
& Ten Wolves for a Hatchet He traded with me 50 Wolves and a
few Parchment Beaver I made him a present of Several Things
but he told me often and at parting that his Countrymen would
never come down they not knowing how to Paddle but told me to
talk to the Trading Natives to get Wolves from his Countrymen
& bring them down." (HBCA B.239/a/59, 19 June 1766)

C YF post journal (Jacobs): "I must acquaint Y^r Hon^rs that a very
considerable part of ye furrs these men bring down is privately
conveyed into ye Factory notwithstand^g my best endeavours to
prevent it. I have also been informed that not one of those
men had any Tob^co or any thing else left to present to ye Ind^ns
to encourage them to come down here to Trade or even to prevent their Trad^g wth ye Canada Pedlars & ye very Ind^n Familys
they were wth Traded wth the Pedlars in their presence nor did
they endeavour or could prevent it for want of goods & as I
always understood those men were sent up into ye Country to
promote your Trade & to Encourage ye Ind^ns to come down to
your Factory & not as private Traders as they really are is y^e
reason I lay ye True State of this affair before you & I hope y^e
Gentle^mn of ye Comite has a better opinion of me than to
think I would use any of ye natives ill or even disoblidge them."
(HBCA B.239/a/59, 8 July 1768)

W Smith: "We heard Guns, We thought it was Ind^s; but it was the
french, going down with their Goods, Att night we Came to
them, as Soon As the master heard we Were Come, he Sent for
us, We went Immediatly, And he Gave Me Some Muskesew
meat and it eat very well then some of his tobacco he beheaved
very well . . . the Ind^s traded brandy, Att night the Master
Invited us both in to his house, there was meat and fatt, but
for bread he had none, then we Smoakt and drank brandy All
together." (HBCA B.239/a/43, 17 and 19 May 1757)

W Pink: "this Day j moved with the Other three English men and
80 Canewes of Jndaines in Companey with us wich was More
than j Did or Could Exspect when j See that those people of
Cannada had a Great Maney Things to Give to them for
Encouradgment and Like wise, a Great deal of Goods to Trade
with them, <but> j has Nothing onely heare and thare a peace

of tobacoo Laying up as j Gow down to the Forte and that j
Smoke all with them For Encouradgement as fast as j Come to
it, but it Cannot be Exspected out of what few Things we has
Gave us when we Come from the Forte <up> in Land with
those Natives and then Travel up and Doun to & frow this in
Land Contrey with them, and all wayes are Seeing of Difrent
and Difrent Bodeys of Jndaines, that we Can Save Much til this
time of the Yeare for when we See or heare of jndaines, why
then j Cot Down a pease of Tobacoo aCording to the Nomber
of jndaines and then S<m>oke it with them and then Gives
tobacoo to on and a knife to a Nother & pouder and Shot to a
Nother and So on, all is for Encouradgement." (HBCA
B.239/a/58, 27 May 1768)

W   Pink: "this Day we Came by the upper House Where the People
of Mountreale did Stay But j Found None Heare Now wich j was
feary Glad of." (HBCA B.239/a/63, 21 May 1770)

W   Tomison: "in the fornoon 3 Indians Came, who informed us
that 150 tents is now pitching towards the trading house . . .
they are all going to ware in the first of June, what I must
observe nothing more incourages these natives to go to ware
then trading Houses being Settled inland." (HBCA B.239/a/64,
29 March 1770)

W   Cocking: "In the afternoon arrived at the Pedlar Franceways
Settlement where we Landed. . . . On our arrival Franceway
introduced the Indians into his House giving each about four
Inches of Tobacco but nothing more gratis. afterwards they
made a Collection of Furrs . . . by the Bulk one hundred
Beaver: He in Return giving them about four Gallons of Adulterated New England Rum, and Cloathing two each with a Hat
& a small Serge Coat. I endeavoured all in my power to prevent
the Natives giving their Furrs but in Vain, Liquor being above
all perswasion with them. and I believe if the Pedler would have
owned to have & given them Liquor after they were intoxicated, some of them would have expended all they had." (HBCA
B.239/a/69, 20 May 1773)

M   Graham: "A Canoe usually brings down from eighty to one
hundred made Beaver in various species of furrs; three fourths
of this number is sufficient to purchase necessaries for his
Family until the next year, the remainder he expends in super-
fluities. The Cub Beaver, Musquashes [muskrats] and the like
are esteemed the Womens property who barter for Beads, Ver-
milion, Medals, Bracelets and other trinkets. I will enumerate
the Articles usually purchased by an Indian: 1 Gun (14 MB), 2

Hatchets (2 MB), 4 Ice Chissels (1 MB), 72 lb Tobacco Brazil
(10 MB), 4 Knives (2 MB), 4 Fishing Nets (3 MB), 10 Flints (1
MB), 1 File (1 MB), 1 Looking Glass (1 MB), 6 Powder (6 MB),
20 lb Shot (5 MB), 1 Powder horn (1 MB), 22 Y^{ds} Cloth (10 MB),
1 Comb (1 MB), 6 Awls & Fire steels (1 MB), 1 Bayonet (1 MB), 1
Kettle (6 MB), 1 Burning glass (1 MB), 12 Beads of sorts (3 MB).
Besides these things he expends a great deal in Brandy to
drink at the Fort and carry to his Friends inland." (HBCA E.2/9.
f. 92r, p. 177)

M Umfreville: "The Company signify to their Factors, that they
have an indisputable right to all the territories about Hudson's
Bay, not only including the Straits and the Bay, with all the
rivers, inlets, &c. therein, but likewise to all the countries,
lakes, &c. indefinitely to the westward, explored and unexplored. They therefore stigmatize the Canadian merchants
with the insulting epithets of pedlars, thieves, and interlopers;
though the quantity of furs imported by themselves bears no
comparison to those sent from Canada." (73)

H Burpee: "Cocking . . . gives us three French posts between The
Pas and the Forks. Hendry for some reason does not mention the
middle fort. Possibly he passed the spot after dark; or may have
been hugging the other bank of the river and so missed it; or,
again, it may have been built after his visit. . . . Below the Forks
[Henday] visited a French trading post, an outpost of the main
establishment at the mouth of the Pasquia." (310, 318)

H Morton: "Henday's flotilla reached La Corne's post." (249)

28 May 1755

W Pink: "this Day we pitched on the North Side of this River,
Cloes to a Carrying plase whare the Jndaines that Gow Down
to the Chourchill Forte Car<r>y thare Canewes over <in to a
Leak> . . . this Leak is Called Eth,Caw, a,moo,Cock,ha,Can.
This is whare we Came to our Fameyleyes the First Yeare that j
Came <in> with those Natives." (HBCA B.239/a/58, 31 May
1767)

W Pink: "this Day the Beaver Jndanes parted with me and Carred
thare Canewes over in to the Leake as they did Last Yeare and
So Gow down the North River." (HBCA B.239/a/63, 28 May 1770)

M Isham: "I do not think itt unpracticible for the English to
make a Setlement at the head of port Nelson River, & to be sup-
ply^d from the Lower parts &c where they might send the Indians
to which place they please, or traffick with them thier,— being a
branch almost all Indians seperates Either to go to York fort,

or Churchill,—this proceeding wou'd be of great service, for by
so doing they might gett double the fur's, they do now,—by
Reason of the Difficulty's the Indians meets with in Comming
to the Lower parts, & in a few years might with god's will,—be
able to roat the french out . . . these proceedings I think reasonable, for if we was never to make such Discovery'^{s} in Land,
itt'^{s} certain we shou'd never Reap the Benefit of what might be
Discover'^{d}—But what is the most Concer'n is to see us sitt quiet & unconcern'^{d} while the french as an old saying, not only
Beats ye Bush but run's away with the Hair also.'' (HBCA E.2/I.
ff. 45v-46r, pp. 82-83)

29 May 1755

T mss   E.2/4: the note, in Graham's hand, is at the foot of the page, in
the middle of the entry for 30 May following the line ''little
water . . . one of them.''

T xref   E.2/4 and E.2/II: cf B.239/a/40, 22 July and E.2/6, 23 July 1754.

P   Graham, ''Plan'' 1774: ''Mr Corry's house 1771'' (HBCA G.2/17)

C   see Isham, ''Remarks'' (B.239/a/40)

C   Graham to the HBC London Committee: ''The Canadians are
chosen Men inured to hardships & fatigue, under which most
of Your Present Servants would sink. A Man in the Canadian
Service who cannot carry two Packs of eighty Lbs each, on &
an half League losses his trip that is his Wages. But time &
Practice would make it easy, & even a few Canadians may be
got who would be thankful of Your Honours Service. John Cole
[a Canadian] informed me that the traders above in their Discourse concerning the Little North (meaning Hudson's Bay
wondered that we lay along the Sea & did not Penetrate
Inland.'' (HBCA A.II/II5, 26 August 1772)

W   Smith: ''came foour mean from the freanh and the brot word
as the indens had brock in to the freansh hous and had took all
the things as the had'' (HBCA B.239/a/45, 10 April 1758)

W   Pink: ''this Day we Came to the Loer house whare the one
English man was Staying But thare was Now Canewes Came up
in the Fall With Goods, But Yestday thare was a Canew Came
up with Four French Men to take Down this yonge Man that
Stayed heare, and Broate Tobacoo to Smoke with the Chiefs,
they Say that in the Fall of the yeare the Frenc Man Called
Sarchshrew is Comeing up with Four Canewes Lodan with
Goods and the Say that thare ware 16 Canewes on the way But
the Winter Came up on them before the Could Get up the Say
that a Great Deale of thar Goods ware Taken from Them a

Comeing up i Cannot Give no Other ACount of them. i heare
that the <See> an English man be Low that Come from one of
the Fortes at the Bottom of the Bay and <he> Should Give a
Truer aCount than j Can do for Onley hared what These had to
Say." (HBCA B.239/a/63, 30 May 1770)

W   Tomison: "The Trader bought 4 bags of rice from my Old
Leader . . . ; he refused the Summer Beaver skins which the
Young men offered him; the Old man asked him where he was
going to winter he said at Basquea; his Indian name is
Saswow . . . his dress was a Ruffled Coarse white shirt a Blanket Jacket, a pair of long vittery [canvas] trousers without
stockings or shoes, his own hair and a hat bound about with
green worsted binding; a poor thin looking man about 50 Years
of age, he seemed to have a great command over the men . . .
the Canadians have all the Actions &c of the Indians and are
dressed in the same manner only they have a Speckled ruffled
shirt and round their heads a silk handkerchief, and they all
know the Indian languages." (HBCA E.2/6, 2 October 1767)

W   Cocking: "Franceway's Dwelling is a long square Log House,
half of it appropriated to the use of a Kitchen & the other half
used as a Trading and a Bed Room; with a Loft above the whole
Length of the Building where he lays his Furrs. Also three
small Log Houses, the Men's Appartments; the whole enclosed
with ten foot Stockades forming a square of about twenty
Yards. His Canoes twenty-four feet long measureing along the
Gunwale five Quarters broad and twenty-two Inches deep. . . . I
believe Franceway has only about twenty men with him altho'
he might endeavour to make the Natives believe he had
thirty." (HBCA B.239/a/69, 20 May 1773)

M   Umfreville: "The great imprudence, and bad way of living of
the Canadian traders have been an invincible bar to the emolument of their employers. Many of these people, who have been
the greatest part of their lives on this inland service among
savages, being devoid of every social and benevolent tie, are
become slaves to every vice which can corrupt and debase the
human mind; such as quarrelling, drunkenness, deception, &c.
From a confirmed habit in bad courses of this nature, they are
held in abhorrence and disgust, even by the Indians, who finding themselves frequently deceived by specious promises, never
intended to be performed, imagine the whole fraternity to be
impregnated with the same failing, and accordingly hold the
generality of the Canadian traders in detestation and contempt." (209-10)

H   Burpee: "[Hendry] was entertained by the officer in charge of the district, who had been absent on his outward journey. This officer was no doubt La Corne." (318)

H   Morton: "Henday breakfasted with the Master, who must have been La Corne himself, for this was the chief post of the district." (249)

H   MacGregor: "Henday commented that this strange building of the French was built 'Log on Log'. What he meant was that it was built like any Alberta settler's log shack . . . the buildings of the Hudson's Bay Company were not put up in this manner. Their logs were cut into lengths of about ten feet and the walls were built in panels of about this length. Each log had a tongue on each end which slid into the slotted uprights." (263)

30 May 1755

T mss   E.2/11: "much I" and "they" written above the line, over carets.

M   Graham: "I am certain from my long knowledge of the Natives indolence &c numbers of them would never come down to the Forts when supplyed with brazile tobacco so nigh hand; by which supply of tobacco, and their own indolence we would scarcely add to our present trades what the Canadians now gets, and the goods that must be got up in large birch rind canoes with great trouble and expence, could not be managed without the assistance of the inland trading Natives who would then be cut off from getting furrs, as they would depend upon us as the worn out degenerated home Natives now does." (HBCA E.2/5. f. 11r, p. 15)

H   Rich: "[Henday's] experience with the French on his return journey was . . . illuminating, for then he saw them during tradetime, and his conclusion was that although during his wanderings, especially at the rendezvous where canoes were made on the North Branch of the Saskatchewan, many Indians 'in the French interest' had accepted his presents and had promised not to trade with the French, yet they could not hold to their resolution." (1: 638-39)

3 June 1755

W   Pink: "this Day we Came out in to the First Leake Called Out.tetouton Cock hagan." (HBCA B.239/a/63, 3 June 1770)

W   Cocking: "I find it impossible to make any remarks, as quitting the Paddle might endanger the breaking of the Canoe in the Falls & Shoals; but I hope those I have made in my passage up as Pr Log may be esteemed sufficient." (HBCA B.239/a/69, 31 May 1773)

H   Burpee: "From Fort Poskoyac Hendry seems to have followed
         substantially the same route as on his outward trip, and
         reached York Fort on June 20th, 1755 . . . In the course of this
         eventful and very important journey, Hendry explored an
         immense extent of new country. It is a dabatable point
         whether he was the actual discoverer of the South Saskatch-
         ewan and the North Saskatchewan. Certainly his is the only
         description we have of any portion of either branch, up to the
         year 1754." (318)

11 June 1755
W   Pink: "this Day we Came out in to the Second Leake, Called
         pemmichogomou." (HBCA B.239/a/63, 9 June 1770)
W   Cocking: "Paddled out of Sequisew Sepy and part of what they
         call Saskachiwan and entered Pimmochicomow Sackaeagan.
         The Indians all complain, saying they have preserved very little
         Provision & saying they shall be starved for Want in going up
         again: to satisfy them, I have promised the Chief at the Fort
         will give them small Supplies." (HBCA B.239/a/69, 5 June 1773)

15 June 1755
T mss   E.2/6: "*met*" written over erasure.
C   YF post journal (Isham): "Making a tomb to put over the Late
         deceased, the Inscription Viz^t

                    In Memory of Saml Skrimsher
            second att York fort and Master of flambro house,
                    Who died May ye 18th 1755
                          Aged 34 Years.
                     Vehement after pleasures
                     I seek for treasures Below
                      Which Caused my asshes
                       Here to Lye in oblivio.
         (HBCA B239/a/39, 6 August 1755)
W   Pink: "Came out in to the Thirde Leake Called a Teack o Cock
         hagan." (HBCA B.239/a/63, 13 June 1770)

16-20 June 1755
T mss   E.2/11: a note is pencilled in the left margin: "NB. See 209.
         Arrival at fort 23rd June"
T xref   E.2/11: cf. B.239/a/40, E.2/6 and E.2/4, 23 June 1755.
M   Isham: "Discourses on Different Subjects [conversation
         between an Englishman and an Indian]:
         E.   here is Indians padling down
              E'thinuwuck, petche, pemiskian

A. where
   tanta
E. they are under the shore . . . where is the Captⁿ or Leader
   shaw, shie nash. patimick . . . tonnewa' U'kemaw
A. See yonder he sitts
   mattacaw nema Kawapitt
E. how do you freind/Watcheer Coshock
B. thank you how do you
   ho', watcheer, watcheer
E. how many Cannoes is come along with you
   tantarto, utuck, Cawwichawutt
B. Sixty four Cannoes or Seventy I believe
   Coote washick metennaw, navo shoputuck, Eskoneder,
   neshuwashick meten na . . .
E. Why you was not here Last year
   Donna nepanoak nema Kemaw hum
B. I was not well was ye Reason I was not here the Last sum^r
   my Cannoe mate Brought my goods did you not see him
   Entawkoshin wache nema mishacott nepanoak entartewitt,
   tatta peshuwuck, enchemawgan,—nema na Kewoppama
   Weder
E. I did see him . . . will you trade to Day
   tatta wappamow . . . anoach keshekaw, na' Kokawtaway
B. no tomorrow . . . we'll trade some brandy now the young
   men wants to Drink
   nema wappakee . . . Anoach Skuttawappo Enkokatawan,
   Kuskathatum wiskaneck a weminequitt
(HBCA E.2/I. ff. 29v-31v, pp. 52-54)

M Graham: "Being now come within two miles of their Journeys
end a point of land prevents their being seen by the English;
here, they all put ashore; the Women go into the woods to get
Pine-brush for the bottom of the Tents, while the Leaders
smoak together and regulate the procession. This being settled they reimbark and so after appear in sight of the Fort to
the number of between twenty and fifty in a line abreast of
each other; if there is but one Captain his station is in the cen-
tre, but if more they are in the wings also, and their Canoes
are distinguished from the rest by a small St George or Union
Jack hoisted on a stick placed in the Stern of the Vessels. . . .
Several fowling-pieces are discharged from the Canoes to
salute the Fort, and the compliment is returned by four small
cannon for each division, the great Flag flying during the
trade." (HBCA E.2/9. ff. 84v-85r, pp. 162-3; cf. Umfreville 58-60)

H   Morton: "On the 20th of June this flotilla reached York Fort
         and 'were kindly received.' So ended one of the most astonish-
         ing journeys in the astonishing history of the fur trade of the
         North-West." (249)

23 June 1755

T mss   B.239/a/40: a single ruled line is drawn beneath this entry; the
         journal is followed by Isham's "Remarks" and Henday's log.
T mss   E.2/6: a double ruled line is drawn beneath this entry, followed
         by the positions and distances of "Basquea House" and the
         "greatest distance."
T mss   E.2/4: below a single ruled line following the journal entries,
         the summary of positions and distances is given in Andrew
         Graham's hand.
T xref   B.239/a/40, E.2/6 and E.2/4: cf. E.2/11, 20 June 1754.
C   YF post journal (Isham): "46 Cannues of pegsgoma Ind^s Came
         to trade, with whom Captn Anthony Hendey att the Head of
         them, who went Last Year with the Ind^s, Informed me Another
         Gang which parted from them will be here in a Small time (ie)
         in a Journal and Captn Hendeys Acc^t in this packet)." (HBCA
         B.239/a/39, 23 June 1755)
C   HBC London Committee to Isham: "We have also Continued
         the following Persons from the Expiration of their present Con-
         tracts whose wages we have raised Viz . . . Anth^y Henday for 3
         Years at £15 if a good Net Maker . . . the above continued Per-
         sons are to Sign Contracts Accordingly which send home in
         the Packet." (HBCA A.6/9, 27 May 1755)
C   HBC London Committee to Isham: "We have perused Hendays
         Journal, & Examined a [map] Draft (which We judge to be of your
         making) of his 12 Mo^s Travel up Inland to Incourage the Natives to
         come down to the Factory and trade, in which We think he has
         and (by continuing the same) may be of service to the Companys
         Interest, In Consideration of which, and the hardships he may
         have undergone: We have Allowed him a Gratuity of £20 over and
         above his Wages. And we will furthur reward him for what future
         Services he shall do the Company by his Travels hereafter, in
         bringing down Indian strangers at the Fort to Trade, which we
         judge to be the only means of enlarging the York Fort Cargoes. for
         we cannot find by his said Journal or Draft that any Settlement
         (the thing you seemed so desirous of) can be made with the least
         Appearance of Advantage . . . We have Entertained . . . Anthony
         Henday Nettmaker and Labourer for 3 years at £20. Pr Ann."
         (HBCA A.6/9, 12 May 1756)

C   Isham to Joseph Isbister (master of Albany): "Captn Anthony
        Hendey . . . is an English Man, and one of the Company's Ser-
        vants, its also for truth that with the Earchithinues he was, &
        See Archine Wache, which I doubt not but you have heard of."
        (HBCA B.239/b/14, 25 July 1756)

C   Isham, instructions to Smith and Waggoner: "I hope not to be
        deceived again in what I am possitive (if wrightly aply^d) will be
        greatly to the Advancement of Trade, and hope to See You once
        more at the Head of Those 75 Cannoes, or more, by Encourage-
        ing and Exhorting those Indians to Trade, by so doing You may
        depend upon it, the Company will sufficiently Reward You for
        eny service You may do the Company by such a Journey,
        Besides which You may depend upon Encouragement from/
        Your Friend and Wellwisher/ James Isham." (HBCA A.11/115, 20
        August 1756)

C   Graham to the HBC London Committee: "The Situation of
        your Affairs in this Country is very unpromising. I have not
        been Indolent, I have gained certain Information of what is
        doing Inland, & think it my Duty to lay before <You> the suc-
        cess of my Enquiry. Your Trade at York Fort & Severn is greatly
        diminished, the Keskochewan Indians Who are the Support of
        it being intercepted by the Canadian Pedlars who are yearly
        Gaining fresh Influence over them by Supplying them with
        Goods Inland. The Indians resort thither in the Winter for
        Ammunition & the whole body of the Natives build their
        Canoes not far distant from the residence of the Traders to
        whom they resort to Purchase Ammunition & other Articles in
        the Spring, & finding they can procure Tobacco & other Neces-
        sarys so near & being kept in Liquor, every Inducement to visit
        the Company's Factorys is forgot, & the prime furs are picked
        out & traded, the refuse is tied up & brought down to us by
        the Leading Indians & their followers: of such as these is Your
        Honour's Trade composed. . . . The Indians that did come
        down never offered to deny having traded their Prime Furrs
        with Canadians but seemed to Manifest an Uncommon Indiffer-
        ence about coming down, & when trading I overheared them
        Say to each other, 'Purchase only this or that Article as for the
        rest we can get them Yonder.' . . . The Number of Years I have
        been acquainted with York Fort & the Attention with which I
        have viewed Your Honour's Affairs I hope will warrant the offer-
        ing of my Sentiments on this occasion. It appears to me that
        the only way of increasing the Furr Trade is to have an Inland
        Settlement to supply the Natives with Necessarys, Ammunition

Tobacco & Brandy would be the Principal Articles, without the
latter the Indians would not resort to Your House if they could
Procure it else where. In an undertaking of this kind Your Honours have many advantages over the Pedlars, Your distance
would be small in comparison to theirs, . . . the falls and carrying Places are far less Numerous, no Natives to Pass but such
as annually take Debt at the Fact^y & are in friendship with us;
the Brazile Tobacco would be a strong enticement to the Indians, & the largeness of the Company's Standard seems likely
to deter the Canadians from Pursuing a traffick which must be
carried on under many disadvantages." (HBCA A.II/115, 26
August 1772)

W   Cocking: "a Yeachithinnee Indian Leader whom I met with in
the Winter, and did endeavour to perswade to come down with
me to the Fort; but in vain at that time: Had since I left him
changed his intent, collected a Stack of Furrs and is coming
down with the Indians he left. This I hope may be of Service, as
this Leader who is a principal Man amongst his Countrymen
will Relate to them, on his Return, the Usage to Meet with at
the Forts; which may induce others also to come down. . . . The
Yeachithinnee Indian Leader mentioned this day to be coming
down was obliged by Sickness to return back, as the Indians
whom he was accompanying said on their Arrival at the Fort."
(HBCA B.239/a/69, 10 June 1773)

M   Robson: "It is universally believed among the [Hudson's Bay
Company] servants, that the French travel many hundred
miles over land from Canada to the heads of our rivers in the
Bay, and that they have erected huts and settled a considerable
factory upon a lake at the head of Nelson-river; trading with
the natives for the lightest and most valuable furs, which they
carry a long way before they find a conveyance by water: and
this general opinion is not taken up at random, but supported
by particular incontestable evidences of the fact. I have seen
French guns among the natives that come to York-fort; and
once I heard Mr. Brady, the surgeon, converse with one of them
in the French language. I have also frequently seen in the governor's hand, a letter addressed to him from the chief factor at
the French settlement on Nelson-river. It was written in French
and Indian; and the purport of it was to establish a trade
between them and the English at York-fort, for those heavy
goods whch the French stood in great need of . . . The governor told us, that he had sent a copy of the letter to England;
and added that, if the Company consented to such a treaty, we

should get no furs but what came through the hands of the French, who would soon have huts all the way down Nelson-river." (62-63)

M   Graham: "Since Anth^y Hendey's visiting the inland Country, Servants hath been sent yearly inland to promote the furr trade, by making presents and inviting down strange Indians, but have increased the trade at York fort nothing worth notice, and indeed I don't know how it should rise by their means, they being ignorant poor labouring men of no abilities, who likes to go for no other reason but to lead an idle and vagrant life amongst the natives, and to get a few furrs for themselves, which they partly trap and buy from the Natives." (HBCA E.2/5. f. IIV, p. 16)

M   Umfreville: "I resided seven years under one of the Governors of [York Fort], during which time, I can with the greatest truth declare, that the trade yearly decreased, and that entirely through his repeated bad treatment of the Indians. . . . Another reason why the Company's trade is so very insignificant, is a total want of spirit in themselves, to push it on with that vigour the importance of the contest deserves. The merchants from Canada have been heard to acknowledge, that were the Hudson's Bay Company to prosecute their inland trade in a spirited manner, they must be soon obliged to give up all thoughts of penetrating into the country; as from the vicinity of the Company's factories to the inland parts, they can afford to undersel them in every branch." (68-69)

H   MacGregor: "A man such as Henday, who had made such a trip as he did, deserved more acclaim than came to him. As far as the world was concerned, the Hudson's Bay Company treated his trip in much the same light as if Henday had been out for a stroll in the back pasture. . . . Except for the long memory of the archives of the Hudson's Bay Company, Henday's great feat was forgotten." (270-71)

H   Rich: "It was a prosaic end to a prosaic narrative. But the achievement completely outshines the narrative in which it is told. In just under a year this Englishman, with only four years' experience of the country, had travelled over a thousand miles alone with his Indians to the foot of the Rockies, had wintered there with them, and had safely returned. He was able to speak French, but the Committee had doubted his ability to measure his journey at all accurately, and he seems to have been such a man as was capable of doing and of feeling far more than he could commit to paper—so much so that the Committee

confidently assumed that it was Isham who drafted his Journal
[*sic*]. Even so, Henday's matter-of-fact narrative repays
detailed study, for he was a shrew observer and in his own cryptic way he got his thoughts on paper. . . . Even the detailed and
important evidence which Henday brought, however, did nothing to change the Committee's attitude or intentions." (1:
637-38)

Commentary

Commentary

Historians and anthropologists have regarded Henday's record as a valuable source of information on British exploration of the continental interior, Native plains cultures and French-British commercial rivalry. The three essays of this section take stock of almost a century of historical and anthropological reference to Henday's year inland. This commentary reviews the topics discussed in scholarly studies on Henday: the explorer's route, the Native groups he encountered, and his influence on mid-eighteenth-century fur-trade policy.

The historians and anthropologists most frequently referred to in the commentary are Henday's editor Lawrence J. Burpee, A. S. Morton, E. E. Rich, Arthur J. Ray and Dale R. Russell.

In the introduction to his edition of the E.2/11 text published in the *Transactions* of the Royal Society of Canada, Burpee made much of the historian's obligation to work from "original documents," but he gave no textual description of his source and seems to have been unaware that there were any other copies of the journal. Instead he summarized Henday's trip inland, identifying the explorer's route and instances of French trade along the Saskatchewan River. Burpee regarded the journal as a reliable witness to events and places. *The Search for the Western Sea*, a general history of French and British exploration beyond the Great Lakes, appeared in 1908. In the preface, Burpee explained that he was moved to write this book "because the story of the exploration of North-Western America had never been told, and because it seemed so well worth the telling." He assured his readers that "in every case the original documents, in whatever form they might be, have been made the basis of the story, secondary authorities being used only to supplement the material obtained from

---

Notes to this section are on p. 323.

the original documents."[1] Burpee considered these "original documents" to be unquestionably reliable evidence of past events and situations.

Twenty-five years after Burpee's history appeared, Arthur S. Morton also insisted, in his *History of the Canadian West to 1870-71*, that
"it has been the aim to base the history entirely on the primary
sources." Unlike Burpee, Morton had access to the Hudson's Bay
Company Archives, then housed in London. Morton was able to un-
earth not only the original of Burpee's copy of Henday's journal but
two more texts, B.239/a/40 and a second text from Graham's "Observations." Morton relied on a Cree name in one of the newly discovered texts to claim that Henday had travelled within sight of the
Rocky Mountains. But Morton's privileged access to the company
archives was not passed on to the reader; his *History* was presented
"without plaguing [the reader] with the bibliographical footnotes."[2]
Although historians have taken him to task for this omission, Morton's construction of a general reader is a spectre that has been
repeatedly invoked in Canadian historical writing.

In 1967 E. E. Rich, the historian who to date has worked most
closely and extensively with HBC material, published a commissioned
two-volume *History of the Hudson's Bay Company, 1670-1870*. Rich
repeated Andrew Graham's characterization of Henday as "a bold and
enterprising man," followed Morton's lead and maintained that Henday "was almost certainly within sight of the Rockies." Rich focussed
on Henday's character as a way of explaining (away) textual and
generic problems. He noted that "Henday's gifts were not literary";
although Henday's account was "a prosaic narrative," Henday was "a
shrewd observer and in his own cryptic way he got his thoughts on
paper."[3]

Henday's journal has also furnished critically important evidence
for studies in ethnohistory, archaeology and anthropology concerned
with the movements, trading patterns and living conditions of Plains
Native groups during the fur trade era. In his *Indians in the Fur
Trade*, Arthur J. Ray bases his analysis of Native/European commercial exchange on HBC lists and accounts; as far as Henday is concerned, Ray follows Rich's lead in analyzing the role of Cree and
Assiniboin as middlemen for fur-hunting groups farther west. Henday
"took detailed notes on the nature and organization of the inter-
change of goods between tribal groups." The explorer's journal can be
considered a valuable source of information: "his notes provide us
with a particularly good picture of the winter activities of the parkland Indian middlemen at mid-century." Relying on the route of travel
traced by Morton, Ray concludes that "the Parkland Assiniboine and

Cree were thus able to spend the winter in comparative ease subsisting on bison." Ray reiterates a hypothesis long held by anthropologists, notably David Mandelbaum, that these tribes, armed with trade guns, moved from the forest and parkland onto the prairies and displaced other plains groups. As for rivalry with the French, Ray maintains that "Henday's observations also give us a good indication of the nature of the effects of French competition. . . . The French were skimming off the higher quality furs."[4] In *Eighteenth-Century Western Cree and Their Neighbours*, Dale R. Russell questions the Mandelbaum hypothesis of tribal displacements. At the same time, Russell traces Henday's route as far west as Alberta, just as earlier historians did, and this far-western reach is critical to his argument: "What is apparent from Henday's journal is that [already by 1750] both the Cree and Assiniboin were living in and south of the Edmonton area in sizeable numbers."[5]

Since 1907 scholars have presented Henday as an important explorer whose journal describes travel and trade as far west as the Rocky Mountains as well as conditions of Native life in the early contact period. But the journal's textual problems make it a risky source. A close look at these problems reveals that historical and anthropological studies using Henday's journal as factual evidence have built on a dubious and elusive foundation.

Notes

1 Burpee, *The Search for the Western Sea*, vii, viii.
2 Morton, xiii-xv, xix, xxii, 244-50. Under pressure to provide sources, Lewis G. Thomas added notes to his revision of Morton's book published in 1973.
3 Rich, I: 632, 637.
4 Ray, *Indians in the Fur Trade*, 89-91. This text best represents Ray's work on Native participation in the fur trade; it supersedes Ray's earlier collaboration with Freeman. The argument of *Indians in the Fur Trade* is summarized in Ray, *I Have Lived Here Since the World Began*, 78-111.
5 Russell, iv, 93-96, 144-45.

Tracing Henday's Route

Isham's instructions drawn up for Henday's departure on 26 June 1754 ordered the explorer to travel with a "Leading Indian" to "his Country" with the object of persuading inland Natives to trade at the Bay. The only specific geographical feature for which he was to search and enquire was an inland sea, the fabulous "mer de l'ouest" which had so intrigued La Vérendrye. Henday was to keep a careful record of his progress: "having a Compass, hand Line paper &c &c along with you, therefore be Very Exact in Keeping a Journal of your travels and observations Daily, observing the Courses." Distances were to be judged on the basis of Henday's trip along the Hayes River earlier that year: "as you know the Distance a Considerable way up the River, you may therefore by a Day or two at first Setting out Know how many miles you go in a Day hereafter, by which you may Compute the miles by padling or travelling by Land all the way."[1] For this earlier trip in February and March, Henday had been provided with "wheel and compass." The measuring wheel was an attempt to imitate the procedures for triangulation used for contemporary British surveys, although the compass was apparently a mariner's instrument registering only the winds, not a surveyor's compass marked off in degrees.[2]

Despite Henday's pilot survey in February 1754, the London Committee was not satisfied with reports of the navigability of inland waterways. Their General Letter of 1755 recommended that Isham conduct a detailed examination of the Hayes and Nelson rivers, since "Nelsons River on your said draught must be laid down from Indian information only, and how much that is to be depended on, we are Annually convinced, and doubtless so are you to."[3] The following year, the Comittee's response to Henday's year inland was no more confi-

---

Notes to this section are on pp. 338-42.

dent: "We have perused Hendays Journal & Examined a Draft (which We judge to be of your [Isham's] making) of his 12 Mo[s] Travel up Inland . . . We cannot help observing the course of Hayes and Seal Rivers are in this draft laid down very differently from any we have heretofore seen or any Information we have ever yet received, therefore . . . we apprehend Henday is not very expert in making Drafts with Accuracy or keeping a just Reckoning of distances other than by Guess which may prove Erroneous."[4]

The London Committee's doubts contrast oddly with the assurance of twentieth-century historians who have mapped Henday's route in considerable detail. Burpee declared that "it is possible to follow him almost step by step, from the time he left York Factory, in June 1754, until he returned to it in June of the following year."[5] Morton suggested an itinerary as precise as Burpee's though quite different in its critical locations.[6] For the bicentennial of Henday's journey, James G. MacGregor traced the explorer's route across the prairie provinces, again "follow[ing] Henday more or less step by step" but deciding for the most part in favour of Morton.[7] Clifford Wilson's article in the *Dictionary of Canadian Biography*, which appeared over twenty years later in 1966, approved MacGregor's "convincing attempt to trace [Henday's] wanderings."[8] Contributing to the *Historical Atlas of Canada*, published in 1987, Richard Ruggles traced a route that conforms with Wilson's description.[9]

Burpee's route takes Henday up the Hayes River to Knee Lake (his identification of "Attick-Sagohan" or Deer Lake), over to Cross Lake, though "for some reason he makes no special mention of it," then up the Minago River to Moose Lake, and by connecting lakes to The Pas ("Basquea" or "Fort Paskoyac"). The explorer paddled a few miles up the Carrot River ("Peatago River") and soon struck overland in a southwesterly loop, crossing the South Saskatchewan River at Saskatoon and reaching the North Saskatchewan halfway between Prince Albert and Battleford. At this point Henday again turned southwest and eventually crossed the Red Deer River ("Waskesew River") above Knee Hills Creek. He met a large group of Archithinues a few days later, then travelled west and northwest to about latitude N51°50′ and longitude W114°, the farthest point of his journey. He returned to the Red Deer River, where his party built canoes, then paddled down the Red Deer River to the South Saskatchewan, on to the forks and Basquea, finally taking "substantially the same route as on his outward trip" from The Pas down to York Fort.

Morton corrects Burpee's identifications of the canoe route from York to Basquea[10] and differs over the identification of the "Waskesew River": Burpee reads this as the Red Deer River of Alberta and keeps Henday along the South Saskatchewan, whereas Morton follows Andrew Graham in identifying "Waskesew" as a name for the Saskatchewan River. According to Morton, after crossing the Eagle Hills Henday followed the south bank of the Battle River ("Countenack River") and forded the Red Deer River near Nevis, just days before meeting the Archithinues west of Balermo. Henday then crossed the Blindman River and "from a high knoll he bade farewell to the Rocky Mountains under their Cree name . . . Arsinie Watchie."[11] For the rest of the winter Henday's party drifted northeast to the North Saskatchewan below Edmonton, where they built canoes and undertook the return trip to York.

MacGregor's prairie itinerary is closer to Morton's than to Burpee's, just as precise as theirs and much more detailed. MacGregor specifies the exact spots of river crossings and camping places, and like Morton, he refuses to admit that his locations are tentative and speculative. Burpee's numerous qualifying phrases—"it can safely be assumed . . . As far as one can judge . . . presumably . . . It is pretty safe to assume . . . "[12]—are brushed aside and replaced by details designed to convince. MacGregor's four small route maps mark each day of Henday's advance along the North Saskatchewan and Battle rivers, his designation of Henday's westernmost point not far from the Clearwater River, and the explorer's cross-country return to the canoe-building location near Edmonton.

Wilson and Ruggles are duly persuaded. Wilson's article in the *Dictionary of Canadian Biography* and Ruggles's plate in the *Historical Atlas of Canada* follow MacGregor's impossibly precise route in all essentials. In his note to the plate, Ruggles cites several sources, primary and secondary, none of them Wilson's *DCB* article. Ruggles's accompanying statement is ambiguous: either his primary sources confirmed Henday's route as stated by Wilson and suggested by Mac-Gregor, or they yielded no new evidence.[13] But his map clearly follows the MacGregor-Wilson line.

MacGregor's book therefore merits a closer look. It is an informal compilation of travelogue, anecdotes, legends, deductive arguments and feverish descriptions of the parkland landscape, all tied together by the thread of the author's quest for Henday's "exact route." For MacGregor, this search was a spare-time project dedicated to Alberta (the province) and Frances (his wife), which occupied his winter evenings and focussed excursions on summer weekends. "Sometimes," he remarks, "I think that we used the pretext of tracing out Henday's route as an excuse for driving through this beautiful countryside."[14] MacGregor's field work led to his exact locations even as it produced disappointment and unheeded failure.

Two examples will illustrate MacGregor's method. The first is his specification that Henday crossed the Red Deer River "about ten miles downstream from the Content Bridge"; MacGregor reasons that "[Henday's] description of the stones of an iron colour would fit this place, as well as the veins of iron running along the surface of the ground." MacGregor nevertheless admits that "this [presence of iron] is a very common phenomenon almost anywhere in this stretch of the Red Deer River."[15] A second example shows MacGregor's tenacious defence of a previously selected location even when he fails to confirm its most important feature. Henday's 7 October 1754 entry in the E.2/11 text reads, "Here is a ridge of fine flint stone," and MacGregor's commentary for 7 October affirms, "That night [Henday] camped two or three miles north and east of the Town of Stettler." But MacGregor is not entirely happy with this important location; on his field trip he could find only bands of sandstone in the river banks, not a hint of flint. He reflects, "If I were on the trail of Henday and could finally hit on this flint ridge, I would feel pretty certain that I was on the right track. This ridge was to be one of my key points in pinning Henday down. Alas for my hopes and plans and intentions! I cannot be certain that I have found it."[16] He is forced to speculate that Henday came across quartzite beds (which *are* to be found at Stettler) or "merely a gravelly ridge." MacGregor consoles himself with the thought that "the particular [ridge] on which Henday camped must have had more flinty pebbles than the majority of [the ridges near Stettler]."[17] His conclusion: despite the lack of flint in the Stettler area, Henday camped near Stettler beside a somewhat flinty gravel ridge.

A similar process of rationalization characterizes MacGregor's discussion of the Rocky Mountains, which Henday is said to have glimpsed for the first time in October and the last time in December. MacGregor is following Burpee's edition of the E.2/11 text, in which there is mention only of the "Muscuty Country" on 24 December 1754. But MacGregor is also aware of Morton's research. Morton discovered two earlier Henday texts mentioning, in the entry for 24 December, a view of "Arsinie Watchie." These are the Cree words for stony hill or mountain, which Morton quickly identified with the Rockies. MacGregor plots Henday's route west of the Red Deer River to a place near Eckville: here was the "Last Hill" marked on Palliser's map a century later.[18] Although he confesses to "going . . . out on a limb and pull[ing] an explanation out of the air," MacGregor argues that the toponym must have survived since the time of Henday's visit in December 1754.[19]

MacGregor's location of the viewpoint of 24 December 1754 derives from the same sort of association and compromise by which he works through the flint ridge problem. He builds on Morton's association and muses, logically enough, "Why is it that Henday's Journal does not refer to his first sight of the mountains? . . . If Henday had been attracted to the mountains to the extent that he would comment on his last view of them, why does he not make some reference to them when he first saw them?"[20] To answer these questions, MacGregor brings Henday farther south and west in October 1754 than either Burpee or Morton does. Henday's first sight of the Rockies must have occurred a few days after the meeting with Archithinues. In Burpee's edition of the E.2/11 text, Henday's journal entry for 17 October 1754 reads: "Thursday. 322 tents of Archithinue Natives unpitched and moved Westward; 17 tents of Asinepoet Natives moved Northwards; and we moved S.W.b.W. 9 Miles. Level land with ledges of Poplar and willows. Passed two creeks, but little water in them; and none to be got anywhere else."[21] On this day, says MacGregor, Henday travelled to a point "about ten miles east of Innisfail." Before they made camp, the explorer's Cree companions led him up a hill from which he gazed spellbound at the line of peaks fringing the western horizon.

> What must Henday have thought as . . . the mountains burst upon his view? . . . On foot and by canoe Henday had travelled fourteen hundred miles for this view. It was worth every paddle stroke, every step. . . . Henday remained apart—silent and reverent—contemplating. . . . It was long before he could tear himself from that hilltop. He had seen the Shining Mountains. Of all white men, he was the first to see them. Through all his future years that view would remain with him. The memory of this day in October would never dim. He had seen the Shining Mountains.[22]

MacGregor includes a photograph of mountains and foothills on the facing page. This photo is not the view to be had from the hill near Innisfail, at least not with the naked eye. Instead it offers a visual clue to MacGregor's account of the explorer's supreme moment: it is a telephoto exaggeration of some part of the front ranges.[23] Even if MacGregor's claims about Henday's viewpoint near Innisfail were justified, the proximity of the mountains in the photograph is not.

It seems odd that MacGregor's book should have been considered authoritative—that professional historians should rely so unquestioningly on this admittedly amateur investigation. Their complaisance may originate in a shared view of Henday's historical importance. MacGregor twice lists Henday's achievements in terms of "firsts": "Two hundred years ago Anthony Henday crossed our prairies, the first white man to do so. . . . He was the first white man to see the main chain of the Rocky Mountains north of Colorado; the first to see Indians with horses on the Canadian prairies; the first to meet the Blackfoot Indians. . . . What a trip this had been—first white man to pass all the way across the Muscuty Plains, first to see Indians with horses, first to meet the regal Blackfeet, and first to see the Shining Mountains."[24] Burpee and Morton list the same "firsts." For Burpee, Henday was "the first British trader upon the waters of the highway of the west [Saskatchewan River]"; for Morton, "one and three-quarters of a century ago English eyes first rested on the beautiful South Saskatchewan . . . it was left to English eyes to see the Rocky Mountains of the north before any other European."[25] Wilson echoes these earlier claims, and referring to Ray's just-published *Indians in the Fur Trade*, adds to them: "Henday had been farther into the western interior than any other European, and he had made valuable discoveries about the Indian economy and the nature of the company's French competition."[26] Ruggles notes that "Anthony Henday may have been the first European to see the Rocky Mountains from the Canadian plains."[27] Although Ruggles qualifies his statement, his "may have been" does not quite offset the force of repeating the Henday-sees-Rockies idea.

These historians subscribe to a sort of explorational Olympics: the west was a cartographic blank on which the heroic European explorer established a record for the first and farthest route. Burpee in particular saw exploration in obviously imperialist and gender-driven terms: "This [the continental interior] is the stage; and the men who move over it are men of . . . heroic build, strong, fearless, clear-eyed, endowed with masculine faults and masculine virtues, dominated by the spirit of adventure of two great races, fit men to break a path through a continental wilderness."[28] Of the "two great races," Morton considered the British to be greater and the role of the fur trade companies to be of critical importance; exploration was a team sport, not just a contest of individuals. Wilson's summing-up of Henday's achievement might be read as less jingoistic, but its terms and distinctions (farther/other, European/Indian, French/British) fall within the same tradition. To get the British trader farthest first, Henday's journal is made to yield evidence of long distances travelled and great aims accomplished, even at the price of overlooking textual ambiguity (Morton), imagining features and occasions (MacGregor), and playing down the divergence of Burpee's and Morton's route-finding (Wilson).

Little or no historical comment has been made on the London Committee's concern that "Henday [was] not very expert in . . . keeping a just Reckoning of distances." Burpee, for example, simply states that the explorer's directions and mileages were "entirely wrong" and overlooks the incongruity of attributing discoveries to an explorer whose record was so unreliable.[29] More investigation into the method and limitations of Henday's route-finding is needed.

The Henday texts indicate the explorer's route as daily notations of courses (compass directions) and distances (miles travelled). There is also a log appended to B.239/a/40. To record his directions, Henday had only a "Boat Compass," and he seems to have made no adjustment for magnetic declination as he moved west. The declination of York Fort was effectively 0°, but there would have been a difference of 15° from Saskatoon west and up to 19° for locations in Alberta.[30] Another difficulty is a zigzag pattern of travel on the plains that belies the purposeful forward movement attributed to European explorers. Isham read Henday's year inland as a search for Archithinues; once the explorer had met these strangers, "Here was the End Captn Hendey's Journey . . . after this they only pitcht too & fro to Get furrs and provisions."[31] But his directions change daily and travel is interrupted; in his entry for 8 August, Henday jokingly reported "all hands Employed eating & smoaking, and I am not behind hand."[32] Cocking protested such delays when his band enjoyed successful hunts: "the Natives are very delatory in proceeding," he complained, "their whole delight being in indolently sitting Smooking or Feasting."[33] Like all the HBC employees sent after him, Henday's route reflected a Native pattern of needs and habits. "We travell as the Cattle [Buffalo] goes," he noted in the entry for 17 January 1755. During the coldest winter weather, Henday's tent-mates refused to stir outside; in the spring, construction of canoes took weeks because the boatbuilders were also hunting, trading and feasting.[34] Burpee and MacGregor smoothed out the route in order to emphasize a western direction, so that, just as for Isham, Henday's exploration assumed an air of determined advance. This emphasis misreads not only the wandering directions of Henday's course notations but the evidence of pauses and expedient decisions also recorded in the journal.

At the same time, distances noted in the E.2/11 text made Burpee suspicious of the explorer's mileages. How much more suspect must Henday's distances seem when compared with the variant figures of the three earlier texts. Of the eighty-five entries in Henday's log (B.239/a/40), forty-one distances have been altered in E.2/11— almost half the total. Nearly every one of these alterations mechanically reduces the earlier figure by half; for example, from 22 July to 5 August the distances travelled according to the earlier texts are 22, 26, 24, 20, 21, 20 and 22 miles; in E.2/11 these appear as 11, 13, 12, 10, 10, 10 and 11 miles, while the courses remain the same. For the pedestrian part of Henday's journey, the E.2/11 text offers more reasonable distances than do the earlier texts, though a corrected, reduced average of eleven miles per day overland was still strenuous. Henday travelled with a numerous crowd that must have included old people and children; heavy burdens had to be transported; there was a daily need to hunt for food.

Graham must have known the London Committee's reaction to Henday's route-finding, expressed in their letter of 1755; if he altered the figures in E.2/11 to allay the doubts of his contemporaries, we can wonder why he did not do so in the journal texts included in earlier states of the "Observations." One reason might be that in 1767-69, when he was compiling the E.2/6 and E.2/4 manuscripts, Graham had no standard by which to judge Henday's distances. Other winterers had followed Henday to the western interior, and some had kept journals—Joseph Smith from 1756 to 1758, William Pink from 1766 to 1770, and William Tomison from 1767 to 1769. But they too were far from being "expert in making Drafts with Accuracy or keeping a just Reckoning of distances." In 1772 Graham sent Matthew Cocking, who was more articulate, more literate and more competent in navigation than any of the previous winterers, to spend a year along the Saskatchewan River.[35] Cocking returned to York with a detailed journal and log: like Henday, he had travelled the "middle track" from York Fort to Basquea, and like Pink, he had gone west to the Eagle Hills. Cocking's average distance on the plains, walking over open level ground with the families, is more credible: on an average day, "the young men hunting as we go," Cocking's party covered six to seven miles.[36]

Cocking himself was diffident about his route-finding skills. Two days upstream from York Fort he remarked, "NB my Courses and distances very incorrect for these Canoes have such a motion in paddling the Compass was never still, and I find it impossible to have the Log at present."[37] And when his band set out on foot after abandoning their canoes, he commented, "Our Courses very uncertain, I found it inconvenient to use the Compass in travelling, so was obliged to set our Courses as well as I could by the Natives direction in the morning, which I find very incorrect scarcely two of them agreeing in one direction."[38] On 26 August and 21 September 1772, Cocking corrected his dead reckoning with observations; once again he emphasized that conditions made these observed positions approximate at best:

> [26 August 1772] This day I took an Observation with a bad Horizon three miles distant . . . Latitude 52°37′ North, As it is not all to be depended on I have not corrected . . . The great Error which seems to be in my Account by Dead Reckoning as p[r] Log must be imputed to my want of proper Instruments, and besides having but little skill in Navigation.

[21 September 1772] This day I took an Observation with an Artificial Horizon in water as p^r Log, but notwithstanding there was but little wind it was less perfect than I could have wished. Latitude 52°13´ N supposing 52°00´ to be nearest the truth I have corrected for that Latitude, taking no notice of the odd thirteen miles.

The September observation encouraged Cocking to correct his distances: by dead reckoning he had gone 744 miles; he corrected this figure to 536 miles.[39]

Since Henday made no observations, he could not correct his dead reckoning of either courses or distances; his later estimates were built on whatever errors had been made earlier in the journey. Overestimating distances without any means of adjusting them is a consistent pattern in all the journal texts. The B.239/a/40 log gives the distance from York Fort to Basquia as 529 miles; in notes at the end of the journal, the E.2/6 and E.2/4 texts estimate this distance as 535 miles; in contrast, Cocking's log gives the same distance as 351 miles. Henday's estimated mile is 1.5 times longer than Cocking's, and as we have just seen, Cocking's observation on 21 September 1772 proved to him that even his mile was too long. Graham included an abridged version of Cocking's journal together with Henday's in the E.2/11 text of the "Observations." Cocking's ability to correct his courses and distances by taking observations, together with the detail of his journal and log, may have encouraged Graham to adjust the overland distances in the E.2/11 text of Henday's journal.

Cocking's journal entry for 13 September 1772 counts 13 minutes as 13 miles; these would be nautical miles, 60 to a degree of longitude, and longer by 576 feet than the statute mile of 5,280 feet. However, there is no indication that Henday was trained enough to measure his distances in nautical miles; it is much more likely that he used the common or London mile, counted as 1,000 paces, the equivalent of 5,000 modern feet or .95 of a modern statute mile.[40] By this calculation alone, the distances recorded in the early winterers' journals must be translated and reduced. Moreover, the length of each pace—two steps—may well have been five feet only under ideal conditions. This length could be altered by many factors (elevation gain or loss, rough ground, extremes of heat or cold, heavy loads, fatigue, hunger, disease, bugs), all of which would shorten the pace considerably even as they lengthened the time it took to move from a point of departure to a destination. This combination of shorter steps and delayed movement under adverse conditions means that measurement of a mile was uncertain when distance was calculated as a lapse of time. From York Fort to Basquea, Cocking noted that they tracked "about three Miles p^r Hour [against] a strong Current."[41]

Cocking's companions travelled fast enough to make him wonder if he could keep up with them, yet the variety and difficulty presented by the rivers and lakes they ascended meant that his rate of
three miles an hour must have been a very rough estimate. An additional reason for inflated distances by canoe is not hard to find. There
were too many variables at work: going upstream or downstream, the
variety of canoeing techniques (paddling, poling, lining and carrying),
the number and strength of the paddlers, the size of the loads, as well
as seasonal changes in water levels. Henday's measurements during
his winter pilot survey in 1754 did him little good during his trip up
the Hayes River the following June. His distances, as the London
Committee suspected, are "by Guess, which may prove Erroneous,"
when they are not simply the copyist's invention.

Burpee, Morton and MacGregor relied on landscape descriptions
to compensate for the explorer's confusing courses and distances.
The "character of the country" may be no more certain a guide, however.[42] Even the key lakes and rivers mentioned in Henday's journal
have been variously interpreted. Misled by later accounts of travel
from York Fort, Burpee assumes that "Attick Sagohan" is Knee Lake,
the first lake inland on the "lower track," but it is fairly certain that
Henday, like Pink and Cocking after him, travelled up the "middle
track" from the Hayes and Fox rivers to the Bigstone River and then
to Utik ("Attick" or Deer) Lake. Burpee identifies the "Wapesew-
copeto" and "Sechonby" rivers as the North and South Saskatchewan, and the "Waskesew" River as the Red Deer River. But the
"Wapesewcopeto" River is called "Waskesew" in the earlier E texts—
E.2/6 and E.2/4. Graham noted in E.2/4 that "this river is
Keskachewan river and only goes by this name in the muscuty country," a reading supported by reference to "ye farthest Branch/the
northernmost branch of Wykasew River/the N branch of waskesew
river" in B.239/a/40, E.2/6 and E.2/4 respectively.[43]

Most problematic of the landscape references is, of course, mention of "Arsinie Watchie" in B.239/a/40 and "Arsinee Warchee" in
E.2/6. Morton, MacGregor and Wilson all identified this landmark
with the Rocky Mountains, and the "muscuty country" with the open
plains. Glyndwr Williams explains why Henday might not have mentioned the Rockies even if he had seen them: "Henday's journal
throughout is a 'nose-to-the-ground' document; he mentions rivers,
lakes and hills as he comes to them. . . . Difficult though it may be to
a modern observer, it is quite conceivable that Henday, whose references to the prairies across which he was travelling were fleeting
enough, never thought it worth while to describe the mountain range
he could see many miles farther west."[44]

Williams's "nose-to-the-ground" interpretation is the opposite
of MacGregor's superheated descriptions in *Behold the Shining Mountains*. But it still does not account for the textual discrepancies present in entries for two dates. B.239/a/40 first gives this Cree name in
the entry for 29 October 1754, which is given as "muscuty plains" for
the same date in E.2/6. The Cree name appears again in the entry for
24 December 1754 in both B.239/a/40 and E.2/6; the other E texts substitute "muscuty country." Yet E.2/6 considers the Cree name and
"muscuty country" to be equivalent, interchangeable terms for the
same feature: in the 29 October entry, Henday comments, "I have
been since the 13th of august in muscuty plains; the Indians calls the
Archithinue Country by another name, which is Arsinee Warchee (ie
dry Country)"; the 24 December entry in E.2/6 records, "I had a fine
prospect of Muscuty or Arsinee Warchee Country," but adds that Henday also "seed the Archithinues smoak" in this last view of "that
delightful Country." Earlier entries (1 August 1754 and 21 September
1754) contain remarks that the plains are "pleasant Country" and
"beyond description": these analogies would weight the identification
in favour of the plains rather than the mountains. The 29 October
entry in B.239/a/40 seems to confirm this: "took my departure from
Arsinie Watchee and steered W^t 10 M fine Levell Land."

Although we cannot rule out the possibility that Henday saw the
Rocky Mountains, it is just as likely that "Arsinie Watchie" referred to
stony hills of quite different proportions. For HBC men used to the
flat shores of the Bay, any height of land was impressive. Peter Fidler
compared the Rockies, when he saw them in 1792, to "dark rain like
clouds rising up above the Horizon."[45] Cocking had used the same
simile twenty years earlier to describe the relatively modest Pasquia
Hills: "high Land appeared at a distance like a Cloud."[46] And although English makes a distinction between hill and mountain, Cree
does not; for example, Pink and Cocking, who recorded their place
names in Cree, passed by the "Mous,wa,Chee" (Moose Hills) as well
as the "Wusquit Wachy" (Birch Hills), and camped for some time in
the "Mekisew Wachy" (Eagle Hills).

Moreover, the generally reliable notations of Cocking's 1772-73
journal indicate a considerable distance between the geographical
features of Manitou Lake and the Rocky Mountains. The version of
Cocking's journal included with Henday's in the E.2/11 text of Graham's "Observations" records: "We separated, part going Westerly towards Manito-Sakehagan & Assine Wache," while Cocking's holograph
journal entry for 9 September 1772 announces, "We seperated the
Beaver & other Indians going Westerly others SW." Manito Lake was a
few days' travel from the Eagle Hills, while a journey of several weeks

separated "the Beaver & other Indians" from the Rocky Mountains. Cocking previously noted that the "Beaver Indians" lived in a range of "large Hills": "this high land is the termination of the Barren Land that way, the Country beyond being woody."[47] The "high land" might be read as referring to the Rockies, but at the latitude Cocking was travelling, "the termination of the Barren Land" would have been far east of any point at which the mountains could serve as a landmark. Inexplicably, the reference to "Assine Wache" appears in Cocking's text at the time it was abridged and copied into Graham's E.2/11 "Observations," while "Arsinie Watchie"/"Arsinee Warchee" is omitted from the later E.2/4 and E.2/11 texts of Henday's journal.

Henday's own association with the Beaver Hills is affirmed on "Moses Nortons Drt. of the Northern Parts of Hudsons Bay laid dwn on Indn. Information . . . ," a map drawn by the Métis governor of Churchill in 1760. The map follows the North American Native cartographic convention, and includes the continental interior from the Arctic Ocean to the prairies.[48] The route from York Fort to "an old French House" (Basquia) divides into a northwesterly line leading to the Athabaska River, the tar sands, Great Slave Lake and a westerly line following the North Saskatchewan River. Branching from the North Saskatchewan is the "Beaver River," on which is placed a "Beaver Mount." A dotted line, labelled "ye track to Hendeys tent," connects with another dotted line called "The Leaders track to ye french house"; together they join via "ye Leaders tent" a line west of the lake-and-portage route to the Athabaska River. Since the "Beaver River" (Amisk River) connects with the North Saskatchewan River from the northwest, it is difficult to identify the "Beaver Mount" with the Beaver Hills lying south of North Saskatchewan. At the same time, the inclusion of three French trading posts on the Saskatchewan River may indicate that the reference to Henday is to his inland journey 1759-60, when he might have followed a different route.

A second Company map, drawn by Andrew Graham in 1774 and titled "A Plan of Part of Hudson's-Bay, & Rivers, Communicating with York Fort & Severn," shows the route from York Fort to The Pas and up the Saskatchewan River as far as the Eagle Hills.[49] The map's western border follows the meridian of W110°, a location much farther east than the westernmost points of Henday's journey as reconstructed by Burpee, Morton and MacGregor. As well as the Eagle Hills, where Cocking wintered in 1772-73, the only other feature shown beyond the river forks is the "Sakatow" (Thickwood) Hills, also mentioned in Cocking's journal. No mountains are shown, no inland sea. This map sums up the few features of the continental interior that Graham could believe in and rely on.

In 1756 Isham had written to the factor at Albany that "its also for truth that with the Earchithinues [Henday] was, & see Archine Wache, which I doubt not but you have heard of."[50] But no matter how often he copied Henday's journal and referred to it in support of his views on inland trade, Graham seems to have dismissed any geographical indications the journal could have supplied. The western blank of his 1774 map indicates a judgement of Henday's route-finding skills similar to that of the London Committee in their letters of 1755 and 1756. Lest any doubt remain that Graham's map omitted the Rocky Mountains but that they were known to lie west of the hundredth meridian, Graham's categorical statement in the E.2/12 text of his "Observations" should confirm his continued ignorance even as he recorded the last text of Henday's journal: "Mountains are not met with nigh the sea-coast [Hudson Bay], and none have been discovered by the Company's servants who have travelled far inland to the distance of 1200 miles WSW from York Fort."[51]

Given the undependable mileages and vague landscape descriptions of Henday's journal, together with equivocal contemporary maps, a more reliable (though still far from certain) method of estimating the extent of Henday's explorations may be to count days of travel. If stages of the winterers' journeys are compared, then some idea of the their rate of travel between known points emerges. Distances to or from unknown points can then be projected. Between known points, Henday's progress up the "middle track" from York Fort to Basquea was equalled by Pink in 1769: their parties made this trip in twenty-six and twenty-four days respectively, while Cocking's group, hampered by illness, took thirty-five days. The return from Basquea to Hudson Bay took Henday almost as long as the trip inland (twenty-five days). Pink in 1770 and Cocking three years later each took eighteen days, although Pink in 1767 also took twenty-five days.[52]

From their various unknown embarcation points along the Saskatchewan River, these same winterers recorded the number of days it took them to reach an "upper French house," usually identified as Fort à la Corne, just below the forks, and the "lower French house" or Pedlars' house at Basquia (The Pas). Cocking's party built their canoes on the banks of the North Saskatchewan and embarked in mid-May, three days above the forks, that is, eleven days distant from The Pas. On the basis of Cocking's times, knowing that he spent the winter in the Eagle Hills, and assuming that Henday also embarked on the North Saskatchewan, we might be able to estimate very roughly how much farther upstream Henday's party built their canoes. Henday embarked on 28 April; he reached the upper house on 23 May and the lower house on 29 May, with five days during which his party did not travel. Henday's travelling time was thus twenty-two days' travel to the upper house and four days more to the lower house—twenty-six days in all. By his time between the French houses, Henday was moving twice as fast as Cocking; he was also much farther up the North Saskatchewan River than Cocking ever travelled. This comparison appears to leave the door open to the possibility that Henday had wintered very far west, or northwest, of the forks and the two trading houses.

A comparison can also be made with the number of days Pink travelled downstream each spring between 1766 and 1770. On his first journey Pink embarked in mid-May and took seventeen days to reach The Pas; on the next two trips he embarked much sooner, in early May and late April, and took much longer to arrive at The Pas—twenty-three days in 1768, more than twenty-seven in 1769. On his last trip in 1769-70, Pink embarked on 28 April, reached the upper house on 21 May and the lower house on 30 May, taking twenty-three days and nine days respectively—thirty-two days in all. Pink's final trip seems to have taken him much farther inland than the previous ones, and is comparable to Henday's record in 1755.[53] We can conclude that both Henday and Pink must have travelled much farther up the North Saskatchewan River than Cocking, who did not go beyond the Eagle Hills. But we must also note that Henday could not have travelled farther than Pink did during his 1769-70 season. Remarkably, no one has suggested that Pink ever came within sight of the Rocky Mountains.

Beyond this rough comparison of travel times, we are left with no way of determining Henday's route. We cannot know with any certainty how far west or north Henday travelled, what route he followed, or what places he visited between August 1754 and April 1755. Burpee, Morton and MacGregor have produced only conjecture, despite their confident declarations that the explorer can be followed "step by step" across the plains. Beyond the "French house" at The Pas, Henday's directions are vague, his distances misleading, his descriptions inadequate. We are not much farther ahead than the HBC London Committee in 1755: Henday's route remains problematic, one of the several unsolved puzzles of his journal.

Notes

1 HBCA A.11/114, Isham, instructions to Henday, 26 June 1754; cf. HBCA A.11/114, Isham, instructions to Henday, 19 February 1754; and HBCA B.239/a/40, E.2/6, E.2/4, E.2/11, Henday, journal, 28-29 June 1754.
2 But cf. A.11/114, Isham to the HBC London Committee, 4 August 1756: "Have sent the measuring wheel home being broke when rec^d." Cf also HBCA B.239/a/69, Cocking, journal, 7 August 1772: "The small compasses that I brought with me and which for handiness I have hitherto used; are

both become useless: at present a small Boat Compass which is very imperfect; these were the only ones I could take with me on this Journey." See Greenhood, 56-59, for descriptions of compasses. A scientific survey of Britain had its beginnings in the aftermath of Culloden: as an engineer of the British Army, General William Roy was employed as of 1747 to survey for roads into the Highlands. Sponsored and aided by the Royal Society, Roy planned and lobbied for a general survey; at Roy's death in 1791, the Duke of Richmond, Master of the Ordnance, assumed direction of the project.

3 HBCA A.6/9, HBC London Committee to Isham, 27 May 1755. Needless to say, the Committee's remark on Native mapping was ironic: among company employees, a belief that Natives were prone to lying was common— for example, HBCA E.2/1, Isham, "Observations on Hudson's Bay," f. 58r, p. 107: "The worst property that attends these Natives is their false information, for if you put a Question to them, as I have Done oft'n, they will answer to what I Desir'd." Such mistrust may have been far from warranted: the traders asked leading questions, underestimated the role of cultural difference in such "simple" informational exchanges, and thus misunderstood Natives who were doing their best to communicate what they knew. Scientific exploration was against hearsay: only the explorer's own measurements and impressions, recorded on the spot in his journal, could be relied on (see Belyea, "Inland Journeys, Native Maps"). By its reference to Native mapping, the Committee was condemning Henday's geographical findings in the strongest possible terms. Isham's reply deflected the issue to trade: "Altho Ind^n Information, we Are well Convinced, that the french Are actually <are> upon all quarters of us, otherwise where could those Indians Gett those french goods new, . . . if there was not a french Settlement near, now by Captn Hendeys Acc^t its for truth, Such french Housses, their is, in plenty" (HBCA A.114, Isham to the HBC London Committee, 2 September 1755).

4 HBCA A.6/9, HBC London Committee to Isham, 12 May 1756.

5 Burpee, "York Factory to the Blackfeet Country," 307.

6 Morton, 245-49.

7 MacGregor, 19-20.

8 Wilson, "Henday," 286. This text supersedes Wilson's earlier article, "Across the Prairies Two Centuries Ago."

9 Ruggles, in Harris, plate 58.

10 See Thomas Fisher Library, Tyrrell-Isbister correspondence, 26 March-24 December 1909; Tyrrell, 6-13; Morse, 36-40. As Morton was to do, Tyrrell distinguished the "middle track" leading from Hudson Bay to the area north of Lake Winnipeg from the "lower track" to Lake Winnipeg later followed by Smith and Waggoner (1757-58) and Tomison (1767-68). The "upper track" went up the Nelson River via Split Lake to Cumberland Lake.

11 Morton, 246; cf. MacGregor, 67.

12 Burpee, "York Factory to the Blackfeet Country," 315.

13 Ruggles, in Harris, 195n. Ruggles, *A Country So Interesting*, 10, 36-37, notes that Henday drew a map of the Saskatchewan River (since lost), but that he was considered a poor draughtsman.

14 MacGregor, 76.

15 MacGregor, 139.

16 MacGregor, 133.

17 MacGregor, 133.

18 MacGregor, 193-96.

19 MacGregor, 167.

20 MacGregor, 167.

21 Burpee, "York Factory to the Blackfeet Country," 340.

22 MacGregor, 168, 171. The provincial government of Alberta has installed a large sign near Innisfail, suggested in MacGregor's book as the place from which Henday viewed the "shining mountains." The sign reads, "ANTHONY HENDAY. As it lost an increasing share of the fur trade to French forts in the northwest, the Hudson's Bay Company tried to encourage more inland Indians to bring their furs to Hudson Bay. Anthony Henday, who had joined the Company in 1750 as a labourer and net-maker, volunteered to journey into the western interior. In June 1754, he left York Factory with a Cree trading party, travelling along river routes to a place near present-day Battleford, Saskatchewan, and on foot across the prairie to a large Blackfoot camp southeast of present-day Red Deer. The Blackfoot refused Henday's invitation to travel to the Bay to trade. They simply traded the best pelts at the French posts along the inland waterways and the remainder were traded to Cree middlemen. Returning to York Factory in June 1755, Henday reported the need for Hudson's Bay Company posts in the interior. Although Henday's journal contains no obvious reference to a mountain range, he may have been the first white person to set eyes on the Rocky Mountains' majestic peaks, perhaps from this very spot!" The sign summarizes Henday's year inland as researched, constructed, imagined and accepted by leading fur-trade historians.

23 Cf. Williams, "The Puzzle of Anthony Henday's Journal," 40: John Kabatoff's photograph of the front ranges appears as a frontispiece to the article; the caption reads, "This view of the mountains is from Carstairs, Alberta, the point farthest west reached by Henday on his journey."

24 MacGregor, 15, 198.

25 Burpee, "From York Fort to the Blackfeet Country," 314; Morton, 246, 250.

26 Wilson, "Henday," 287.

27 Ruggles, plate 58.

28 Burpee, *The Search for the Western Sea*, vii; cf. Ryan, 21-26, 41-42.

29 Burpee, *The Search for the Western Sea*, 130; cf. Morton's assertion, 463-69, that David Thompson, as representative of the North West Company, was engaged in a "race to the sea" with John Jacob Astor's Pacific Fur Company in 1812, discussed in Belyea, "'The Columbian Enterprise' and A. S. Morton."

30 Comparison of David Thompson's calculations from 1790 to 1812, which experts regard as reliable (see Gottfred), and current declinations (taken

from Newitt and Haines, map 10) shows there has been very little change of declination in western North America since the end of the eighteenth century. I have assumed a similarly slight rate of change from 1750 to the period of Thompson's observations.

31 HBCA B.239/a/40, Isham, "Remarks."

32 HBCA E.2/6, Henday, journal, 8 August 1754.

33 HBCA B.239/a/69, Cocking, journal, 19 August 1772.

34 HBCA B.239/a/40, Henday, journal, 27 December 1754, 17 January 1755, 18 March-27 April 1755.

35 HBCA E.2/12, Graham, "Observations on Hudson's Bay," pp. 648-49: "I have often reflected that the accounts given us by the men sent inland (Anthony Hendey and William Tomison excepted) were incoherent & unintelligible. I thought therefore that a sensible Person might Answer the purpose much better & make many observations that may be of utility . . . Mr Cocking readily offered himself for any service to promote your Interest. I have therefore sent him inland with a Leading Indian. He will give a rational Account of things, and endeavour to find the Lat. & Long. of the several places." See also Burpee, "York Factory to the Blackfeet Country," 309.HBCA B.239/a/69, Cocking, journal, 10 and 12 August 1772.

37 HBCA B.239/a/69, Cocking, journal, 29 July 1772.

38 HBCA B.239/a/69, Cocking, journal, 14 August 1772.

39 HBCA B.239/a/69, Cocking, journal and log, 21 September 1772.

40 Heidenreich, 121-37.

41 HBCA B.239/a/69, Cocking, journal, 4 July 1772.

42 Burpee, *The Search for the Western Sea*, 130.

43 HBCA B.239/a/40, E.2/6, E.2/4, Graham, note appended to Henday, journal, 11 October 1754, and 20 February 1755.

44 Williams, "The Puzzle of Anthony Henday's Journal," 56.

45 HBCA E.3/2, Fidler, journal, 20 November 1792.

46 HBCA B.239/a/69, Cocking, journal, 1 August 1772.

47 HBCA B.239/a/69, Cocking, journal, 29 August 1772.

48 HBCA G.2/8, "Moses Nortons Drt. of the Northern Parts of Hudsons Bay . . . " (1760); Warkentin and Ruggles, 86-89; Helm, "Matonabbee's Map"; Lewis; Belyea, "Inland Journeys, Native Maps"; Belyea, "Mapping the Marias"; Warhus.

49 HBCA G.2/17, Graham, "A Plan of Part of Hudson's-Bay . . . " (1774).

50 HBCA B.239/b/14, Isham to Joseph Isbister, 25 July 1756.

51 HBCA E.2/12, Graham, "Observations on Hudson's Bay," p. 4: cf. HBCA E.2/9, Graham, "Observations on Hudson's Bay," f. 4v, p. 2: "Wachee Mountains are not met with any where near the sea-shore and are very rare Inland."

52 HBCA B.239/a/56, 58, 61, 63, Pink, journals, 1766-67, 1767-68, 1768-69, 1769-70.

53 Tyrrell, 6-11, suggests that Pink spent the winters of 1767-68 and 1768-69 in the Moose Hills, and the winter of 1769-70 in the Eagle Hills; however, these locations do not tally with the distances in days' travel just enumerated. Russell, 105, summarizes Pink's four trips: "From [Pink's journals]

we learn of the wide spread of country he covered in his four journeys inland: from the mouth of the South Saskatchewan where he built his canoes in 1766 to the country between Vegreville and Edmonton where he wintered in 1769. Yet Pink always seemed to winter in the same general area—the open country either west or south of the Eagle Hills." For Henday's route Russell, 95, follows Wilson, who follows MacGregor in claiming that Henday travelled as far west as the Red Deer area and wintered near Edmonton.

Indians, Asinepoets and Archithinues

More than a decade before Henday left York Fort to winter inland, James Isham interviewed an Earchithinue man whose "Country Lyes on the back of this Land, and to the westward of Churchill River, where the Spaniards frequents those seas." Isham learned that the Earchithinues did not trade at the Bay forts because they were often at war with "Sinnepoets and other Indians," so he reasoned that enticing them to trade at the Bay "was not unpossable, if peace was Concluded betw^n them and other Nations." The western strangers, who "have no trade with any Nation as Yet," might be drawn into the English company's commercial network if an inland settlement were built or if a party of men were sent to their distant "Country."[1]

Isham's description of the continental interior reveals how little the Hudson's Bay Company knew of the vast region to which its charter lay claim. It also shows what aspects of "the back of this Land" interested the factors at the Bay forts. They were vaguely aware of Spanish settlement in California, but since Isham and his colleagues were in the fur business, their focus was on trade, hence on the inland Native groups who might contribute to higher returns. Isham later bowed to outside pressures and instructed Henday to enquire after an inland sea, but his own description of the hinterland was in terms of the people who lived in it. He listed eighteen "different Nation's or countery Indian's that usses the English settlements, in these norther^n parts": Nakawawuck, Moquo, Muskekowuck, Keiskachewon, poetuck, Cawcawquek, Nemau', wappuss, sinnepoet, Earchetinues, Missinnepee, Gristeen, pennesewagewan, Quashe'o, Pechepoethinue, wunnuskue, unnahathewunnutitto and Uchepowuck. In a note added to the main text of his "Observations," Isham also mentioned "the

---

Notes to this section are on pp. 363-68.

Eagl^d Ey'^{d} Indians which I never see, but are Sensible they are the same Nation as the sinepoats, or stone Indians, speaking the same Language."[2]

Isham identified Native groups in two ways: he first differentiated local Indians, trading Indians and those who "have no trade . . . as yet"; he further divided them into "nations." In 1755 Samuel Johnson defined "nation" in his new *Dictionary of the English Language* as "[a] people distinguished from another people; generally by their language, original [*sic*], or government. . . . A nation properly signifies a great number of families derived from the same blood, born in the same country, and living under the same government."[3] Johnson's criteria of distinction—language, kinship, sociopolitical organization and territory—are optional in the first part of the definition ("or"), cumulative in the second ("and"). There is thus some latitude in use of the term, ranging from the European state, for which all criteria were applicable, to non-European societies, which might be identifiable by only one characteristic: language, kinship *or* government. Isham's catalogue associates the Sinepoets and "Eagl^d Eye'^{d} Indians" because he thought they spoke the same language—a language other than that spoken by other groups known collectively to the Bay factors as Indians. This different language shared by the Sinepoets and "Eagl^d Eye'^{d} Indians" defined them as one nation, although they were distinguished from each other by their dress (or lack of it).[4] In contrast, "Earchithinue" was a single designation applied to a number of Native groups who were not related by blood, language or even temporary political alliance. The name is derived from the Cree word for "stranger"; it was applied to Natives living beyond the other groups already named, and who were not yet trading Indians. "Earchithinue" is therefore not the name of a nation. For the traders it was a temporary, purely commercial designation; for the trading Indians, it appears to have been a blanket term that could be reduced to a simple we/they differentiation.

Many of the eighteen nations Isham named spoke mutually understandable dialects of Cree, yet were differentiated in his list. Several of them were identified with geographical areas. For each group, the "Country" by which they were named appears to have been the farthest point from which they travelled to Hudson Bay, and the area in which they normally lived. The Keiskachewon, with whom Henday travelled, were a geographically identified group. As well as the names listed in his "Observations," Isham's canoe tallies kept between 1757 and 1761 mention "Sturgeon & pegsgoma" and the "Bloody Ind^s."[5] Isham's letter to Jacobs after Henday's departure announced that Henday was "at this time amongst the Pegogamy and

Earchithinue Indians."[6] It could be that the Pegogamy had become important traders in the decade that separated the letter from the "Observations," just as the "Bloody Ind[s]" were newcomers to the Bay. It is also possible that Isham's list in the "Observations" was not exhaustive at the time it was drawn up, and that Isham overlooked them in his summary because these two groups were poorly represented at the Bayside forts.

In contrast to Isham and later Graham, both of whom had only a few days' contact each summer with the trading representatives of inland Native groups, Henday and the winterers who followed him spent most of the year with certain bands, travelling with them as far as their "Country." The position from which the winterer observed Native people inland depended on the extent to which he was accepted within the group, and adapted to their way of life. The HBC winterers were not allowed to forget their "duty to God" and their job to protect and pursue the interests of a British business. The purpose of their presence inland was to smoke with "strangers"and exhort them to trade at the Bay, distribute presents and occasional supplies of ammunition and tobacco, and enquire about Canadian rivals, when possible keeping a detailed account of their movements and transactions.[7] This company mandate created an unbridgeable division of mentalities between the winterer and the band with whom he travelled. Cocking, for example, observed and carefully recorded details of Native ceremonies such as the Wippetanassowin (offerings to the earth at the beginning of winter), the Buffalo Pound calumet and "God songs" for cure of sickness, but he also remarked on the uselessness of such ceremonies. And he plainly pitied "a poor forlorn Frenchman" who had lived for seven years with Assinnee Poets.[8]

Henday's journey set certain precedents, but effectively it had none to follow. According to Isham's instructions, Henday was recommended to the care of Connawappa, "a trusty home Indian" from York Fort, and a "Captn or Leading Indian" named Attickosish. With Henday's help (his presence and his presents), this leader was supposed to persuade "Kisckachewon, Missinnippee, Earchithinue, Esinepoet or any other Country Indians" to trade at the Bay.[9] Very quickly, if we can believe B.239/a/40, Henday was active in persuading inland "leaders" to trade at the Bay. Near Basquia, within three weeks of setting out from Hudson Bay, he smoked with a leader for the French who "behaved very civilly," telling him about the open country that lay ahead. By early August Henday was invited to a feast at which he "was not behind hand" in his enjoyment of the occasion, and where he was "looked on as a Leader."[10] When he met with Asinepoets, some of whom had not been to the Bay for years (they found trading

with the French more convenient), Henday's sales pitch may have
been persuasive. They promised to go to York the following summer,
and according to the E.2/6 text, Henday returned "in Company with
20 Canoes Asinepoet Indians." Henday also encountered "5 tents of
mirthco (ie bloody) Indians" in September. Attickosish and Connawappa separated from Henday in late fall. Over the winter the HBC
employee urged his tent-mates to hunt for beaver and deplored their
laziness, while he trapped furs on his own account and improved his
hunting skills. His verbal "encouragement" was not heeded, even re-
sented. Essentially Henday remained an outsider, for whom the condition of acceptance was superficial conformity with Native habits and
culture. His wistful comment in E.2/4—"the Frenchmen are masters
of all the Indian languages & have greatly the advantage of us"—indicates the explorer's awareness of his own disabling ignorance and
inexperience.[11]

Henday's meeting with a large Archithinue band may or may not
have persuaded these equestrian buffalo hunters that their interest
lay in trade with the Hudson's Bay Company. On 14 October 1754,
Attickosish, Connawappa and Henday entered the Archithinue camp
of 200 tents where they smoked, feasted on buffalo tongues, and tried
to persuade the "Great Leader" to send two young men to the Bay.
Attikosish delivered the message from Isham while Henday distributed
trade goods, as prescribed in his instructions. Depending on which
text of Henday's journal is consulted, the Great Leader accepted or
refused the invitation from York. In the E texts the Archithinue leader
is said to have declined, explaining that his people followed the buffalo and could not paddle canoes. In B.239/a/40 Isham's supplementary "Remarks" insist on the exceptional and admirable qualities of
this equestrian culture which had "no trade with any [European]
Nation *as yet.*" Either way, the "significance" of Henday's journey
depends on the Archithinues' distinctive status. Following Isham and
their own impermeable romanticism, historians have expatiated on
the Archithinues' prosperous self-sufficiency while overlooking the
important part in these people played the fur trade network. Already
they were implicated in the fur trade, as hunters and trappers.

The groups whom Henday, Pink and Cocking accompanied transported the Archithinues' furs to the Bay forts. Bands of Archithinues
who camped near boat-builders along the Saskatchewan River each
spring were there to trade, albeit through middlemen and for used
goods.[12] At one of the canoe-building camps the Archithinues "Joined
the bloody Ind^s" whom Henday had met in September but whom, following Isham, he had likened to Asinepoets. "I could find no difference between them and the Asinepoet Indians," his journal reads,

"only they do not cover their private parts, they are the only Natives that ever I seed here or other parts that does not conceal their naked-ness, Indians [Henday's companions] seemed to be afraid of them."[13] Henday does not comment on their language. Like some Asinepoets and unlike the Archithinues, at least five tents of the "bloody Ind[s]" could paddle in canoes and go down with Henday to Hudson Bay. The E texts also note that the Archithinues "have other Indians beyond them who are their Enemies, they are also called Archithinues and by what I can learn talks the same Language and hath the same customs &c."[14]

The same assortment of Native groups mentioned in Henday's journal is found in the records of Pink and Cocking. Like Henday, the later winterers smoked with Sinnapoits/Assinnee Poets shortly after reaching the prairies, and came across Yeartchethynnewock/Yeachi-thinnees farther west. The groups of "Jndaines" and Sinnapoits tend-ed to be small (5 to 20 tents), although Pink saw a combined group of "Fiftey Tents of Jndaines Twenty of Sinnapoits" assembled to build canoes in the spring of 1769. These canoe-building Sinnapoits con-trasted with 150 tents of Sinnapoits encountered in August 1769, "a great Nomber that Never se the Forte the Cannot paddle."[15] Pink also named "A Bodey of Jndaines Called Black footed" with whom his group pounded buffalo, and "a Bodey of Yearchethynnawock Called Mithquothanawock."[16] In contrast to Henday, who thought the "mirthco or Bloody Ind[s]" indistinguishable from Asinepoets except for their "nakedness," Pink classified the Mithquothanawock as Archithinues, though he gave no reason. The winterers tried to fit the people they had just met into the three categories they had learned at the Bay: Indian, Asinepoet and Archithinue. Since Henday's Mirthco and Pink's Mithquothanawock were not Indians, they had to be forced into one of the other two categories.

Cocking met Yeachithinnees in December 1772, as he moved between the Mikesew Wachy (Eagle Hills) and Sacketakow Wachy (Thickwood Hills). He had heard about "their Enemies the Snake Indians" who raided from the south, and was shown "a Coat of war which . . . formerly belonged to the Snake Indians; several folds of Leather stitched strongly together in the form of a European Coat without Sleeves, Arrow proof."[17] In Graham's E.2/11 abstract of this journal, Cocking is shown "a Coat without sleeves six fold leather quilted, used by the Snake tribe to defend them against the Arrows of their adversaries"; a month later, Cocking describes the Archithinues he met as dressed in "Jackets of Moose leather six fold, quilted, and without sleeves."[18] It is evident that in a few pages the copyist has transferred a curious, distinguishing characteristic of one Native group, the enemy "Snake Indians," to another, the Yearchithinnee "friends" with whom Cocking's group pounded buffalo. In the same abstracted entry, Cocking is made to observe that the Yeachithinnees are "well mounted on light sprightly Animals . . . [and] appear to me more like Europeans than Americans," a phrase that recalls Henday's remark in the E.2/11 text of his journal: "These brave Natives [the Archithinues] swimmed their horses across the river, they look more like Europeans than Indians."[19] This textual pattern of borrowing and copying from one journal to another does not inspire confidence in the exactitude of descriptions that have come down to us. Even so, the winterers' journals, taken collectively, present a picture of inland groups more complex and varied than that of Isham's and Graham's "Observations."

Meeting with Yeachithinees in December 1772, Cocking welcomed a chance to learn what distinctions these people made within the blanket term "strangers" assigned to them by Cree middlemen and the English traders. Henday had merely noted that there were "other Indians beyond" the Archithinues he met in October 1754;[20] with the help of an interpreter who was "thoroughly acquainted with the Assinnee Poets . . . [and] that tongue," Cocking was able to question his Yeachithinnee hosts and record no fewer than eight subdivisions:

> These Natives are called Powestick Athinnewach, or Water-Fall Indians. The People I am with inform me there are four Nations more which go under the name of Yeachithinnee Indians with whom they are in friendship, Viz^t Mithcoo-Athinneewock or Blood Indians: Koskiketew Watheessituck, or black-foot Indians; Pigonew Athinnewock, or muddy Water Indians and Sussewuck, or woody country Indians. Their Enemies also go under the general name of Yeachithinnee Indians, four Nations. Kanapick Athinneewock, or Snake Indians; Wahetee, or Vault Indians; Kuttunnayewuck; and Nah-puck-Ustiquanock, or flat Head Indians so called they tell me from their foreheads being very flat.[21]

In this account, neither the general Yeachithinnee grouping nor the subgroup distinctions can be explained according to a single characteristic (language, kinship, alliance or territory). "Water-fall," "muddy Water" and "woody country" are geographical names; "flat Head" refers to physiognomy, "black-foot" to dress. "Snake Indians" are the enemies most feared. In Cocking's list the Natives' own criteria of relationship and distinction jostle with the winterers' conceptions formed and modified by Isham and Graham.

Cocking's account, written almost twenty years after Henday made his first trip inland, repeats many elements of Henday's meeting with the Archithinues—the strangers' hospitality, their dress, their tobacco and ceremonial smoking of it, and their refusal to travel to the Bay, "these People being entirely unacquainted with Canoes." Cocking's journal also registers certain changes, however. While Henday and Pink were obliged to buy pack animals from Assinipoets, Cocking's own companions (Indians) not only pounded but ran buffalo: in August 1772, "Indians killed ten [buffalo] some with Guns & others with Bows, hunting on Horseback."[22] Quite possibly, the account of mid-September buffalo hunting in the E texts of Henday's journal is a description dependent to some degree on reports of such hunts that postdated Henday's mid-century experience.[23] Dating change in Native cultures is difficult not only because it is invariably documented as an outsider's impression, but also because the terms used to designate these cultures are more often than not imprecise and *un*changing. By the time of Cocking's first journey inland, riding horses no longer served to distinguish Archithinues from other Native groups. Yet in the E.2/12 volume of his "Observations," written long after Cocking's return, Graham still refers to only the Archithinues as "these Equestrian Indians." The Asinipoets, he notes carefully, like to steal horses from the Archithinues "which serve to convey their baggage about the country: but I must mention that they never ride on them." In contrast, Graham recalls that "the Company's servants who have wintered inland with the Natives have seen above three hundred Archithinue Indians on horseback in one body."[24] The splendid October meeting described in Henday's journal is again evoked. But by the time Graham was writing E.2/12, horses had modified hunting and travelling patterns of all the plains groups.

In HBC journals, correspondence and memoirs, the term "Archithinue" gradually took on a new distinction, no longer referring simply to little-known or unknown Natives, but to specific groups on the western plains, while "stranger," the English translation, defined the trade relationship. More than once Cocking remarked in his journal that soon they would meet up with "Yeachithinnee Indian Friends . . . with whom these people [his companions] are in friendship." Cocking also smoked with "Assinnee Poet Strangers," urging them to trap furs and visit the Bay forts, "most of them being Strangers; but they were seemingly unwilling, saying they were unacquainted with the method of Building Canoes and Paddling."[25] The association in Cocking's statement between "Strangers" and an ignorance of canoes associates the Assinnee Poets with characteristics that formerly distinguished Archithinues from other Native groups, including Asinepoets who traded at the Bay forts; at the same time Cocking's Yeachithinnees had become "Indian Friends."

At York Fort and Severn House, Graham's direct contact with Native groups was restricted to their representatives who traded at the Bay. But unlike Isham, he could supplement his own experience and improve on Isham's categories by consulting the winterers' reports. How much he learned from the winterers, how much he shaped their expectations, and how much he modified their journal descriptions are of course open questions. In his "Observations," Graham undertook "to enumerate the various nations with their tribes which resort to the settlements . . . and specify what part of America is the usual residence of each." As well as referring to "nations" he introduced the term "tribe," which Johnson defined as "a distinct body of the people as divided by family or fortune, or any other characteristick." Johnson noted that "tribe" was "often used in contempt."[26] Graham did not treat the two terms as synonyms. In the E.2/6 text of his Observations he referred to "the Archithinue Indians and Asseenepoet Indians" as "tribes" (each a "distinct body" of the "Indian" people), but a few lines later he corrected his use of the term: "the Aforementioned tribes or more properly nations."[27] Cultural as well as physical distance could have contributed to his choice of a more generous and respectful designation for the Archithinues and Asseenepoets. In his E.2/5 text, Graham contrasted "the inland trading Natives" with "the worn out degenerated home Natives" who lived all year close to the Bay forts.

For Graham, "tribe" was primarily a subdivision of "nation." His list contained forty tribes grouped into six nations: Keishkatchewan, Assinepoet, Wechepowuck, Archithinue, Nakawawuck and Oupeeshepow. Graham normalized their names and slotted them into easily recognizable categories. The winterers had begun this trend towards descriptive and relational simplification by reporting on certain prescribed aspects of Native life: language, dress, remarkable customs and organization for war. Graham thus distinguished one nation from another according to language, "usual residence," trading role and alliance/enmity. The nations which figured on Graham's list were his own constructions imposed on the largely self-defined tribes. Of particular note is Graham's modification of the sense of the Native groups' "usual residence" to conform with the European concept of territorial possession. His "Plan of Part of Hudson's-Bay" drawn in 1774 includes the names of his nations: Nekawawuck, Northern and Southern Keskachewans, Eastern and Western Asenepoets, as well as Ateemouspecky or Dog-Rib Indians farther north.[28] The "Country" of each nation is demarcated by territorial borders drawn as heavy lines. This rationalization of Native groups and their assignment to discrete territories provided a systematic, Europeanized understanding of Native societies on which subsequent traders such as Edward Umfreville and Alexander Mackenzie built their recollections and admonitions. In turn, Umfreville and Mackenzie paved the way for the categories and theories of twentieth-century anthropologists and ethnohistorians.

Of the western nations in Graham's enumeration, the Keishkatchewan were the greatest contributors to HBC trade. Graham remarks that their response to contact with European trade was "gradually to retire farther inland until they came amongst the Buffalo." Although they were said to have migrated from the coast of Hudson Bay to the continental interior, "yet the language has undergone no alteration." The Assinepoets, whose "Language is quite different from the Keiskatchewan or Na heth eway tongue," were "more powerful and numerous."[29] Graham was personally acquainted with these two groups because they visited the Bay forts annually. Knowledge of other Native groups south and west of Hudson Bay could be found in the winterers' journals and gleaned from news exchanged with other factors.

> These Indians [says Graham of the Archithinues] possess an extensive Country beyond that of the Asinepoets to the Southward and Westward; they have plenty of Buffalo, and never eat Beaver or Fish; have no water carriage, and know nothing about managing a Canoe; some Englishmen have been sent amongst them to induce them to come down to the Forts; but they answered, that, they lived very well; know not how to manage a Canoe, nor were willing to undergo the inconveniences of such a journey: however one or two have had the curiosity to come to York Fort but never repeated the visit.[30]

Graham mentions the Archithinues' spring trade, which also figures largely in Henday's journal: "They are expert hunters, and procure many Furrs which they exchange at a dear rate with the Keiskatchewans for Guns, hatchets, and other goods."[31] Graham's interest is narrow: his descriptions include only those Native traits and circumstances that were relevant to trade. He dismisses Cocking's list of enemy Archithinues: "We have advice of other Nations beyond these, but as they contribute nothing towards the Trade of Hudson's Bay, and the accounts are very imperfect and dissatisfactory, I shall say nothing more about them."[32] Thus Cocking's detailed information was again reduced, in Graham's abstract, to Henday's vague indication that there were "other Indians beyond" the strangers he met. It is ironic that Graham's commercial interest—his efforts to organize the company's trading network as an outreach from the Bay forts—should have acquired lasting value as anthropological documentation.

The description of inland Native groups in Edward Umfreville's long polemical pamphlet, published in 1790 and entitled *The Present*

State of Hudson's Bay, repeats Graham's exposition and simplifies further. Umfreville, like Graham, was employed at the Bay as a "writer" (clerk and accountant) for eleven years, but saw the plains for himself in the 1770s. His book contains detailed descriptions of inland Natives after traders had built posts up the Saskatchewan River, but prior to the devastating smallpox epidemic of 1781. Umfreville distinguished seven kinds of Indians with whom the English traded: Nehethawa, Assinne-poetuc, Fall, Sussee, Black-feet, Paegan and Blood Indians. Like Graham, he devoted most of his discussion to the Nehethawa, since these people were best known to the trade, and remarked that the names he gave to more distant people were often those assigned to them by the Nehethawa.[33] Umfreville's list corresponds to Graham's western nations and the groups identified in the winterers' journals: Indians, Asinepoets and the four friendly Archithinue groups noted by Cocking. Umfreville defined the tribes he listed according to language and speculated on their origins; for example,

> Ne-heth-aw-a . . . is the name they give to themselves, and their language. They are scattered over a very extensive country, for which reason they do not appear to be numerous, but were the different tribes to be collected, this nation would hold much greater influence among others than they seem to do.—I am of opinion, that the Ochipawa Indians . . . inhabiting the countries to the south-eastward, sprung from the same original stock with the Ne-heth-aw-as. The great affinity of their language seems to confirm this conjecture . . . These two nations have always been in strict alliance with each other. . . . But it is a certain fact, that when the French possessed Canada, they never named any nation of Indians with propriety. [These] people they termed Crees; but their doing so is known only to themselves, unless it was from the Ochipawas calling them Cristineaux, which may probably be the case.[34]

For details Umfreville relied on Graham's "Observations," just as Graham seems to have relied on the winterers' reports. With each new formulation, puzzling details and anomalies were set aside in favour of categorical generalizations. Umfreville was intent on describing the "collected . . . nation," not the "different tribes." He might be thought commendable for his caution in relaying less-than-dependable information, much as contemporary cartographers were considered scientifically responsible because they left blank spaces for unexplored territory: "On the other, or western side of the Stony Mountain are many nations of Indians, utterly unknown to us, except by Indian information, which we cannot enough rely on to justify us in advancing for facts, what may, perchance, be founded in error and misrepresentation."[35] Unfortunately Unfreville's arrogance in mistrusting "Indian information" resulted in the trader's refusal to record what he was told about far western Natives by those Natives themselves or their longtime neighbours.

Alexander Mackenzie's introduction to his *Voyages from Montreal* drew heavily on Umfreville's pamphlet, as a similarity of content and even turns of phrase reveals. This introduction contains a brief, schematic account of the plains Native groups engaged in the fur trade.[36] It describes the "extent of country" into which traders had penetrated and lists the human inhabitants along with the flora and fauna. According to Mackenzie, there were ten plains tribes: Algonquins, Nadowasis and their relatives the Assiniboins, Knisteneaux, Fall or Big-bellied Indians, Stone Indians, Sarcees, Picaneaux, Blood-Indians and Black-Feet Indians. Mackenzie dispensed with the earlier distinction between "nation" and "tribe," using the terms interchangeably and naming each tribe in association with the country it occupied. At the same time, he stated that seven of the ten tribes had migrated or were still migrating from one region to another.[37] Oddly enough, he did not include the Knisteneaux among those tribes on the move, although Graham gives as common knowledge the retreat of the Keiskatchewan from Hudson Bay.

Twentieth-century anthropologists and historians have continued the simplifying, solidifying trend of the fur-trade summaries: plains "tribes," their "tribal range," their "core areas" or zones of "occupation," and their history of migration are now established terms and categories of modern anthropological research. There is some skittishness about using the term "tribe," but no other word or concept has been adopted in its place. As editor of the *Handbook of North American Indians: Subarctic* (which includes discussion of Cree living between the coast of Hudson Bay and Lake Winnipeg), June Helm considers

> the identification and demarcation of "tribes" . . . [to be] in most cases a matter of judgment. . . . Any set of families immediately coresident as a local group had wider sociocultural affiliations and identities with like, neighbouring groups, but there was no political integration or unity among them, so this often-invoked criterion cannot be used in this region to delimit sets of local and regional groups as "tribes." For some sets there is enough similarity of dialect, social contact and amity, and common historical experience among the units to justify readily enough their inclusion in one "tribe," "people," or "nation."[38]

The reader is left wondering which "cases," if any, are so certainly defined and demarcated as not to be "a matter of judgment." Helm plays with the same criteria of language, kinship and political organization by which Johnson defined "nation" even as she uses "nation," "people" and "tribe" as synonyms.

The implication of this discussion of tribal organization is that while there is no defining authoritative structure, there are temporary instances of propinquity, contact and association among "like, neighbouring groups." But this is to beg the question: what after all constitutes likeness, similarity, commonality? Are we to imagine that of a number of "neighbouring groups" in a certain area, only "like" groups would interact, cooperate or form alliances? Simplification of relationships among Native groups always tends to "tribal" categorization, even among anthropologists. Each volume of the *Handbook of North American Indians* opens with a map, baldly labelled in the *Subarctic* volume as a "Key to Tribal Territories" and very reminiscent of Graham's "Plan of Part of Hudson's-Bay." A disclaimer accompanies the map, announcing that it is merely a "diagrammatic guide":

> Tribal units are sometimes arbitrarily defined, subdivisions are not mapped, no joint or disputed occupations are shown . . . the ranges mapped for different tribes often refer to quite different periods, and there may have been many intervening movements, extinctions, and changes in range."[39]

However, the disclaimer cannot overrule what the map clearly shows: the cartographic scheme of tribes and their territories denies Helm's verbally expressed scruples and persuasively reinforces the timeworn concepts. As Morton Fried suggested in 1975, the tribal territory is not foreign to the European state but a reflection of it.[40]

Divisions of Cree, Assiniboin, Peigan, Shoshoni and others, reported and reiterated for centuries, have become so familiar as to go unquestioned. Moreover, recent adoption of traditional names has not modified the concept of tribe for Natives any more than for anthropologists. For example, in an *Encyclopedia of North American Indians* published in 1996, the entry "Blackfoot," written by Darrell Robes Kipp (identified as Blackfoot), specifies that the traditional self-designation is Nizitapi: the real people. In describing his people, Kipp echoes the HBC description of Archithinues: "The Blackfeet were people of the plains and buffalo. They never used canoes or ate fish." Kipp explains the aversion to canoes and fish not in material terms (ignorance of paddling, dietary preference, self-sufficiency) but as spiritual respect:

> To the Blackfeet, rivers and lakes hold a special power because they are inhabited by the Suyitapis, the Underwater People. Painted lodge covers, medicine bundles, and other sacred items were transferred to the tribe from the Suyitapis. In turn, their power and domain are respected by the tribe. Today, the [Montana] reservation waterways and lakes are touted as

premier fishing spots. Yet most tribal members maintain the traditional ban on fishing.[41]

The Archithinues' steady refusal to take to canoes, recorded as early as Isham's "Observations," is thus illuminated. Nevertheless Kipp employs the term "tribe" no fewer than three times in this one short passage. He explains how tribal membership is defined in terms of lineage measured by "blood quantum," a criterion of identification "inspired by the Bureau of Indian Affairs." Despite their own name and the maintenance of traditional beliefs, Kipp's people have accepted the name "Blackfoot" and the concept of tribe imposed by an outside authority. In Canada, the old designations of Blackfoot, Blood and Peigan have given way to Siksika, Kainaiwa and Piikani; the Sarcee tribe traditonally associated with the "Blackfoot Confederacy" is now called Tsuu T'ina First Nation. A current website groups the four renamed tribes of the Confederacy with the Stoney tribe as the five signatories of Treaty Seven, negotiated in 1877. Recent self-definitions have not obviated the European concept of "tribe."[42]

The process of hardening earlier remarks and observations into systematic, identifying categories has produced widely accepted if problematic theories. The most tenacious is the thesis of eighteenth-century Cree expansion from the Canadian Shield onto the plains. It can be traced back to Mackenzie's assertions that plains Natives had moved quite recently to the countries they occupied in his time; beyond Mackenzie to Umfreville's contention, based on affinity of language, that Nethewas and Ochipawas must be related; and even farther back to Graham's remark that the hunt for furs around Hudson Bay had forced the Keiskatchewan nation "gradually to retire inland." Anthropologists have filled out the picture: armed with trade guns, Cree middlemen are supposed to have displaced Natives to the west who were equipped with traditional weapons and weakened by European diseases, particularly the smallpox epidemic of 1781. The modern Cree expansion thesis was explicitly formulated as early as 1932, by Diamond Jenness in his *Indians of Canada*:

> As soon as they obtained firearms from Hudson Bay, [the Cree] expanded westward and northward, so that by the middle of the eighteenth century they controlled northern Manitoba and Saskatchewan as far as the Churchill river, all northern Alberta, the valley of Slave river, and the southeastern part of Great Slave Lake. Some of them had even raided up the Peace river into the Rocky mountains, and others down the Mackenzie . . . The acquisition of firearms by surrounding tribes, and a terrible epidemic of smallpox that devastated them in 1784 [sic] checked their further expansion.[43]

Mandelbaum's historical and ethnographic study of *The Plains Cree*, published in 1940 and reprinted several times in the last fifteen years, relies on the expansion thesis to explain "why and how Cree culture was changed when some of the Cree changed their habitat, economy and general environment." Mandelbaum is sure that Cree reached the western interior and evolved culturally much later than Jenness estimates:

> The Plains Cree live on the northern edge of the Great Plains, chiefly in the Park Belt, the transitional area between the forest and plains. They have occupied this territory only since the beginning of the nineteenth century, for it was formerly inhabited by the Assiniboin and Gros Ventre in the eastern part and by the Blackfoot in the western section. . . . the tribal range may be defined in terms of the valleys of the Qu'Appelle, the lower North Saskatchewan, and the lower Battle rivers. . . . The northern limits of the Park Belt also marked the boundary between the Plains Cree and their congeners, the Western Wood Cree.[44]

Mandelbaum builds on the link between tribes and territories that was cemented in Umfreville's and Mackenzie's publications. Ray's *Indians in the Fur Trade* makes use of the expansion thesis, but pushes the period of plains acculturation back to 1720.[45] John Milloy's study, titled (like Mandelbaum's) *The Plains Cree*, briefly and unquestioningly reiterates Mandelbaum's assertion that Cree movement onto the plains began in the 1730s and continued for the rest of the century.[46] Laura Peers traces the western movement of Ojibwa in the late eighteenth century, though she suggests a Native relationship to the fur trade that is much subtler than the Cree expansion thesis of Jenness, Mandelbaum and Milloy:

> Dependence . . . is a simple term for a complex series of changes and choices that enmeshed Native peoples in the fur trade. The Ojibwa, like other Native peoples, chose to participate in the fur trade at this level for their own ends—even if some of those motivations and goals were products of cultural changes set in motion by the fur trade itself. . . . the Ojibwa were intertwined in the fur trade, were changed by it, and were to some degree reliant on it; but they were also stimulated by the aspects of it that resonated with their own goals and perceptions of the world.[47]

Nevertheless Peers insists on a continuing identity: "Though their way of life changed, in some cases drastically, they were still Ojibwa. Even those bands that adopted 'plains' cultural features did so as one dons a new coat."[48] Thus there are differences of historical detail, but all of these scholars favour a linguistic basis of definition. They identify "Cree" and "Ojibwa" as large social networks who speak dialects of the same language, despite other cultural differences between the plains groups and forest communities of the Canadian Shield.

In *Eighteenth-Century Western Cree and Their Neighbours*, Dale Russell criticizes the thesis of Cree expansion as "fundamentally misconceived." Russell maintains that the common error, which has permeated previous discussions of the history of the Cree, can be avoided. This is the mistake of treating any and all western Cree groups as being alike. . . . [I]n the identity of, and their relations with, their immediate neighbours, the faunal resources which they utilised, and in their exposure to the fur traders . . . their specific histories vary widely, and it is not useful, except on a most general level, to speak of "the Cree moving west" or "the dependency of the Cree on the fur trade" without specifying which Cree groups are meant.[49]

Russell remarks that much of the evidence for movement of the Cree is simply the result of European penetration from east to west. It was not the Native groups who moved west but advancing Europeans who put them on record: the impression of migration was produced by "displaced observation."[50] Russell's stated aim is to show is that the earliest European observers found Cree already living in the western interior—having migrated from the east, certainly, but not at the time of or because of the fur trade. Hence the importance of Henday's journal, the earliest record of European travel into this region. "It is most surprising," Russell comments, "that Mandelbaum . . . fails to discuss the lengthy journal of Anthony Henday . . . who . . . shows that in 1754, the Cree and Assiniboin were not only wintering in the Red Deer and Edmonton areas but were accompanying local Indians, probably Blackfoot or Gros Ventre, on their raids further to the southwest."[51]

By referring in detail to the journals of Henday and other HBC men who wintered west of Lake Winnipeg and up the Saskatchewan River, Russell demonstrates convincingly enough that the Indians who traded at the Bay between 1754 (Henday's first journey) and 1773 (Cocking's winter in the Eagle Hills) lived for three seasons out of four on the prairies and in the parkland farther north and west. However, despite his criticism of the "common error" of tribal generalization, Russell himself falls into it time and time again. In the sentence quoted above, for example, he refers to Cree, Assiniboin, Blackfoot and Gros Ventre—that is, to anthropologically defined tribal categories rather than to specific communities. Nor does Russell question the association of tribe and territory; instead he recognizes tribal subdivisions and determines the "location" and "distribution" of each. What Russell successfully disproves is Mandelbaum's timing of the migration from eastern forest to western plains, and its cause. But he does not dismantle the concept of "tribe" fundamental to the expansion thesis, a concept based on language regardless of geographical separation, acculturation or immediately operative social structures. Out of long habit and common practice, anthropologists continue to use the tribal designations inherited from Graham, Umfreville and Mackenzie; even Russell fails to break free of the conceptual limits they impose.

In order to rethink the social structures and relationships of western Native groups so that the puzzling anomalies of the winterers' journals are not papered over with familiar anthropological labels, we need to read their texts without the reassurance of the tribal identifications and descriptions so readily furnished in editors' notes and commentaries. To explain that Henday travelled with a Cree band, smoked with Assiniboin leaders and tried to entice Blackfoot young men down to Hudson Bay misleads more than it enlightens: the tribal divisions named in this explanation seriously distort the winterers' own accounts of plains cultures. Nor do the winterers' journals attest to a wave of Cree newcomers whose presence west of Lake Winnipeg and up the Saskatchewan River had the domino effect of pushing other tribes south and farther west. Instead the journals indicate that Native groups were organized in very small units which congregated, then separated, at various times of the year. Moreover, the pattern of association was not limited to "like neighbouring groups" as Helm suggests, but also involved the frequent interaction of unlike groups, distinguished from each other by all the characteristics that have defined "nation" and "tribe."

The basic unit of social organization seems to have been the family, or household—about eight persons occupying a single tent.[52] When Henday reached the "muscuty plains" he travelled with "the families," in a crowd numbering more than four hundred; by early December, he was living with only one family of twelve people: in all, three men with nine women and children. The Natives he had accompanied from York did not reassemble until they met to build canoes in March. In contrast, the Archithinues are mentioned only on occasions when they came together in large numbers—two hundred tents in October, almost three hundred in May. Isham attributed the characteristics of a European state to the Archithinues' fall reunion: "there are as much discipline observed as in some other parts of y[e] world: their Monarch or King is obliged by all, he is seated att times on the throne where he gives out orders to his officers for his Men . . . some on y[e] paroll, others Rideing round the borders of their Country to see if any Enemies are att hand."[53] Only B.239/a/40 gives such an impression, however; the E texts of Henday's journal present the Archithinue camp as a meeting of chiefs and an agglomeration of smaller social units which dispersed once more as Henday's party moved away.

The journals of Pink and Cocking describe a similar pattern of aggregation and separation for all the Native groups they met, including the Archithinues. While Isham insisted that Archithinues were "quite different to all other Ind[s] in Regard to their Customs, manners, Behaviour &c,"[54] Pink and Cocking considered the Yearctchathynawock/Yeachithinnees together with the other Native groups they met while they were inland. Pink noted on 24 December 1769 that "this Day Came and put up By us a Bodey of Jndaines Called Black footed," and a week later "we Mooved a way with the Black Footed Jndaines whare the ware a Gowing to a pound for Pouning of Bofflow."[55] In October 1772 Cocking's party travelled to an old Yachithinnee pound; six weeks later twenty-one tents of Yachithinnees arrived and camped on the other side of the pound; the men of both parties smoked and then everyone tried to drive buffalo into the pound, without much success. In March Cocking's companions camped by another pound together with four tents of Neheathaways and twenty tents of Assinnee Poets; this time a number of buffalo were slaughtered, the calumet was smoked, and the meat was divided equitably among all the households: "The pound belonging to the Assinee Poets they had the Produce at their direction, altho the others sometimes drove the Beasts into it; but the Buffalo were seemingly impartially Divided according to the number of People."[56]

The winterers' journals attest to a surprising degree of cooperation exhibited by people who were not related by blood or marriage, who did not speak the same language or practice the same customs. Building a pound, driving the animals, killing them and preserving the meat required the most complex social organization of any sequence of activities in traditional plains Native life.[57] Moreover, the elaborate network of fur-trade relationships that extended over plains and parkland by the time of Henday's journey—a network which nominated trade leaders, specified hunters and middlemen, and decided between French/Pedlar and English interests—was clearly based on previous trading relationships.[58] Both pre- and post-contact trading networks must have relied on this elevated degree of intercultural cooperation. And to ensure the organizational flexibility necessary for such cooperation, in all of the various Native groups described in the journals any assembly beyond the basic household unit appear to have been temporary. These groups fluctuated in size but were always much smaller than the tribal organization suggested by the Bayside memorialists and later commentators. A map drawn in 1801 by a "Blackfoot chief" named Ackomokki, copied by Peter Fidler, locates the "Different Tribes that inhabit on the East & west side of the Rocky Mountains with . . . the Number of tents." The "Tribes" that are named on this map do not correspond at all to the tribal names and large territories assigned by Mackenzie, Umfreville and twentieth-century anthropologists. Instead the names more closely resemble band identifications—for example, the Mud House Indians, the Wrinkled Indians, the Grey Fox Indians, the Hairy, Rib and Scabby Indians, the Grass Tent Indians.[59] The winterers observed larger, culturally homogeneous "tribal" groups only as seasonal aggregations, of short duration, and in not a few instances prompted by the fur trade itself: reuniting the families at the eastern edge of the plains, assembling to build canoes for the return journey to Hudson Bay, meeting the canoe-builders to trade with them as middlemen, travelling as far as the French/Pedlar posts.

By the mid-eighteenth century, all of the plains groups were implicated to some degree in the fur trade. Isham's rough classification of home Indians, inland trading Indians and Archithinues who "have no trade with any Nation as yet," was the limited view from Hudson Bay. Even the impressive Archithinues of Henday's journal met the canoe brigades hundreds of miles from their "pleasant country" in order to exchange goods with the middlemen. The Asinepoets' ambiguous position—some going to the Bay, some saying (like the Archithinues) that they could not paddle canoes—continued for the twenty-year period between the journeys of Henday and Cocking. The Asinepoets' promises were also ambiguous: Cocking was sure, for example, that the Natives he smoked with traded with the pedlars, though they denied it, and that they would not travel to York, though they vowed they would: "they are such notorious Liers there is no believing them."[60] The variant texts of Henday's journal project this ambiguity onto the Archithinues in their record of conversations between the "Great Leader," Attickosish and Henday: the B.239/a/40 success version records the promise, while the E texts (and Cocking's journal as well) dramatize the Archithinues' non-appearance at York in a speech of refusal. This was not a refusal to trade, however, as proved by the brisk business of the middlemen and the traders from Canada.

Paradoxically, various kinds and levels of cooperation, including adaptation to the requirements of the fur trade might not have been possible without the frequent skirmishes that characterized Native warfare. The Bay factors thought otherwise, and instructed the winterers to discourage war in favour of hunting for furs and trading at the forts.[61] Although the best furs were taken in winter, war and the journey to Hudson Bay competed for the months of fine weather. As Henday and all his successors observed, tensions could and often did run high. Two Asinepoets reported that Archithinues had killed six Indians in September 1754; in December Henday was told that the Archithinues would kill his tent-mates if they hunted in that country; two months later, "4 Ind^n men brought ye news of 30 Earchithinues & 7 of our Ind^s were killed, and that they were going to Warr again, for they Came away to Acquaint all the Ind^s of it . . . 2 Indian tents was pitch beside us, brought 3 Earchithinues they had taken in Warr, and 3 Scalps."[62]

Many of the fuller entries in Pink's journal mention how wary each of these plains groups was of the others, and how easily friends could become enemies. On 13 May 1768, as Pink was returning to York by canoe, two hundred tents of Yeartchathynawock decamped from the river side, "being in fear of these Jndaines as they were at warr wth them some years ago."[63] This avoidance contrasts with the lively trading that took place when Henday's Indian party met Archithinues along the river in May 1755. Thirteen years later Pink's own group was equally cautious: "The Jndaines heare Now Constantley Keep garde in the night time for Fears of the other Jndaines Called Yeartchethynnewock and Cenepick we ethynewock for Feare they should Come up on them all on a Suden in the night time."[64] Pink's names and description indicate that the equestrian people his party feared were probably a group of the enemy Archithinues later figuring in Cocking's list:

> j Heare by thes Jndaines that to the South and SWwarde of whare we are now, thare is plentey of Beaver and Woulves, Neare hand, But being allways in Feare of the Jndaines Called Kene,pick,we,e,thyn,na,wock is the Reason that the Jndaines Dos not Gow after them, the Contrey Quite Open and those Jndaines Southwarde having all horses is the Reason the Jndaines that j am With are in Fear of them.[65]

Russell argues that "the fear [which Pink reports] seems based more on caution than the actual presence of these groups," since Pink's group was in its own territory and the "dangerous country" lay to the west and south.[66] But caution is a behaviour prompted by fear, and Russell's assumption that the Kenepickweethynnawock were at a considerable distance is based on the anthropological association of tribe and territory. At the same time of year Henday had recorded that "the Archithinues had killed, and scalped 6 Indians, and that there were a great many nigh us."[67] There is no reason to understand the passage from Pink's journal other than literally: Pink reported "Feare," and his party set a watch because they anticipated a sudden attack from enemies nearby.

Cocking also noticed a readiness for war and repeatedly urged the people with whom he smoked to hunt and trade, not to fight. In October 1772 he noted, "See several Stone Heaps on the tops of the Hills which the Natives tell me were gathered by the Yeachithinnee Indians, who used to lay behind these Heaps reconoitering the Country."[68] Two months later he heard from the hospitable Yeachithinnees with whom his party had tried to pound buffalo that they planned a raid.

> Three Yachithinnee Indians came from the Westward. they inform us that many of their Countrymen are sickly and Buffelo very scarce that way so as they are greatly distressed for want of food. On this account they say the

War Pipe has been smooked and several are intended to go to War. they have brought a present of Tobacco to be smooked by their Friends here with a desire that they will accompany them in this Expedition.[69]

Again, at the Assinnee Poet buffalo pound, the second scene of inter-cultural cooperation, Cocking learned that "it is the professed intent of most of the Natives to go to War next Year. They own these Expeditions cause them to undergo great hardships, and besides are distressed for want of Ammunition and Tobacco for two Years after; but the Loss of their Friends seems to be above all difficulties."[70]

The reasons given for going to war are illuminating: sickness, famine and the "Loss of their Friends." Pink previously noted such connections:

Yesterday night Dyed an Jndaine Man . . . all theare Tolck is Now a bout War, the Say that this is the Reason of it, that is jf a ney porson dyes With Sickness or is Killed a Mongst them the Must Gow to war With the Other Natives Called Y,artch,a,thyne,a,Wock and Kill as Maney as the Can of them and then the Say that the are Eavin with them for the Dearth of thare Frend or Frends.[71]

The picture that emerges from the winterers' journals is of war as a response to privation, illness and death *within* the group initiating conflict. Grief was translated into anger and directed towards a foreign enemy, so that it could be externalized and dissipated. The enemy group was set up as a collective scapegoat. As well, males of all groups were driven by the perennial need to show how valorous they could be. The conflict might have little or nothing to do with the previous interaction of the two warring groups, and was not necessarily an expression of enduring cultural animosity. Peaceful interaction could follow and alliances could be negotiated again after some time had passed. That death from hunger or disease could be compensated by war obeys a logic that escapes us, and that may have puzzled the winterers as well. They were curious enough to question their companions and diligent enough to note down the responses. The reasons they recorded did not include the inveterate enmity of large, culturally distinguished groups. War, at least on the attacking side, concerned warriors more than general populations: Cocking's Yeachithinnees were recruiting volunteers for raids and skirmishes, and the emphasis was on individual prowess rather than destructive manoeuvres. The prizes of war were scalps and captives (women, children and horses) taken as personal trophies and goods. As Henday noted, "They are like the rest of the Natives murthering one another slyly; seed several pretty Girls that had been taken in war, and many dryed scalps with long black hair displayed on long poles round the Leaders tent."[72] And as Umfreville later observed, "When several tents or families meet to go to war, or to the Factories to trade, they choose a leader, but . . . everyone is at liberty to leave him when he pleases, and the notion of a commander is quite obliterated as soon as the voyage is over."[73]

Small, murderous, profitable forays seem to have satisfied impulses of aggression and acquisitiveness. Without these sporadic safety-valve operations, the mix of people in the plains and parkland, all of whom were exploiting seasonally scarce resources, could not have coexisted the rest of the time. The same groups who camped, traded and hunted together could war on each other, and eventually renew their previous cooperative relationship. In the long run both kinds of activities ensured survival, flexibility and adaptation to changing circumstances.

All of the winterers' journals responded to conventions of observation and notation that prescribed what their writers saw and experienced. When they noted the structure and relationships of plains groups, however, the winterers from Henday to Cocking left a remarkably consistent record: their journals make very similar comments on the household unit, the varying size and cultural diversity of groups who camped together, the network of trading middlemen and the reasons for going to war. These repeated elements have not found their way into the studies of ethnohistorians and anthropologists; instead, regardless of the winterers' finer distinctions, modern scholars are reluctant to abandon the concept of territorially defined tribes inherited from later commentaries. Interpretation according to these concepts carries the risk of distorting and obscuring what knowledge the winterers' texts can be made to yield.

Notes

1 HBCA E.2/1, Isham, "Observations on Hudson's Bay," ff. 71v-72r, pp. 134-35.

2 HBCA E.2/1, Isham, "Observations on Hudson's Bay," f. 71r, p. 133; also HBCA E.2/2, f. 42v, p. 250. The spellings given in journals and commentaries are given here, and they change as each text is discussed. There is no right way to spell any of these names—see Wolfart and Carroll, xvii-xviii. Nor is there a right description of the groups they refer to: traders at Hudson Bay, winterers and subsequent commentators gradually learned to separate the unknown "Other" according to language, customs and trading alliances. Isham recognized that Asinepoets spoke a language quite different from the Indians; Henday further distinguished the "Bloody Ind^s" from Asinipoets by their dress (or lack of it) while insisting that these plains groups spoke the same language. Henday also differentiated between English Earchithinues and "forregn" Earchithinues; later Cocking divided the Yachithinnees into eight subgroups. The process of renaming and redefining continues. There are Canadian and American spellings for Ojibwa/Chippewa, Blackfoot/Blackfeet and Peigan/Piegan, while many of the "tribal" names assigned in the *Handbook of North American Indians* are no longer recognized by the "tribes" themselves.

3 Johnson, "nation." Twentieth-century definitions of "common" words
   may be deceptive. Cf. Black-Rogers's exploration of "starving" and related
   words in fur trade documents dating from 1750 to 1850: Black-Rogers
   explores specialist usage by European traders and Natives, but for
   "primary . . . definition" relies on modern dictionaries. The research technique of upstreaming (i.e., defining and describing past conditions, practices, concepts, etc., in terms of present concepts as well as observed conditions and practices) can downplay or ignore changes in denotation and
   implication from one century to the next. In the "starving" example,
   Johnson's eighteenth-century definition, which insists on death from
   hunger or cold ("to die" being the root if obsolete sense of the verb "to
   starve"), is at odds with Black-Rogers's contention that "usage of the
   term /STARV-/ appears to *begin* with food deprivation sufficient to
   threaten the *start* of such a sequence" (359, original emphasis). By referring to Johnson, Black-Rogers could have shown that traders' reports of
   "starving," if they do in fact indicate "the *start* of such a sequence," of
   hunger rather than its fatal outcome, mark a shift away from the usage
   noted by Johnson and towards the modern sense of the word.

4 HBCA E.2/2, Isham, "Observations on Hudson's Bay," f. 42v, p. 250; HBCA
   E.2/4 and E.2/11, Henday, journal, 6 September 1754; HBCA E.2/5, Graham,
   "Observations on Hudson's Bay," f. 34v, p. 62: "The assenipoet Indians . . .
   one of the tribes that comes to York Fort does not cover their private
   parts." Perhaps it needs to be underlined that the association of "Sinepoets"
   and "Eagl^d Eye'^d Indians" depended on Isham's view of them from the
   Bay. Whether or how the groups Henday met were related in some way (by
   blood, marriage, language, customs, geographical region) depends on the
   criteria used for identification.

5 HBCA B.239/a/42, 44, 47, 48, Isham, canoe tallies, 1758-61.

6 HBCA B.239/b/11, Isham to Jacobs, 17 August 1754; Russell, 148.

7 HBCA A.11/114, Isham, instructions to Henday, 26 June 1754, Isham, instructions to Smith and Waggoner, 19 August 1756, and Graham, instructions to
   winterers, June 1766.

8 HBCA B.239/a/69, Cocking, journal, 20 October 1772, 3 September 1772; cf.
   HBCA E.2/11, Cocking, abstract of journal, insertion into the entry for 31
   July 1772 (not in B.239/a/69): "Basquia . . . is a long frequented place
   where the Canadians randezvous and trade with the Natives. Many of their
   Superstitious and Fanciful marks are seen here."

9 HBCA A.11/114, Isham, instructions to Henday, 26 June 1754.

10 HBCA B.239/a/40, Henday, journal, 15 July 1754, 8 August 1754, 21 September 1754; cf. 26 March 1755.

11 HBCA B.239/a/40, Henday, journal, 9 and 23 December 1754; HBCA E.2/6,
   Henday, journal, 23 December 1754; HBCA E.2/6, E.2/4, E.2/11, Henday, journal, 28 December 1754-4 January 1755; HBCA E.2/4, Henday, journal, 30 May
   1755. Stephen states that "by and large, [Henday] used Cree place names,
   and where he does seem to have applied his own place names, they are not
   very imperialistic" (92). For Stephen, use of Cree names shows how Henday "became a sense part of the landscape itself," an ecological image of

the explorer apparently far removed from the British hero of Burpee, Morton and Rich. Yet Stephen's renovation of Henday's image is based on the unchanged ("imperialistic") fusion of Natives with the land they inhabit; both are seen as aspects of "Nature," the inverse of civilization.

Before he went inland in June 1754, Henday was not familiar even with Cree, the language of the "Home Guard Indians" who lived around York Fort. Isham had urged him to "Converse with the guides as much as you can, that you attain the Language" (HBCA A.11/114, Isham, instructions to Henday, 19 February 1754). Before the year was out Henday was also conversing with his "Bedfellow," but his journal compares poorly with Cocking's, Fidler's or even Pink's journals in terms of reported information about Native attitudes, customs and social organization. There are seventeen Cree placenames (not counting variant spellings) in the four journal texts, and a total of fifty placenames listed in the B.239/a/40 journal and log. Clearly, most of the B.239/a/40 names are impromptu inventions, not transcriptions of traditional Native names—examples are Hair Hill (where a hare was sighted) and Accident Creek (where a boy was shot inadvertently). We are left to speculate on Maidenhead, though it may refer to the English town west of London, just as St Caterns Hill recalls a landmark on the Isle of Wight.

The spelling of Cree words was necessarily phonetic, and depended on the writer's facility in hearing the language. In Henday's case this facility was not great, and quite apart from problems related to dialectical differences, Graham may have had to guess at many of the words. Most of the Cree place names apply to landmarks between Hudson Bay and Lake Winnipeg; with few exceptions, the names for this route cited by Pink and Cocking are not the same as those given in Henday's journal. Some English equivalents can be found in the Henday texts, others in contemporary documents such as the "Observations" of Isham and Graham; I have also scanned Faries and Rayburn; for additional words I am grateful to Charles V. Fiddler, principal of the Plains Indians Cultural Survival School in Calgary. But a number of names in Henday's journal have eluded these attempts to translate them; see Hall, Munro and Rouillard on the problems of transcribing Amerindian place names.

The seventeen more or less recognizably Cree placenames of Henday's journal are as follows: Mistasinnee or Amista Asinee (Great Stone), Mistick-Apethaw Sepee (Wood Partridge River), Apet Sepee (Steel River), Atticksogohegan (Deer Lake), Monokausokohigan (prairie lake), Mono ko tuskey or Muskuty tuskey (grassy prairie region), Attinum Sokahigan or Outtenum Lake (wind across lake), Keskachewan River (swift-current river), Peatago River, Wonman Sokahigan (. . . lake), Swatagan Sokahigan (Salt Lake), Wapesu Copeto Seepie (white "thrown-down" river—i.e., rapids), Arsinie Watchee (stony hill/mountain), Chacutena or Cunekagan Creek, Constenak or Countenack River, Baskquea or Basquea or Paskeway Yay (river narrows), and Mukekemen Sogohigan (. . . lake). The journal includes Cree terms for fish and animals: tickameg (whitefish), waskesews ("red deer" or elk), mustuce (buffalo cow), quiquakah (wolverine), wejack (fisher), as well as ruhigan (dried beat meat). It also includes the names of Native groups: Keskachewan Indians (people from the swift-flowing river), Asinepoets/Senipoets (stone people), Archithinues/Earchithinues (strangers, those who speak a foreign tongue) and Pegogamaw Indians. Finally, the journal names Henday's companions and other Native leaders: Attickasish (little deer), Connawappa, Cocamanakisick (little . . .), Shenap, Maconsko and Wappenessew (white . . .).

On personal names, HBCA E.2/12, Graham, "Observations on Hudson's Bay," p. 304: "They have all a name given to them when young, that is a month or two after their birth . . . but perhaps as the Child grows up he will have another or two names; the signification of them are various & taken from Animals, Vegetables, fossils, or remarkable actions or events." Cf. Derrida's analysis of Lévi-Strauss, *Tristes tropiques*: "La guerre des noms propres suit l'arrivée de l'étranger et l'on ne s'en étonnera pas. Elle naît en présence . . . de l'ethnographe qui vient déranger l'ordre et la paix naturelle" (166).

12 HBCA B.239/a/40, E.2/6, E.2/4, E.2/11, Henday, journal, 24 December 1754-4 January 1755 and 12-21 May 1755; HBCA B.239/a/58, Pink, journal, 2-4 and 13-14 May 1768; HBCA B.239/a/69, Cocking, journal, 26 May 1773.

13 HBCA E.2/6, E.2/4, E.2.11, Henday, journal, 5-6 September 1754.

14 HBCA E.2/4, Henday, journal, 15 October 1754.

15 HBCA B.239/a/61, Pink, journal, 8 March and 6 April 1769; HBCA B.239/a/63, Pink, journal, 26 August 1769.

16 HBCA B.239/a/63, Pink, journal, 13 October and 24 December 1769.

17 HBCA B.239/a/69, Cocking, journal, 4 November 1772.

18 HBCA E.2/11, Cocking, abstract of journal, 4 November and 4 December 1772.

19 HBCA E.2/11, Henday, journal, 15 May 1755.

20 HBCA E.2/6, Henday, journal, 15 October 1754.

21 HBCA B.239/a/69, Cocking, journal, 1 December 1772.

22 HBCA B.239/a/69, Cocking, journal, 3 and 5 December 1772; cf. HBCA E.2/6, E.2/4, E.2/11, Henday, journal, 14-15 October 1754.

23 HBCA B.239/a/40, E.2/6, E.2/4, E.2/11, Henday, journal, 13-14 and 26 August, 10-15 September and 20 September 1754; HBCA B.239/a/58, Pink, journal, 7 August 1767; HBCA B.239/a/69, Cocking, journal, 25 August 1772.

24 HBCA B.239/a/69, Cocking, journal, 25 August 1772, 4 November 1772; HBCA E.2/11, Cocking, abstract of journal, 4 November 1772; HBCA E.2/12, Graham, "Observations on Hudson's Bay," pp. 36, 332-33, 349.

25 HBCA B.239/a/69, Cocking, journal, 19 September and 17 October 1772.

26 Johnson, "tribe."

27 HBCA E.2/6, Graham, "Observations on Hudson's Bay," f. 43r, p. 84.

28 HBCA G.2/17, Graham, "A Plan of Part of Hudson's-Bay . . . ," (1774).

29 HBCA E.2/9, Graham, "Observations on Hudson's Bay," f. 82r, p. 157.

30 HBCA E.2/9, Graham, "Observations on Hudson's Bay," f. 82v, p. 158.

31 HBCA E.2/12, Graham, "Observations on Hudson's Bay," p. 349; HBCA B.239/a/40, E.2/6, E.2/4, E.2/11, Henday, journal, 12-21 May 1755.

32 HBCA E.2/12, Graham, "Observations on Hudson's Bay," p. 350.

33 Umfreville, 178-302.

34 Umfreville, 179, 195.

35 Umfreville, 176-77. Umfreville was content to plagiarize Graham's descriptions of specific Native groups, even though Graham had relied in part on "Indian information." For Umfreville's plagiarism of Graham, see Glover, introduction to Graham, *Observations on Hudson's Bay*, ed. Williams, xxx-xxxii, and Williams, "Andrew Graham and Thomas Hutchins," 14.

36 See Lamb, ed., introduction to *Journals and Letters of Alexander Mackenzie*, 33, 515-16, for evidence of authorship by the explorer's cousin Roderic McKenzie, who wished to write a book-length history of the fur trade.

37 Mackenzie, lxvi,lxx-lxxii, lxxxi-lxxxiii, xci-cxvi.

38 Helm, introduction, *Handbook of North American Indians/Subarctic*, 1-2; Helm, ed. *Essays on the Problem of Tribe*; cf. Fried, 86: "I must confess that my major misgiving in attacking the concept of tribe lies in the possible deletion of this word in the service of the comparison of cultures. The fact that the word tribe in its conventional sense is rendered meaningless by the arguments [of *The Concept of Tribe*] does not mitigate the sense of loss, curious as that may be." See also Rousseau; Greenberg and Morrison; Morantz; Parks, 180; Peers, xv-xviii.

39 Helm, ed., *Handbook of North American Indians/Subarctic*, viii-ix; see also maps in the following: Scaglion, 24-31; Ray, *Indians in the Fur Trade*, 95-101; McMillan, 115; Cruikshank, 60; Dickason, 64-65.

40 Fried, 101-2, 110-11. Defining other cultures in terms of one's own has been one of the themes of postcolonialist commentary: see, for example, Clastres, de Certeau, Todorov. Cf. Peers, xviii.

41 Kipp, 76.

42 Kipp, 76. Kipp's article is illustrated (uncaptioned and unattributed) by Mary Shäffer's photograph of Samson Beaver's family, taken in 1907 and conserved in the archives of the Whyte Museum of the Canadian Rockies, Banff, Alberta. If tribal designations are used, the Beaver family were not Blackfoot but Stoney. No clearer proof can be found of cultural simplification, here to the point of generic Indianness, than the indiscriminate use of this photo. Dempsey, 8, describes the "Blackfoot Confederacy": "The Blackfoot nation consists primarily of three tribes, the Bloods, Blackfoot and Peigans, all of whom speak the same language. . . . Allied to them are the Sarcee Indians, who speak a different tongue, and the Gros Ventres . . . The Blackfoot, in their own language, refer to themselves as *Soyi-tapi*, or Prairie People. An older term *Nitsi-tapi*, or Real People, was once a self-identification but is now used to describe any Indian person, regardless of tribe." See http://www.treaty7.org (9 June 1999) for grouping of the five Treaty Seven signatories and current self-definitions.

42 Jenness, 284.

43 Mandelbaum, xiii.

45 Ray, *Indians in the Fur Trade*, 23.

46 Milloy, xv.

47 Peers, 13-14.

48 Peers, xi. Peers criticizes the "culture area" approach, which emphasizes the formation of cultural values in response to geographical and

economic imperatives. Cf. Russell, 5-6, who ascribes importance to cultural diversity within the Cree linguistic group.

49 Russell, 2, 5.

50 Russell, 47; Greenberg and Morrison; Peers, xvi-xvii, 4-5.

51 Russell, 47, 24.

52 Johnson, "family": "1. Those who live in the same house; household; 2. Those that descend from one common progenitor; a race; a tribe; a generation; 3. A class; a tribe; a species."

53 HBCA B.239/a/40, Isham, "Remarks."

54 HBCA B.239/a/40, Isham, "Remarks."

55 HBCA B.239/a/63, Pink, journal, 24 December 1769 and 1 January 1770.

56 HBCA B.239/a/69, Cocking, journal, 29 March 1773.

57 Frison, 211-37. However, Frison offers a preliminary caution, which is of interest given the frequent instances noted in winterers' journals of a scarcity of buffalo or other big game: "The present evidence strongly indicates that prehistoric economic strategies were seldom limited to any given life zone or food source. Narrow economic specializations were often the road to disaster, and broad spectrum hunting and gathering is proposed here as having best characterized most of prehistoric life on the Northwestern Plains. The balance between the two strategies [hunting and gathering] changed in response to climatic conditions which directly affected the animal populations" (14).

58 Meyer and Thistle.

59 HBCA G.1/25, Ackomokki, transcribed by Peter Fidler. "An Indian Map of the Different Tribes . . . " (1801). For comment, see Belyea, "Mapping the Marias." Only "Sessew's Indians" can be identified with a tribe, the Sarcees, now known as Tsuu T'ina First Nation.

60 HBCA B.239/a/69, Cocking, journal, 23 August 1772.

61 HBCA A.11/114, Isham, instructions to Henday, 26 June 1754; HBCA B.239/b/27. Graham, instructions to winterers, June 1766.

62 HBCA B.239/a/40, Henday, journal, 10 and 22 February 1755.

63 HBCA B.239/a/58, Pink, journal, 13 May 1768.

64 HBCA B.239/a/61, Pink, journal, 22 October 1768.

65 HBCA B.239/a/63, Pink, journal, 18 September 1769.

66 Russell, 101.

67 HBCA E.2/6, Henday, journal, 18 September 1754.

68 HBCA B.239/a/69, Cocking, journal, 6 October 1772.

69 HBCA B.239/a/69, Cocking, journal, 16 December 1772.

70 HBCA B.239/a/69, Cocking, journal, 28 March 1773.

71 HBCA B.239/a/58, Pink, journal, 26 September 1767.

72 HBCA E.2/6, E.2/4 and E.2/11, Henday, journal, 15 October 1754.

73 Umfreville, 43.

Uses of Henday's Journal

During the middle decades of the eighteenth century, would-be competitors criticized the Hudson's Bay Company for its lack of interest in exploration; the company, they said, monopolized trade while it "slept at the edge of a frozen sea."[1] At the same time, French advances west of the Great Lakes caused trade returns to fall; Natives who had previously made the difficult, dangerous journey to the Bay were now intercepted at the edge of the prairies. Clearly the company had to explore the western interior and to modify its trade strategies, or at least make some gesture towards doing so.

The wintering policy that Henday's trip inaugurated was not a new idea: following the French precedent of *coureurs de bois*, Henry Kelsey and William Stewart had travelled inland half a century earlier. Their journeys did not materially alter the Hudson's Bay Company's habits of trade, nor did those of Henday and the young men who wintered with Natives for almost four decades after him. This practice continued even after Cumberland House was built, west of the old French post of Basquia, in 1774. The company preferred to attract visitors from the interior to the Bayside forts rather than to organize a network of inland posts. Sending young men inland appeared to respond to French competition, and could be done at low cost, with little change in annual administrative routine. Any initiative to bring about real change in HBC trading practice would need to satisfy the London Committee's inclination for caution, thrift and business as usual. Henday's journal was useful to the Bayside factors in two ways. First, its status as an empirical report ensured its acceptance as a reliable account of inland conditions. And second, Henday's commercial failure reported in the journal texts of Graham's "Observations"

Notes to this section are on pp. 390-94.

(E.2/6, E.2/4 and E.2/11), no less than his success announced more than a decade earlier in the text sent to London (B.239/a/40), justified contemporary views on trade held by Isham, Graham and Ferdinand Jacobs, all associated with York Fort and therefore concerned with the Saskatchewan trade.

The empirical status of Henday's journal reflected a double tradition of ships' logs and the Royal Society's scientific interest in such accounts as records of exploration. Henday's year inland was not only a response to the French commercial threat; as with Hearne's exploration of the Coppermine River two decades later, the Hudson's Bay Company also hoped to win wider political recognition of its charter right to monopolize the vast continental interior west of the Bay. While the British public and its political representatives hoped for territorial annexation and a northwest passage, the company thought in terms of trading relationships with the people who lived "on the back of this Land, and to the westward of Churchill River."[2] A record which could satisfy these various aims of scientific curiosity, imperial ambitions and commercial expansion would go far to justify the expense of an employee's annual wage and the goods he would need to distribute as "encouragement" to Native leaders. Henday's instructions enjoined him to chart his progress using "a Compass, hand Line paper &c &c" and to "be very exact in Keeping a Journal of your travels and observations Daily, observing the Courses, trying the Depth of water in the River or Lakes when in your Cannoe," then every evening "to Remark Down Every thing that occurs to your View Daily, mentioning when you Come to any River or Lake the name, when you meet with any Natives what Nation &c."[3]

Isham's instructions to Henday touch on all of the categories of eighteenth-century scientific reporting: logging courses and distances, sounding bodies of water, cataloguing soils and flora, enumerating large animals, describing Native customs, noting opportunities for resource exploitation and trade, together with the injunction to keep a careful account of all these details each day. Henday's journal responds faithfully, even mechanically, to these categories of enquiry, as sample entries in the four texts demonstrate:

> Wednesday fine weather, wind NW^t. took my departure from Jack Island, att the Entrance of Nelson pond, and steered WSW^t 25 Miles, when we Came to ye River on the West side which is Nelson River, goes through the middle of it; this Day past 28 Islands, the water very deep all this days paddle, the Currant but small, fine tall woods on both sides of ye River. (B.239/a/40)

> Frid^y moderate weather, wind W. travelled none, went a hunting with the Men, killed a great many Waskesews, seed above 300 feeding in one plain,

the Ice is 4 Inches thick on the ponds, and the ground Covered with snow but not so deep as to use snow shoes. At night a grand feast &c. (E.2/6)

Tuesday a strong gale wind W. Traveled 15 miles WSW level land, short grass and several salt water lakes; we are now entered muscuty plains, shall soon see plenty of buffaloe and the archithinue Indians hunting them on horse-back. (E.2/4)

Thursday Wind West and moderate weather. Two Young Natives in the french interest brought 12 Beaver skins to trade with me for Ammunition, I gave them a little & told them to go down with me to York Fort with their furs, where they would receive more goods for them in barter than they did from the French. They gave me fair promises. (E.2/11)[4]

Henday's journal seems to be a straightforward, unadorned recital of events and observed details, yet we would be naive to think that what he tells us is in simple fact what he saw and did. The very strictness with which the empirical categories are accounted for is an indication of the degree to which the journal *prescribed* what the explorer was to observe. Its conformity with Isham's instructions shows the extent to which initial expectations guided the explorer's comportment as scientific explorer and trading agent. There is very little descriptive variation or spontaneous action, except perhaps in details of Henday's hunting adventures.[5] Nor is there reason to believe that Henday or other inland journalists kept a more primitive and personal record than their journals. No "field notes" survive for any of the winterers, from Henday to Fidler—no evidence that any of these men ever formulated their experience according to narrative or observational expectations other than those of the empirical journal. On the contrary: Isham's instructions to Henday mention the format of each entry as a pattern or grid, to stimulate and guide the winterer's activities of observation and negotiation as much as to record them.[6] At its most informative, as seen in the examples above, Henday's journal registers signs of his acculturation ("hunting with the Men," the newly acquired Cree word "muscuty"), anticipation and relaying of hearsay knowledge ("we shall soon see . . . "), as well as awareness that "Natives in the french interest" were polite but not always sincere. Perhaps one aspect of the journal's importance as a historical reference lies in these very modest accommodations of its prescribed categories of enquiry.

The journal's empirical status, with its claim to furnish a true, direct, on-the-spot and as-it-happened account of Henday's inland experience, has encouraged twentieth-century historians and anthropologists to search it for evidence of European knowledge of the continental interior as well as of mid-eighteenth-century Native soci-

eties and trading patterns. Henday's journal has proven more than
usually recalcitrant: scholars' insistence that what Henday did and
saw is more than minimally recoverable has led to some dubious conclusions. We have seen what little sure knowledge can be had of Henday's route inland. Following Morton, Rich affirms that Henday "was
almost certainly within sight of the Rockies . . . though his Journal
does not mention the fact," and then, to support this unfounded
assertion, Rich speculates on Henday's character: observant, sensitive, yet inarticulate, the explorer "seems to have been such a man as
was capable of doing and feeling far more than he could commit to
paper."[7] With each statement, the distance between historical reconstruction and textual proof widens.

Moreover, the empirical claims of documents such as Henday's
journal have led historians, anthropologists and geographers to imitate scientific values of neutrality and objectivity in their own work.
But a review of the positions taken by commentators on Henday's
journal demonstrates that the past is always conceived and evaluated
with reference to scholars' own cultural values, problems and questions.[8]

Burpee pictures Henday as participating in a series of adventur-
ous explorations which laid western North America open to European
conquest. Removed from us by almost a century, Burpee's concern for
"the destiny not merely of a colony, but of an empire" strikes us with
all its outmoded enthusiasm. So does Morton's pro-British contrast
between Henday and La Vérendrye: "The one went to view the country and bring the Indians to trade. The other went as a Commandant
with his staff and bodyguard to annex the land. Consequently the
French advance westward was slow, and it was left to English eyes to
see the Rocky Mountains of the north before any other European."[9]
Those "English eyes" were Henday's. Burpee and Morton scrutinize
the explorer's journal for evidence that the HBC employee, as a representative of Britain's commercial domination, had for all practical
purposes "annex[ed] the land" that would later be claimed politically.
Saskatchewan and Alberta, with ethnically mixed immigrant populations, had joined Confederation only three years before Burpee's book
appeared. Henday's early exploration justified the prairie region's
integration with a British dominion.

Closer to our way of thinking, Ray's and Russell's positions are
less obviously biased and limited. Ray sees the fur trade as "an inte-
grating force between Indians and Europeans. To be successfully pros-
ecuted, the fur trade required the cooperation of both parties. . . . Although it was not an equal partnership, nor one in which the same
group always held the upper hand, at no time before 1870 would it

have served the interests of one party to destroy the other. . . . The various Indian groups were continually adjusting to the transformations of their environmental and cultural surroundings . . . various opportunities which the fur trade offered them."[10] In his detailed account of this succession of exchanges, Ray emphasizes the canniness and discrimination of Native traders in their choice of trading partners, as well as their insistence on high-quality goods. Ray's picture of cooperation is a revision of the older view that Europeans overwhelmed primitive savages in their march across the continent. This "partnership" view is dictated by the historian's own political climate of treaty negotiations and recognition of Native roles in past events and situations. At the same time, the positive value attributed to such mutual responsibility is modern and non-Native rather than aboriginal; Native traders are redrawn as sophisticated shoppers at the Bay. The view of the fur trade that Ray expounds "corrects" the imperialism of Morton and Rich as it reflects the uncertainty and ambivalence of a non-Native majority in the face of new Native demands for justice and redefinition.

Russell's study, published almost twenty years after Ray's, seems to us the least biased of the commentaries on Henday. Russell goes even farther than Ray to revise the older political theme of European domination; his aim, he says, is to reassess Mandelbaum's thesis and to study the eighteenth-century geographical distribution of western Cree. "It was erroneously assumed," concludes Russell, "since early data placed the Cree to the east while later data placed them in the west, that the Cree themselves had migrated." He shows that the Cree were less subject to "transformations of their environmental and cultural surroundings" than Ray has claimed, and able to resist much of the shock of European contact.[11] Russell's picture of the western Cree as a stable, powerful group is subtly anti-imperial, calmly post-colonial, sensitive to the agenda of an increasingly influential constituency in Canadian politics and society.

Study of a document such as Henday's journal is clearly a process of successive reinterpretations. Historical revision is inevitable and necessary: from one period to the next, even from one decade to the next, changing sociopolitical values are decisive in determining the focus and judgements of any enquiry. Moreover, documents are themselves changed by this process: they are read with different questions in mind; they are edited and re-edited; they are even rewritten. In practice the scholarly distinction between text and interpretive commentary (primary and secondary sources) can be blurred. Reading can be selective, and in making edited texts more "readable" than "faithful," editors choose among textual variants, explain anomalies, bridge gaps, and generally play down strangeness or difficulty. In these ways the manuscript artifact is clothed in familiar terms and encouraged to "speak" in a relevant, acceptable way.[12]

Henday's journal is of particular interest in this regard, because the process of interpreting it began as soon as the explorer returned to York Fort in 1755 and continued as Graham wrote it into successive states of his "Observations." To follow this process, the journal needs to be situated in the mass of records and correspondence documenting eighteenth-century Bayside trade, politics and exploration. There is a good chance that investigating the documentary context of contemporary "Letters, Books and Papers"[13] will shed more light on Henday's year inland than treating the journal as an "objectively" reliable reference. His journal may be as close to pure textuality and non-referentiality as an empirical document can get. Yet clearly it was useful as a political tool in the Bayside factors' lobbying for a change in the company's trading practices.

As early as 1743 James Isham suggested "a Setlement at the head of port Nelson River" as a means of obtaining "double the fur's" and eventually, "with god's will," driving the French from their posts along Lake Winnipeg and the Saskatchewan River. "What is the most Concer'n," concluded Isham, "is to see us sitt quiet & unconcern'^{d} while the french as an old saying, not only Beats ye Bush but run's away with the Hair also."[14] Isham proposed this idea again, nine years later, as one of two schemes to increase the company's trade. In a letter to the London Committee, he suggested that outposts be built on the Severn and Nelson rivers, and that a company employee be sent into the Saskatchewan region, in order to discourage Natives from trading with the French.[15] Since he could not make policy decisions, all Isham could do to further these plans was to make a carefully reasoned plea to the company's directors. The London Committee stopped short of approving new posts. But recognizing that some action was required, they allowed Isham to send "a proper Person . . . a great way up into the Country with Presents to the Indians."[16] Henday volunteered for the job, ventured inland in June 1754, and returned to York Fort twelve months later.

Whatever holograph account Henday produced during this year away was copied for presentation to the London Committee during the summer of 1755. To this copy Isham appended a series of explanatory remarks which directed the Committee, none too subtly, to see the year inland in certain flattering ways. Leaving nothing to chance, Isham carefully outlined the economic importance of the wintering initiative, stressing Henday's trading skill as well as his endurance of "great hardships and difficultys." The explorer's meeting with the

Earchithinues was described in terms designed to impress. Henday is pictured as the HBC's ambassador to a foreign court: the inland chief is a "Monarch or King" seated on a throne and obeyed by all around him. Simply by visiting them, Henday transformed these people into "English Earchithinues" and distinguished them from "forregn Earchithinues," who lived even farther away and who carried out occasional raids. Isham's "Remarks" make much of the strangers' unwillingness, presented as inability, to make or paddle canoes. If they were instructed in "the art of Cannues," they could trade directly with the Bay forts. The problem of French inland trade is minimized; it would be negligible "if the English was Inland by about 500 Mile"; but the "Remarks" opt firmly for a policy of sending employees to winter with Native bands. "Severall men" following Henday's example "would be the only Means to Root ye french out, and therefore recover the Trade they have so Long Enjoyed."[17] The "Remarks" reveal that if subsidiary posts could not be built on the Severn and Nelson rivers (his first plan), Isham was intent on making the most of his second project, to send young men inland as winterers. Henday's journal would demonstrate that this second plan was a good one.

The claims and recommendations of Isham's "Remarks" are borne out by the B.239/a/40 text of Henday's journal. It tells of meeting the Earchithinues as well as detailing Henday's relationships with his guides, his tentmates and groups met along the way. As well, the B.239/a/40 journal minimizes the French threat: Henday's bravado when meeting French traders at Basquia on his way inland is complemented by his successful dissuasion from trading there on his return. Instead of exchanging their furs at this conveniently situated post, B.239/a/40 reports (rather improbably) that the Indians were "busy talking" and "Mending their Can^s" when they stayed there for several days. Henday arrived at York "att the Head" of an impressive brigade, having attracted all the way to York at least those Natives who could make and paddle canoes.[18]

Despite Isham's appended "Remarks," the journal text sent to London presented such serious problems that its usefulness as a reliable record was questioned immediately. Although they had no sure knowledge of the continent's dimensions, the London Committee were skeptical of Henday's directions and distances.[19] Nor did the journal's geographical descriptions give a clear impression of the "dry inland Country" so different from that of the Bayside forts.[20] The Committee found the journal's the only reassuring element to be its report of trading success: apparently Henday had exacted promises from Archithinue leaders and had persuaded his brigade to pass by the French posts. Since trade was, after all, the company's priority,

Henday was richly rewarded for his efforts: his annual wages were increased from £15 to £20 and he was given a "Gratuity" of £20 more. Comparison can be made with Graham's salary: as "Assistant Writer" at York, the largest of the Bay forts, Graham earned only £15 annually.[21]

There is reason to suspect, as Williams suggests, that Isham's lobbying may have been furthered by alteration of Henday's original journal. Although there are hundreds of variants in the four Henday texts, for historians the most significant divergence—contradictions over the issue of trade—is between B.239/a/40, the text sent to London in 1755, and the E texts of Graham's "Observations." Williams speculates that Henday himself tampered with the truth recorded in his "notes" (the text written inland) in order "to show his achievement in a dishonestly optimistic light."[22]

What is just as possible and more likely is that Graham, who prepared a fair copy of the journal for York's year-end report to London, complied with Isham's directions and modified at least certain passages of Henday's original journal with a view to supporting the chief factor's contentions: the wintering experiment would be presented in a positive light. In any case, Isham was given permission to send more men to the western interior. As if to confirm the wisdom of this initiative, more Native groups from the Saskatchewan region began visiting the Bay.[23] The London Committee, so sharply suspicious when it came to Henday's distances, were perfectly accepting of the explorer's success at dissuasion. Henday's trip re-established a trading strategy that the Bay posts employed for another forty years.[24]

Ultimately the policy of sending winterers inland proved inadequate as a measure to reduce Canadian rivalry. But the company came to this conclusion very slowly. The London Committee and the Bayside factors weighed the merits of both options for a long time before Graham finally argued openly in favour of inland posts, eighteen years after Henday's first trip. The copies of the journal in Graham's "Observations," all three of them registering a failed venture, served as evidence at that time to justify growing disillusionment of the Bayside factors with the official policy that regularly sent several employees "a great way up into the Country" at considerable expense, and with no marked improvement in trade.

Both Isham and Graham had long noted that the winterers who went inland in the twenty years following Henday's first journey made little difference to returns at York Fort. More people made the journey and had to be entertained, but they did not bring more furs. Trade remained steady for several years: from 1746 to 1754 returns averaged 25412 "made Beaver," and from 1755 to 1759 the average number was

26320. From 1760 to 1767 there was an encouraging increase followed by a sharp decline.[25] In 1766 Graham, interim chief at York, confided to Moses Norton, the factor at Churchill, "Have had a good many Canoos but many of them poorly Gooded nay some of them hardly anything to Trade and had it not been for 47 Canoos of Sinnepoet Indians should have had no Beaver."[26] The probable reason for this up-and-down curve was not the effectiveness of HBC winterers so much as war with France and the British victory at Quebec. For a time war broke French supply lines; after the conquest French investors could no longer support the trade. But the French inland network was soon reinstated, thanks to refinancing by British entrepreneurs.[27] Just as the French had done, British "Pedlars" from Montreal robbed the Bay posts of their best furs.

Yet the London Committee continued to favour the policy of wintering employees. Their General Letter of 1756 praised Henday and concluded that "bringing down Indian strangers at the Fort to Trade . . . we judge to be the only means of enlarging the York Fort Cargoes."[28] Several years later, in response to Isham's report that the number of canoes arriving at York (however poorly provided with furs) had increased from 244 in 1758 to 321 the following summer,[29] the London Committee wrote approvingly, "Experience having confirmed to you the great Advantage arising from some of Our Servants Annually sent up a great Distance inland among the Natives agreable to Our repeated Directions on that head, whereby many Indian Strangers have been brought to Trade at the Factory. We therefore strictly Order, that the same be Encouraged and continued at all proper opportunitys."[30] The London Committee chose to react with complacency despite Isham's repeated statements that an increase in the number of canoes was no indication of a rich cargo.

Any innovation of trading practice continued to be narrowly defined as individuals' contact with Native groups of the interior, even though Isham seems not to have abandoned the more ambitious plan of settlements to follow. Referring to Henday's attempt at a second journey in 1755 (cut short by his partner's illness), Isham repeated that sending young men to winter with Natives "will, and is the only Means to Recover & Enlarge the trade att York Fort. . . . " But in the next phrase of the same sentence he reiterated the idea of inland posts: "and [I] shall put such in force the first oppertunity when the Season permits taking Care this fall to Gett a Quantity of Birch Rhyne in order to make proper Vessells, for ye Same grand Design; the which I hope will put a Stop to the Surprizing Encouragements of the french, on the Borders of our Lands."[31] Isham's plan of an outpost on the Saskatchewan River would not be realized for two more decades.

The London Committee permitted only "prudent Endeavours" even as they declared themselves "determined to Encourage every thing that hath the least shadow of Encreasing the Companys Trade to advantage."[32]

In 1768 the London Committee was still endorsing only the narrow policy of individuals wintering with Native groups: "We approve Your continuing to send out Servants Inland with the Natives in order to promote the Companys Interest;—We are glad You have met with no Interruptions the last year, and recommend your prudent Endeavours to enlarge our Trade as much as possible."[33] The Committee was responding to continued good cargoes from York Fort as reported by Ferdinand Jacobs, the successor to Isham as governor of York, in his General Letter of August 1767 ("31640 Skins made Beaver besides 942 Skins more now Sent home") and to the assurance that Jacobs had "heard nothing this Year of any English Trading with the In-Land Indians that frequently come to York Fort to Trade."[34] Jacobs's satisfaction was short-lived. The following year, when returns plummeted to 18324½ made Beaver, he hastened to explain why: "the case of so sudden & great a Fall in the Trade is, the Canadian Pedlers are with large Quantities of Trading Goods in different parties, all over the Heart of the Trading Indians Country." Jacobs questioned the wintering policy, observing, "We have sent the same Men Inland this Year, but cannot say much with regard to their Influence in promoting Your Honours Trade." The initiative for change still had to come from the London Committee: "whatever Measures Your Honours should take to prevent the future Loss of your Trade and to remove those thieves off Your Land that we will be ordered to do We will execute with the greatest care & Expedition if practicable."[35] In a supplementary letter, Jacobs once more put forward Isham's plan "to build a House or Houses on the most Convenient Places to stop the Pedlars robbing you of your Trade."[36]

During most of his time of interim command at York Fort, in 1761-62, 1765-66 and 1771-72, Graham complied with, even defended, the pattern initiated by Henday's mid-century journey and approved by London. Williams offers a psychological explanation for this position: Graham was against inland posts because they were once more suggested by Jacobs, whom Graham apparently disliked and wished to supersede.[37] But among other things, this scenario of personal antipathy overlooks the ambivalence and complexity of Graham's own position, hinted in early states of the "Observations" dating from 1767-69. Already Graham was admitting that some new action to counter inland competition was necessary: "Before the Conquest of Canada the French had houses for trade above us, and since the year 1765 have returned again, and now under the English government seems to be carrying trade on with our Indians amongst the lakes &c with greater vigour than before, which will certainly oblige the Hudson's-Bay Company to take some method to hinder the Canadian Traders from running away with the prime furrs."[38] Obviously the current wintering policy was not working. In theory the policy was a good one, yet experience had shown that volunteers for the job were inefficient: the trade they brought to the Bay was not worth the "expence" of their outfits and wages. "Since Anth.y Hendey's visiting the inland Country, Servants hath been sent yearly inland to promote the furr trade, by making presents and inviting down strange Indians, but have increased the trade at York fort nothing worth notice, and indeed I don't know how it should rise by their means, they being ignorant poor labouring men of no abilities, who likes to go for no other reason but to lead an idle and vagrant life amongst the Natives, and to get a few furrs for themselves."[39]

The alternative, to build inland posts, did not seem more hopeful. "I am certain," argued Graham, "that inland Settlements would be more for the Native interest than for the Company's advantage, as their being supplyed so nigh would encourage their wretched Indolence [and] prevent them from visiting the lower Forts. . . . All the discovered Rivers are so shoal, full of cataracts and long land carriages, that with great difficulty, expence and attended with the utmost confusion, birch rind canoes would not be got up to Keskachewan river with a trifle of goods in less than 4 months."[40] At the same time Graham wrote suggestively, "The Canadian Traders being returned to the lakes and rivers above us are now carrying on trade with more vigour than when they were under a French Government which will make the Company take some method to extirpate them out either by legal authority or by making settlements inland; the first would be the best way to do; the second way would be attended with great trouble and expence. I own it would banish away the Interlopers but would not encrease the Furr trade one skin, excepting they could get the Archithinue Indians and Aseenepoet Indians to come to trade at Basquea."[41] Thus Graham echoed Jacob's disillusionment with the wintering policy as early as 1768, in response to the sudden fall in returns that year. It was obvious even then that the "Pedlar" successors to the French inland trade were taking the best furs of the Saskatchewan region because they already had inland posts, and their increased trade in the late 1760s seriously reduced the trade at York. Prudence and habit nevertheless anchored the Hudson's Bay Company "at the edge of a frozen sea."

Although Isham, Jacobs and Graham pressed for a change in policy, all three were playing the company's game: they had to accommodate the London Committee's antipathy to the risk and expense of new posts even as they tried to overcome it. In order to effect change while insisting on their obedience to Committee directives, Isham and Graham invoked empirical testimony which would carry some persuasive weight: they cited winterers' reports of the inland trade. Although he found reasons for dismissing the idea of inland settlements, Graham suspected all along that the wintering policy had not measurably promoted trade; his interview with a lone Archithinue visitor in the summer of 1766 changed doubt to certainty. But the HBC London Committee had not been convinced by the Bay factors' own views on inland trade. To his remarks in the "Observations" Graham added two winterers' journals that would justify his own growing pessimism: William Tomison's report in 1768 that "Pedlars" had captured the Saskatchewan trade, and the failure version of Henday's journal. The wintering policy had always been flawed. "Since the year 1756 [*sic*] several Englishmen hath been sent annualy inland to endeavour to promote the Company's trade, and to invite down the Archithinue Indians to trade, but have not yet succeeded, and am certain never will," explained Graham. "I did my utmost endeavour to search and find out the reason why the archithinues could not be got down to trade, and the reasons they gave me were the same as mentioned by Anth^y Hendey in his Journal wrote out in full in the first book of this work."[42]

It is possible, though far from certain, that the failure version of Henday's journal found in Graham's "Observations" is closer to Henday's original than is the version sent to London in 1755. Certainly the failure version is more logical and coherent, and by the late 1760s it presented the problem of inland trade more eloquently. Where, for example, B.239/a/40 records for 21-25 May 1755 that the French traders at Basquia "got but very Little trade" though Henday's brigade "Lay by" for three days, the E texts detail the Natives' trade at Basquia despite Henday's best efforts to prevent them. The delay at the French house is therefore more plausible in the "Observations" texts, which clearly describe the middleman trade and explain the lack of fine furs traded at York Fort. York's trade returns and correspondence during the years immediately following Henday's journey reflect the E texts more closely than the curiously inconsequential account in B.239/a/40. Shortly after Henday's return to York, Isham wrote to the London Committee that "the french by their Surprizing Encouragements on the Borders of our Country, trades in Reality for great Quantitys, the real proof of which is plain by the Acc^t of Captn

Hendeys Journey &c."[43] The emphasis of Isham's remark is still on French competition, not on Henday's successful deflection of this trade. Isham's instructions to Joseph Smith and Joseph Waggoner, who wintered on the plains in 1756, conclude with his hope "not to be deceived again in what I am possitive (if wrightly aply^d) will be greatly to the Advancement of Trade";[44] Isham's deception might refer to Henday's abortive second attempt to go inland in 1755, but since it is written into instructions to two other winterers, the reference is more plausibly to Henday's inability, so far unacknowledged, to stop Natives from dealing with French traders.

If indeed Henday's original journal recorded the explorer's failure to lure Natives from the French trade, Graham, the second-in-command at York Fort, may have transformed Henday's pessimistic but honest report into the "dishonestly optimistic" text sent to London. Graham could then have returned to Henday's original journal twelve years later and copied it more or less verbatim into several states of his Observations. But another possibility is that in 1767 Graham returned to B.239/a/40 and altered key passages to reflect the threat to trade posed by the post-war "Pedlars."

The extent of Graham's alteration of the journal can never be known for sure. However, it is not only because of such alteration that Henday's journal is an ambiguous, mysterious document. Even Henday's lost original could not be taken as a transcript of the explorer's experience, and Henday's own superiors were aware of this—far more acutely, it would seem, than twentieth-century scholars have been. Although Henday's instructions repeatedly urged the explorer to describe in accurate detail what he saw and did, Isham and his second placed little confidence in verbal accounts. In 1756 Isham sent a French coat to London as material proof of trade rivalry; ten years later, Graham sent a ruffled shirt and a length of cloth. These artifacts have disappeared, leaving (ironically) only written testimony of the disbelief they were meant to allay.[45] We must accept that all documents are more or less elusive simply by virtue of their being textual records. We cannot treat these letters and journals as if they were windows, and see "through" them to the events, places and situations they mention. Nor can there simply be adjustment for "bias." No facts rush to the rescue. All we can do is to account for these texts *as texts*, carefully avoiding the strong temptation to dismiss or play down awkward assertions and downright contradictions. Regardless of Henday's role as the first of a continuous line of HBC winterers, his journal is an important document precisely because its multiple texts resist explanation and resolution: they cannot be made to tell a simple or coherent story.[46] The best understanding we can come to is a contextual one, in the strict sense of the word "contextual": we can read Henday's journal together with contemporary texts that have been preserved in the archival collection, and consider the possibilities that this comparison suggests.

Graham copied, condensed and may have altered several winterers' reports—not only Henday's but the journals of Joseph Smith (1756-57 and 1757-58), William Pink and William Tomison (late 1760s) and Matthew Cocking (1772-73). In the E.2/12 "Observations" Graham recalled, "I have often reflected that the accounts given us by the men sent inland (Anthony Henday and William Tomison excepted) were incoherent and unintelligible."[47] The second of Smith's two extant journals fall into this category of borderline literacy, while the first is a far more articulate fair copy in Graham's hand. A collection of executive summaries, again in Graham's hand and catalogued as HBCA B.239/a/59, consists of abstracts of Pink's journals for 1766-67 and 1767-68 together with highlights from the York Fort and Severn House post journals for 1767-69. Graham marked what he considered important passages in Pink's journals by enclosing them in square brackets, and then copied these passages into B.239/a/59; the result is a condensed, focussed account of trading relations with "strange Indians" and "Pedlar" occupation of former French posts. Graham abstracted Tomison's journal of 1767-68 in the E.2/6 and E.2/4 "Observations"; he also included a summary of this journal in the Severn House post journal of 1767-68. In his E.2/11 volume, Graham abstracted and considerably altered Cocking's journal of 1772-73; as with Pink's journals, both Cocking's full account and the abstract are extant and can be compared.[48]

Smith's journals are close counterparts to Henday's. His first journal survives only in Graham's copy, and begins as follows: "1756 Augst ye 23^d We took our Departure from York fort, and in 4 days Reached Steal river, seed two tents of Ind^s. Stayed there two days, the wind blowing hard att NW^t."[49] Its geographical descriptions are reasonably detailed and informative; for example—

> 17 In the Morning Steered Away WNW^t, Came to the falls, no Water to go with the Canues, obliged to Carry our things over them, and after that to go into the woods to pull down a beaver Dam as we had the day before, from this place, our Course NW, and nothing growing ashore but willows, Cross'd a narrow Creek then Steered West, untill we past one Bay, then WSW^t, Cross'd another Creek, put up for this night Low Shore and Burnt woods[50]

—while reports of Natives and the French resemble various entries in Henday's journal:

9 This day Came one Ind^n from the french, brought word, the french had no powder, att there house, and the had never heard of us before, the french Men that was in our Company All winter always told us he would Certainly kill us, but the Ind^s Said if they did or offer'd to do any harm to us, they would kill them all.

10th & 11th Smoakt it, and then Six tents Sett out on purpose to go to Warr, having no Goods to trade, that is to Come to ye factory with.[51]

In contrast, Smith's second journal, apparently a holograph, begins, "June ye 30 in the year of 1757 we tuck our daperter from the factory and thasdey ye 30 we leay at the big stone and fridey ye 1 we lea in Stell rever and seatedy 2 day we lea in Stell rever a litel be yand the crick. . . . "[52] Marginally literate as it is, this opening passage is eloquent compared with the rest of the journal, a sample of which reads as follows:

Seatedy the 17 we moved and want SSW and Sundey the 18 we lea by and mondey the 19 we moved and want south and tusedy the 20 we moved and want SbW and wandey the 21 we lea by and thasdey the 22 we lea by and fridey the 23 we moved and want SW and Seatedy the 24 we moved and want SSW and Sundey the 25 we moved and want SbW. . . . [53]

Landscape description for the river ascent to the plains is limited to repeated mention of "fourls [falls] and ileands" and one reference to the "Baren grownd." Reporting on French traders and inland Native groups is brief and confusing: "mondey the 25 we want SW over that Lak and a bout noun cam to the Large caring pleas a[nd] Sear the freanch at and we was forct to ceary our things a bout three mile and on the other Side ther was sixteen tennts of indens and we geave tham backe[y]."[54] It is tempting to conclude that in copying Smith's journal Graham heavily edited it, even effectively rewrote it, not only normalizing its spelling but inserting remarks that were appropriate responses to the winterer's instructions. The heaviness of Graham's editorial hand can be judged not only by comparing Smith's two journals; Graham's abstract of Cocking's journal of 1772-73 can also be compared with Cocking's extant holograph. It is possible that Henday's journal was subjected to similar treatment.

For years Graham vigorously pursued the wintering policy that Isham had recommended. Pink, one of the six young men sent from York Fort in the summer of 1766, obeyed point by point Graham's instructions "to Encourage the Indians to get all the Furrs they can, & use Your best endeavours to prevent their going to War. You are to make enquiry & get what intelligence You can of the Approaches of the People of Canada, how far they have penetrated into the Country."[55] Graham's careful questioning of an Archithinue who had travelled with the "Trading Indians" to York Fort dates from that summer:

> I had one Archithinnee Man down here this Summer He told me that He was not afraid of the Trading Indians and said they were more obliged to Him & his Countrymen than he was to them. He told me Furrs especially Wolves were plentifull and that the Trading Indians might get them and bring them down to the Fort . . . I made him a present of Several things but he told me often and at parting that his Countrymen would never come down they not knowing how to Paddle but told me to talk to the Trading natives to get Wolves from his Countrymen & bring them down.[56]

Pink returned from wintering along the Saskatchewan River and was sent inland again. On both trips Pink "heared of a Nother Bodey of those people Called Ye,artch,athin,na,wock" which made him resolve "to Gow a way up inland for to acquaint the Rest of those Contrey people . . . to Trap an Catch what Fores they Can and Give to those people that I am with . . . Ye,artch,e,thyn,na,wock Cannot paddle in a Canoe."[57] As he was returning to York Fort, Pink came upon "Some of the people of Cannada and Likewise a Little up from the Rivers Side j See thare house." The urge to trade was too much for the Natives he was with.

> heare j has Some Trobel with those jndaines now upon the aCcount that the are for Tradeing of thare fors with those people, and Likewise Some are for Staying heare and not for Coming Down to the Forte, but j Dos my best indeavor to bring those Jndaines frome those people Down to the Forte, but it is in vaine for me or aney Other English man to Do our best Endeavours in Encouredging of <them> Down, unless thare is the Same <done> thare.[58]

Jacobs, who assumed command of York Fort again in 1767, also perused Pink's journals and cited this last passage in the York Fort post journal as evidence that the wintering policy did not work. Jacobs added, "I have also been informed that not one of those men . . . [was able] even to prevent [the Indians'] Trad^g wth ye Canada Pedlars & ye very Ind^n Familys they were wth Traded wth the Pedlars in their presence."[59]

Meanwhile, back at Severn House, Graham continued the company's wintering policy by sending Tomison to Lake Winnipeg. Graham admitted that the main motivation for ordering Tomison's journey was to discover what the "Pedlars" were up to. Tomison kept a journal which Graham summarized in the Severn post journal sent to London:

> ye particulars of his Journey I shal give you wch will further enable you to Judge what game ye Pedlars are playing above us . . . ye English & French

Pedlars . . . were arrived at their Houses in Misquegamaw River on ye west Side of ye Lake . . . Octr 2^d passed by his Tent Saswe a French Pedlar 10 French Servants 12 Ind^n Assistants an Ind^n guide or conductor wth 6 large Canoes well loaded wth all sorts of Goods . . . Saswe declined Speaking to him but one of his men who spoke good English & told him that they were going towards Basquea . . . he see many Ind^{ns} some Albany some Severn some York Fort Ind^{ns} who kept continually Trad^g what Furrs they caught wth ye Traders at Misquegamaw River & that when he went Paddling among them to get them down they had no Furrs to come wth so finding nothing was to be done he set out for Severn House June ye 6th he arrived wth 3 Canoes wch was 5 Canoes less than what he set out with.[60]

The failure version of Henday's journal copied into Graham's "Observations" is remarkably close to Tomison's report as Graham summarized it in 1768.

The journals of Smith, Pink and Tomison, as well as the interview with the Archithinue man, form a context produced by Graham himself and supported by correspondence among the Bayside factors. The journals of this context repeat four narrative elements: a company employee winters with a band of "Trading Indians"; Native groups who "Cannot Paddle" barter their furs with these middlemen; the middlemen pass by a "French House" and many trade their best furs despite all efforts of the HBC man to dissuade them; the middlemen who continue with the winterer have only a few poor furs to trade at the Bay. In the 1755 text of Henday's journal (B.239/a/40), two of these elements are awkwardly denied and reversed: the Natives who "Cannot Paddle" agree to learn this skill so they can visit the Bay forts, and the HBC employee manages to lure his band away from the French inland traders. The Henday texts included in Graham's "Observations" contain all four elements as they appear in the other accounts written in the late 1760s. The early states of the "Observations" (E.2/6 and E.2/4) include the abstract of Tomison's journal for 1767-68 together with the failure version of Henday's journal. Although there is no proof that Graham rewrote either Henday's or Smith's journal, the textual comparisons are suggestive. To produce the failure version of Henday's journal, Graham had only to stitch together what he had learned from Pink, Tomison and the Archithinue visitor. Graham's role in producing the four texts of Henday's journal may have ranged from careful copying, to amplification of certain statements, to borrowing from other sources, to deliberate invention.[61]

At first glance this last possibility may seem far-fetched, but we need to consider Henday's journal in the context of Graham's statements on trade and the remarks of his Bayside colleagues. Especially interesting are the documents which antedate Henday's return. In the

E texts of the journal, it is claimed that the Archithinue chief whom
Henday met in October 1754 refused to let his men travel to Hudson
Bay because they were unacquainted with canoes. Isham's instructions to Henday foresaw this objection: "I have been Severall times
inform'd that the Earchithinues who are perdigious Numerious, and
which is my View in Sending you to bring them to trade, has no
knowledge, or at Least can not padle in Cannoes; if this be true and
you have the oppurtunity of seeing some of them, Let your Guides
Show and Learn them, also Exhort them to practice it, that they may
be able to padle Down to the fort &c."[62] When Henday disappeared up
the Hayes River in the summer of 1754, Isham wrote to Jacobs, who
was then factor at Churchill: "By Anthony Henday who is gone in
Land, and is at this time amongst the Pemogamy and Earchithinue
Indians I hope Good success . . . my Chief View is this is not only to
Exhort and Encourage the [Pemogamy] Indians to come to Trade, but
to bring the Earchithinues to a Trade, who are very Numerous."[63]
Jacobs answered by return:

> I wish Anthony Henday may meet with the success You expect, hope he
> Will encourage the Indians to come and Trade, but Sir, pardon my freedom
> in saying, am of Opinion those Earchithinue Indians will never be brought
> to Trade at either of theese Factoryes (I say, never) my reason stands
> Good, they being a very Timerous People, and make no use of Canoes, nay,
> nor won't be perswaded to Venture in one, besides the Indians which
> trades Yearly with t[hem] get great Quantity of Furrs (Catt in particular)
> from the above said Earchithinues, and trade from them for Our Goods,
> and may probably be the reason for their not encourageing them to come
> Down to Trade, by which means the Indians keep the Benefit of that Trade
> amongst them selves.[64]

In this reply, written while the first winterer was still inland, Jacobs
anticipated the failure version of Henday's journal as it appeared fifteen
years later in Graham's "Observations." What Graham learned from his
Archithinue visitor in 1766 and from the journals of Pink and Tomison in
1768 added nothing to what Isham and Jacobs had already written in
1754, on the basis of conversations with earlier Native visitors to the Bay.
For twenty years after Henday's first trip inland, winterers informed the
chief factor at York of the same conditions, in exactly the same phrases,
as if this information were news. In turn, the London Committee was
informed, in the Bayside year-end reports, of these conditions as evidence that the wintering policy was not successful.

   As with their reporting of trade conditions, Henday and the winterers who followed him did not record new facts about the continental interior or its inhabitants. Since their accounts followed a prescribed pattern by which information was solicited and collected, the

inland explorers simply reiterated what had been perceived and suspected all along. The winterers were first and last true to their formal
instructions when they wrote up their journals. In the best empirical
tradition, they saw what they were told to look for and made their
experiences fit the model of action allowed in their orders. They also
looked for confirmation of stories and rumours they had heard in conversations during their Bayside service. For example, Matthew Cocking, who wintered in the Eagle Hills in 1772-73, essentially repeated
Henday's conversation with the Archithinue leader and Henday's description of the Archithinues' tobacco, smoking ceremony, dress and
cooking utensils. As well, Cocking echoed the statements of all earlier
winterers that traders from Montreal were doing a brisk business. It is
worth noting that Cocking was Graham's copyist—of the B.239/a/59
summaries and parts of the E.2/9 "Observations" before he travelled
inland, and the E.2/10 "Observations" after he returned. He would
have been well aware of Graham's picture of the continental interior
and of Graham's views on trade.[65]

By 1768 Jacobs was writing to the London Committee that "your
servants that goes inland would be of more service in stopping the
progress of these pedlars were they to be sent up in a body with a
careful prudent man to command them, and to build a house or houses inland."[66] His letter played up to the Committee's fondness for
thrift and caution, but it brought no change in policy. Since the parliamentary enquiry of 1749 and Isham's prosperous time as governor
of York Fort, the company had made it appear to its own personnel, as
well as to critics and the public, that it was indeed meeting the oppo-
sition from Canada and exploring the Bay hinterland. After 1768, however, trade continued to fall off and something had to be done about
it. In the end, a factor's career depended on his cargoes.

As master of Severn House, Graham was aware of Jacobs's fruit-
less effort to make the London Committee aware of just how serious
competition had become in the Saskatchewan region. Graham may
well have decided against simple advocacy and in favour of Isham's
backup tactic: using Henday's account as a reference tool and vehicle
of persuasion. In 1755 Isham had forwarded the journal to the London
Committee and had referred to it as evidence of French pressure on
York's trade: "the french by their surprising Encouragements on the
Borders of our country trades in Reality for great Quantitys [of the
best beaver], the Real proof of which is plain by the Acc^t of Captn
Hendeys Journey."[67] Graham used Henday's journal in the same way.
He included a text of the journal in his "Observations" and used it as
proof that the pedlars traded the best furs inland and that Archithin-
ues would never trade at the Bay.[68]

In August 1772, with Jacobs's approval, Graham wrote a supplementary letter included in the York Fort annual report to the London Committee. In his letter Graham described the inland competition in considerable detail and openly recommended a new outpost at Basquia.

> The Situation of your Affairs in this Country is very unpromising. I have not been Indolent. I have gained certain Information of what is doing Inland, I think it my Duty to lay before <You> the success of my Enquiry. Your Trade at York Fort & Severn is greatly diminished, the Keskochewan Indians Who are the Support of it being intercepted by the Canadian Pedlars who are Yearly Gaining fresh Influence over them by supplying them with Goods Inland. The Indians resort thither in the Winter for Ammunition & the whole body of the Natives build their Canoes not far distant from the residence of the Traders to whom they resort to Purchase Ammunition & other Articles in the Spring, & finding they can procure Tobacco & other Necessaries so near & being kept in Liquor, every Inducement to visit the Company's Factorys is forgot, & the prime furs are picked out & traded, the refuse is tied up & brought down to us by the Leading Indians & their followers: of such as these is Your Honour's Trade composed.[69]

The situation sketched here repeats earlier annual reports by the Bayside factors, the journals of Pink and Tomison, and the failure version of Henday's journal included in Graham's "Observations" since 1768. Far from opposing each other, Graham and Jacobs had identical reactions to the prosperous trade returns of the early 1760s and to the sharp decline after 1767. Both recommended a post to capture the Saskatchewan trade. Graham's letter of August 1772 supported this change in policy by citing a letter from Thomas Corry, a Canadian trader on the Saskatchewan River, as reinforcement of the remarks furnished several years earlier by Pink, Tomison and the Archithinue visitor to York. Corry's account of the Montreal traders' long and difficult route to the Saskatchewan River dispelled any doubt that the shorter route from Hudson Bay was too rugged to supply an inland post.

As for the effect on plains Native groups, Corry and the winterers testified to a situation that stretched back to Henday's inland journey almost twenty years before. The link was Wapenessew, the "French Leader" mentioned by both Henday and the pedlar Corry. Henday had met him in February 1755 and had enticed him down to York; since then, as Graham noted in the E.2/4 text of Henday's journal, this leader had traded at the Bay and was "greatly esteemed." Graham's letter of August 1772 recalled that

> Wappenasew the Indian mentioned in Corry's Letter is a Person of Prime Consideration with the Natives, & his Influence is very extensive. He came

to York Fort in 1755 & continued Yearly with us until two Years ago, when the Canadians who have great need of his Assistance to promote their Trade & protect their Persons, tried every means to attach him to their Service, & they have succeeded. . . . It appears to Me that the only way of encreasing the Furr Trade is to have an Inland Settlement to supply the Natives with Necessarys, Ammunition Tobacco & Brandy would be the Principal Articles . . . In an undertaking of this kind Your Honours have many advantages over the Pedlars, Your distance would be small in comparison to theirs. . . . the Canadian traders having got up the Country are settled above us right in the track of the Indians . . . & unless Your Honours exert your selves speedily, the trade at York Fort will be ruined; for otherwise (tho' it may rise for one Year) it will never be uniformly large as usual.[70]

Graham's urgent recommendation strained the limits of the respectful subservience expected of a company "servant" writing to his employers. Where Jacobs and Graham differed appears to have been in their willingness to act according to their changed perception. Jacobs recommended gradual change, hesitated to seize the opportunity offered by Canadian defectors, and waited for the Committee's direction. Graham hired the Canadian defector Thomas Corry, and even recommended him to the London Committee as "a strong, tall, able Man, speaks the English, French & Indian Languages . . . & can write a little, & very much belov[d] by the Natives."[71]

The timing of Graham's letter is of particular interest. A few weeks earlier he had sent Cocking to winter on the plains; at last a company employee who was literate and relatively "expert in . . . keeping a just Reckoning of distances" would provide a detailed report of the geography and the trade conditions inland. But the interim governor of York did not wait for Cocking's report to urge a change in strategy: he referred instead to the journals of earlier winterers, and came to the same conclusion in August 1772 that Cocking did in June 1773, after a year of on-the-spot investigation. The winterers' accounts, ostensibly personal, eye-witness reports of places and conditions, revealed little if anything that had not been known and anticipated by the factors who sent them inland. The abiding interest of the winterers' journals does not therefore lie in their empirical record of the continental interior, but in the extent to which various offices and functions of the Hudson's Bay Company trading operation were sustained by a network of reiterative, mutually confirming "Letters, Books and Papers."

Graham did not need Cocking's evidence to urge a change in policy. Instead, what is remarkable about his August 1772 letter and the variant texts of Henday's journal is that Graham drew on the reports and correspondence already available to him. Moreover, he used these documents to bring about change rather than to conserve a long-standing practice. After 1768, Jacobs and Graham looked for an alternative to the wintering policy for which Isham had campaigned using Henday's journal (the success version) as proof of its effectiveness. While Jacobs's plea for a trading settlement on the Saskatchewan River fell on deaf ears, Graham's letter persuaded the London Committee to approve this plan. Graham's recommendation was carefully prepared. Together with other inland reports, Henday's journal (the failure version) was used to demonstrate how ineffective the wintering policy had been from the beginning. Both Isham and Graham used the same technique to urge a change in policy. Both won their point because they put their weight behind the empirical claims of the journal form and presented innovation in the form of reportage.

Notes

1 Robson, 6. Cf. Dobbs; Great Britain, parliamentary *Report* of 1749; Umfreville, 68-9. For a summary of the controversy leading to the government enquiry, see Rich, 1, 533-86.
2 HBCA E.2/1, Isham, "Observations on Hudson's Bay," ff. 71v-72r, pp. 134-35. For the mid-eighteenth-century scientific, political and economic climate in which the company was operating, see Williams, *The British Search for the Northwest Passage in the Eighteenth Century*, 31-78, 109-29; Rich 1: 549, 556-609, 630-47.
3 HBCA A.11/114, Isham, instructions to Henday, 26 June 1754; cf. HBCA A.11/114, Isham, instructions to Henday, 19 February 1754, and HBCA A.11/114, Isham, instructions to Smith and Waggoner, 20 August 1756.
4 HBCA B.239/a/40, E.2/6, E.2/4, E.2/11, Henday, journal, 10 July 1754, 3 January 1755, 13 August 1754, 13 March 1755.
5 HBCA B.239/a/40, Henday, journal, 22 November 1754 and 17 April 1755; cf. the typical description of buffalo hunting in HBCA E.2/6, E.2/4 and E.2/11, Henday, journal, 16 October 1754.
6 HBCA A.11/114, Isham, instructions to Henday, 19 February 1754 and 26 June 1754.
7 Rich, 1: 632-37; see also Stephen, 93; cf. Glover's personality profile of David Thompson, discussed in Belyea, " 'The Columbian Enterprise' and A. S. Morton," 23-25.
8 Foucault, *Les Mots et les choses*, 143; see also Crary, 25-60; Adolph, 78-128, 242-303; Duggan; Edney; Ryan, 38-53, de Certeau, 3-23, 63-120; cf. Sande Cohen, 19-21, 63-173.
9 Burpee, *The Search for the Western Sea*, vii; Morton, 250.
10 Ray, *Indians in the Fur Trade*, xi.
11 Russell, 1-3, 213; see also Peers, *passim*.
12 Brown, "Documentary Editing," 5-8; cf. Shanks and Tilley, 7-28.
13 HBCA A.6/10, HBC London Committee to Isham, 26 May 1761.
14 HBCA E.2/1, Isham, "Observations on Hudson's Bay," f. 46r, p. 83.
15 HBCA A.11/114, Isham to the HBC London Committee, 6 August 1752.
16 HBCA A.6/8, HBC London Committee to Isham, 24 May 1753.

17 HBCA B.239/a/40, Isham, "Remarks."

18 HBCA B.239/a/40, Henday, journal, 30-31 May 1755, 23 June 1755.

19 HBCA A.6/9, HBC London Committee to Isham, 12 May 1756.

20 HBCA A.11/114, Isham, instructions to Henday, 26 June 1754.

21 HBCA A.6/9, HBC London Committee to Isham, 12 May 1756; Stephen, 40-41.

22 Williams, ed., appendix A to Graham, *Observations on Hudson's Bay*, 335n., simply states that the theory of Isham's modification of B.239/a/40 is not "completely satisfactory"; in a later article, Williams, "The Puzzle of Anthony Henday's Journal," 52-53, 56, suggests that Henday himself altered his journal to placate Isham's desire for the commercial success of his year inland.

23 An indication of this development is given in Graham's note on Wappenessew, a "French Leader" who promised Henday that he would trade with the HBC from then on—see HBCA E.2/11. Henday, journal, 2 February 1755. See also Williams, ed., appendix A to Graham, *Observations on Hudson's Bay*, 335n.

24 Peter Fidler was the last HBC winterer: see HBCA E.3/1, Fidler, journal, 1791-92; and HBCA E.3/2, Fidler, journal, 1792-93.

25 HBCA B.239/a/42, B.239/a/44, B.239/a/47, York Fort "General Letters" to the HBC London Committee include Isham's canoe tallies for the years 1756-57, 1758, and 1760.

26 HBCA B.239/b/27, Graham to Norton, 26 July 1766.

27 Rich, 1: 648-61; Morton, 254-55.

28 HBCA A.6/9, HBC London Committee to Isham, 12 May 1756.

29 HBCA A.11/115, Isham to the HBC London Committee, 29 August 1759. See also HBCA E.2/6, Graham, "Observations on Hudson's Bay," 45v-50r; Umfreville, 204-5.

30 HBCA A.6/9, HBC London Committee to Isham, 15 May 1760.

31 HBCA A.11/114, Isham to the HBC London Committee, 2 September 1755.

32 HBCA A.6/9, HBC London Committee to Isham, 27 May 1755.

33 HBCA A.6/11, HBC London Committee to Jacobs, 19 May 1768.

34 HBCA A.11/115, Jacobs to the HBC London Committee, 5 September 1767, and Jacobs to the HBC London Committee, 7 September 1767.

35 HBCA A.11/115, Jacobs to the HBC London Committee, 23 August 1768.

36 HBCA A.11/115, Jacobs to the HBC London Committee, 20 August 1768.

37 Williams, ed., notes to Graham, *Observations on Hudson's Bay*, 337, 339, 344-46.

38 HBCA E.2/5, Graham, "Observations on Hudson's Bay," f. 10v, p. 14.

39 HBCA E.2/5, Graham, "Observations on Hudson's Bay," f. 11v, p. 16; cf. HBCA B.239/a/69, Cocking, "Thoughts on Making a Settlement Inland," written after his return to York Fort in 1773: "As to sending Servants Inland, in the manner that has been already established, to encourage Trade. I am of Opinion it will Answer no end, for the Persons who have been upon this Service only liked to continue as it skreened them from Duty at the Fort: and they were most of them disliked; as they never endeavoured to gain the Affections of the Natives, and converted the Goods they were

furnished with to the Purpose of Collecting Furrs for their own private Emolument."

40 HBCA E.2/5, Graham, "Observations on Hudson's Bay," f. 13r, p. 19.

41 HBCA E.2/6, Graham, "Observations on Hudson's Bay," f. 42v, p. 83.

42 HBCA E.2/5, Graham, "Observations on Hudson's Bay," ff. 8r-8v, pp. 9-10.

43 HBCA A.11/114, Isham to the HBC London Committee, 2 September 1755. See also HBCA A.11/114, Isham to the HBC London Committee, 2 September 1755, written as a supplement to the annual YF "General Letter": "really Gentlemen the fault [of poor returns] is not mine but the Natives themselves, who actually trades great Quantity of beaver with the french; as to their Setlm^ts its too true, Such their is in abundance, the truth of which please to observe Captn Hendeys 12 Months travels in Land."

44 HBCA A.11/114, Isham, instructions to Smith and Waggoner, 20 August 1756.

45 HBCA A.11/114, Isham to the HBC London Committee, 4 August 1756; HBCA E.2/4, Graham, "Observations on Hudson's Bay," f. 60v, p. 114. Cf. Williams, "The Puzzle of Anthony Henday's Journal," 52-56; Stephen, 17-24, 69-88.

47 HBCA E.2/12, Graham, "Observations on Hudson's Bay," p. 648.

48 HBCA B.239/a/43, Smith, journal, 1756-57; HBCA B.239/a/45, Smith, journal, 1757-58; HBCA B.239/a/56, Pink, journal, 1766-67; HBCA B.239/a/58, Pink, journal, 1767-68; HBCA B.239/a/61, Pink, journal, 1768-69; HBCA B.239/a/59, abstracts of post journals for York Fort and Severn House, as well as of Pink's journals, 1766-68; HBCA B.239/a/64, Tomison, journal, 1769-70; HBCA B.239/a/69, Cocking, journal, 1772-73; HBCA E.2/6 and E.2/12, Graham, "Observations on Hudson's Bay."

49 HBCA B.239/a/43, Smith, journal, 23-27 August 1756.

50 HBCA B.239/a/43, Smith, journal, 17 September 1756.

51 HBCA B.239/a/43, Smith, journal, 9-11 February 1757.

52 HBCA B.239/a/45, Smith, journal, 30 June-2 July 1757.

53 HBCA B.239/a/45, Smith, journal, 17-25 September 1757.

54 HBCA B.239/a/45, Smith, journal, 25 July 1757.

55 HBCA B.239/b/27, Graham, instructions to winterers, June 1766. Cf. HBCA A.6/10, HBC London Committee to Graham/Jacobs, 13 May 1767: "We approve of your having sent 6 of our Servants Inland with different Sets of Indians, and hope that material advantages will arise in future from those Journeys.—Mr Graham in his Journal 29 June last advising that he had been informed by some Indians . . . of their trading in the Winter with some English [inland] . . . , We expect that You will use your utmost endeavours to induce the Indians to bring all their Goods to the Factory and prevent if possible any Diminution of the Companys Trade."

56 HBCA B.239/a/59, Graham to the HBC London Committee, 19 June 1766.

57 HBCA B.239/a/58, Pink, journal, 4 and 25 May 1768.

58 HBCA B.239/a/58, Pink, journal, 26 May 1768.

59 B.239/a/59, Jacobs to the HBC London Committee, 8 July 1768; cf. HBCA B.239/b/29, Jacobs to Moses Norton, 25 July 1768: "the Canada Pedlers have got into the Center of the Indians that usually come down to this Factory to Trade, & carried off a great part of the Trade of this Place . . .

Our Men Inland are of such Service, as to see the very Indians they were with all the Year, as well as Numbers of others, Trade with those Interlopers & Had not the least influence to prevent it, Nor had they any thing left of the large Quantities of Goods they Receive when they proceed Inland to induce the Indians not to Trade with them or perswade them to proceed on their Journey to the Factory. You see by this Account what hopes I have of a Trade next Year, And the Leading Indians were unreasonable in their demands of Presents which I was obliged to comply with . . . that they should have no Plea to desert the Factory & go to the Pedlers . . . I have been particular on this Melancholy affair as It gives Me great concern."

60 HBCA B.198/a/9, Severn House post journal (Graham), 4 August 1768.

61 Williams: "Graham was treating Henday's notes [*sic*] . . . in the same way that he treated his own . . . , a process summed up by the present writer in his preface to the published edition of Graham's 'Observations': 'A short paragraph in one volume may swell to several pages in a later; new information appears and disappears; revisions are made, and then apparently unmade . . . '" ("The Puzzle of Anthony Henday's Journal," 55).

62 HBCA A. 11/114, Isham, instructions to Henday, 26 June 1754.

63 HBCA B.239/b/11, Isham to Jacobs, 17 August 1754.

64 HBCA B.239/a/11, Jacobs to Isham, 23 August 1754.

65 HBCA B.239/a/69, Cocking, "Thoughts on making a Settlement Inland."

66 HBCA A.11/115, Jacobs to the HBC London Committee, 20 August 1768.

67 HBCA A.11/114, Isham to the HBC London Committee, 2 September 1755.

68 Cf. HBCA E.2/6, E.2/4, E.2/11, Henday, journal, 14-15 October 1754, with HBCA B.239/a/69 and E.2/11, Cocking, journal, 3 and 5 December 1772.

69 HBCA A.11/115, Graham to the HBC London Committee, 26 August 1772; HBCA E.2/4 and E.2/11, Henday, journal, 2 February 1755; HBCA A.11/115, Jacobs to the HBC London Committee, 29 August 1772: "the reason of this decline appears to be owing to the Canadian Traders for the Particulars of which we refer you to Mr Graham's Letter." Rich, 2: 34, considers Graham's letter a sudden change of position; in his notes to Graham, *Observations on Hudson's Bay*, Williams adds, "The very fact that Graham had hitherto opposed the idea of inland settlement may have given this letter more weight" (344). Williams does not suggest any reason why Graham would suddenly have changed his mind on this issue. Cf. HBCA A.11/115, Jacobs to the HBC London Committee, 20 August 1769: "It is a very Provoking thing to See your Hon^{rs} Trade Carried off in this manner, and what is most Vexatious I have it not in my Power to put a Stop to it, ad to this the overbearing Demands of the Trading Indians who having So ready a Supply from the Pedlers are now Prodigious hard to Please . . . there is a place Called Pow wis tick Assinee'cup, that is the Fall Carrying Place, where the men inland tells me there might be a house built to oppose the Pedlers, but if only to live in quietly and Encourage the Indians to Come to Trade there is many Places Nearer hand to this Factory would do . . . I must not Pretend to Say that the Same number of Indians would Come was none of your Servants to be Sent inland, therfore I shall Continue to Send them, but they may be Gradually decreased, and in a Little

time might be Totaly Laid aside if the Indians Continues to Come without them"; cf. also HBCA A.11/115, Jacobs to the HBC London Committee, 20 August 1772: "Some of the Pedlers men have Run away from those that Employ'd them, One of them Came to York Fort, Mr Graham Employ'd him in your Service and Sent him inland . . . I am . . . in hopes your Hon^{rs} will Let me Know whether you approve of Employing these Runaways in your Service." As of the late 1760s, both Graham and Jacobs questioned the wintering policy, were dissatisfied with the winterers' performance, and seriously considered the alternative of inland posts.

70 HBCA A.11/115, Graham to the HBC London Committee, 26 August 1772.

71 HBCA A.11/115, Graham to the HBC London Committee, 26 August 1772.

List of Sources

List of Sources

Manuscript Sources

Hudson's Bay Company Archives, Provincial Archives of Manitoba

HBCA A.6/8-10. HBC London Committee to York Fort. 1753-61.

HBCA A.11/114-15. York Fort to the HBC London Committee. 1752-72.

HBCA A.11/114. James Isham. "Instructions to Anth^y Hendy, Dated at York Fort, Feby ye 19th 1754."

HBCA A.11/114. James Isham. "A Copie of Orders and Instructions to Anth^y Hendey upon a journey in Land, Dated att York Fort, June 26th 1754."

HBCA A.11/114. James Isham. "Orders to Joseph Smith, and Joseph Wagoner." 20 August 1756.

HBCA B.49/a/1. Samuel Hearne, journal. 1774-75.

HBCA B.198/a/9. Severn House post journal. 1767-68.

HBCA B.239/a/40. James Isham. "Remarks."

HBCA B.239/a/43. Joseph Smith, journal. 1756-57.

HBCA B.239/a/45. Joseph Smith, journal. 1757-58.

HBCA B.239/a/42-7 York Fort post journals. 1757-67.

HBCA B.239/a/56. William Pink, journal. 1766-67.

HBCA B.239/a/58. William Pink, journal. 1767-68.

HBCA B.239/a/59. abstracts of York Fort post journals, Severn House post journals, and William Pink, journals. 1766-68.

HBCA B.239/a/61. William Pink, journal. 1768-69.

HBCA B.239/a/64. William Tomison, journal. 1769-70.

HBCA B.239/a/69. Matthew Cocking, journal. 1772-73.

HBCA B.239/a/72. Matthew Cocking, journal. 1774-75.

HBCA B.239/b/11-29. Bayside correspondence. 1754-68.

HBCA B.239/d/44. York Fort Account Book. 1754.

HBCA E.2./1, E.2/2. James Isham. "Observations on Hudson's Bay."

HBCA E.2/4, E.2.5, E.2.6, E.2/11, E.2/12. Andrew Graham. "Observations on Hudson's Bay."

HBCA E.3/1. Peter Fidler, journal. 1791-92.

HBCA E.3/2. Peter Fidler, journal. 1792-93.

HBCA G.1/25. Ackomokki, transcribed by Peter Fidler. "An Indian Map of the Different Tribes that inhabit on the East & west side of the Rocky Mountains . . . " 1801.

HBCA G.2/8. "Moses Nortons Drt. of the Northern Parts of Hudsons Bay laid dwn on Indn. Information & bro^t Home by him anno 1760."

HBCA G.2/15. Andrew Graham. "A Plan of Part of Hudson's-Bay, & Rivers, communicating With the Principal Settlements." 1772.

HBCA G.2/17. Andrew Graham. "A Plan of Part of Hudson's-Bay, & Rivers, communicating with York Fort & Severn." 1774.

HBCA G.1/20. Samuel Hearne. "A Map of some of the principal Lakes River's &c leading from YF to Basquiaw . . . " [1775]

Huntington Library

HM 1720. "Remarks on Hudsons Bay Trade by Andrew Graham many Years Factor at York Fort and Severn House for the perusal of his Employers 1769."

Thomas Fisher Rare Book Library, University of Toronto

Box 90. Correspondence between J. B. Tyrrell and William Isbister, 26 March-24 December 1909.

Printed Sources

Adolph, Robert. *The Rise of the Modern Prose Style.* Cambridge: MIT Press, 1968.

Belyea, Barbara. "The 'Columbian Enterprise' and A. S. Morton: A Historical Exemplum." *BC Studies* 86 (1990): 3-27.

Belyea, Barbara. "Amerindian Maps: The Explorer as Translator." *Journal of Historical Geography* 18:3 (1992): 267-77.

Belyea, Barbara. "Inland Journeys, Native Maps." *Cartographica* 33:2 (1996): 1-16.

Belyea, Barbara. "Mapping the Marias: The Interface of Native and Scientific Cartographies." *Great Plains Quarterly* 17 (Summer/Fall 1997): 165-84.

Belyea, Barbara, ed. *David Thompson: Columbia Journals.* Kingston and Montreal: McGill-Queen's University Press, 1994.

Black-Rogers, Mary. "Varieties of 'Starving': Semantics and Survival in the Subarctic Fur Trade." *Ethnohistory* 33 (1986): 353-83.

Bowers, Fredson. *Essays in Bibliography, Text, and Editing.* Charlottesville: University Press of Virginia for the Bibliographical Society of the University of Virginia, 1975.

Brown, Jennifer S. H. "Ethnohistorians: Strange Bedfellows, Kindred Spirits." *Ethnohistory* 38:2 (1991): 113-23.

Brown, Jennifer S. H. "Documentary Editing: Whose Voices?" In *Occasional Papers of the Champlain Society*, 1-13. Toronto: Champlain Society, 1992.

Brown, Jennifer S. H., and Robert Brightman, eds. *"The Orders of the Dreamed": George Nelson on Cree and Northern Ojibwa Religion and Myth, 1823.* Winnipeg: University of Manitoba Press, 1988.

Brown, Jennifer S. H., and Elizabeth Vibert, eds. *Reading beyond Words: Contexts for Native History.* Peterborough: Broadview Press, 1996.

Brown, Mark R., and Jerry Honeycutt. *Using HTML 3.2.* 3d ed. Indianapolis: Que, 1997.

Bumsted, J. M. "Clio and the Historical Editor." *Acadiensis* 9 (1980): 92-101.

Burpee, Lawrence J. *The Search for the Western Sea.* Toronto: Musson, 1908.

Burpee, Lawrence J., ed. "York Factory to the Blackfeet Country—the Journal of Anthony Hendry, 1754-55." *Proceedings and Transactions of the Royal Society of Canada*, 3d series I (1907): II, 307-64.

Certeau, Michel de. *L'Ecriture de l'histoire.* Paris: Gallimard, 1975.

Clastres, Pierre. *L'Etat et la nation.* Paris: Minuit, 1966.

Cohen, Philip. "Textual Instability, Literary Studies, and Recent Developments in Literary Scholarship." *Resources for American Literary Study* 20:2 (1994): 133-48.

Cohen, Sande. *Historical Culture: Of the Recoding of an Academic Discipline.* Berkeley: University of California Press, 1986.

Cole, Douglas, and Bradley Lockner, eds. *The Journals of George M. Dawson.* 2 vols. Vancouver: University of British Columbia Press, 1989.

Coles, Laura Miller. "The Decline of Documentary Publishing: The Role of English-Canadian Archives and Historical Societies in Documentary Publishing." *Archivaria* 23 (1986-87): 69-85.

Coles, Laura Miller. "Looking Backward, Reaching Forward: The Champlain Society and Documentary Publishing." In *Occasional Papers of the Champlain Society*, 15-35. Toronto: Champlain Society, 1992.

Crary, Jonathan. *Techniques of the Observer: On Vision and Modernity in the Nineteenth Century.* Cambridge: MIT Press, 1990.

Cruikshank, Julie. *Reading Voices/Dän Dhá Ts'edenintth'e̲: Oral and Written Interpretations of the Yukon's Past.* Vancouver: Douglas and McIntyre, 1991.

Cullen, Charles T. "Casual Observer Beware: The Need for Using Scholarly Editions." *Prologue* 21 (1989): 68-73.

Cutler, Wayne. "The 'Authentic Witness': The Editor Speaks for the Document." *Newsletter of the Association for Documentary Editing* 4 (February 1982): 8-9.

Davis, Richard C., ed. *Sir John Franklin's Journals and Correspondence: The First Arctic Land Expedition.* Toronto: Champlain Society, 1995.

Dempsey, Hugh A. *Indian Tribes of Alberta.* Calgary: Glenbow Museum, 1979.

Derrida, Jacques. *De la grammatologie.* Paris: Minuit, 1967.

Dickason, Olive Patricia. *Canada's First Nations.* Toronto: McClelland and Stewart, 1992.

Dobbs, Arthur. *A Short Narrative and Justification of the Proceedings of the Committee Appointed by the Adventurers, to prosecute the Discovery of the Passage to the Western Ocean of AMERICA.* London, 1749.

Duggan, Graham. "Decolonizing the Map: Post-Colonialism, Post-Structuralism and the Cartographic Connection." *ARIEL* 20:4 (1989): 115-31.

Dunlap, Leslie W., and Fred Shelley, eds. *The Publication of American Historical Manuscripts.* Iowa City: University of Iowa Libraries, 1976.

Edney, Matthew H. "Cartographic Culture and Nationalism in the Early United States: Benjamin Vaughan and the Choice of a Prime Meridian, 1811." *Journal of Historical Geography* 20:4 (1994): 384-95.

Eggert, Paul. "Document and Text: The 'Life' of the Literary Work and the Capacities of Editing." *Text* 7 (1994): 1-24.

Elias, Robert H. "Eighteenth-Century Thorns, Twentieth-Century Secretaries, & Other Prickly Matters." *Text* 3 (1987): 347-53.

Faries, Richard. *Dictionary of the Cree Language.* Toronto: General Synod of the Church of England in Canada, 1938.

Foucault, Michel. *Les mots et les choses.* Paris: Gallimard, 1966.

Foucault, Michel. *L'Archéologie du savoir.* Paris: Gallimard, 1969.

Fried, Morton H. *The Notion of Tribe.* Menlo Park: Cummings, 1975.

Frison, George. *Prehistoric Hunters of the High Plains.* 2d ed. San Diego: Academic Press, 1991.

Gilman, William H. "Review Essay: How Should Journals Be Edited?" *Early American Literature* 6 (1971): 73-85.

Gottesman, Robert, and Scott Bennett, eds. *Art and Error: Modern Textual Editing.* Bloomington: Indiana University Press, 1970.

Gottfred, Jeff. "Understanding How David Thompson Navigated." *Northwest Journal* 9 (November-December 1996): 1-38.

Gough, Barry Morton, ed. *The Journal of Alexander Henry the Younger.* 2 vols. Toronto: Champlain Society, 1988-92.

Graff, Henry F., and A. Simone Reagor. *Documentary Editing in Crisis: Some Reflections and Recommendations.* Washington: National Historical Publications and Records Commission, 1981.

Gravell, Thomas L., and George Miller. *A Catalogue of American Watermarks.* New York: Garland, 1979.

Great Britain. *Report from the Committee, Appointed to enquiry into the State & Condition of the countries adjoining to Hudson's Bay, and of the Trade carried on there.* London, 1749.

Greenberg, Adolph M. and James Morrison. "Group Identities in the Boreal Forest: The Origin of the Northern Ojibwa." *Ethnohistory* 29:2 (1982): 75-102.

Greenhood, David. *Mapping.* Chicago: University of Chicago Press, 1964.

Greetham, D. C. *Textual Scholarship: An Introduction.* New York: Garland, 1992.

Hall, Frank. "Names! Names! Names!" *Bison* (December 1984): 12-13.

Halpenny, Francess G., ed. *Editing Canadian Texts.* Toronto: Hakkert for the Committee for the Conference on Editorial Problems, 1975.

Harris, R. Cole, ed. *Historical Atlas of Canada.* Vol. 1: *From the Beginnings to 1800.* Toronto: University of Toronto Press, 1989.

Hartman, Geoffrey H. *Saving the Text: Literature/Derrida/Philosophy.* Baltimore: Johns Hopkins University Press, 1981.

Hay, Louis. "Does Text Exist?" *Studies in Bibliography* 41 (1988): 64-76.

Heawood, Edward. *Watermarks.* Vol. 1 of *Monumenta Chartae Papyraceae,* edited by E. J. Labarre. Hilversum: Paper Publications, 1950.

Heidenreich, Conrad. "Measures of Distance Employed on Seventeenth- and Early Eighteenth-Century Maps of Canada," *Canadian Cartographer (Cartographica)* 12:2 (1975): 121-37.

Helm, June. "Matonabbee's Map." *Arctic Anthropology* 26:2 (1989): 28-47.

Helm, June, ed. *Essays on the Problem of Tribe.* San Francisco: American Ethnological Society, 1968.

Helm, June, ed. *Subarctic*. Vol. 6 of *Handbook of North American Indians*, gen. ed. William C. Sturtevant. Washington DC: Smithsonian Institution, 1981.

Houston, C. Stuart, ed. *Arctic Ordeal: The Journal of Sir John Richardson*. Kingston and Montreal: McGill-Queen's University Press, 1984.

Houston, C. Stuart, ed. *To the Arctic by Canoe, 1819-1821: The Journal and Paintings of Robert Hood*. Kingston and Montreal: McGill-Queen's University Press, 1994.

Houston, C. Stuart, ed. *Arctic Artist: The Journal and Paintings of George Back*, commentary by I. S. MacLaren. Montreal and Kingston: McGill-Queen's University Press, 1994.

Jenness, Diamond. *Indians of Canada*. 7th ed. Ottawa: Minister of Supply and Services Canada, 1977.

Johnson, Samuel. *Dictionary of the English Language*. 2 vols. London: Strahan, 1755.

Kenny, A., and O. Y. Rieger. *Managing Digital Imaging Projects: An RLG Workshop*. Ithaca: Cornell University, 1998.

Kipp, Darrell Robes. "Blackfoot." In *Encyclopedia of North American Indians*, edited by Frederick C. Hoxie. Boston: Houghton Mifflin, 1996.

Kline, Mary Jo. *A Guide to Documentary Editing*. Rev. ed. Baltimore: Johns Hopkins University Press, 1998.

Lamb, W. Kaye, ed. *The Letters and Journals of Simon Fraser, 1806-1808*. Toronto: Macmillan, 1960.

Lamb, W. Kaye, ed. *Gabriel Franchère: Journal of a Voyage to the North West Coast of America During the Years 1811, 1812, 1813 and 1814*. Toronto: Champlain Society, 1969.

Lamb, W. Kaye, ed. *The Journals and Letters of Alexander Mackenzie*. Toronto: Macmillan for the Hakluyt Society, 1970.

Lamb, W. Kaye, ed. *George Vancouver: A Voyage of Discovery to the North Pacific Ocean and Round the World, 1791-1795*. 4 vols. London: Hakluyt Society, 1984.

Landow, George P. *Hypertext: The Convergence of Contemporary Critical Theory and Technology*. Baltimore: Johns Hopkins University Press, 1992.

Lavagnino, John. "Reading, Scholarship, and Hypertext Editions." *Text* 8 (1995): 109-24.

Lemisch, Jesse. "The Papers of Great White Men" and "The Papers of a Few Great Black Men and a Few Great White Women." *Maryland Historian* 6 (1975): 48, 63-65.

Lewis, G. Malcolm. "Indian Maps." In *Mapping the North American Plains: Essays in the History of Cartography,* edited by Frederick J. Luebke, Frances W. Kaye and Gary E. Moulton, 63-80. Norman: University of Oklahoma Press and the Center of Great Plains Studies, University of Nebraska-Lincoln, 1987.

Maas, Paul. *Textual Criticism,* translated by Barbara Flower. Oxford: Clarendon Press, 1958.

MacGregor, James G. *Behold the Shining Mountains.* Edmonton: Applied Arts Products, 1954.

Mackenzie, Alexander. *Voyages from Montreal . . . with a preliminary account of the rise, progress, and present state of the fur trade.* 1801, facsimile reprint Edmonton: Hurtig, 1971.

MacLaren, I. S. "Exploration/Travel Literature and the Evolution of the Author." *International Journal of Canadian Studies* 5 (1992): 39-68.

McElrath, Joseph R. "Tradition and Innovation: Recent Developments in Literary Editing." *Documentary Editing* 10:4 (1988): 5-10.

McGann, Jerome. *A Critique of Modern Textual Criticism.* Chicago: University of Chicago Press, 1983.

McGann, Jerome. "The Textual Condition." *Text* 4 (1988): 29-38.

McKenzie, Ruth, ed. *The St. Lawrence Survey Journals of Captain Henry Wolsey Bayfield.* 2 vols. Toronto: Champlain Society, 1984-86.

McMillan, Alan D. *Native Peoples and Cultures of Canada.* Vancouver: Douglas and McIntyre, 1988.

Mandelbaum, David. *The Plains Cree: An Ethnographic, Historical and Comparative Study.* 2d ed. Regina: Canadian Plains Research Center, 1979.

Meyer, David, and Paul C. Thistle. "Saskatchewan River Rendezvous Centers and Trading Posts: Continuity in a Cree Social Geography." *Ethnohistory* 42:3 (1995): 403-44.

Milloy, John. *The Plains Cree: Trade, Diplomacy and War, 1790 to 1870.* Winnipeg: University of Manitoba Press, 1988.

Morantz, Toby. "Old Texts, Old Questions: Another Look at the Issue of Continuity and the Early Fur-Trade Period." *Canadian Historical Review* 73:2 (1992): 166-93.

Morse, Eric. *Fur Trade Canoe Routes of Canada/Then and Now.* 2d ed. Toronto: University of Toronto Press, 1979.

Morton, Arthur S. *A History of the Canadian West to 1870-71.* 2d ed. Revised by Lewis G. Thomas. Toronto: University of Toronto Press, 1973.

Moulton, Gary E., ed. *The Journals of the Lewis and Clark Expedition.* 11 vols. Lincoln: University of Nebraska Press, 1983-98.

Munro, Michael R. "Treatment of Toponyms in Manitoba from Languages without an Alphabet." In *Report on Canadian Participation, United Nations Conference on the Standardization of Geographical Names III, Athens 1977*. Ottawa: Canadian Permanent Committee on Geographical Names, 1978.

Newitt, L. R., and G. V. Haines. "Magnetic Declination Chart of Canada, 1990." *Canadian Geophysical Atlas*, map 10. Ottawa: Geological Survey of Canada, 1990.

Nielsen, Jakob. *Hypertext and Hypermedia*. Boston: Academic Press, 1990.

Nordloh, David. "The 'Perfect Text': The Editor Speaks for the Author." *Newsletter of the Association for Documentary Editing* 2 (May 1979): 1-3.

Parker, Hershel. " 'The Text Itself'—Whatever That Is." *Text* 3 (1987): 47-54.

Parks, Douglas R. "The Importance of Language Study for the Writing of Plains Indian History." In *New Directions in American Indian History*, edited by Colin C. Galloway. Norman: University of Oklahoma Press, 1988.

Peers, Laura. *The Ojibwa of Western Canada, 1780 to 1870*. Winnipeg: University of Manitoba Press, 1994.

Phelps, C. Dierdre. "The Edition as Art Form in Textual and Interpretive Criticism." *Text* 7 (1994): 61-75.

Ray, Arthur J. *Indians in the Fur Trade*. Toronto: University of Toronto Press, 1974.

Ray, Arthur J. *I Have Lived Here Since the World Began: An Illustrated History of Canadian Native Peoples*. Toronto: Lester Publishing, 1996.

Ray, Arthur J., and Donald Freeman. *"Give Us Good Measure": An Economic Analysis of Relations Between the Indians and the Hudson's Bay Company before 1763*. Toronto: University of Toronto Press, 1978.

Rayburn, Alan. *Dictionary of Canadian Place Names*. Toronto: Oxford University Press, 1997.

Reiman, Donald H. *Romantic Texts and Contexts*. Columbia: University of Missouri Press, 1987.

Reynolds, L. D., and N. G. Wilson. *Scribes and Scholars: A Guide to the Transmission of Latin and Greek literature*. Rev. ed. Oxford: Clarendon Press, 1974.

Rich, E. E. *The History of the Hudson's Bay Company, 1670-1870*. 2 vols. London: Hudson's Bay Record Society, 1958.

Rich, E. E., ed. *Isham's Observations on Hudson's Bay*. Toronto: Champlain Society for the Hudson's Bay Record Society, 1949.

Robinson, Peter. *The Digitization of Primary Textual Sources*. Oxford: Office for Humanities Communication, 1993.

Robson, Joseph. *An Account of Six Years Residence in Hudson's-Bay, from 1733 to 1736, and 1744 to 1747.* 1752, reprint n.p.: S. R. Publishers and Johnson Reprint Corporation, 1965.

Rouillard, Eugène. "L'Altération des noms de lieux." *Bulletin de la Société de géographie de Québec* 10:5 (1916): 282-84.

Rousseau, Jacques. Review of Pierre Biays, *Les marges de l'oekoumène dans l'est du Canada*. *Revue d'histoire de l'Amérique française* 20:4 (1967): 631-36.

Ruggles, Richard. *A Country So Interesting: The Hudson's Bay Company and Two Centuries of Mapping, 1670-1870*. Kingston and Montreal: McGill-Queen's University Press, 1992.

Russell, Dale R. *Eighteenth-Century Western Cree and Their Neighbours*. Ottawa: Canadian Museum of Civilization, 1991.

Ryan, Simon. *The Cartographic Eye: How Explorers Saw Australia*. Cambridge: Cambridge University Press, 1996.

Said, Edward. *Orientalism*. New York: Vintage, 1979.

Scaglion, Richard. "The Plains Culture Area Concept." In *Anthropology on the Great Plains*, edited by W. Raymond Wood and Margot Liberty, 23-84. Lincoln: University of Nebraska Press, 1980.

Schultz, Constance B. "'From Generation unto Generation': Transitions in Modern Documentary Historical Editing." *Reviews in American History* 16:3 (1988): 337-50.

Shanks, Michael, and Christopher Tilley. *Reconstructing Archaeology: Theory and Practice*. London: Routledge, 1992.

Simon, John Y. "The Canons of Selection." *Documentary Editing* 6 (December 1984): 8-12.

Small, Ian. "The Editor as Annotator as Ideal Reader." In *The Theory and Practice of Text-Editing: Essays in Honour of James T. Boulton,* edited by Ian Small and Marcus Walsh, 186-209. Cambridge: Cambridge University Press, 1991.

Stephen, Scott. "A Puzzle Revisited: Historiographic and Documentary Problems in the Journals [sic] of Anthony Henday." Master of Arts thesis, University of Winnipeg, 1997.

Stevens, Paul, and John T. Saywell, eds. *Lord Minto's Canadian Papers*. 2 vols. Toronto: Champlain Society, 1981-83.

Tanselle, G. Thomas. "The Editing of Historical Documents." *Studies in Bibliography* 31 (1978): 1-56.

Tanselle, G. Thomas. "External Fact as an Editorial Problem." *Studies in Bibliography* 32 (1979): 1-47.

Tanselle, G. Thomas. "Historicism and Critical Editing." *Studies in Bibliography* 39 (1986): 1-46.

Taylor, Robert J. "Editorial Practices: An Historian's View." *Newsletter of the Association for Documentary Editing* 3 (February 1981): 4-8.

Tedlock, Dennis. *The Spoken Word and the Work of Interpretation.* Philadelphia: University of Pennsylvania Press, 1983.

Tedlock, Dennis. "From Voice and Ear to Hand and Eye." *Journal of American Folklore* 103 (1990): 133-56.

Teute, Fredrika J. "Views in Review: A Historiographical Perspective on Historical Editing." *American Archivist* 43:1 (1980): 43-56.

Todorov, Tzvetan. *La Conquête de l'Amérique: la question de l'autre.* Paris: Seuil, 1982.

Trigger, Bruce. "The Historian's Indian: Native Americans in Canadian Historical Writing from Charlevoix to the Present." *Canadian Historical Review* 67:3 (1986): 315-42.

Tyrrell, J. B., ed. *The Journals of Samuel Hearne and Philip Turnor.* Toronto: Champlain Society, 1934.

Umfreville, Edward. *The Present State of Hudson's Bay.* London: Charles Stalker, 1790.

Vinaver, Eugène. "Principles of Textual Emendation." In *Medieval Manuscripts and Textual Criticism*, edited by Christopher Kleinhenz, 139-59. Chapel Hill: University of North Carolina Department of Romance Languages, 1976.

Voigt, George L., and John Bush Jones, eds. *Literary and Historical Editing.* Lawrence: University of Kansas Press, 1981.

Warhus, Mark. *Another America: Native American Maps and the History of Our Land.* New York: St. Martin's Press, 1997.

Warkentin, John, and Richard I. Ruggles. *Manitoba Historical Atlas: A Selection of Facsimile Maps, Plans and Sketches from 1612 to 1969.* Winnipeg: Stovel-Advocate Press for the Historical and Scientific Society of Manitoba, 1970.

West, James L. W., III. "Fair Copy, Authorial Intention and 'Versioning.'" *Text* 6 (1993): 81-92.

Williams, Glyndwr. *The British Search for the Northwest Passage in the Eighteenth Century.* London: Longman's for the Royal Commonwealth Society, 1962.

Williams, Glyndwr. "Andrew Graham and Thomas Hutchins: Collaboration and Plagiarism in Eighteenth-Century Natural History." *The Beaver* 308 (Spring 1978): 4-14.

Williams, Glyndwr. "The Puzzle of Anthony Henday's Journal." *The Beaver* 309 (Winter 1978): 41-56.

Williams, Glyndwr, ed. *Andrew Graham's Observations on Hudson's Bay,* introduction by Richard Glover, appendixes by Glyndwr Williams. London: Hudson's Bay Record Society, 1969.

Williams, Glyndwr, ed. *Hudson's Bay Miscellany, 1670-1870*. Winnipeg: Hudson's Bay Record Society, 1975.

Wilson, Clifford. "Across the Prairies Two Centuries Ago." *Canadian Historical Association Report* (1954): 29-35.

Wilson, Clifford. "Henday (Hendey, Hendry), Anthony," *Dictionary of Canadian Biography*, edited by Francess Halpenny, Vol. 3, 285-88. Toronto: University of Toronto Press, 1974.

Wolfart, H. Christoph, and Janet F. Carroll. *Meet Cree: A Guide to the Cree Language*. 2d ed. Edmonton: University of Alberta Press, 1981.

Websites

http://ota.ahds.ac.uk Oxford Text Archive. King's College, University of London. 9 June 1999.

http://www.uic.edu/orgs/tei Text Encoding Initiative. University of Illinois at Chicago. 9 June 1999.

http://www.treaty7.org Treaty 7 Tribal Council (Calgary). 9 June 1999.

Index

Index

The names of individuals, social groups and places associated with Henday's journal are listed below, together with the names of scholars who have contributed to the study of this document, to the period of fur trade history it represents, and to theoretical positions relevant to its edition.